365 MEDITATI
to NURTURE *the* SOUL

Rhythms of Growth

LINDA DOUTY

Linda Douty Mischke

UPPER
ROOM BOOKS®
NASHVILLE

To my husband,

Walter Mischke

whose deep love and kindness continue to enchant me . . .

Upper Room Books website: books.upperroom.org

UPPER ROOM', UPPER ROOM BOOKS', and design logos are trademarks owned by The Upper Room', a ministry of GBOD', Nashville, Tennessee. All rights reserved.

Cover image: © DeepGreen / Shutterstock.com
Illustrations for July and October: Michael C. McGuire, settingPace
Other month illustrations: Jane Wageman
Cover design: Left Coast Design, Portland, OR / www.lcoast.com

Library of Congress Cataloging-in-Publication Data

Douty, Linda.
  Rhythms of growth : 365 meditations to nurture your soul / Linda Douty.
      pages cm
  ISBN 978-0-8358-1351-8 (print) — ISBN 978-0-8358-1352-5 (mobi) — ISBN 978-0-8358-1353-2 (epub)
  1. Devotional calendars. I. Title.
  BV4811.D627 2014
  242'.2--dc23

                                                                    2014010106

Printed in the United States of America

CONTENTS

ACKNOWLEDGMENTS

This lengthy book was a big hill to climb, and I owe much to those who hung in there through every step. Not many people choose to evaluate 365 meditations with their thinking caps on and a red pencil at the ready! My three loyal readers—Steve Mischke, Anita Fletcher, and Walter Mischke—did just that, taking one month at a time and never flagging in their astute suggestions and "Atta-girls." Their puzzlements yielded greater clarity; their comments enriched the content; their devotion to truth prompted deeper explanations. I hardly know how to express my gratitude. I owe them an unpayable debt.

Hugs and gratitude all around to my wonderful friends who tolerated both my enthusiasm and my occasional whining and pried me loose from my writing blocks with various versions of "You can *do* this!" I appreciate every pithy remark, every brilliant idea, and every kick in the backside. You know who you are and what you mean to me. Your support and encouragement kept me company in my lonely office.

I gleaned the bulk of the wisdom in this book from sessions with clients in my spiritual guidance practice over the past eighteen years. As they allowed me to companion them on their spiritual journeys, I watched their own rhythms of growth unfold. Those hours of sharing provided many of the insights in these pages.

Thanks to the talented team at Upper Room Books, a group of dedicated professionals and tireless cheerleaders. Together, they brought order out of chaos and confidence out of discouragement. They were always ready to respond to a phone call, reply to a panicky e-mail, and answer my questions. Besides, they are endlessly kind.

If there were such a thing as a hug in print, it would go to Upper Room's Editorial Director, Jeannie Crawford-Lee, who believed in the project from the beginning and helped me mold the concept into a reasonable shape. What a friend and ally you are.

Special kudos go to Rita Collett, editor extraordinaire, who patiently worked with my offbeat style and edgy theology and rendered it readable and acceptable. A friend to both writer and reader, Rita embodies the dynamite combination of keen intellect and a warm heart—everyone involved benefits from her expertise.

Most of all, it was Walter who smoothed out the rough places. My long-suffering husband cooked meals, cleaned the house, and picked up all the balls I dropped. When I felt overwhelmed, he patiently altered plans at the drop of a hat with a smile (mostly) on his face. While I holed up in my office, churning out words, he lived a solo life for hours on end. And he never stopped rooting for me. What a guy. . . . I count myself as one very lucky woman.

—LINDA DOUTY

INTRODUCTION

Strange how unrelated ideas can converge into an unlikely alliance. The first thread of thought introduced itself through the casual comment of a friend, "I wish you would write a book of daily reflections that connect spiritual wisdom to the messy life I'm living right now!" That thread intertwined with a second idea that had been rumbling in my head for a long time—the challenge to write about how growth in the spirit actually happens—not what we think about it, but how we experience it in real time and in the complexity of daily living.

Then a third theme started weaving into the mix: the ways the cycles of nature—planting and harvesting, weeding and watering, punishing droughts and nourishing rains—reflect spiritual formation. That pulsing drumbeat of creation speaks to the steady beating of our own hearts. Those sacred rhythms, so evident in the created order, began to suggest this book's structure.

Even though the rhythms of spiritual growth hum with the rhythms of nature's pace, we never seem to cease in our efforts to control the process of our own unfolding. Oh, how we try to make those rhythms adapt to culture's pace—setting goals, measuring spiritual success, micromanaging our life in the Spirit as if it were a business project! But the template just won't fit. We can cooperate with God's holy process, but we can't control it.

The drumbeat of seasons—nature's and our own—stays steady but seldom constant. There are ups and downs, stops and starts, assurances and surprises. The seasons come and go pretty much on schedule, but the events within them are sometimes fast-paced staccatos and sometimes plodding andantes. The rhythm of hurt and healing, for instance, happens to the trees and to us as well. In a single instant, a bolt of lightning can split a massive oak, or a person can trip and tumble down the stairs. However, the pace of healing (for both) is part of an unfolding miracle that we didn't invent and can't control. This erratic change of tempo shows itself in other ways:

- We can experience flashes of inspiration that light up every corner of our lives, much like a pond lily that suddenly bursts open. The flash of inspiration leaves us with the slow task of living out those lofty insights.
- We can vow with utter conviction to become thankful, joyous people, only to hear ourselves complaining ten minutes later.
- Our hearts can surge with love for all humankind, then we blow our top when someone cuts us off in traffic.
- We can feel showered with grace one moment and steeped in spiritual drought the next.

Yet, the beat goes on.

The passages of the authentic spiritual journey require patience and faithfulness. It helps to learn the lessons of creation as it coaxes us into its natural patterns. We allow seasons of the soul to unfold, and we stay alert to the divine invitations hidden there. Winter calls us to reflect and regroup in the stillness. Spring beckons us to tend the seeds of growth that God plants deep within us. Summer says, "Bear fruit and share it with the world!" Autumn invites us to let go with the leaves.

The seasonal themes in the book are supported by both scripture and a brief breath prayer—a kind of prayer that engages the body. The breath prayer method—repeating a short phrase on the inhale and a petition on the exhale—will bring the concepts into the body and enhance their understanding. The beauty of a breath prayer comes in its brevity and portability. We may think or utter it anywhere, anytime—standing in a grocery store line or during a bout of insomnia at 3 a.m. The more often, the better.

At the close of each meditation I provide a suggestion for reflection. Rather than an assignment to be completed, I hope the words serve as a launching point for the leading of the Holy Spirit.

The cycles of the seasons shape the monthly topics:

January invites us to listen to winter, emphasizing the productivity of inactivity. We explore the difficulties and delights of silence, along with practical suggestions for finding the possibilities lurking in the shadows of quiet moments. Tips are offered to declutter minds, calendars, and spirits.

February is dedicated to the topic of discernment and decision making—from listening to the subtle guidance of the body to distinguishing between the whispers of God and the shouts of the ego. We learn to sense when we might be committed to a commitment to which we no longer feel committed! Then we will develop greater clarity in the use of our gifts and graces for the good of others.

In *March* we embark on an "archaeological dig" in the garden of our souls to see what's really there. In the rocky process of exploring the soul's interior garden, we unearth the sticks and stones that litter the path to wholeness.

April deals with the inevitable downpours of despair, the rainy seasons of our lives when grief and loss become part of the soul's landscape. Practical suggestions on coping with dark times and discovering the graces in such upheaval are included.

The entries in *May* help us recognize the sprouts and flowers in the growing garden of the soul—the process of "greening." We'll consider the role of pruning, as well as tolerating imperfect "blooms" and "weeds."

In *June* we learn what it takes to be good caretakers of growth through spiritual disciplines and innovative methods of prayer. Exploration of music, books, sabbath rest, and other practices helps us open windows to the light of God that surrounds us.

July focuses on the formation of fruits of the Spirit—showing how the fruit moves from idea to incarnation—and how we live out those attributes daily in service to others. We delve into the experience of spiritual drought, as well as the ways in which we stunt the growth of our inner garden.

August looks at the value of a change of pace, those times apart that refresh us as we visit the beach, the mountains, the rivers, the desert, or the sanctuary of our homespun holidays. These diversions provide unexpected invitations to stir our souls.

September's theme of letting go explores the territory of loss and gain, with an emphasis on breaking the momentum of old patterns that choke the spirit. These meditations target behaviors related to control, worry, pessimism, and anxiety. They teach us how to move from the desire to let go to practices that enable us to do it.

October celebrates the brilliant colors of creativity and their role in making us artists of life. Pursuits such as painting, music, pottery, cooking, woodworking, and more are introduced as intentional spiritual practices that spark our aliveness.

November contains the many rhythms of gratitude that help transform us from people who simply make a list of blessings into people whose lives are immersed in thanksgiving, from people who habitually say thank-you into people from whom gratitude flows naturally.

In *December*, we celebrate not only the birth of Jesus but the birth of new life within us. Hopefully, the exercises of the previous eleven months will be reflected in subtle shifts of the Spirit that begin to show up in our lives. Each day will feature a different signpost that points to spiritual transformation.

I'm convinced that we weren't put on this earth to be "successful" in our spiritual lives but to surrender to the sacred rhythms of the One who sustains us. This Force that animates everything—the whole of reality—empowers us to grow and flourish. We are cherished offspring of a Love that will never let us go.

Genuine transformation of the spirit is not about getting our ticket to heaven punched. It's about releasing our well-meaning agendas to the One who created these cycles of change in the first place—being wide open to grace.

Living into that stunning reality tunes us to the sacred rhythms of the soul—enabling us to love God, ourselves, and others with the love we were born to give.

January

LISTENING TO WINTER

"Be still, and know that I am God!"
—PSALM 46:10

BREATH PRAYER
Speak, O God, . . . for I am listening.

JANUARY 1 · *A New Beginning*

Winter is quiet. Winter waits. Winter respects the organic changes taking place under the surface. Listening to winter means that we dare to follow its example.

The dawn of a new year always carries the seeds of potential—ready to sprout, eager to grow, throbbing with unrealized life. Twelve fresh months spread before us like a buffet. We learn to write a new year on our checks. We wonder what will fill the sparsely noted calendar pages. Often we rush to figure it out, proclaim resolutions, compose to-do lists. But if we're listening to winter's guidance, we may hear whispers that we're running ahead of the unfolding process. Winter invites us to hold the reins on our runaway spirits, to reflect before we stampede into action.

Expert fire-builders tell us that the empty space between the logs is necessary for fire to kindle. And so it is with us. We must create space to spark the soul's wisdom. The soul, somewhat shy, speaks in whispers not in shouts; it requires unhurried time.

The ego protests this slowdown, shouting at us to get organized, start moving, attack the looming projects. But the soul pulls us in another direction, urging us to carve out a few reflective moments to consider those calendar entries, to become aware of who we are and where the Spirit is leading us.

We make this process a priority because in the soul's growth, it *is*. Prayer, reflection, sipping a cup of tea while staring out the window—anything that allows spaciousness also allows a wisdom greater than we know to pay a winter visit. Be ready to open the door. Slow down and sit a spell.

Reflect: Create a time today (even five minutes) when you can sit in silence and allow your spirit to settle. Don't expect anything; don't evaluate the content of the time. Just know that your soul is opening to love and wisdom.

JANUARY 2 · *New Year's Resolutions*

I've never been a fan of New Year's resolutions. Like many other folks, I make them, usually break them, then wallow in guilt as I revert to business as usual. That being said, it still seems prudent to project some sort of intention as the new year begins, some evidence of movement toward healthy changes.

This year I'm altering my usual program by engaging in times of silent reflection, reviewing the past year's moments of joy and challenge and focusing on the lessons offered. What occasions brought delight? What brought pain or suffering? Did I open myself to greater compassion and love because of them? Through this reflective process, I can sense divine presence moving through life's experiences.

Rather than regarding the difficult times as occasions of God's absence, it helps to recall the support that bore the wings of love during those thorny passages, the kindnesses that made situations bearable—all signs of God's encompassing presence. On the other hand, remembrance of the surprising joys teaches volumes about what nurtures and delights. It's a mixed bag and a total package that spell LIFE, full of light and dark places. Seeing ourselves and our lives as a whole lends a perspective that is illumined by attention and unlocked with the key of gratitude.

So I hope to be a more reflective learner this year—stopping often to do some spiritual fishing, throwing my net into deep waters and seeing what life-giving lessons I can catch. Want to join me?

Reflect: Spend some time reviewing the past year and its events. What invitations to grow did you perceive and accept? How did you change as a result? Give thanks for the ways in which the Spirit can shape you through whatever occurs in your life.

JANUARY 3 • *Fallow Time*

Farmers speak of the value of allowing a field to lie fallow for a while, to remain idle in order to rejuvenate the soil for future productivity. Listening to winter teaches us that we too can find refreshment through lying fallow.

Joining this cycle of nature—work and rest, action and contemplation, productivity and passivity—puts us in harmony with creation itself. Jesus modeled this rhythm for us. On occasion, he left needy crowds behind to commune with God in prayer, to celebrate with friends, or just to be alone for a time.

When our souls lie fallow, they become aware of the quiet infusion of God in and through everything—not merely the moments we might deem spiritual or religious. Divine creative energy is the animating force that undergirds all of life, all the time. Words from the book of Acts give us a glimpse of this life-giving energy: "In him we live and move and have our being" (17:28).

Though we may not have the luxury of a week's retreat or a spa vacation, we can find pockets of refreshment even in a busy day—soaking in a hot bath, reading a few pages from an inspiring book, watching the cardinal flutter at the feeder, petting the new puppy, sitting in silence.

Our souls need the same kind of renewal as the farmer's field. Perhaps we too will be more fruitful if we respect our need to lie fallow occasionally.

Reflect: Make a list of minivacations that can provide respite during your daily round. Post them where you can refer to them often. Find some fallow moments today, simply to *be* rather than to *do.*

JANUARY 4 • *Cocooning*

Once I plucked a cocoon from a tree and pried it open to see what was inside. Bad idea. Inside it was dark, unformed, unfinished. I had disturbed the darkness essential to its unfolding.

The darkness of a cocoon does not reflect an absence of life but rather the activity of life being formed. It takes patience. The gradual maturing of our own souls also takes some cocooning. A time of stillness, even when it feels like a gloomy laziness, allows this process to evolve while we watch and wait and pay attention to what is happening.

Science tells us that each chrysalis attaches to a cremaster—a tiny spiny protuberance that serves as an anchor point to connect the pupa to a stem, twig, or other "holding place"—nature's Velcro™, if you will. We too stay connected in dark times to that quiet core inside our souls where God meets us, comforts us, sustains us, "cocoons" us—with a giant cosmic hug. Spiritual disciplines can strengthen this connection through prayer, meditation, worship, spiritual friendships, and service to others.

Creativity can also serve as that still point. After all, an artist isn't a special kind of person so much as each person is a special kind of artist. Your own soul is the canvas, the weaving, the song, the poem—and with every stroke or word, you're joining the creative dance of life.

Listening to winter leads us to discover a whole host of cremasters—our companions in a growth group, the support of our families, a spiritual director—and above all, our trust in a loving God who champions our wholeness.

Reflect: What connections and creations serve as your anchor points? May you feel blessed today as you allow those still points to nurture your own cocooning process.

JANUARY 5 • *My Soul Waits in Silence. . . .*

It's almost impossible to reflect in the midst of a whirlwind. Every day the noise of crowded homes, busy highways, chattering workplaces, and media entertainment—not to mention our techno-gadgets—bombards us! Sitting in silence invites us to focus on matters of the heart, communing with something greater than the cacophony around us—in other words, listening to winter.

So how do we do that? The first obvious answer comes when we choose to stop talking, which includes the ticker tape running in our heads while our lips are closed. Sacred silence is not the silence of a graveyard but the silence of a garden growing. If you stand in a winter garden, it appears that nothing is happening in the somber stillness. Yet biology reminds us that vigorous activity, cellular movement, and unseen life abound underneath the ground—life that we can neither see nor control. Eventually growth emerges in leaves and flowers and, ultimately, fruit.

Intentionally entering the silence signals radical trust. Do we believe that the Spirit can form us without our expert micromanagement? If so, we offer the garden of our hearts for divine tilling and planting with no questions asked. As we relinquish control and judgment of the process, we find over time that green growth emerges—in the form of answered prayer, fresh insights, and an awakening to God's presence in everything.

It seems as if our souls are shaped just as organically as the flowers in this amazing underground process.

Think about it—a garden offers itself to the light and lets go of control. Lilies turn into lilies, tomatoes become tomatoes. Maybe we too can be shaped into what we were meant to be as we trust the divine Gardener in the silence.

Reflect: Try sitting for at least five minutes in a quiet place with eyes closed. Breathe deeply, imagining that your inner garden is being tilled and planted by One wiser and more loving than you've ever envisioned.

JANUARY 6 • *The Ancient Path of Silence*

Ask for the ancient paths, where the good way lies; and walk in it, and find rest for your souls" (Jer. 6:16). Silence is an ancient path that has stood the test of time.

As an extrovert, I used to consider silent prayer a waste of time, a time I should use more productively. Why sit when I could be feeding the hungry? For compulsive "doers" addicted to productivity and measurable results, stillness is a tall order indeed.

The practice of silence had to change my life before I could change my mind. Studying the witness of others convinced me that God could nurture my hectic soul, if I could learn to be still. The practice didn't seem to fit my wiring, but I felt compelled to give it a try.

My first guide in this endeavor was Father Thomas Keating through his method of Centering Prayer. I rose early each morning, his book *Open Mind, Open Heart: The Contemplative Dimension of the Gospel* in my lap, and sat comfortably—spine straight and feet flat on the floor—trusting that God was tilling the soil of my soul. Keating suggested the choice of a "sacred word" to which I could return when distracted. Since he cautioned against using a word that carried lots of meaning (to avoid thinking about the word rather than emptying the mind), I had to experiment with several words before I found something workable. I finally chose *empty*.

Even though I sensed no results that fit into my usual patterns of evaluation, I continued to show up—first for five minutes, then ten, then twenty. As the practice became more comfortable, I sat for even longer periods of time. I held fast to the perception that something was occurring in the hidden recesses of my spirit. The lengthening silence brought with it a sense of trust. I slowly realized that silence is the true training ground for the art of listening.

Reflect: Take a chance on this ancient practice. Find a quiet spot and commit to a power greater than yourself. Be gentle with yourself as you plow new spiritual ground.

JANUARY 7 · *Drowning in Words*

I love words—the sight of them on the page, the vibration of them in the ear, the delicious feel of them as they roll out of my mouth, their power to describe and enchant. I love water as well, but I try not to forget that I can drown in it as well as delight in it. Truth is, most of us are drowning in words.

We are seduced by sound and print in all its forms—from stimulating discussions to vivid descriptions. We become so enthralled with words that we begin to mistake the "right words" for the real thing. We can easily confuse reading a book about prayer with the practice of praying. Words can become an end in themselves rather than a means to the experience of the holy. On the journey of spiritual formation, words can point to God but not provide the experience of God. In the words of poet John Keats, "Nothing ever becomes real till it is experienced—even a proverb is no proverb to you till your life has illustrated it."[1]

Silence offers the divine language that enriches the growth of introverts and extroverts alike, yet it can be both deafening and disturbing. Being silent can also feel like a colossal waste of time. We usually try to fill it, obliterate it, or enliven it by inner and outer chatter. I once considered silent practice as one of many forms of contemplation, a mere appetizer on the rich buffet of spiritual options that we could take a bite of—or not. I now believe it forms the foundation of true communication with God.

Psalm 46:10 says it plain as day: "Be still, and know that I am God!" Not "Read another book, and you'll know"; "Tackle another worthy project, and you'll know"; or even "Study the Bible more, and you'll know." It says to be *still* and know.

Reflect: Pause several times today to pay attention to your feelings. Sense God's presence in small details: a sudden surge of love for your family, the taste of hot cornbread, the smell of a fresh rose. Just stop and feel it rather than describe it.

JANUARY 8 • *Stumbling through the Silence*

My novice attempts at silence, while sporadic and unsatisfying, encouraged me to "keep my appointment with God." So I did—morning after morning. My mind wandered; I got twitchy. I noticed no immediate change and heard no booming voice from on high. For a person accustomed to being proactive and trying harder, I found it a tough discipline.

At first, silence felt like my enemy; a chorus of chattering voices competed for attention—the "monkey mind." I had to accept that minds just *do* that—leap from thought to thought like monkeys leaping from limb to limb. My spiritual guides urged me to remain patient, releasing thoughts without self-judgment or evaluation—in short, to trust the process. Those who write about the contemplative life refer to silence as "the language of God." To experience this holy voice, I had to present my soul as an empty container to be filled with . . . whatever.

After weeks, I began to notice subtle—almost imperceptible—differences that no one would have noticed but me: a kinder response to an irritation; more patience, less judgment. Not a major spiritual overhaul but slight changes nonetheless. My exterior behavior seemed to receive silent support from inside—oh, so slowly.

But all wasn't roses and light. Along with budding fruit of the Spirit, I experienced a heightened awareness of my real motives and hidden agendas. Ouch. Ultimately, I came to accept this revealing light as part of the process, encompassed not by judgment and shame but by forgiveness and mercy.

Eventually, the silence turned from adversary to adviser, from foe to friend. Rather than inverting a life of service into mere navel-gazing, silence can charge our spiritual engine and set it into motion. Silent practice is far from lazy inactivity. A lifetime endeavor, to be sure, but it begins with that first brave step into the silence.

Reflect: Sit comfortably in a straight chair, feet flat on the floor, settling into the silence with deep belly breaths. Set a timer for ten minutes. As each thought arises, mentally let it go like nudging a butterfly off your shoulder. Then return to your breathing or your sacred word. Don't judge yourself as inadequate or inept—only faithful!

JANUARY 9 · *Trusting the Hidden Process*

So how can we take part in this astounding process of growth? We begin with *patience.* The Spirit's guidance doesn't usually operate in fast mode but rather on "winter time." In silence, we can offer questions and concerns to God's wisdom, not so God will fix us or our problems arbitrarily but so we can take our next step in harmony with divine guidance. The Spirit can comfort us in suffering, come to us through others' actions and words, and nudge us into action in subtle ways. In our microwave minds, we want that guidance pronto and without ambiguity, but patience paves the way.

We offer our full *presence* by noticing what is occurring *now.* We do not regret the past or fear the future but focus on being here *now* in love. Is what we are thinking or doing furthering the service of love?

We open ourselves to deeper *perception.* Our awareness of this growth process sharpens as we acknowledge what energizes us as well as what drains us. What causes anxiety, despair, joy? What triggers our reactions? How does this perception invite us to change?

Finally, the growth process requires our *participation.* Once we perceive the guidance, how can we do our part? We summon the courage to take the next step, to move toward the next point of light that we can see.

Reflect: Creation itself grows in silence—plants, trees, flowers. The sun and the moon move in silence. Silence itself gives us a new perspective. Slowly consider your awareness of God's presence in the silence. Be aware as the vast emptiness, free of sound, fills with a larger and more loving presence.

JANUARY 10 · *Getting Unstuck*

I remember the wise words of a mentor voiced many years ago: "One of the best ways to get unstuck is to take chances." He then posed a question that hit me right between the eyes: "When will you learn to take a risk on your own behalf?"

Struggling with the meaning of that question, I realized that I regarded such questions as selfish and egocentric. I had to learn the hard way that taking a risk on my own behalf is a movement toward wholeness rather than selfishness.

Becoming an authentic person means daring to be your true self—not being less than you are capable of being or pretending to be more. Strength comes in congruence and freedom comes in authenticity, but both are part of a risky business.

As we become more comfortable in our own skin, we gain the courage to say what we mean and mean what we say. In doing so, we risk the reactions of those around us whose love and approval we so desperately seek. Prior to this helpful risk taking, most of us fell into the habit of parsing our words to elicit the best response. To put it bluntly, we tried to manipulate people's feelings toward us.

Rather than using our honesty as a hammer to pound others with our opinions, we can learn appropriate ways to remain true to our values while not leaving ambiguous impressions of who we are and what we think. After all, tact is the intelligence of the heart. As the writer of Ecclesiastes cautions, there is "a time to keep silence, and a time to speak" (3:7). However, sitting on feelings that demand expression can drive them down an emotional rabbit hole, and they often fester into resentment and buried anger—all because we didn't risk speaking authentically.

Yes, getting unstuck requires steadfast loyalty to the true self, guided by God.

Reflect: Notice your communications today. Are they clear and congruent with how you truly feel? Pray that God will teach you the value of honesty in all you say and do so that you can be free of unhealthy mixed messages.

JANUARY 11 • *Stepping Off the Treadmill*

The feeling of mindlessly spinning in circles or running in place is common to all of us. The mundane tasks of living—showering, dressing, driving to work, preparing meals, changing the diapers—seem to drain the hours from the day, as if we are running as fast as we can while getting nowhere. In truth, it's easier to complain about this treadmill than it is to actually break the cycle of running in place.

Dislodging the patterns of "same old, same old" can require some creativity in reframing simple tasks, which enables us to spark new life into a humdrum day:

- Take a different route to work.
- Plan a week's meals at one sitting.
- Introduce a new spiritual discipline into your devotional routine.
- Dress in clothes you haven't worn for a while.
- Get dishes and place mats out of storage and *use* them.
- Eat dinner on a card table in front of the fire.
- Play soft music instead of using the TV as background noise.
- Promote a positive attitude among family members by asking, "What was the best thing that happened to you today?"

A powerful shift in perception can occur by doing an ordinary thing with extraordinary mindfulness. Pay your bills with sincere gratitude for the services rendered; set the table while saying a prayer for the person who will occupy that place; as you wash your face, be cleansed of falseness and vanity.

In other words, allow commonplace happenings to bless you with uncommon meaning. Daily life is more about *loving* what you have to do than *doing* what you love to do. It's more about wanting what you have than having what you want.

Reflect: Be attentive today to the small things, taking nothing for granted— the smile of a loved one, your dog's wagging tail, the sun on your face, your own breath. Breathe a silent thank-you for simple joys.

JANUARY 12 • *A Clean Slate*

Something about a new calendar book brimming with clean blank pages excites me. Or in this digital age, perhaps a smartphone date book with no entries brings joy. Either way, we choose how we will fill the blanks. The new year affords us an opportune time to take responsibility for ourselves. After all, it's our voice that says yes and our hand that writes on the calendar. The new year becomes a good time to quit agreeing to a flurry of activities and then blaming others for putting too much on us. We can take time for deliberate consideration of what brings life to us and others.

First off, we need to fire the interior "drill sergeant" who pushes us around—the one who barks, "You ought to, you need to, you should, you must." We often project that bossiness onto God by assuming the Almighty's displeasure with our errant behavior and our need to "straighten up." But our own inner sergeant, not the loving source of life, motivates us through guilt.

How different it feels inside when we can say, "I choose to, I want to, I will!" instead of "I've got to, they need me to, God requires me to." When we change from the inside out, we can make difficult, sacrificial choices from a loving heart rather than from a grudging obedience. This freedom may seem to run counter to the religious mandate that most of us grew up with: the virtue of obedience. This "virtue," as we have mistakenly defined it through the years, maintains an aura of coercion—doing things because others expect it. My experience has been that the Spirit invites, not coerces. God's guidance comes as invitation not condemnation.

So in these reflective winter moments, consider moving from duty to devotion. We usually do our duty with gritted teeth, but we can choose freely with a smile.

Reflect: Monitor your thoughts and words today, noticing each time you say "ought" and "should." Instead, try saying "I choose," so you can claim responsibility for what you say and do.

JANUARY 13 • *Parable of the Rocks*

A professor stood before his time-management class with an object lesson. He picked up a gallon-sized jar and began to fill it with fist-sized rocks, then asked the class members, "Is this jar full?" They all answered yes. Then he reached for a bucket of gravel and poured it into the jar, allowing the smaller rocks to settle around the larger ones. Again he asked, "Is the jar full?" And again they replied with a resounding yes. He then produced a container of sand, which he added to the jar. It filled in the empty spaces. Again the same question, "Is it full?" This time, only a few participants said yes. Finally he brought in a pitcher of water, which indeed did fill the jar to the brim. His demonstration completed, he asked his class, "Now what is the moral of this lesson?" A clever student immediately raised his hand and proclaimed proudly, "The point of your illustration is that no matter how much you have to do, you can always fit something else in!"

"No," replied the professor. "The moral of the lesson is that if you don't put your big rocks in first, you'll never get them in at all."

In deciding what our "big rocks" are, we're likely to let some lesser things go, at least for a while. Of course, our priorities constantly change as our lives evolve. Tasks like child care, tending a sick family member, starting a new business, completing an important project, convalescing from an illness can occupy prime space in our lives until the need for them disappears. However, if we prayerfully keep our deepest values in view, we are more apt to parcel out our time and energy prudently.

Reflect: What "big rocks" fill your life right now? What activities and tasks can only you do? Which items can you delegate or postpone? Allow the Spirit to reveal what is truly important at this particular time.

JANUARY 14 • *The Stuffed Schedule*

I bumped into a friend in the grocery aisle recently. After the customary hellos and how are yous, she swiped a wisp of hair from her eyes and sighed with exasperation, "I've just been soooo busy!" Then I heard myself saying the same words. It's a recurrent refrain. We rush past the abundant life and jeopardize our own souls when we live such hurried and harried lives.

This flustered attitude is an equal opportunity employer that rules people, regardless of race, creed, or gender. From doctors to doorkeepers, life piles endlessly upon itself until the beautiful experience of being alive melts into one enormous obligation, leaving us exhausted and stripped of joy.

Once in a while we acknowledge the unpleasant truth: Our busyness holds a hidden psychological payoff. Our culture rewards busyness, but another underlying motivation bears scrutiny. We proclaim our "busyness" to one another with some hidden degree of pride; we claim our exhaustion as a trophy; we pretend our ability to withstand stress is a mark of real character. The busier we are, the more important we seem to ourselves and—we think—to others. Unfortunately, this busyness has become the model of a successful life.

When we cram our days full with people, projects, and schedules, we affirm the familiar bumper sticker that mirrors our reality: LIFE IS WHAT HAPPENS WHILE YOU'RE BUSY MAKING OTHER PLANS. Our intuition toward simplicity is not enough. We must act on this awareness rather than pick up yet another catalog and place an order for unnecessary diversion. Simplifying our life doesn't usually mean selling the house and giving away everything we own. It's often enough to begin to clean off the messy desk or pare down the crowded calendar. Old habits will push back, tempting us to return to normal. We smile and say, "I know you!" and then gently let them go.

Reflect: Consider honestly your relationship to busyness. Does it remain a constant in your life or a sometimes occurrence? Each time you feel overly busy, take a deep breath—breathing in peace and breathing out the harried feeling. One step at a time, one task at a time.

JANUARY 15 • *Paring Things Down*

Have you ever noted the correlation between exterior clutter and interior clutter? Studies that try to measure such connections point to one certainty: Disarray in the outer world contributes to confusion in the inner world. No wonder wise teachers through the centuries have lifted simplicity as a virtue and asserted that less is more. The spiritual life is fundamentally one of subtraction, not addition. Simplicity is a simple idea, . . . or is it?

If we start with visible possessions, we know that simple doesn't always mean easy. In married life, if one person is a pack rat while the other is a neatnik, just cleaning out the garage can create trouble. One such couple reached a truce when they agreed on a useful litmus list to guide their cleanup:

- Do I love it? (item of beauty and meaning)
- Do I need it? (How long since I last used it?)
- Does it support who I am now in my life? (Do I still need these ski boots when I've given up skiing?)
- Does it need repair, and am I willing to do so *now*?

Using these questions as a guide, the couple sorted the bounty into containers marked Throw Away, Give Away, Sell, Lend, and Keep, setting a firm date and destination for each collection of goods.

This process involves both reflection and physical activity. It reminds us of what we value and why, with the added benefit of a more serene atmosphere of order and spaciousness.

Reflect: Start with a crowded closet or a cluttered kitchen drawer. Or simply unravel the jumble of computer cords. As you sort and toss and unwind, be aware of the interior release you feel. Give thanks that you are taking a step toward simplicity.

JANUARY 16 • *Programming Your Frustration*

Last January I prayerfully asked, "How is God inviting me to grow this year?" I got a very surprising answer. Over the next few days, a strange phrase kept nudging my consciousness. It returned again and again: *You're programming your own frustration.* When I finally decided to deal with what seemed to be a "message," I noticed a sea of anxiety and hurriedness underlying my days. The outward manifestations may be familiar to you: constant glancing at the clock; driving too fast, trying to make it before the light turns yellow; concern about being late, rushing to finish my to-do list; a slight tightening of the muscles that felt normal. I felt like I was living behind an imaginary eight ball most of the time.

Since the pesky phrase wouldn't leave, I figured the Spirit was inviting me to deal with it—not simply to list all my reasons for feeling that way or all the people and projects that were supposedly responsible for my malaise. I needed to examine my complicity in my condition.

I knew from experience that to wallow in self-judgment (or judgment of others) would only land me in a pit of guilt and resentment. Yet I didn't know where to start. I needed a "tool," a spiritual practice that would facilitate the needed change. Thus evolved the Preparation Prayer.

At first waking, I silently repeated Psalm 118:24, "This is the day that the LORD has made; let us rejoice and be glad in it." Then, with a cup of coffee in a quiet place, I followed this pattern:

1. List all activities/appointments/tasks to be accomplished today. Include everything—even minor tasks: trip to grocery store, dental appointment, picking up the kids, as well as work hours, and so on.

2. Survey list to see if to-do items extend beyond the time allowed. Does the list demand more energy than I have? Will I be running late by afternoon?

3. If there are too many entries, target activities to delegate, move to another day or month, or discard altogether. Eliminate them from the list.

4. When the list is a manageable size, rewrite the entries in chronological order so that you can see the flow of the day ahead.

5. Pray through the list. Imagine the light of God surrounding each activity, as if the Spirit goes before you and beside you, empowering you with energy, focus, and purpose. Inhale each task mindfully and slowly; exhale the sense of urgency.

Affirm that *This is the day the Lord has made. I will rejoice and be glad in it.*

Reflect: While suspending all judgment, put your day under a microscope of grace and wisdom. Then notice ways you may be "programming your own frustration."

JANUARY 17 · *Decluttering the Calendar*

Listening to winter leads us to take responsibility for our own choices. We learn to get real about our physical and emotional limitations. We discover that it's better to do a few things with joy and competence than a bevy of things with fatigue and resentment. We learn that *No* is a complete sentence that doesn't require a string of becauses and excuses. Our false guilt and martyr complexes fade away into authentic living.

Here's a simple beginner's tool. Write down every single item or activity for which you are responsible and the various activities that occupy your time. Then form several lists:

- List items or activities that only *you* can do; if you don't do them, they won't get done. (*Being a loving spouse or responsible parent, caring for an ailing family member, remaining employed . . .*)
- List items or activities that someone else can do. (*President of PTA, committee chair, board member . . .*)
- List items or activities you would like to do but can postpone. (*Taking a weaving course, learning to play bridge, going on a golf outing, helping with the literacy project, teaching a Sunday school class . . .*)
- List items and activities that feed your soul. (*Painting, sports, book club, cooking, gardening . . .*)

Only you can move commitments around on your list and decide where they belong. The list is never permanent or static because life isn't!

Despite the numerous worthwhile tasks, a significant difference exists between seeing what needs to be done and being called to do it. As you make these choices, remember this: If what you're doing has an underlying sense of joy and fulfillment, it's probably yours to do. On the other hand, if joy is missing and you feel like the victim of constant drudgery, then you've probably picked up someone else's task.

As the old adage reminds us, "People begin to cut wisdom teeth the first time they bite off more than they can chew." We need to act on that wisdom!

Reflect: Sit quietly with pen and paper in hand and slowly craft your own list. Allow time for a thoughtful, honest, and reflective process. Pray for the courage to act on what you discover.

JANUARY 18 • *Produce and Possess*

Oh, he's very successful," I heard myself saying as I described an up-and-coming young executive. A red warning light started blinking in my mind. Once again, I had unconsciously reflected our culture's idea of success.

Even though we intellectually embrace the call to simplicity and acknowledge our soul's yearnings for it, we run smack into the cultural message to produce and possess. Regardless of what we say, when we look at how we actually spend our money and time, it appears we've bought into this flawed notion. We accept society's measurement of us by what we generate and accumulate, and we apply the same rationale in our evaluation of others.

The twin imperatives—produce and possess—can lead us away from our authentic selves if we don't pay close attention. They start eating up time and money until our planned purchases, trips, and activities begin to drive all our decisions. Before we know it, life is cluttered with the maintenance of the stuff we've acquired and the life we've enshrined. It can become a vicious cycle indeed.

As we listen to winter's wisdom, we explore ways to reverse this trend, finding real joy in what we have without being caught in the whirlwind of more, more, more. What would it mean in our lives to lean toward less, less, less?

Reflect: Take a few moments to reflect on your relationship to your stuff. Does it own you, or do you own it? Make a realistic plan to reduce the volume of possessions you no longer need.

JANUARY 19 • *The Muddled Mind*

In many ways, the mind is like a whiteboard, and we hold both the marker and eraser in our hands. The thoughts we choose to hold carry incredible power, affecting us and those around us for good or ill. In other words, thoughts produce feelings; feelings produce emotions; emotions produce actions; actions produce experience—a cause-and-effect process that is both gratifying and terrifying.

Addressing a muddled mind requires some serious thought management. A mind full of racing thoughts robs us of peace and stability. When we choose to go over the same hurts and resentments again and again, we deepen harmful neural pathways and can become stuck in a sea of negativity. Unconsciously, an internal victim stance can slowly become part of our identity, and we often wear our victimhood like a badge of honor. Even if the feelings are justified, they do their toxic work in our bodies and minds, plus giving us an aura of "See how much I've suffered."

I'm not suggesting that we suppress negative feelings. However, after some time for venting, exploring the lessons, expressing concerns, making amends—whatever appropriately honors those legitimate feelings—the time comes to "erase the whiteboard." Our continuing to replay grievances in our heads is like drinking hemlock and hoping someone else will get sick!

This "erasing" opens us to the challenging territory of forgiveness. We forgive people, not bad behaviors. We forgive—not for the person who wronged us—but for ourselves. If indeed, God has created us in the divine image, being true to our divine heritage calls us to forgive as God forgives.

So when thoughts of complaint or judgment keep returning, switch gears and choose other thoughts that contribute to healing, such as thanks for what we do have rather than regret for what we don't; gratitude for life as it is rather than complaint about what it isn't.

Reflect: Today pay attention to the terrain of your own mind. As the gatekeeper of your thoughts, do you allow unwanted visitors to enter? Feel the freedom of your soul as you bid farewell to each negative visitor.

JANUARY 20 · *Junk Food for the Brain*

There's no such thing as idle thought. Just as radio waves or telephone transmissions carry messages, so do the invisible vibrations produced by our thoughts. No wonder Paul counseled, "Be transformed by the renewing of your minds" (Rom 12:2).

Our culture seems more obsessed with what we eat than what we think: How many calories? How much fiber? Did we get our five servings of fruits and vegetables today? I wish we paid that much attention to what we feed our minds. We take "bites" from a buffet of offerings—violent movies, ridiculous TV sitcoms, trashy novels, idle gossip—all junk food for the brain. In order to monitor what we feed our minds, we must first become aware of the part we play in the feeding. An old American folktale drives this truth home.

An elderly man listened as his grandson described a battle between two friends on the playground. The grandfather got a faraway look in his eyes and said, "Yes, I know what you mean, but the *real* battle is somewhere else, . . . and it's between the two wolves!"

"What do you mean?" asked the boy.

The old man replied, "We have a battle raging all the time inside every one of us—where no one else can see. One wolf is negative—he wears anger, envy, jealousy, greed, arrogance, self-pity, resentment, false pride, inferiority, superiority, and bravado. The other wolf is positive—he wears joy, peace, love, hope, humility, kindness, generosity, truth, and compassion. It's an ongoing war—a true battle!"

"Well," said the boy, " who *wins*, Granddaddy?"

And the wise man replied knowingly, "Oh, that's easy. The winner is the one you *feed*."

After first hearing that story, I began to notice the subtle (and not so subtle) ways I feed the negative wolf by repeating a criticism, by calling a friend to complain about someone who has slighted me, by engaging in vengeful fantasies. Just as life-enhancing emotions grow by being fed, so do the emotions that choke the life from us. To state the obvious: Energy flows where attention goes.

Reflect: Notice today which wolf you feed through your thoughts. Be compassionate with yourself, even as you become aware of your complicitity.

JANUARY 21 • *Changing Your Mind*

Some folks are fluid and some congeal," said one observer of the maturing process. We often confuse stability with rigidity. Even though we like to think of our values and opinions as the "right" ones, we can remain open to deeper understanding and to refining our positions when reality dictates it.

Oftentimes, we tend to hold on to the familiar, even when it no longer serves us or when modern discoveries shoot our opinions full of holes. When science revealed that the earth was round, many maintained their belief that it was flat so they could "stand on their beliefs." Life surprises us with shifts that may not exist in the script we planned, and we are called to rewrite the lines over and over again.

In our culture of confidence, three phrases we dread confessing are these: "I'm sorry," "I'm not sure," and "I've changed my mind." Unfortunately, we associate them with the weak and lily-livered—people we believe cannot stand up for themselves or stick with a decision. We label politicians as flip-floppers and judge those who compromise as unprincipled. The world might be a better place if folks were willing to change long held opinions when they become untenable.

Being able to consider many points of view is a virtue of the strong, not the weak. The capacity to change our minds reflects humility and the intelligent pursuit of truth. Those who hang on to an opinion like a dog with a bone remind me of the old cliché, "My mind is made up; don't confuse me with the facts!" None of us has a corner on the truth.

Reflect: As you reflect during these winter contemplative moments, notice your own rigid feelings. Summon the courage to consider opening your mind to new ways of thinking.

JANUARY 22 • *The Humble Spirit*

The words of Jesus in the Sermon on the Mount point to the value of genuine humility: "Blessed are the poor in spirit, for theirs is the kingdom of heaven" (Matt. 5:3).

Perhaps being confused and spiritually restless is not such a bad state of being. It implies our acknowledgment that we can always learn something, that we can expand our horizon, and that a wider truth exists. After all, growth of the soul is about expansion, not contraction.

"Poor in spirit" can also mean we're at the end of our rope, out of answers, and uncertain. In that condition, we naturally respond by reaching for something greater and wiser. Being poor in spirit points to true humility and a willingness to subvert our pompous egos. Of course, we usually think that refers to someone else, but what about the times when we think we are better than others—more principled, more "right"?

Spiritual uncertainty leads us to the startling reality that doubt can form the cutting edge of faith. Quite a number of my beliefs have been challenged, dissected, and reshaped during the course of my life. Though it didn't seem so at the time, the intellectual wrestling has strengthened rather than weakened my faith. Our concerns about our beliefs can propel us toward authenticity. Our concerns can rattle our spiritual cages in a way that won't allow falseness or blind belief. The Spirit often uses our failures and doubts to lead us to deeper truth.

A humble spirit also opens us to what I call "nonthinking thinking," which exposes us to intuition, feeling, and deeper divine guidance.

Reflect: Explore the content of your doubts. God may be inviting you to expand and grow!

JANUARY 23 • *Divine Discontent*

Years ago, an insightful spiritual director taught me something profound about spiritual restlessness. I still recall the words of my lament.

"I've sort of 'fallen off the wagon'," I confessed. "My devotional time is dry and boring. My mind wanders, and I feel as if my prayers are bouncing off the ceiling. What used to be so fulfilling just isn't working anymore. There's something wrong with me."

Rather than the concerned response I expected, my spiritual director's lips curled into a soft smile. "Mmmm," she mused, "sounds like you have a serious case of divine discontent!"

My director's response puzzled me. Then she added, "If we never felt a spiritual 'itch,' how could God lead us into deeper truth? We would simply stay with the status quo and never grow. Look at this experience not as a condemnation from the Spirit but an invitation!"

I assumed she would help me fix my situation—give me a stricter discipline, a better book maybe. So I got out a pen and paper, ready to record her cure.

"So what am I supposed to do now?" I asked expectantly.

"I have no idea," she replied. "Just continue to show up, and be open to God's guidance." I was disappointed.

For months, my morning routine had been as precise and punctual as I was, as I studied and prayed in a predictable formulaic manner. That is, until the dryness and boredom set in, accompanied by a vague guilt that somehow I was being lazy or disobedient or not doing it right.

I tried to dismiss my own judgments and pray through the discontent, asking God to reveal unexplored methods of connecting to the sacred. Soon I felt a need to explore my natural ways of feeling and expressing, even incorporating prayer into my walking routine. My body began to connect with the sounds, sights, and smells of creation, breathing fresh energy into my spiritual practice. But the guilt remained—that fear of divine displeasure.

Then a lightbulb flashed. I realized that my belief in God as stern judge was constricting my spirit. I had to let that punitive image go in order to relate to God as enlivening joy. Loosening my demanding grip on myself began to have a domino effect. I became less exacting and legalistic with those around me too. I began to cut us all some slack!

I caught a glimpse of spiritual freedom.

Reflect: When have you experienced divine discontent? Consider the restlessness as an invitation rather than a condemnation. Be open to God's leading to the next step of your faith journey.

JANUARY 24 · *Learned Ignorance*

One hallmark of spiritual growth comes in knowing that we don't know. We make friends with uncertainty and become aware of our own ignorance—even embracing it as necessary to our growth as human beings.

Certainty about what is true pits us against one another and keeps us from learning anything new. Paradoxically, our admitting that we don't have a corner on the truth opens us to revelations of truth.

Over five hundred years ago, the German cleric Nicholas of Cusa was sailing home from Constantinople when a personal experience of God changed his life and philosophy forever. God slipped in past his intellect, bypassing his brainy certainties. Cusa's writings coined the phrase, "learned ignorance." It reminds me of God's warning to Moses on Mount

Sinai, "You cannot see my face; for no one shall see me and live" (Exod. 33:20). Mystery cannot be caught in our net of words or fully known by our finite minds.

Wise sages through the centuries have attested to the value of mitigating intellectual knowledge with experiences of the heart and soul. In contemporary life, we sense this need when we contrast reading a book about prayer and actually engaging in prayer! Whether we call it "holy emptiness" or "poverty of spirit" or "beginner's mind," knowing that we do not know is the beginning of wisdom.

Reflect: Today be willing to suspend your need to know and allow the Mystery to be mysterious. Sense your soul opening to whatever happens, knowing that the Spirit goes with you.

JANUARY 25 • *Being Right*

Being right is highly overrated. Even our cherished dream of being able to say "I told you so" never feels quite as good as we think it will. And sweet revenge is not sweet at all. It leaves a rancid aftertaste in the depths of the soul.

Many of us would rather be right than happy. But our compulsion to be right can thwart our communication with others. We all recall conversations that deteriorated into a ping-pong game of one-upmanship. We know what it's like to give an opinion, only to realize that the other person is busy formulating a rebuttal rather than a response. We also know the feeling of intense competition that wells up inside us as we get attached to winning the verbal battle—the stuff of which ulcers are made and friends are lost.

In addition, the determination to be right—to win—prevents us from learning the crucial difference between tolerance and acceptance. We pat ourselves on the back when we reach a point of tolerance for the opinions of others. We vow to be magnanimous enough to "allow" them to have opinions contrary to ours. We might even go so far as to agree not to interfere with their practice or beliefs, to refrain from trying to convince them of the rightness of our position. However, this level of tolerance still carries an unspoken tinge of judgment, a silent message that "I'm right and you're wrong."

Acceptance goes a step farther. It implies a willingness to consider that others' points of view are as valid for them as yours is for you. It admits the possibility that you may not have all the answers or see the whole picture. We often have much to learn from each other.

Reflect: In dealing with those who disagree with you, notice the difference between tolerance and acceptance. Let grace surround every communication you have today.

JANUARY 26 • *Treasuring Time*

The passage of time can resemble a speeding train or a snail's crawl, depending on whom you ask and what's happening in their lives. Experience dictates time's meaning, no matter what the clock and the calendar proclaim. Consider these comparisons:

- To realize the value of one month, ask a mother with a premature baby.
- To realize the value of one week, ask a person with a project deadline.
- To realize the value of one hour, ask lovers rushing to a dinner date.
- To realize the value of one minute, ask a person who missed the plane.
- To realize the value of one second, ask a person who just slammed on the brakes to avoid a crash.
- To realize the value of one millisecond, ask a person who just won a silver medal instead of a gold.

You get the idea. And what's the point of all this? The awareness and appreciation of the power of experience to alter our concepts of time. That knowledge can lead us to suspend our judgments of others who are living through events that affect their sense of time differently.

For example, someone who has recently lost a spouse through divorce or death often eagerly seeks companionship or desires to start dating. To them, three months may feel like an eternity, while observers with busy lives may regard it as "too soon." A healthy person may experience time as fleeting, while someone with chronic pain agonizes through laborious moments, one at a time.

We can deepen our compassion when we make an effort to walk in someone else's shoes as the clock ticks.

Reflect: Notice your awareness of time as the day unfolds. When does it speed up or slow down? Allow yourself to breathe a prayer of compassion for others who may be caught in a time trap different from yours.

JANUARY 27 • *And Then the Phone Rang*

The day spreads out with every moment planned, when the inevitable happens—an unexpected interruption upends your tight schedule. A sick child needs to be picked up at school, a snowstorm approaches, an accidental bump shatters cabinet glass, a friend needs to talk. An old adage states that you can tell a lot about a person by the way he or she handles three things: stalled traffic, a rainy day, and tangled Christmas tree lights. I would add a ringing telephone.

Interruptions dot life's landscape. We can approach them as land mines or oases, as reasons to explode or to take a breather. An intrusion tests our ability to shift gears, to be flexible in order to accommodate someone's needs. Above all, it invites our presence in the moment rather than wishing to be elsewhere.

Part of our growth in the Spirit comes in recognizing how small our world can become—that is, we all tend to interpret everything in terms of how it affects *us.* Why is the mail carrier so late when *I* need that letter *now*? Why didn't she call someone else to help—I have things to *do*! Why can't this line move faster so I can get on with *my* day?

So the next time the phone rings, take a deep breath and welcome it as fodder for the soul's growth in patience and flexibility—not to mention grace! Your tense muscles and harried spirit will thank you as they relax.

Reflect: Observe your normal reaction to interruptions. Consider moving from irritation to an invitation to be present and grace-filled.

JANUARY 28 • *Inner Assets*

In the aftermath of 9/11—that is, before anger, before analysis, before retribution—an automatic human response erupted all around us, regardless of politics or religion. People acted in a similar and instinctive way: They didn't call their stockbroker; they called *home*.

People reconnected with old friends in Oregon; they asked forgiveness of someone they had wronged; they mended family fences; they said thank-you; they slowed down; they went to church. And they *hugged*. They hugged their children, strangers on the street, trees.

In individual ways, we all began to wonder not only what our "big rocks" were (see Jan. 13) but beneath that, what our inner assets were. What would remain if all externals disappeared? Many people found they had *undervalued* those basic assets. They didn't know they had them until their own behavior surprised them—when helpful, often heroic deeds instinctively came forth as those inner assets became actions. On the other hand, many *overvalued* their inner assets, assuming they existed but finding they had atrophied from disuse and benign neglect while they had focused on other matters. In either case, people were struck with the need to invest in assets that really counted, those with long-term yields.

This primal reaction to tragedy revealed a transcendent bottom line that speaks about the nature of our spiritual wiring, the way we're created as human beings. God built something potentially magnificent into our human DNA. Some might call it a survival instinct. Maybe. But it seems higher on the evolutionary scale than that. We evidence an impulse toward life, beauty, love, and compassion that goes beyond cognitive decisions. It's not about what we believe but about what we are as God created us.

At a basic level, we seek connection to people, to nature, to God, to community. On 9/11 that yearning for belonging and connection filled us with a patriotic surge. And the connections felt good, real, true . . . evidence of an inner reservoir of valuable assets that help us not only survive but *thrive* in this complex world of ours—that is, if we nurture those inner sparks of goodness.

Reflect: Ponder the value of your inner assets. What are they? Today intentionally invest some time and energy in strengthening those assets.

JANUARY 29 · *Investing in Bonds*

If asked the value of our portfolios or how much cash is in our bank account, most of us could spout a number, perhaps even naming our investments. We're accustomed to attending to that part of our lives, checking on it, celebrating it, or agonizing over it. We give it the time and focus we think it deserves.

The *inner* asset stuff doesn't organize well into columns of figures or predictable formulas. But when something rocks our world, what's inside us helps us cope with questions like these: What does all this *mean*? What really *matters*?

Our inner assets involve family, relationships, community, and the divine love that cements those bonds. What keeps us from making regular investments in these lasting assets?

As a young person, I remember the glow I felt when standing in a circle of friends, arm in arm, singing "Blest Be the Tie That Binds." I felt a sense of belonging, of caring, of common purpose to love God and others. Perhaps we need to recapture the value of those bonds of friendship and mutual encouragement.

A much-repeated sentiment at funerals is, "I wish I had one more chance to tell this person how much they meant to me." Say it *now*, tell someone *today* how much you care. Don't be stingy with your thank-yous and I love yous. You're investing in valuable bonds of connection with yourself, your Creator, and the world around you.

Reflect: Review the precious bonds that bind you in your life. Make a conscious investment in those bonds through a phone call, a hug, a word of encouragement, or simply a smile.

JANUARY 30 · *Investing in Securities*

What spells security for us: a gated community, a hefty bank account, an efficient alarm system, good medical coverage? We yearn to feel protected against calamity and harm.

Understandably, we pray that God will keep us safe from all harm, though assurance of that doesn't mesh with the facts of life. For reasons we can't comprehend, events take place that are not God's will, and the world is a dangerous place. We are not puppets on a string, nor are we entitled to divine protection by virtue of Christian belief or our supposed goodness. We all share the divine gift of free will, which fills our world with uncertainty and saps our feelings of security.

But we have sacred foundations to stand on. Years ago teacher and author Flora Wuellner responded wisely to a question about God's role in times of turmoil. The questioner implied that many mishaps were God's way of helping us grow, of "teaching us valuable lessons." Flora disagreed, encouraging us to focus not on causation or protection but on the ongoing presence of the holy—no matter what happens or why.

Wuellner's explanation went like this: It's one thing to say that if my child falls down the concrete stairs and breaks his leg, I as a good parent will do everything in my power to bring good out of that experience. I'll help him heal, teach him that he shouldn't have left his Rollerblades™ at the top of the stairs, encourage him to learn life lessons through the experience of pain and recovery. However, it's quite another thing to say that as a good parent, I would push that child down the stairs so that he could learn those valuable lessons!

We rest secure in the words of Romans 8:28: "All things work together for good for those who love God." No matter how the circumstances came about—through our mistakes or someone else's or a random event—God will help us pick up the pieces of whatever has shattered and fashion them into something new.

The security this world offers is an illusion because it is all subject to loss. God offers the security and promise of eternal presence.

Reflect: What makes you feel secure? Spend time today investing in a deeper connection with God, who will always support you.

JANUARY 31 • *Investing in Trust*

When a friend and I explored the meaning of trust recently, she confided, "Sometimes we think things to death. I try not to stick my head in the sand. I know there's meanness in the world, but I also see unexpected explosions of grace all around me!" The reality of trusting in God puts us in league with Albert Einstein, who is credited with saying, "The most

important question a person can ask is, 'Is the universe a friendly place'?"
Do we trust that a mysterious benevolence lies at the heart of life? Does
Somebody up there like us?

We know plenty of reasons to answer no to those loaded questions.
People's inhumanity to others is well-documented. But wisdom through
the ages comes down on the side of yes. To answer yes changes the way
we view life and the way we live it. Something harmonious happens
when we lean into that affirmation with heart, soul, and mind. Science
tells us that our cells actually change structure, the immune system is
strengthened, relationships deepen, and irrational joy and peace emerge.
Surely these characteristics are evidence of God's healing, justice, peace,
compassion—and a love greater than any concept we can imagine.

Even though we can't always understand the divine Mystery at the
heart of things, we can trust it. When we take the radical leap of faith, we
find our true home, as reflected in the final stanza of the familiar hymn
by Isaac Watts, "My Shepherd Will Supply My Need":

> The sure provisions of my God attend me all my days;
> O may thy house be my abode and all my work be praise.
> There would I find a settled rest, while others go and come;
> No more a stranger, nor a guest, *but like a child at home.*

When we know how much God cherishes us, love finds its way into
the pulse of our lives and moves us into the world with compassion.

Reflect: What does it mean to you to trust God? Pray that your understanding of that reality will grow and deepen so that you feel like a child in a nurturing home.

February

DISCERNMENT
AND DECISIONS

"Now to him who by the power at work within us is able to accomplish
abundantly far more than all we can ask or imagine. . . . "
—Ephesians 3:20

Breath Prayer
Guiding Spirit, . . . show me the way.

FEBRUARY 1 · *A Tricky Business*

What should I do with my life? What is God's will for me? Should I take that job or not? Read to the kids or do the laundry? No matter what personal phrases we use, the question of discernment frequently visits all of us—dressed in all sorts of clothes. Whether our decisions are trivial or weighty, making them is an ever-present endeavor.

Any thinking person embarks on a discussion of discernment with fear and trembling and, I hope, some genuine humility. All we have to do is check the history books or the daily newspaper to see some horrendous behaviors committed under the banner of "God told me to . . ." or "I just felt I should do it!" The territory of discernment is filled with uncertainty and devoid of easy formulas.

I've heard countless sermons telling me that the way to make good decisions is to find out God's will and *do* it. The speaker would usually emphasize the amount of courage and self-sacrifice necessary to *obey*. As a young person, I believed that God's will for my life would most likely be something terribly costly—that my life as I wanted it or presently knew it would be *over*. Obeying God carried all sorts of negative baggage. I recall many teachings about obedience and few suggestions about how to listen for the authentic voice of God.

So how do we open ourselves to the influence of the Holy Spirit? To move from merely making decisions to living in the divine flow involves the development of our listening skills. When we learn to listen with the ears of the heart, we can take the next small step forward. This month, we'll open the door to deeper discernment.

Reflect: How do you presently listen for God's still small voice? What seems to stand in the way of deeper listening? Today, pay attention to how you make decisions, asking God to enter your personal process of discernment.

FEBRUARY 2 · *Some Measuring Sticks*

Though no magic formula for discernment exists, the Christian tradition offers some time-tested tools to guide the process. The Wesleyan quadrilateral urges us to consider an issue or question in light of four areas: scripture, tradition, reason, and experience—and not to trust only one area as a single measuring stick. The truth often suffers when we don't respect the balance offered by employing all four areas.

Scripture: Holy texts inspire and guide us, but verses taken out of context have often led us to poor judgment and violence. We can hold any number of positions on an issue and "prove" it with biblical texts, giving us reasons to exclude folks, wage wars, and spread all manner of divisiveness in the name of God. For this reason, reliable spiritual leaders encourage choices out of the spirit of the law, rather than the letter of the law. Is the action or position loving? Does it lead to wholeness? Does it expand the heart? Does it represent our highest values? Does it encourage community?

Tradition: We reap enormous benefits from the experience of those who have gone before us. Which traditions support the way of love? How does the wisdom of the faith community help us discern? We speak of the priesthood of believers. We attend church; we study the lives of the saints, all in an effort to discern the will of God in concert with others who can hold us accountable.

Reason: In discerning God's will, we don't have to check our brains at the door. We need intellectual scrutiny rather than naive thinking. The Spirit often guides us through thought processes.

Experience: Here the rubber meets the road. How does my experience compare with what I've learned from scripture, tradition, and reason? Because if my experience doesn't resonate with these other approaches, then it remains merely a good idea, something that we ought to do, should do, talk incessantly about doing but never actually experience in our everyday lives. We can attend Bible classes, study the words of our elders, and think issues to death—all worthy pursuits—but unless we experience the divine voice at our own "center of consent," we rarely live out our intentions in daily life.

Reflect: Take time today to consider your own measuring stick for discernment. In what ways do scripture, tradition, reason, and experience act as signposts in your search for truth? How might you include them in a way that leads to balance?

FEBRUARY 3 • *Deprogramming*

A woman gazed out her kitchen window one morning and remarked to her husband, "Look at that laundry on the neighbor's clothesline. It isn't clean—looks like she needs some new detergent!" She continued with the same commentary day after day. "Would you look at those dingy clothes on the line? Someone needs to teach her how to do the wash!" After a week or so, the woman was surprised to see a clothesline full of bright, clean garments and remarked, "Well, looks like she finally learned how to do her laundry properly!" Her husband smiled and replied, "I cleaned our windows this morning."

The point is obvious—it matters which lens we look through as we make judgments. So, as we begin delving into our own process of discernment, we may need to "clean the window." Some of our own distortions may come from faulty assumptions that cloud our vision.

Most of us have been both formed and de-formed by our religious traditions, making it wise to do a little deprogramming. Those who grew up with an image of God as punitive and demanding may have regarded divine guidance as counsel to dread. It's difficult to trust someone you fear.

Do we dare to believe with the writer of Ephesians 3:20 that God's will for us is "far more than all we can ask or imagine"? We yearn for the abundant life that the scriptures promise, but we usually want what we want! In other words, we'll gladly sign on to the abundance, but we would like a photo of it before we do! We crave control.

Reflect: Breathe deeply, trusting that God's definition of abundance is indeed more than you can imagine. Let go of preconceived notions so that you can be open to God's grace.

FEBRUARY 4 • *Trusting Your Feelings*

Our feelings are a powerful creation—a kind of inner compass. Surely they are part of the avenue of guidance and a priceless gift from the One who formed us as human beings. However, if we were taught to ignore or diminish our feelings, then that teaching needs to be deprogrammed if we are to be open to divine leading.

Feelings themselves are neither bad nor good, but they point to an issue that requires our attention. Our response to our feelings marks the measure of our discernment. Look at the natural emotion of anger, for instance, which many of us were taught to treat with disdain. (Bury it, ignore it, get rid of it—good people don't get angry.) However, anger can provide significant information for us in the discernment process, teaching us vital truths about ourselves. Rather than rushing to judgment and blaming others for the feeling, we can use our anger as a blinking stoplight, which prompts us to ask, "What in me is reacting so angrily? What wound in me is reopening?" The emotion itself bears no fault; our automatic acting out gets us in trouble. Sometimes, rather than act on the anger in a responsible and grace-filled way, we choose to feed the negativity.

Even the feeling of love can emerge from a variety of inner causes. It may be sexual attraction; it may be neediness. It can also be part of the greater love that dwells within us and longs for expression in the world.

Though people have warned us that trusting our feelings is foolish or selfish, our remarkable emotional system is part of the process of listening to God. So let's remember that God speaks not in spite of our feelings but often through them.

Reflect: Be especially aware of the power of your emotions today. What might God be inviting you to learn through them? Allow divine guidance to speak through your feelings.

FEBRUARY 5 • *God Is in Control?*

Well, yes, . . . and no. Close examination of this glib assumption that "God is in control" leads any thinking person to some questions and caveats. Does this mean everything that happens is God's will, so we accept it as holy decree? What about the gift of free will?

One signpost of spiritual maturity comes in our increasing capacity to embrace paradox and mystery. Consideration of God's "control" offers one opportunity. As human beings, we want to know why events happen the way they do. We often rush to distorted answers to gain intellectual satisfaction. We want to make sense of it! Whether we're considering triumph or tragedy, we tend to think in terms of reward or punishment from an all-powerful God. The question Why? can trigger spiritual paralysis.

We want to hold something or someone accountable for life's puzzling events. In our quest to find the cause or place the blame, some of us malign God's nature by making God responsible for everything—in other words, in control.

Recently, while sitting with a young couple whose only child had been killed in a traffic accident, I met a friend who came by to offer comfort. This well-intentioned but misguided person told the hurting parents that the certainty that this tragedy was God's will should offer reassurance. How could this hurting couple receive consolation from the Person who willed (supposedly) their daughter's death?

Things don't always happen according to our plans and desires. Because we feel that we lack control over our lives, we want someone to be in control. But complexity and uncertainty are part of life.

Still, God is not absent or uninvolved. The divine heart breaks along with ours in times of trouble and celebrates with us in times of joy. We stand on the solid rock of God's loving presence, and God's desire for relationship is nothing short of a miracle. True discernment then takes root in our relationship with the Divine. Attempting to figure it out by listing pros and cons may contribute to decision making, but spiritual discernment involves far more than that.

No matter how circumstances evolve, we receive the invitation to participate (free will) in our own recovery process by working with a God (divine Sovereign) whose very nature is healing and whose will for us is wholeness. Perhaps that is the ultimate "control" that God exercises as part of God's loving nature.

Reflect: Explore your feelings about God's control, affirming both divine sovereignty and free will—embracing both as true and life-giving.

FEBRUARY 6 • *My Purpose*

Another popular idea that begs for deprogramming is the belief that "God has one purpose for me, and it's up to me to find it." This sets up yet another distortion of God's nature—that of One who plays hide-and-seek with us, requiring us to search for a destiny hidden in the clouds.

A wise friend confronted me years ago when I was pursuing that elusive blueprint called "my purpose." His words turned my thinking and my theology around. He countered, "What kind of God do you worship—one who teases and hides things from you? What if your real purpose is to be loving and faithful and to make compassionate use of your God-given gifts? In many ways, God may leave it up to you whether that happens in Cincinnati or Seattle—or whether you become a social worker or a stay-at-home mom. God's will for you to be a channel of love in the world can be lived out in any number of ways. Remember, we are not puppets!"

My friend's words invited me to take responsibility for discovering and acknowledging the way I had been created by God and being available to the flow of divine love, whether I sold shoes or ran for the Senate. Once again, we encounter God's omnipotence and the free will of human beings in a creative dance of cooperation. To step into the dance of grace, we must learn the meaning of trust and willingly embrace our freedom to choose.

Though God may not have a specific road map laid out for us, God does have hopes and desires for us—a divine dream for us. It doesn't matter so much what we do to earn income; rather, it's what we do to be ourselves, the persons God created us to be. When we focus only on finding a fixed purpose, we miss the many possibilities that await us.

Reflect: Consider your purpose as it relates to the great commandment to love God with all your heart, soul, and mind, and your neighbor as yourself. How are you fulfilling that purpose in your life?

FEBRUARY 7 • *Incomplete Images of God*

Faulty assumptions, which are reflected in our limited images of God's nature, can lead to faulty discernment. We can be sure that the dynamic Water of Life (the Spirit of God) will overflow the edges of any container we construct. If we think we can fully define God or catch the sacred in a net of words, we deceive ourselves. A word simply points to something beyond itself. The word *sugar* is not sugar itself—we have to taste sugar to know its sweetness.

We experience God in countless ways—as comforter, as judge, as friend, as peacemaker, as creator, as source of all, as loving father, as nurturing mother—an inexhaustible host of spiritual "containers." As human beings, we naturally tend to describe God with human characteristics because that's our primary frame of reference. But we need never lose sight of the fact that God is more than the Bible, more than the church, more than any definition—no matter how grandiose— that we can devise. When we take one facet of God's nature and make it the whole, we distort the image of the One who said, "I AM WHO I AM" (Exod. 3:14).

Our words and limited images will always fall short. A profound difference exists between our experience of God and the way we explain the experience, between knowing God and talking about God. Simply put, our words and images of the holy mystery are far less important than our relationship to it.

Reflect: Call to mind your favorite names and descriptions of God. Do they define your relationship with the Holy One in a limiting way? List as many images as you can, reflecting on the times you have experienced God in those ways. Experiment with new images in your prayer today, knowing that God is always more.

FEBRUARY 8 • *Expanding the Divine Image*

Though Sally had been on a serious, intentional spiritual journey for years, she kept snapping back to a distorted image of God she had formed in her early years: a strict heavenly Father who demanded obedience—the primary purpose of the relationship.

In an honest conversation, Sally sounded exasperated as she spoke of her many family duties: helping to care for her grandchild, church demands as chair of an important committee, and overseeing some home renovations—all of which had usurped her usual devotional time. "I guess I would describe myself as a backslider!" she said with an attempt at humor. Her words conveyed her belief that God was disappointed in her. Her old image of God had returned, one of God as a kind of school principal who would stand her in the corner to do penance for her sins of omission.

Old habits and images die hard. Time and again, we must return to the true experience of God not as one who condemns but one who invites us to grow—in whatever circumstances occur. Sally did this by committing to more "grace on the go" prayers for this busy time of her life, breathing a prayer of gratitude for the sweet smell of the baby's skin and the blessing of this new life and escaping the noisy renovation for a brief walk in a quiet park. As she told me later, "I found that God can run as fast as I can!"

Reflect: As you go about your daily round today, formulate brief "grace on the go" prayers so you can experience the companionship of the Spirit everywhere you go and in everything you do.

FEBRUARY 9 • *Feminine Aspects of God*

A few years ago, some young seminarians—both men and women—expanded the container of my God image by urging me to pay attention to the feminine aspects of the divine nature as well as the familiar masculine images.

These young people pointed me to scripture citations like these: "I have calmed and quieted my soul, like a weaned child with its mother" (Ps. 131:2) and "'How often have I desired to gather your children together as a hen gathers her brood under her wings'" (Luke 13:34). Part of God's nurturing nature surely resembles a mother caring tenderly for her offspring. By associating God with masculine images only—King, Conqueror, Prince, Lord, Judge, Sovereign, Father—we limit the wholeness and inclusiveness of divine presence.

Rather than having me give up my accustomed address to God (Heavenly Father), the seminarians encouraged me to *add to it* more and more aspects of the divine. In truth, honoring the feminine aspects didn't change my God "container" so much as enlarge it. I began to appreciate the truth that God is neither male nor female; "God is spirit, and those who worship [God] must worship in spirit and truth" (John 4:24).

When we open our hearts to ongoing revelation, we claim mother-like attributes of God in addition to father-like qualities. Our relationship to God is enriched, and the avenues to spiritual experience become boundless.

Reflect: Recall times when you have experienced the nurturing, motherly aspects of God. Expand your notions of who and what God is, honoring more parts of the divine mystery as the boundaries blur.

FEBRUARY 10 • *The Whole Shebang*

Not only do we limit our images of God, we also limit our sense of God's presence. No matter how we express it, we often posit the notion that God is present when things are going well and absent when things are not.

When we feel inspired or happy or fulfilled, we equate those feelings with being "close to God" or saying "God was with me." By contrast, when we feel depressed, sad, angry, or defeated, we tend to feel abandoned, separated from divine presence.

Before we can discern God's will for us, we must begin to see life as a whole—both the light and the dark, success and failure, illness or health. As Romans 8:38 affirms, "Neither death, nor life, nor angels, nor rulers, nor things present, nor things to come, nor powers, nor height, nor depth, nor anything else in all creation, will be able to separate us from the love of God."

We can understand our human, knee-jerk reaction during hardship, "How could God let this happen? What did I do wrong? Where is God?" Our persistent questioning why often blocks us from the redemptive ongoing presence that shows us the next step, that heals our wounds, that weeps with us.

One function of faith is to ground us in a love that will not leave us or let us go, even if for a time we cannot feel that comforting companionship. In those dark times, we trust that God participates with us as we pick up the pieces of whatever is broken.

Reflect: Ponder times in your life when you have felt separated from God. How did God's love reach you during those times? Did that love come to you through family, friends, neighbors, your own resilience? As you look at those times in retrospect, express gratitude for the grace that emerged in surprising ways.

FEBRUARY 11 • *The Three-Storied Universe*

Heaven is up there; hell is down there; and I'm right here in between." So goes our traditional rendering of the structure of the spiritual cosmos.

Our literal acceptance of this language may reflect a notion we need to reexamine and deprogram.

Jesus never offered only one definition of the kingdom of heaven. He expressed its many facets through a variety of rich metaphors, likening the kingdom to a mustard seed, a pearl of great price, a portion of yeast, and other images—all hidden treasures that, when honored, have a larger effect on the external world. While we see evidence of the kingdom at work in the visible world, its germination begins in the heart: "The kingdom of heaven is within you." No amount of forced external "good behavior" makes up for the fact that the kingdom of heaven has its roots in the soul. It is an inside job.

In like manner, the Sermon on the Mount records Jesus' response to specific sins like murder and adultery by pointing to the recesses of the heart where hatred and lust reside before they blossom into actions. (See Matthew 5:21-48.)

Jesus' specificity about the importance of the inner world suggests that we need to take notice and allow the barriers of space and time to disintegrate. Let's face it; we know when we experience heaven or hell in our daily lives; we use those words to describe an inner condition. As we come to realize that God's omnipresence supersedes our childish image of "a white-bearded man on a faraway throne," we make room for the power of mystery.

The poet Elizabeth Barrett Browning said it well: "Earth's crammed with heaven, and every common bush afire with God." Rather than being tethered to physical descriptions and locations of heaven and hell, spiritual maturity invites us to see them as part of the human condition—right here, right now.

Reflect: Take a few moments to mull over your sense of heaven, hell, and earth. How have you experienced each of those places in your life?

FEBRUARY 12 • *Disarming Our Defenses*

The path to spiritual discernment involves some deprogramming and some disarming—letting down our defenses, taking off the armor of control, trusting that God's Spirit can lead us in the direction of a whole-ness we can scarcely imagine.

Prayerful discernment needs to be more than asking God to approve our agendas. Entering the decision-making process under the guidance of the Spirit means we make room for such guidance by letting go of our idea of what we need to happen or want to happen. Being sincerely open is a difficult matter; self-deception abounds in the unconscious. Being wide open allows the Spirit to shape what we want and leads us to love and growth. We surrender to a wisdom greater than our own.

The word *surrender* has gotten a bad rap. It conjures up images of a defeated soldier waving a white flag in utter helplessness. But surrender to a loving God involves saying "Yes!" rather than "I give up."

Surrender to God need not mean we'll board the next ship to the Congo or quit our jobs. Most likely we'll stay in the same place and look the same; but instead of an agenda-driven life, we will move toward a soul-centered life guided by the Spirit.

Life is not a secret blueprint but a process of becoming all God created us to be, no matter where we are or what we do. As we disarm ourselves and become cloaked in genuine humility, we will gain the wisdom to discern the things that foster faithfulness.

Reflect: Fling open the door to your heart today, releasing preconceived notions, worn-out ideas, judgments, resentments . . . making a gracious space for divine guidance.

FEBRUARY 13 • *Disarming the Ego*

A minister-friend confessed recently, "When I pray for discernment as I write a sermon, the process can get contaminated pretty easily. Instead of listening to the Spirit's leading, I can get derailed by unspoken questions like, 'Will the congregation like this? Will so-and-so go ballistic if I say what I really believe to be true? If I use that commentary, will I sound more academic and intelligent?' I have to get my ego out of the way, or I can't really listen!" These are the words of an honest and self-aware person.

Praying for guidance requires that we let go of "What will they think?" as the major aspect of our attitude. The same goes for the shoulds and oughts and supposed-to-bes of our lives. And the pride. And the control.

Being completely disarmed strips us of our defenses and barriers, making us vulnerable and alert for the still small Voice.

In terms of self-knowledge, the ego can be a wonderful servant. However, when it sits in the driver's seat, it's a dangerous master. Discernment on our part comes in sensing when the ego takes control of the wheel. God invites us to listen to the whisper of the soul rather than the shout of the ego.

Reflect: Notice any thoughts today that relate to the ego, such as *How am I coming across? Do I look okay? Do they like me?* Smile at your humanity as you assign the ego a lesser role in your decision-making process.

FEBRUARY 14 • *Distinguishing among the Voices*

It's hard to distinguish the divine voice of discernment from the clamor of other compelling voices: "Mother and father expected me to . . . , the advice of my friends leads me to . . . , my doctor instructed me to . . . , the culture around me influences me to . . . , the preacher warned me about . . . , my counselor encourages me to. . . . " Some of these external callings provide valid food for thought; some lead us to guilt, self-criticism, and anxiety.

Deep within each of us is a hidden place where the Holy Spirit communes with us. In our January reflections, we explored the necessity of visiting this inner soul space where we listen to the loving wisdom of the Holy One. In John 14:16-17, scripture tells us we are not alone in this cave of the heart: [The Father] will give you another Advocate, to be with you forever. This is the Spirit of truth . . . , he abides with you, and he will be in you.

However, our own ego can block the door to discernment, shouting its own message, such as, "How can I get what I want?" If the projected action will polish our halo, we can be sure an ego investment is infusing the process. If we listen in an atmosphere of complete honesty and vulnerability, the Spirit will reveal the identity of this ego-dominated voice so we learn to recognize it. Though this ego-centeredness is a part of the human condition, it's important that we can distinguish its interfering influence when that occurs. God's voice leads to authentic behavior, fullness of life, love, compassion, and spiritual freedom.

Reflect: Get to know the voice of your ego with a sense of compassion for your humanness. Open your heart to God's ongoing acceptance and forgiveness as you travel the path of self-knowledge.

FEBRUARY 15 • *Through a Spiritual Lens*

Discerning the Spirit's movement in your life resembles donning a different pair of glasses as you consider where you are being led. For instance, you might be deciding whether or not to accept a particular job offer. One valid lens for discernment would include the following questions: Can I live on that salary? How does my family feel about moving to Cincinnati or Santa Fe? Do I possess the skills for this position?

The spiritual lens, however, would address such concerns as these: Do I feel invigorated when I consider doing this work? Is this job consistent with my highest values? Will this environment allow me and my family to grow into richer relationship? Will this vocation allow my heart to expand and my compassion for others to grow? Is there a feeling of peace and challenge when I imagine being in that position?

As mentioned before, seeing something that needs to be done is one thing; being called to do it is another. In order to sense a magnetic invitation to do something—whether it's a paid job or a committee chairship or a volunteer activity—we must expand our ways of listening to the movement of the Spirit. We gather pertinent information; we notice the reactions of our body and emotions; we consider the opinions of those we love and trust. Then we bring all that assessment to the center of our souls in prayerful openness. We cannot allow money and prestige to overwhelm the voice of the Spirit.

Reflect: Mull over a decision—large or small—that you may be facing. Take some time to view it through the lens of the Spirit as you prayerfully consider all factors. Beware of an urgent feeling that you "ought" to do it.

FEBRUARY 16 • *The Body Speaks*

Part of distinguishing the voices that affect our discernment comes from honoring the guidance our bodies offer. The body, created by God, resembles a radar system that can detect divine nudges and invitations in profound ways.

The body constantly speaks to us, and part of the task of discernment comes in learning to hear and heed its messages. How does our body signal our stress levels: a tension headache, lower back pain, tight shoulders, queasy stomach, nervous fidgeting, a racing heartbeat? In my thirties, an intuitive physician helped me discover my own stress indicator. During a time of "burning the candle at both ends" and trying to do too much too fast, I developed a throbbing sore throat that sent me in search of antibiotics for what I assumed was a strep infection.

It wasn't. Noting no inflammation or physical cause, the doctor explained the source of the pain as "esophageal spasms," my body's personal response to stress. "But it hurts!" I argued. He agreed that the spasms created pain, and he urged me to focus on the cause of the stress and act on it. "If you learn to recognize your own body's stress signal—and honor it—it can make a difference in your entire life. Learn to take responsibility for it."

My doctor's wisdom came as a gift for me that day. From that moment to this, when that familiar aching in my throat gets my attention, I breathe deeply and relax. Then I summon the courage to face the stress and find ways to identify and address the actual cause of the condition. Your stress signals may be more subtle but still noticeable.

When the psalmist proclaimed that we are "fearfully and wonderfully made" (Ps.139:14), he wasn't kidding. The intricate web of connections among body, mind, and spirit form a reliable network for divine guidance—one that we ignore at our peril.

Reflect: How does your body speak to you in times of stress? Honor it as an avenue of guidance created by a loving God, and be thankful.

FEBRUARY 17 • *The Brain Speaks*

Medical science and spirituality are not enemies. Study after study unites the two disciplines or at least calls them into meaningful dialogue, inviting us to view the miraculous interactions of the body with awe and wonder.

God created us in this interrelated way, so that our bodies, minds, and spirits provide vital information in the discernment process.

Research on the amazing aspects of the brain is coming out faster than we can digest the implications. A major finding focuses on the adaptability of the brain to changes in its environment (neuroplasticity), which indicates that we can play an active role in altering the brain by paying attention to what we "feed" it. Scans have revealed that prayer and worship engage particular neural pathways that affect the area of the brain that lodges empathy for others. We can enhance the neural structures that make us calmer and more compassionate, as well as improving memory and cognitive skills.

One of the findings reported in *How God Changes Your Brain* indicates that participation in fear-based religions that stress God's anger and punitive nature can stimulate the part of the limbic brain that creates anxiety and dread. However, the authors suggest ways that help us collude and cooperate in positively affecting the brain:

- Faith: be hopeful and optimistic (affirming the unconditional love of God)
- Dialogue: communicate with others (especially your faith community)
- Aerobic exercise: use movement to improve cognition and reduce anxiety
- Meditate/Pray: still the body and mind
- Yawn: breathe in oxygen to affect relaxation and help in focusing[1]

Science can play an integral part in how we understand the intricacy of creation. Though science can never tell us who or what God is, many of its findings can plunge us further into the wonder of the Mystery that sustains us.

Reflect: Consider your own body as "a temple of the Holy Spirit" (1 Cor. 6:19). In what ways can you honor the ongoing revelations offered by science?

FEBRUARY 18 • *Resonance and Dissonance*

In surprising ways, our bodies mirror the messages of the soul. Saints of old referred to this process as having feelings of "consolation" and "desolation," which they regarded as reliable nudges from the "still small voice" of the Spirit. These days, we're more likely to say, "That really rings true for me" or "That doesn't feel right to me."

We experience and describe the positive responses of resonance (consolation) personally—a feeling of aliveness, a lifting of the spirit, an expansion of the heart, being pulled upward toward the Light, an unusual peace, the felt presence of God, a sense of Yes. On the other hand, we experience dissonance (desolation) as darkness, constriction, resistance, narrowness of spirit, absence of energy, heaviness, a sense of No.

To use these feelings as one barometer of divine guidance, we must learn to identify them and also notice the ways our bodies and behavior register them. I learned that I was ignoring the signals one day during a memorable conversation with one of my sons.

During a time when I intentionally sought "God's will for my life," I was talking with my son about my day at Perkins Theological Seminary attending a conference. I launched into a lively account of what the professors said, even mentioning the wonderful "smell of old books" in the building. I gave a very long answer to his short question, "What did you do today?"

My son's follow-up comment sparked a shift in perception that has stayed with me through the years. He said, "Mom, just listen to yourself! You're wondering where God is leading you, and you assume it has to involve pain and sacrifice! Don't you think God can speak through your joy, your love of learning, and the pleasing odor of books? For goodness sake, pay attention!"

God's ways of speaking are much greater than our powers of listening!

Reflect: How does your body register feelings of resonance? dissonance? Begin to notice and name these feelings as you develop a greater capacity for hearing divine guidance.

FEBRUARY 19 • *Skills and Passions*

Mary, a retired accountant, wanted to invest some of her newly discovered extra time to be of service to her church. Because of her expertise with numbers, the pastor asked her to chair the finance committee. Mary described her feelings of dissonance: "My heart sank. I knew I had the skills to do it. I felt I should do it, but I just didn't want to! I've always yearned to work with young children. I had to put my own kids in daycare when they were young because of my career, and I missed that playful experience of being with toddlers."

In truth, the accountant side of Mary's life had received plenty of room to grow, but her circumstances had buried her passion for children. It's a useful illustration of the difference between skills (what we're capable of doing) and passions (what we long to do). At that point in Mary's life, one option carried feelings of dissonance and the other of resonance. Knowing the difference between those feelings helped her distinguish the difference between her skills and her passions. Most people in her position would do as they were asked. Instead, she told her pastor she wanted to volunteer in the nursery rather than chair the finance committee.

Often we can combine our skills and passions. But sometimes we mistake one for the other, assuming that we must pursue our vocational skills for a lifetime simply because they exist. Buried creative desires to paint, knit, do woodworking, teach, cook, plant a garden—you name it—go ignored as we focus on what we think we *ought* to do. The God whose very nature is abundance and wholeness invites us to discover all that we are.

Reflect: Make an honest list of your skills and a separate one of your passions. What steps, even small ones, can you take to honor your curiosity and yearning?

FEBRUARY 20 • *Decision Drivers*

We are shaped by the questions that sit, day after day, deep within us—often beneath our awareness. For instance, if we seek a life of more pleasure or greater comfort or more approval or dependable safety or financial security—even peace of mind—those inner desires will drive the decisions we make. Their silent influence will infuse the discernment process with their preferences.

Consider the revealing story of an elderly monk whom others admired for his keen spiritual wisdom. A young novice in the monastery, eager to discover the old man's secret, hid outside his hermitage to spy on him. He heard a thump as the monk's knees met the floor at prayer time. Then he heard these words: "Who are you, God, and who am I?" Moments later, there came the same question: "Who are you God, and who am I?" All day long, those were the only words the young novice heard.

If the prevailing question in our lives centers around our desire to know God and to know who we are in relation to God, that central yearning will color our decisions. Surely this intent of the heart reflects the words of Matthew 6:33: "Strive first for the kingdom of God and his righteousness, and all these things will be given to you as well." This kind of seeking is not a one-time intention; it's a way of life.

Reflect: Think honestly about the factors that drive your decisions. In what ways does your desire for divine truth affect the way you approach discernment?

FEBRUARY 21 • *Your Vocation*

The word *vocation* shares the same root with the word "voice." This shared connection implies a difference between our job and our vocation. How does our connection to the Spirit allow the divine voice to speak in and through us? On our path to deeper discernment, we're invited to look at how God calls us to participate in the healing of the world.

Our job provides a way to pay the rent. Our unique voice, or vocation, focuses on how we live out our particular gifts and graces. An ongoing life of listening helps us to express the divine dream in any circumstances. A woman in my community spent her entire life teaching. She inspired students for decades, garnered countless awards, and was honored by her peers. She felt fortunate to have significant overlaps between her job and her vocation.

However, now well into her nineties, long retired from teaching, she continues to live out her vocation—that of inspiring others and spreading joy in the extended-care facility where she lives. I'll never forget her response to my question about her life at this final stage. With a gleam in her eye, she described her first waking moments each morning: "When I see the light of dawn, I wonder what gift I can give today to someone who needs it—even if it's as simple as a smile."

We often think we must live out our purpose in neon lights or through some grand accomplishment. However, it's less about what we do and more about who we are.

Reflect: Ponder the ways God invites you to be who you were created to be, to use those gifts to express love and healing in the world. What one specific action can you take today to live out your vocation?

FEBRUARY 22 • *Taking the Next Step*

Imagine that you're standing at the edge of a dark forest. You want desperately to reach freedom on the other side (an answer to discernment), but you don't know exactly how to navigate the tangle of trees. All you have in your jeans pocket is a tiny flashlight. The woods look daunting, scary, perhaps even impossible, but you're committed to the journey. Then imagine a Voice giving you encouragement and instructions:

- Take out your flashlight and shine it on the path before you.
- Step into the small circle of light that you can see.
- Shine the flashlight forward again; step into the circle of light.
- If you stumble and fall, simply smile and breathe a forgiving "oops!" (No guilt or remorse allowed; it's a waste of time).
- Dust yourself off and get back on the path.
- Repeat the process again and again and again.
- You will reach the other side of the forest, one point of light at a time.

In other words, act on the light you have now. It doesn't have to be the final word, the clearest word, or the most profound word. You don't have to wait until the situation improves or until you feel like it. The road to release doesn't require a meticulous map. In fact, knowledge of the path is no substitute for placing one foot in front of the other. You simply proceed with the light you've been given. Take a risk and act.

Oddly enough, people usually think that taking action involves fixing a problem or finding a solution. In the process of discernment, that approach may be counterproductive. The procedure seems to be best served by opening yourself to divine direction then aligning with positive, life-giving energy and acting in cooperation with God's guiding light. God is always inviting us beyond where we are—one small step at a time.

Reflect: Recall a situation of discernment that you're presently considering. What one action would move you forward? a phone call? a contact to give you essential information? a time of reflection and prayer about the possibilities? Just take one step.

FEBRUARY 23 • *Getting It Wrong*

But what if I think I'm doing the will of God, and I get it wrong? What if it doesn't turn out well?" she asked.

"Join the club," I responded.

Sometimes we learn as much from getting it wrong as getting it right. Failure is a rich seedbed of personal growth. A noted *Peanuts* cartoon shows Sally sitting at a table with two pieces of paper—one large and one small—in front of her. As she writes diligently on the large piece, she says to Charlie Brown, "I'm making a list of all the lessons I've learned from life. Well, actually, I'm making two lists." Charlie Brown asks, "Why is one list so much longer than the other?" Holding up the long list, Sally says, "Oh, these are the things I've learned the hard way!"

In the arena of human behavior, we learn from experience. And how do we get experience? Through trial and error, through failure as well as success. Even if we offer an act of kindness that is rebuffed or doesn't produce the desired result, the action itself may not be misguided. When acting from a motivation of love and compassion, we learn to let go of the outcome.

One mark of spiritual maturity is a willingness to take risks, to get it wrong, to believe that God's forgiving spirit will pick us up, dust us off, and set us on the path again. If we remain at the starting gate for fear of making a mistake, our souls will congeal into something lifeless and fearful. We move forward in faith with the light that we have. Second chances abound in the arena of divine grace.

Ask, pray, watch, act. Don't allow fear to paralyze you!

Reflect: Think of times in your life when you have learned valuable lessons from your mistakes. Give thanks that God's loving presence helped your soul grow from your choices.

FEBRUARY 24 • *Judgment or Discernment?*

There are contrasts between *judgment* and *discernment,* even though we often use the terms interchangeably. Judgment usually involves a sense of distance from the thing or person being judged that emphasizes it as "other." It has an aura of put-down, condescension, or fear. Discernment, on the other hand, identifies "with," seeing a behavior or situation as it truly is and choosing an appropriate course of engagement or disengagement accordingly.

For instance, judgment might label someone as an "incorrigible gambler," while discernment would involve understanding that the person has a gambling problem and deciding not to go to a casino outing! I might judge my financial adviser as a thief because I lost money or, after considering his financial advice, my discernment might lead me to give him another chance or to find another consultant.

Here's a checklist for determining the difference between judgment and discernment:

- Judgment is a reaction; discernment is a response.
- Judgment is unreflective; discernment is thoughtful.
- Judgment is hasty; discernment takes time.
- Judgment jumps to conclusions; discernment thinks it through.
- Judgment contains our own biases; discernment is open to the Spirit.
- Judgment carries a sense of superiority; discernment seeks equanimity.
- Judgment stems from emotion; discernment desires wisdom and insight.
- Judgment labels; discernment seeks understanding.

Before we take the familiar leap to judgment of a person, the law of love would have us affirm that person's essential goodness before assuming the worst. After all, there's some good in the worst of us and some bad in the best of us.

Reflect: Consider the difference between judgment and discernment in your own life. The next time you feel tempted to make a quick judgment, take time to respond with discernment rather than reaction.

FEBRUARY 25 • *The Discernment Prayer*

In the old days before processed milk, my grandmother would wait for the thick cream to slowly rise to the top of the container before skimming it off to enrich her cup of coffee. Discernment is like that; it takes patience and attention. You wait until the cream rises to the top. Or, to use another metaphor, it's a bit like standing in a muddy puddle, waiting for it to clear up. If you stand still long enough, the dirt settles to the bottom as you watch. In like manner, good decisions require stillness and waiting.

In making decisions, the pertinent data can swirl into a mass of confusion. We receive external data in the form of advice from those we trust, factual aspects to consider, scriptural principles, and life values. Internal data comes from the body's reactions and the soft voice of the soul where the Spirit speaks to us. As all this input merges, a decision will begin to form.

A familiar prayer facilitates this process of guidance, relying on our sensitivity to God's interior influence. It assumes a belief that the Spirit speaks through our soul, body, feelings, intellect, and the yearning of the heart. Based on a verse from Psalm 37:4 ("Take delight in the LORD, and he will give you the desires of your heart"), it can point the way forward.

We clear our minds of cluttering thoughts and set aside our own preference regarding the answer. Then we pray the following prayer for discernment with patience and persistence for days or even months:

Loving God, if this course of action is for my highest good and those involved, I pray that you will *increase* my desire for it; if this is not for the highest good, I pray that you will *decrease* my desire for it. Amen.

Then we patiently pay attention.

Reflect: As you consider a question, a choice, or a decision, pray The Discernment Prayer faithfully, noting any changes in the desires of your own heart under the influence of the Spirit. Listen for the still small whisper of God.

FEBRUARY 26 • *Deciding*

There comes a moment when it's time to make a choice and step forward in faith. If we wait for absolute certainty, we'll wait forever! Prolonged hesitation and constant second-guessing can make it impossible to act.

An old saying states, "Leap and the net will appear!" Being overly cautious stunts our courage and corrals us in mediocrity. We take the next step, trusting that we'll be shown the one after that and the one after that. We're called to faithfulness, not perfection.

We can foster a deepening trust by praying the following prayer:

O Holy One, be with me in my uncertainty. Though I'm ready to move forward, my willingness sometimes feels weak and tentative. But somehow, I trust that you will honor my intention because that's all I have right now. Even if I make a misstep and stumble, I trust your gracious Spirit to steer me back on the path to authentic discernment.

So accept my feeble effort, my availability, my desire to honor your words, "Do not be afraid." I no longer ask for a vision of the whole journey, but simply for the next step. As you shine your holy light on my path forward, I will take that step with your loving, forgiving Spirit ever at my side. Amen.

Reflect: Meditate using one of the following verses: "'Do not be afraid, little flock, for it is your Father's good pleasure to give you the kingdom'" (Luke 12:32) or "The Lord is my helper; I will not be afraid" (Heb. 13:6) or "O Most High, when I am afraid, I put my trust in you" (Ps. 56:3). Allow your fears to melt into life-giving trust.

FEBRUARY 27 • *Litmus Test for Listening*

In any process of discernment, the inevitable question arises: Am I on the right track? Am I moving in a healthy direction?

Even when a path forward seems clearly indicated, signposts that provide encouragement and confirmation of the decision exist:

- An interior sense of joy and peace (resonance) rather than feelings of heaviness and dread (dissonance)
- Something I deeply desire
- A sense that the fruit of the Spirit (love, joy, peace, patience, kindness, generosity, faithfulness, gentleness, self-control—Galatians 5:22-23) can grow on this path
- A feeling of spiritual freedom rather than duty and obligation
- Energy and courage to move forward
- An awakening to heightened awareness and understanding
- A clarity of motives. Is my aim to gain approval, to "look successful" to others? Is this decision merely more comfortable and less challenging, therefore I'm assuming it's "peaceful"?
- An assurance that the decision honors others and is compassionate.
- A strengthening of personal commitments
- An avenue that fosters love in the world
- Trust in the Spirit's involvement in the process

A few final questions about our decision can jolt us into action: How will I feel about this on my deathbed? What path will I wish I had taken? This line of questioning diminishes the fear of taking a risk. Even if it's a difficult path, the repeated encouragement of scripture is "Be not afraid."

Reflect: Move through the signposts slowly and prayerfully, being as honest and vulnerable as possible. Trust that God's will for you is wholeness and abundant life.

FEBRUARY 28 • *The Dance of Discernment*

The merging of divine guidance and our free will is like many mysterious concepts—best expressed through imagination and metaphor.

To me, it resembles a sacred dance. When we dance to music, we simply take the next step in the rhythm of the tune rather than knowing where we're going to end up on the dance floor! The dance of discernment is no ordinary movement. It is intimate and instinctive—much like a tango, where the partners move in sync with each other and the dance is seamless. If we can imagine ourselves as a partner, with the Holy Spirit leading the dance, then each time the Spirit shifts, we automatically flow with the music. We do not stop to analyze (two steps forward, one move backward, now turn?).

Perhaps initially we sense this remarkable union for only an instant, but over time we learn to recognize the overwhelming resonance. We come to understand that it is rooted deeply in our soulful relationship with the One who created us for this intimate journey. The nudge from the Spirit usually leads only to the next move, not the entire dance!

I believe our dance with the Spirit can be just as instinctive as a tango if nourished and practiced for a lifetime. As our relationship with God grows stronger, we gradually begin to move as God moves, see as God sees, hear as God hears, love as God loves. Of course, like any dancer, we sometimes make a misstep. But when we stumble, we come to depend even more on the wisdom and wonder of the leading partner. And, like any skill, the more we practice, the easier it becomes.

Spiritual discernment is an art, an ongoing engagement with the Creator. It isn't a list of dos and don'ts designed to lead us to the right answer. Over time, this holy partnership can become a way of life rather than a list of decisions.

So may we flow with the pace of guidance, and step onto the dance floor!

Reflect: Engage your imagination and allow yourself to dream about your own dance with the Divine. How would close partnership with the Holy Spirit affect your relationships, your thoughts and statements about others and your view of the world?

FEBRUARY 29 • *A Bonus Day*

Every four years, we receive the gift of an extra twenty-four hours. How will we use this bonus day?

We affirm that the Holy Spirit desires our wholeness as human beings so we can serve the world with love and compassion. We remind ourselves that the guiding love of God wants us to experience life in greater abundance—the divine measure of abundance, not the world's measure. With that unconditional love as our foundation, we take time to recap our own process of discernment—not simply what we know about spiritual decision making but how the process operates in our particular lives.

As we listen for the Spirit's gentle nudges, remember to notice the following:

- Flashes of emotional "electricity"—intense curiosity, sudden bursts of joy, sincere interest, deep desire
- Recurring thoughts that continue to visit, unbidden
- Persistent urges of fear and resistance that may cloud your vision.
- Messages from your environment—scripture, songs, advice of those you trust
- Moments of frustration, obligation, the burden of duty that stifle your peace
- Feelings of harmony with your values and beliefs

As you consider these movements in your own soul, listen for God's invitation embedded within them. What is the still small Voice beckoning you to notice? to grow or learn from? How is God inviting you to take risks, to act on faith?

Another revealing exercise involves imagining other people in your situation—persons toward whom you feel love and goodwill—who seek counsel from you. What advice would you give? What wisdom would you share? What might God lead you to say? Allow the inspiration intended for them to wind its holy way to you.

No matter how difficult our dilemmas of discernment, no matter how many troubling aspects a decision may contain, we are never alone in the messiness. God is with us—guiding, inspiring, cajoling, forgiving, loving. What a glorious gift on this bonus day!

Reflect: Allow courage and gratitude to emerge from your heart. With a knowing smile, embrace the truth that God's guidance is not simply a sweet idea but an abiding reality.

March

TILLING THE
GARDEN

"You will know the truth, and the truth will make you free."
—John 8:32

Breath Prayer
Open my eyes. . . . that I may see.

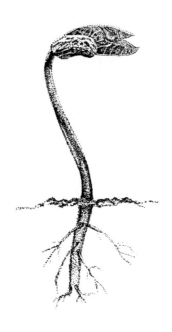

MARCH 1 • *Breaking Ground*

It's quite daunting to stand before an untilled plot of land. Your mind swims in possibilities—yellow zinnias, juicy strawberries, bright green beans. But you also know that hours of digging and weeding, planting and watering loom ahead first. Finally, with a deep breath and a sharp spade, you turn over that first mound of dirt.

Our souls want to blossom too. And, like a plot being readied for plants, we prepare our souls. We must clear the inner garden of debris and weeds that can choke tender seedlings. We uncover and set aside stones and boulders before fruits of the Spirit can flourish.

When we courageously dig inside ourselves—through the dirt, if you will—interior spaciousness opens up. Air can get in. Sunlight can penetrate through the muck. Hard-packed soil is loosened.

This digging opens a pathway to the holy and to the true self at the same time. When folks come in for spiritual guidance, some desire a more meaningful experience of God. Others enter with the questions "Who am I? Who is the self that God created in me?" No matter which yearning is conscious, both the desire for relationship with God and the desire to discover who we really are become part of the same process. On the journey to God, we find our true self. On the journey to our true self, we encounter the holy. The searches weave in and out of each other in a remarkable fashion—an organic unfolding and blooming.

So pick up the spade and turn on the tiller. It's time to break ground.

Reflect: Take some time to contemplate the reality of your inner garden, where the treasure of your true self and the richness of divine relationship await you. Pray for the courage to start digging through the dirt.

MARCH 2 • *The Holy Gardener*

We aren't alone in the tilling and planting of our soul's soil, thank goodness. The Holy Gardener not only invites us into the growth process but accompanies and guides us through it. The image of God as one who fosters our flourishing is far from the demanding taskmaster we habitually envision:

- Rather than a strict supervisor who requires slave labor under threat of punishment, we encounter One who patiently allows us to work at our own pace.
- Rather than a greedy "boss" who focuses on proof of productivity, we find One who celebrates the emergence of every tiny green shoot.
- Rather than a distant dictator who watches while we sweat, we meet One who is digging at the roots along with us to discover what's there.
- Rather than one who issues threatening ultimatums, we hear a voice of gentle encouragement.

God's nourishing presence filters out our own self-judgment. On our trek to the truth of ourselves, we will surely dig up unpleasant discoveries. Those moments of confrontation can mire us in shame and discouragement, and we revert to the self-condemnation that brings the growth process to a standstill. At those times, we need to feel the sacred arms around us forgiving our foolishness, accepting our human impulses, loving us in spite of our weakness.

Do we dare see ourselves through the eyes of the Holy Gardener? It seems too good to be true that divine perfection can love our human imperfection. It plays havoc with our sense of fairness, our notion that we must earn love or at least deserve it somehow. Yet, accepting that we are accepted—unbelievable though it is—is the only antidote to our self-condemnation.

Reflect: As you "till the soil" of your inner garden, notice any moments of interior self-judgment today, your times of saying (or thinking) "I'm such a klutz"; "I'm an incorrigible sinner"; "I'll never be any better." Stop and affirm that you are a beloved child of God—cherished and accepted.

MARCH 3 • *Sifting through the Stones*

As we begin this archaeological dig into the inner garden, we may overturn rubble that we somehow recognize. In other words, we bump up against barriers that we've encountered before, core issues that keep returning. Familiar stones litter the soil of the soul.

Through the years, I have thought many times that I had slain the dragon of perfectionism, for instance, only to face it again, this time with a different face and a new costume:

- I cut my kids some slack to "be who they are," only to find myself irritated that my coworkers don't meet my expectations.
- I present a workshop and feel encouraged by most of the feedback, yet I wake at 3 a.m. obsessing over one critical comment.
- The pastor's sermon was inspirational, yet I harbor the criticism that his illustration was offtrack.

We know how it goes . . . the same personality traits and tendencies keep resurfacing. Yet, each time that core issue returns, hopefully we notice it sooner and can call it by name! Spiritual growth is so incremental that it feels like watching the grass grow.

So, we will not permit the familiarity of some of the debris to discourage us in our digging. We greet the discovery with an "Aha!" rather than an "Oh, no!" An "aha" moment opens our spirit to a glimpse of gratitude because we can recognize something true about ourselves that may need to be changed.

The soul wants to deal with what is authentic, real, true. Letting go of a disagreeable trait is almost impossible unless we can first recognize it and name it. We learn to accept the truth about ourselves by dealing head-on with our issues and being willing to celebrate the growth—even the tiny victories.

Reflect: Consider a basic personal characteristic that you keep bumping up against. Be thankful that the Spirit has guided you to recognize it and that you have the courage to name it. How might you respond to the transformation that the Spirit offers?

MARCH 4 • *The Poison of Unforgiveness*

A familiar adage notes that "resentment hurts the vessel in which it is stored more than the object on which it is poured." Chronic resentment and anger are toxic not only to our souls but to our bodies. That makes unforgiveness a formidable boulder to remove during the inner journey of tilling and discovery.

Forgiveness often feels like condoning. The truth is, we forgive people, not bad behavior. We don't have to manufacture warm fuzzy feelings, nor do we have to like the person! Forgiveness entails letting go of the toxicity.

As human beings, we seem honor bound to justify our hurt feelings and nurture them in every way possible. It reminds me of scratching a raging case of poison ivy—it feels so good to scratch it, but that only makes it redder and hotter. As we "scratch" these negative feelings by thinking them to death and describing them in repeated episodes, they naturally become angrier and darker. We'll just call one more person to tell him or her what happened. We'll plan all the things we might say at our next encounter with the offender and imagine the response. All the while, the toxic feelings do their dirty work until we realize the toll they are taking on us.

Once we become clear about how unforgiveness affects us, it becomes a bit easier to begin the process of laying that burden down. Forgiveness frees the forgiver from emotional entanglement in someone else's issues. We no longer choose to carry that heavy baggage. Is it as simple as setting down a heavy suitcase? No. Will we succumb to the temptation to pick that bag up again? Probably. But we can be willing to be willing.

Jesus modeled it dramatically for us on the cross, embodying a forgiveness that included even his murderers. He never condoned their behavior! Even as we accept God's forgiving love toward us, it's hard to accept the fact that God forgives others in the same way when they have hurt us or those we love. When we acknowledge the divine river of forgiveness, we can join the powerful flow. We begin by sticking a toe in.

Reflect: With complete honesty, consider your own challenges in the area of forgiveness. How is resentment affecting your relationships and spiritual growth?

MARCH 5 • *The Freedom of Forgiveness*

I once heard a story that illustrates the imprisoning nature of unforgiveness. In a war's aftermath, one previous prisoner of war asked another, "Have you forgiven your captors?" The person replied emphatically, "No!

I could never forgive those horrid people!" "Oh, I see," replied the first man. "Then they still have you in prison, don't they?" Forgiveness can set the soul free. Here's a way to begin:

- Feel the pain in your body. Find a safe place, a trusted friend, a wise counselor, and get the feelings out. Tell what happened. Own your story. You can't forgive a wound that you don't feel. Stay with this part of the process until you feel emptied of it.
- Join the flow of forgiveness that belongs to a loving God. You don't have to generate forgiving feelings. Admit that you can't forgive under your own steam, and unite with a divine forgiveness greater than your own.
- Swim with the current, not against it. Make concrete plans to move out of the victim mode. *Am I repeatedly telling the story, casting myself as a victim?* Try to talk about the situation less, and when you do, speak from a place of peace, praying for a gentler approach. Try to move toward ways of talking about it that no longer disturb you.
- Release the baggage into God's hands—over and over, if necessary. Choose to carry the burden no longer.

Create an interior prayer container for healing. This is not an inner space where you go over your list of complaints or prayer petitions about that person but space where your soul meets with the Spirit residing within you. Remember, at your core, you are made in the image of a forgiving God. That authentic soul has the capacity for love and forgiveness. Begin to live out of the bottomless well of compassion.

Forgiveness can become a way of life rather than merely an act of the will. Despite our tendencies toward vindictiveness, one-upmanship, and tit for tat, we have access to a power than can enhance our best intentions. At the same time, our resistance dissolves like melting snow, and we begin to accept the past for what it is—the past—and to prepare our garden for new growth.

Reflect: Center on a person or situation that you want to forgive. Go through the steps slowly and prayerfully, feeling the expansion of freedom in your soul and body.

MARCH 6 • *Reactionary Anger*

Anger is a wicked warlord when it takes charge of us. It can even become our default setting, an automatic reaction to anything that appears to threaten us—a critical comment, a differing opinion, a remark that challenges our status quo, a driver who cuts into our lane. Chronic anger is one stone we need to remove to enter the serene soil of the soul.

Anger can wreak havoc in our bodies. Medical studies catalog the physical consequences of habitual anger: tension headaches, stomach upset, muscle constriction, high blood pressure, and a host of other damaging ailments. The price we pay for our complicity in grasping this negative energy comes not only in diminished health but in persistent unhappiness and poor relationships.

The positive aspect of anger is that this natural emotion can provide information for us. We listen to the voice of anger and notice the knowledge about ourselves that it signals. We can ask ourselves some probing questions: What does this anger tell me about myself? Does it reveal fear of disapproval or abandonment? evidence of some unhealed wound from way back? a challenge to my sense of entitlement? We need to recognize, feel, and accept those angry places inside us without judgment. Only then can the healing begin. We can't choose a reconciling response to an emotion we haven't felt and owned.

Anger tells us that something is amiss and needs to change. We summon the courage to focus on our response rather than another person's behavior, which we can't change anyway. Then we commit to getting off the merry-go-round of chronic anger that robs us of joy.

Reflect: The next time you experience anger, take a deep breath and get some emotional distance from the issue. Feel the pain or guilt in your body, and ask it what it wants. Choose a healthy, loving response that contributes to your spiritual health.

MARCH 7 • *On the Defensive*

I once heard someone described as "bristly," and I have some idea what that means. It refers to living out of a default setting of defensiveness, particularly in regard to a slight or a challenge—an attitude that automatically rejects instead of accepts. It's certainly one of the stones that stand in the way of the soul's growth.

We naturally tend to defend ourselves against anything that threatens our treasured status quo. We exhibit an automatic push back as our egos rush into combat mode. This defensiveness can surface when someone mentions our bad habits, challenges our political opinions, or questions our religious convictions. We want to be right; we want to win the argument; and, most of all, we don't want to change.

Often, this self-justification shows itself in "yes, but . . . " statements:

- Yes, but they shouldn't have done that. (*Shifting the focus to another's behavior.*)
- Yes, but something bad might happen. (*Cataloging all the reasons why it won't work or wouldn't be safe.*)
- Yes, but Mama taught me to be like that. (*Detouring away from our own responsibility into the sins of our family of origin.*)
- Yes, but you hurt my feelings. (*Failing to examine the source of our own reactive behavior.*)
- Yes, but that's just the way I am. (*Refusing to engage the work of growth.*)

A phrase beginning with the word *but* is like putting the brakes on a moving car, halting its momentum, keeping it from reaching its destination of truth or change. Though the conjunction sometimes introduces an important exception or a warning, most of the time it's an excuse not to move ahead into the uncharted territory of new ideas or attitudes.

This pessimism is like wearing a pair of gray-tinted glasses that throws a murkiness over everything, that dims the radiance of relationships, work, and spiritual health. To deal with our own defensiveness, we must affirm that the dark glasses are ours. This tedious inner work offers a liberating payoff in the sense of buoyancy and openness that will take its place.

Reflect: Today, be willing to monitor your own complaining, listening for "yes, but." Take off your dark glasses, and consider the invitation to be open to change.

MARCH 8 • *Picture Perfect*

Perfectionism fits the description of the proverbial "wolf in sheep's clothing." It usually masks as excellence, and who doesn't want to be excellent? Our culture encourages us to aim high and never give up! We're reared on the notions that only losers settle for second place and anything worth doing is worth doing well. Perfectionism ranks among the most serious barriers to love of self and neighbor.

Those who tend toward compulsive perfectionism often grow up unconsciously worshiping some false idols:

- Do it better, and you'll be noticed.
- Be the best, and you'll win the prize.
- The more perfect you are, the more love you'll get.
- The more right you are, the more you'll garner divine approval.

Perfectionism can separate us from others and starve our souls. And it can take a tragic toll on our relationships. If we're always trying to complete tasks perfectly, we often want others to mimic and match our level of productivity. Failure becomes intolerable, so we limit our risks by attempting only those feats we can do well. We start sugarcoating our problems (perfect people don't have any). We polish our performance. Any chink in our armor results in self-criticism and an interior feeling of not measuring up to our own standards.

Inadvertently, perfectionism creates an unwelcoming atmosphere for others—they don't feel free to express their own shortcomings. In trying to be efficient and competent, perfectionists forget to be real. We usually admire them rather than cherish them, appreciate them rather than love them. We envy their accomplishments, but those accomplishments distance us from them. The love perfectionists hope to receive often dies on the vine; they attract only those who love them conditionally.

The good news is that we perfectionists can break this vicious cycle. We can learn, even the hard way, that we live in an imperfect world as one of its flawed inhabitants—and that's okay.

Reflect: Take time today to reflect on your own need to be perfect. Does it show itself in constant self-evaluation, self-criticism? Notice the ways it makes you feel both inferior and superior.

MARCH 9 • *The Boulder of Busyness*

The good is often the enemy of the best. Or, as one person told me, sometimes we're so busy with the work of the Lord that we forget the Lord of the work!

Jesus' parable of the good Samaritan (Luke 10:25-37) illustrates this human dilemma. Misfortune befalls the man traveling from Jerusalem to Jericho. He is severely wounded, and a Samaritan (a social outcast) stops to help him. The story tells us, however, that a priest and a Levite (respectable churchgoing folks) pass him by. I've often surmised that since they were good, responsible people, they probably had more important things to do—perhaps even at their place of worship. They may have been engaged in significant, community-building work to which they felt dedicated. In other words, they were busy.

Our busyness can often prevent us from noticing urgent needs that cry for our attention. We look the other way or, like the priest and the Levite, we "pass by on the other side." We find it challenging to balance the busyness of our lives with a spaciousness that allows us to respond to others. The Samaritan obviously had "margins" in his life—a little wiggle room. Plus, his lack of preoccupation with his own agenda allowed him to see the need right in front of him.

It's easy and often admirable to overcommit ourselves to worthwhile projects. However, it can create the kind of chaos that prevents us from being our neighbor's keeper or an attentive spouse, from connecting to the spiritual Source that nurtures and feeds our good works.

Reflect: Is busyness a boulder on your path to deeper growth? If so, with God's guidance, select one change in your lifestyle now that can make a difference.

MARCH 10 • *The Little Things*

It isn't merely the big boulders that block us in our digging expedition to the center of ourselves where the divine meets us; little gravelly things also litter the way. Seemingly trivial reactions and responses scatter the terrain, usually unnoticed.

Recently I overheard a group of adults engaged in a lively discussion about the need for more kindness and graciousness in today's culture, the imperative for love and compassion for others. As they enjoyed their lunch, offhand comments interspersed the positive conversation:

- Couldn't our waiter speed things up a little?
- Can you believe he hasn't refilled my coffee yet?
- I think that table by the window is being served before we are!
- Wonder why they serve this inferior kind of mayo?
- Really, they shouldn't allow their waiters to wear jeans!
- Whatever happened to good manners in this country?

Harmless comments, maybe. But they represent a habitual grumbling that inhibits the growth of the spirit in insidious ways. We often whine our way into attitudes of entitlement and criticism that deter the flowering of grace in our lives.

Weeding out those tiny thoughts and mutterings can create wide open space for the pursuit of love and compassion. Slip an unexpected five-dollar bill to the young person who is feverishly clearing the tables.

Reflect: Consider your own level of grousing around. Has finding fault become a habit? As you observe your behavior today, try replacing complaints with compliments.

MARCH 11 • *Ignore It, and It Will Go Away*

Do you remember the legendary words of Scarlett O'Hara in *Gone with the Wind*? "I'll think about that tomorrow." That famous phrase captures our human tendency to procrastinate.

Procrastination serves as a major defense mechanism when we bump up against qualities or characteristics we don't want to face in ourselves. We'll just put it on a shelf until some imaginary "later."

As we discover the blocks to growth—perfectionism, judgment, resentment, busyness, whatever—it's not surprising that we shrink from engaging the changes we need to make. "I've always been this way . . ." or "It's not my fault . . ." or "I don't know how . . ." are all familiar avenues of avoidance. The avoidance itself becomes a major hindrance.

Likewise, pretending the problem doesn't exist doesn't make it disappear. Refusing to think about it or ignoring its drain on our spiritual lives can shelve it for the short run, but it keeps returning until it's dealt with. It isn't easy to corral the courage to confront our own demons and negative patterns, but courage clears the way to the core of who we are—human beings created by love and for love. We weed out everything that impedes or obscures that love as we till our inner garden.

So pick up those stones; identify the blocks, name them, and face them head-on. The Spirit of God, who invites us to wholeness, will empower us with the courage we need.

Reflect: What patterns of thought and behavior in your life do you habitually ignore? Enlist the Holy Spirit's empowerment to take specific steps and turn avoidance into action.

MARCH 12 • *Don't Feel It*

I remember my spiritual director's words as if it were yesterday—though it was actually twenty years ago. She had asked me how I felt about a particular wounded time in my life. I launched into a fairly accurate description of the pain involved.

"You know what?" my director noted. "You describe feelings—you don't feel them!" I had no idea what she meant. Besides, I had no clue about how much my lack of feeling inhibited my spiritual and emotional growth. The disconnect between what I knew in my head and what I felt in my heart and body was the way I had learned to deal with life's wounds.

Thankfully, with wisdom and compassion, she helped me recognize the pattern. Since words came easily for me, my safe go-to place during times of struggle and stress was straight to my head, where I could think about it, analyze it, articulate it, and—to be honest—control it. Heaven forbid that I should open the door to unbridled emotions!

I still have trouble summoning the strength to allow myself to feel pain and disappointment. I still prefer to describe it so that I won't have to feel the searing discomfort. I'm chickenhearted that way. But I've learned to seek the support of caring friends, understanding family, and, above all,

God's boundless grace. The only way to find healing is *through* the pain, not around it. Rather than analyze things *ad nauseam*, I need to say, "Ouch."

Reflect: Remember times when you have stuffed your feelings inside, hoping they would disappear. What safe places could provide healthy outlets for your pain?

MARCH 13 • *Distraction*

Our culture has mastered the art of distraction. Often our first reaction to someone who has suffered a loss is to say, "Just try to stay busy!" We tend to admire those who have the ability to mask pain and keep a stiff upper lip, to somehow transcend the hurt. In like manner, when faced with daunting or painful issues, we sometimes reach for the nearest distraction or panacea.

Most of us have a low tolerance for pain, and we just want to get rid of it. Whether it's a headache or a heartache, we seek something to make it better—right now. Though a pill or a pint may be the usual choices, we often turn to more subtle addictions to provide the emotional anesthesia we seek.

We have quite a catalog of possibilities: a chocolate pie? a luxurious trip? a shopping spree? mindless TV? a new romance? workaholism? a time-consuming project? compulsive cleanliness and neatness? an exhausting exercise routine? Since these addictions don't carry the social stigma of drugs, sex, and alcohol, we may fail to see them as detrimental. The capacity to ride the crest of the pain or to just hang in there and be present to it is countercultural.

Identifying our own patterns of distraction may be murky, since they can appear to be reasonable choices. If, however, they are preventing the tough work of confronting boulders that are blocking our path, they usurp our journey to the wholeness we are digging to find.

Reflect: To what activities or items do you turn when you want to feel better? In what ways are you using those as distractions from what you need to feel and face? Pray for the clarity to see your distractions for what they are.

MARCH 14 • *Weeding Our Neighbor's Garden*

Instead of pulling the weeds in our own garden, we prefer to weed someone else's. The most familiar path of diversion comes when we switch our focus from us to them:

- If he hadn't done that, I wouldn't harbor this resentment.
- If she hadn't said that, I wouldn't be so angry.
- If they hadn't piled all this work on me, I would have more time for my family.
- If those kids weren't so violent, we wouldn't have rampant crime in our city.
- If I didn't have this illness or limitation, I could help someone else.

Even when statements like these carry some truth, we can use them to avoid tackling the issue of what we *can* do. In order to defend ourselves, we move our attention from our choices to theirs. Jesus' metaphor found in Matthew 7:3-5 hits us all where it hurts:

> "Why do you see the speck in your neighbor's eye, but do not notice the log in your own eye? Or how can you say to your neighbor, 'Let me take the speck out of your eye,' while the log is in your own eye? You hypocrite, first take the log out of your own eye, and then you will see clearly to take the speck out of your neighbor's eye."

This counsel calls us to identify our own "logs" so that we can engage the wrongs of society with integrity and compassion. We don't shift the blame from others to ourselves or to God. We suspend blame altogether so that we can see matters as they are. Only as we clear the air of finger-pointing can we open our hearts to clear and loving choices.

Reflect: Notice both the overt and the subtle ways that you shift focus from your own responsibility to that of others. As you willingly release these judgments, move bravely into the territory of dealing with your own logs.

MARCH 15 • *Bless Her Heart*

As a daughter of the South, I'm quite familiar with the sugary phrase, "Bless her heart." Only lately have I begun to recognize the hidden messages that lurk beneath the surface of a number of our lovely sentiments—a clever way to mask our real feelings by saying one thing while meaning another. Part of our tilling-the-garden task is to strip away all pretense and recognize these hidden motives and messages:

- Bless her heart: She's doing the best she can, though it's obviously inadequate or ill-informed.
- I really don't care what they do, but . . . : I *do* care, but I'll somehow tolerate their errant behavior.
- I'm doing great: I'm actually hanging on by a thread, but I want to appear to have everything under control.
- All I can do now is pray: I've exhausted every reasonable option and now have to resort to what seems less effective.
- I have nothing against female ministers, but . . . : I prefer male authority in the pulpit.
- And what do *you* do?: What matters to me is what you do, not who you are.
- I don't want to hurt your feelings, but . . . : I'm about to hurt your feelings—big time.

In the Sermon on the Mount (Matthew 5–7), Jesus employs the technique of peering beneath the surface of words and actions. Repeatedly, he unmasks the hidden motives: "You have heard that it was said . . . , 'You shall not murder . . . ' But I say to you that if you are angry with a brother or sister, you will be liable to judgment." In the ensuing verses, he moves from the act of adultery to the emotion of lust, shifting the focus from outward action to inner motivation.

As we approach the process of discovering who we really are, it's necessary to shine light on the hidden motives that may be unconscious to us. The truth can surely set us free!

Reflect: As the day unfolds, ask yourself: Am I saying what I really mean, or are my words masking a hidden message? Be confident that the arbiter of all truth, the Spirit of God, will lead and guide you with heartwarming compassion.

MARCH 16 • *What Will They Think?*

A friend's motto is this: "What other people think of me is none of my business!" A lofty ideal and cleverly stated, but truthfully, most of us want the approval of others. In fact, we want that approval so desperately that we easily fall into the trap of assuming we know what others think about us. Then we go on to suppose what they want and expect from us. It's a deadly spiral of projection that leads us away from the authentic self we yearn for.

As we let go of our tendencies to please, it doesn't take long to realize that the driving force behind such behavior is an insatiable need for approval—from the church, from our parents, from a spouse, from children, from the culture around us. We deplete our centeredness by giving away our power in tiny bits and pieces. Before we know it, we have adapted to this or agreed to that and have placed our sense of worth in the hands of others. We find ourselves in the precarious place of allowing others to tell us who we are and believing it, enslaving us to their expectations. Plus, it makes chameleons of us. I'll be this for that person and that for another.

At what point does flexibility become adaptation to the wishes of others? And when does that adaptation become toxic to the soul? The pivotal point varies with each person, and no one can define it for another. It's a matter of sensing that fine line where the cost is too high, when we are not being true to ourselves and our values. Then it becomes our responsibility to cry "Enough!" Adaptation can produce accolades, but we can lose ourselves in the process. Unfortunately, many of us habitually say "yes" when our silent souls are urging no. It's up to us to set boundaries to safeguard our health and integrity. We can learn that no is a complete sentence that requires no excuses, manufactured or real.

Our culture teaches us to live a divided life, to play our cards close to the vest and not wear our hearts on our sleeves. So we learn to pretend and edit our behavior for maximum effect. However, when we can no longer live with these gaps between inner and outer, circumstances begin to change.

We may find that perhaps it's better to be disliked for who we really are than to be liked for who we are not.

Reflect: Today, notice times when what you say on the outside and what you feel on the inside don't match.

MARCH 17 • *Criticism and Flattery*

Mary, an aspiring poet, thought she had her need for approval under control. As she read one of her poems to a discussion group, a member felt so moved that she requested a copy. The leader, however, offered a criticism that ripped open Mary's inner wound (a desperate need for approval). Our need for affirmation rarely leaves us permanently. It surprises us with sneak attacks.

We are vulnerable at both ends of this spectrum—both criticism and flattery. As we become more comfortable in our own skin, we can take in criticism and flattery as information to consider rather than allowing them to define us. Maybe that challenging comment has a valid point; maybe that affirmative comment can tell us about our gifts. In both cases, we can receive valuable data that need not pull us off center.

The development of our needy perspective starts early. As a youngster, I had an unusually strong desire for approval. I recall my constant compulsion to be the best speller, to know the right answer, to wear the appropriate clothes, to have the proper belief, to make a good impression—all in an unconscious effort to gain others' esteem. The thought of disappointing someone filled me with a sense of anguish and unworthiness.

This fragile sense of self followed me into adulthood as I repeatedly sought to shape my behavior into conventional compliance. As a woman schooled in the notion that a good wife and mother puts the wishes of her husband and children first, I shushed my inner opinions and needs. According to my upbringing, the proper course of conduct was smile and submit, submit and smile. I wasn't willing to give my family a single opening for criticism if I could possibly help it. After all, I depended on their approval to make me feel worthy.

The truth is that while others can disappoint us, disapprove of us, or even reject us, we must not allow them to tell us who we are. We are beloved children of God. We remain true to ourselves when we live out of that relationship as our primary grounding.

Reflect: As you go about your day, consider your reactions to others' comments. Are your feelings easily hurt? Do you allow perceived slights to define you? Each time you feel off center, return to the core where you are grounded in God's love.

MARCH 18 • *Barrier to Being Real*

The need for approval can spread its tentacles into every part of our lives. Most of the time, we don't realize how it subconsciously drives our actions and shapes our self-image.

One serious barrier to being authentic is the psychic presence of the question, How am I coming across? We then see the world through an egocentric lens that leads straight to self-deception and eventually to distortion and manipulation.

This tendency reveals itself in insidious ways that seem acceptable to us because they are such familiar mental companions:

- Should I have worn a tie?
- Did I say something wrong?
- Is anyone going to talk to me?
- I don't think they like me.
- They're avoiding me.

Conversely, the ego can grab flattery for affirmation:

- They complimented my speech, so I must be a good speaker.
- I got invited to that party, so I'm important.
- She saved me a seat, so I'm accepted.
- I made a bundle on that business deal, so God is blessing me.
- I've read all those books, so I'm smarter than they are.

When we direct our energy toward the protection of our fragile egos, we constrict our freedom to be true to ourselves and to love our neighbors with sacred abandon.

Reflect: Imagine yourself walking into a room of strangers at a reception of some sort. Suspend thoughts of how you are coming across, and replace them instead with a genuine desire to connect with people, discover their interests, and help them feel accepted and worthwhile.

MARCH 19 • *The Treasure of the True Self*

Who am I—really? Who is this self that God created? We become who God created us to be by discovering our essential wiring—our gifts and graces as well as our particular pitfalls. We awaken to what is already there, hidden in the soil of our souls.

This discovery is not like switching on a lightbulb but about embarking on the intimate quest of getting acquainted with what is true about us. We hear the whispers of God's guidance and know the reality of divine love and acceptance through this authentic identity. In this spacious safety zone, we are free—free to hear God's invitations to grow, to take chances, and to see the possibilities in ourselves.

The authentic self is as elusive as a butterfly. We get glimpses of it—times when such joy fills us that we forget who is watching us, times when our defenses melt away, times when wonder leaves us speechless. These uncalculated responses come from a place that is free from our orchestration and management. They bubble up from a natural well deep inside us—like unedited responses to life.

People have offered many definitions of the self. The ones here are but a few options:

- Inherent identity
- Immortal soul
- Divine indwelling
- Cosmic Christ within
- Essential "me"
- Sacred essence
- Divine DNA

If the authentic self represents who we *really* are, then we can define the false self as who we *think* we are! We spend the first half of our lives building the false self, the ego self, as part of our human condition. That part consists of education, money, job, body image, social identity, sexual identity, successes, failures. It isn't bad, but it isn't our essence. We don't have to destroy the false self; we simply recognize it as incomplete. Once we encounter and embrace the true self, the false self will no longer be in charge.

The words of 2 John 2 affirm this divine indwelling: "Because of the truth that abides in us and will be with us forever." Each of us manifests this internal truth in unique ways. We also hear it in unique ways. Over the coming days, we will explore ways to recognize this beautiful core within us.

Reflect: Think of the unique characteristics that make you *you*. Begin making a list of the ones you are presently conscious of and get ready to add to what you know!

MARCH 20 • *Our Natural Wiring*

Once we dig up some of the items that hamper and hinder the discovery of the true self, what then? How can we develop a sensitivity to the signals that point to authenticity? How can we wake up to our God-inspired wiring?

One of the best tools I know to guide this search is the spiritual practice called the Examen—a positive treatment of the age-old spiritual discipline known as the Examination of Conscience. The old form tends to focus on failure to honor God during a particular day, more like a confession of sins.

This adaptation of the Daily Examen helps us figure out how we're wired, how the Creator has endowed us. If God created us as complex networks of body, mind, and spirit, then God can speak through our bodies, minds, and emotions. When we participate in an activity that engrosses us in a healthy way, God is saying, "Listen; this is the real *you*! This is how I created you! Pay attention to what lights your fire!" The Daily Examen helps us pay attention. This particular version focuses on the life-giving moments we've experienced. It also addresses our likes and dislikes. Most of us go through life doing our duty as "good" people and often fail to ask the following questions: What do I really want? What do I truly like? We've been taught that raising those questions is a selfish pursuit rather than a matter of sound spiritual discernment. We get caught up in what we *should* want and like.

Answering honestly the same few questions on a daily basis, even for two or three weeks, can provide a treasure trove of information about our natural wiring. Noticing our patterns of response in various settings and with diverse people is like being introduced to who we really are—under the surface, beneath the ought-tos and supposed-tos.

Reflect: Purchase a small notebook that you devote especially to recording your responses to this practice. Let go of any notion that you're allowing yourself to be selfish, trusting that God will use your aliveness to bless the world around you.

MARCH 21 • *Life-Giving Moments*

The first question for consideration while practicing the Daily Examen sounds deceptively simple: What moments today felt life-giving?

When answering, try to avoid generalizations, such as "Everyone was nice to me today" or broad concepts such as "It's good to be alive." Notice times when your pulse raced, when you felt your body surge with energy, when you felt full of light or love. Be as specific as you can:

- When I felt the baby burrow her face in my neck
- When I saw a crocus that had pushed up through the snow
- When Mary called me and asked how my bad cold was
- When I heard my favorite song on the radio
- When I bit into the first ripe tomato of the summer

Not all life-affirming moments are pleasant. Sadness and physical strain are also parts of life:

- You may have attended the funeral of a friend and felt a surge of gratitude for the sanctity of life.
- You may have had surgery and felt strangely elated at the first twinge of painful awakening, grateful to be alive!

- A friend may have confided in you about a family problem, swelling your heart with compassion.
- You may have toiled in your garden all day long, trimming hedges and bagging leaves, yet felt very alive in your exhaustion.

This attentive practice trains us to notice the activities and feelings that we usually ignore, tethering us to the present moment. Life often passes us by while our focus is elsewhere.

Reflect: Today pay special attention to the signals of aliveness, both positive and negative, that your exquisite network of mind, body, and spirit brings to you.

MARCH 22 • *Instants of Inspiration*

The second question is this: What inspired me today? I watched a patient mother settling a spat between her twin toddlers in the grocery store recently. Holding their tears and tantrums at bay, she gently quieted them, oblivious to the staring strangers around her. Somehow, she put her embarrassment aside to soothe them into remarkable calmness. I later said to her as we waited in the checkout line, "This too shall pass. You're a great mom!" A host of experiences can gift us with instant inspiration:

- A kind shopper holds the door for you as you struggle with too many packages.
- A minister utters a phrase in the sermon that is just what you needed to hear.
- A symphony swells, and the music makes your heart sing.
- The evening news carries an image of a soldier returning home to loved ones.
- A robin heralds the onset of spring.

The simple act of seeing and honoring these inspiring instances can in itself provide inspiration. We so easily coast along on automatic pilot that we fail to notice the times when people, sights, and sounds touch our spirits. As we pay attention to those moments, we learn valuable lessons about what inspires us. Why did we feel it? What in us responded? What exactly did we appreciate?

We don't all experience the same reactions to the same stimuli. Pausing to detect our particular responses tells us volumes about the way we are put together and invites us to open ourselves to more inspiration!

Reflect: As you consider the second question in the Daily Examen about what inspired you today, take a moment to observe how inspiration feels in your body. Let that recognition lead you as you list your instances of inspiration.

MARCH 23 • *Smiles and Tears*

The third question is this: What caused you to break into a smile today or moved you to tears? Nothing is quite as spontaneous and resistant to our control as laughing and crying. This particular question deals with what touches or delights or moves you. Identifying those moments involves following the trail left by your smiles and tears.

We don't plan our bursts of laughter; the chuckles just bubble up. Neither do we orchestrate our tears, saying, "I think I'll cry about this." The tears simply well up and overflow. Intellect does not determine smiles and tears; they are natural reactions of the heart and soul. That's why they reveal so much about who we are.

One Sunday soon after the onset of the Iraq war, I was sitting in church alone—on a back pew near the exit (thank goodness). As we stood for the closing hymn and began to sing, tears began to stream spontaneously and uncontrollably down my face. The emotional upheaval was visceral and overwhelming; I didn't know what was happening to me. I made a hasty exit to my car, still crying.

The hymn was "Onward, Christian Soldiers," a hymn I had sung since childhood. I had long ago committed all the verses to memory. As I reflected on the *why* of my reaction to the lyrics, I realized my soul was speaking in no uncertain terms through its language of tears: I could no longer tie my Christian faith to battle images, words that could harm and maim and separate humanity from humanity. Some essence or core inside me wasn't going to stand for it. I received a message from my soul, delivered by my tears.

In like manner, the people or situations that bring a spontaneous smile to our faces disclose our capacity for delight. What we smile at speaks to us of our particular wiring for joy—or maybe sarcasm or wicked comedy! In this remarkable messaging system, God uses our natural responses to tell us who we are, whether we like the revelations or not.

Reflect: Today, as you "notice," concentrate on those situations or people or words or thoughts that coax a smile or a tear. Write them down in detail, so you can see what the emerging patterns have to say to you.

MARCH 24 • *Losing Track of Time*

The fourth Examen question seeks to uncover those aspects that totally capture your attention and imagination. What are you doing when you seem to lose track of time?

My husband, Walter, likes to eat lunch at twelve o'clock sharp. One day when our usual noon lunchtime came and went, I discovered Walter still squirreled away in his garage workspace, sanding a beautiful piece of wood for the umpteenth time. He had worked for hours—measuring, cutting, gluing—lost in the myriad steps of creating a new table for the living room. Though normally a left-brain guy, this artistic pursuit satisfied such a significant part of him that he lost track of time as well as his hunger.

When we develop activities that sustain our focus, we are on the road to tracking our deepest passions—and that tells us about our personal uniquenesses. Pursuit of passions doesn't fall into the category of "one size fits all." A mere ten minutes of toil at Walter's workbench would have sent me around the bend! Yet here I sit in my office where I've been all day long—totally engrossed in penning this paragraph, fulfilling my own passion.

A few years ago, a scientific study of the attributes of contented centenarians produced some startling revelations about the value of finding our passion. The respondents were folks who were thriving well past the one-hundred-year mark and were from all corners of the globe. (The four attributes that outdistanced all the rest had nothing to do with diet (surprisingly enough). They were as follows:

- A basic optimism about people and life in general
- A capacity for letting go

- Daily mobility
- Pursuit of a passion

The activity itself doesn't matter as much as the degree of enthusiasm with which it is engaged. Whether the activity involves gardening, golf, church work, painting, hiking, whatever—the crucial element is that it completely captures our attention and interest. In other words, we lose track of time while doing it.

Remember, the Spirit uses many avenues to tell us about our specific wiring—including our creative yearnings.

Reflect: When do you lose track of time? How are you honoring the passions in your life?

MARCH 25 • *Draining and Dreading*

Both joy and despair are contagious, which makes it imperative to notice the people and circumstances that drain you. Acknowledging those can supply clues in getting to know the real you.

So the next question is this: When do you feel like your energy is being sapped out of you? What were you doing? Who was with you? Where were you? By noting the details of the "drained" feeling, you may discover the types of people and situations that undermine your energy and enthusiasm.

In keeping her Daily Examen notes, Marian noticed the same friend's name appearing repeatedly as she listed these times of depletion. She loved this dear, lifelong friend, but every time she conversed with her, Marian's aliveness plunged. Rather than terminate the friendship (the woman meant a great deal to her!) or try to figure out a way to change her friend, Marian made a more responsible and loving choice. She took the time to discern why she reacted in such a negative manner.

Marian realized that her friend, a compulsive pessimist, always imagined the worst, spinning each negative scenario in a downward spiral. And Marian joined her in that gloomy spiral. To change the dynamic Marian decided to deflect the negativism by inserting a positive statement or gently changing the subject. In addition, she promised to refrain from joining in the downbeat comments. Over the ensuing months, the friend remained basically her same pessimistic self, but Marian's conversations with her took on a healthier tone.

This same question may disclose physical surroundings that bring you down. Does your office need better lighting, a new coat of paint, a bouquet of flowers? Do you need to find a few moments each day to feel the sun on your face? Do you need to clear the clutter?

Our bodies and spirits convey a sense of dread to us in a variety of circumstances. Perhaps you feel burdened every time you head to a particular gathering or participate in a certain activity or attend a specific kind of meeting. Notice, notice, notice.

Reflect: Pay special attention today to the things that seem to depress and deplete you. Even if it's a person or situation you can't avoid, think of creative ways to alter your susceptibility or improve the circumstances.

MARCH 26 • *Curious as a Cat*

The final probing question is: What piques your curiosity? Sometimes a tiny spark of interest can point to a hidden part of yourself. And it may make no sense whatsoever.

Several years ago, while perusing a continuing education catalog from a local college, a course grabbed my attention. It still makes me laugh. I noticed a four-session class on quantum physics in the senior adult offerings. Nothing could have been further from my previous realms of interest, but my curiosity compelled me to read the course description. I had always avoided scientific subjects and had never taken high school physics, much less a college-level class. Yet I found myself musing over the possibility.

Just four classes, I reasoned, *with no prerequisites or exams or papers to write. I could merely walk in, button my lips, sit on the back row, and listen. What did I have to lose by taking a chance?* So I enrolled.

The class introduced me to a world I didn't know existed. Talk of atoms, waves, particles, and quarks fascinated me. Did I understand *all* of it? No way. Did I contribute one smidgen to the class discussions? Absolutely not. However, I figured that getting 50% of challenging material beat getting 100% of a boring topic. Little did I know that in the years following, I would encounter many theologians who were beginning to relate quantum physics to a deeper appreciation of the Spirit and the dazzling nature of creation. Who knew?

See what curiosity is lurking inside you. Maybe you will pick up a paintbrush or a writing pen or a hammer.

Reflect: Try to follow your glimmers of curiosity without dismissing them as ridiculous or illogical. Maybe there's a secret part of you that wants new information or a surprising activity!

MARCH 27 • *Befriending the Shadow*

This month's inner exploration may have surfaced some parts of you that don't particularly please you. But self-knowledge involves owning all parts of yourself—the dark as well as the light. It's time you met a bit of your shadow side.

I once heard a teacher on this subject warn that if you think you know all about your shadow self, you are sadly mistaken. We never complete our shadow work, no matter how much spiritual growth we've experienced. In the journey to wholeness, human beings come to full consciousness in part by facing their own mistakes and failings. We can't kill off the shadow parts of ourselves, nor should we. But we need to know their names and their wily ways.

We may define the shadow in a variety of ways—the unexamined parts of ourselves, those parts that reside in the dark, parts that are hidden to us. Often a shadow trait is the underbelly of a basically good characteristic that slips into shadow behavior when carried too far. Allow me to illustrate.

I've already admitted to being a reasonably efficient person, which I've learned to regard as gift. However, I've become aware of its nasty shadow side: Making others feel diminished or put down through my overblown expectations or bossiness. As I began to pray for the Spirit to show me when my perfectionism slipped over into shadow, I became more and more aware of its insidious nature. Time after time, when I perceived my words or actions as "helpful," others perceived them in a way that diminished them. I'm still working on it! Every trait, no matter how lofty it seems, has a shadow side. Consider these:

- Love can become jealous and possessive.
- Goodness can become spiritual pride. (No wonder Jesus mentioned it so often!)
- Discernment can become judgmentalism.
- Beauty can become vanity.
- Truth can become a weapon against people.
- Loyalty can become blind trust.
- Tolerance can become indifference.
- Self-confidence can become arrogance.
- Faith can become self-righteousness.

Awareness is key; we can't deal with what we don't know. The closer we get to the light of God, the more sharply our shadows will be illuminated. As Paul warned in Romans 12:3, "I say to everyone among you not to think of yourself more highly than you ought to think, but to think with sober judgment."

Reflect: Think about your best traits—those attributes for which you are grateful. What are their shadow components? Ask for divine guidance in this deepening knowledge of yourself, trusting that it will lead to true humility and strength of character.

MARCH 28 • *Putting the Pieces Together*

The time comes when, rather than merely reading words about the true self, we take on the task of becoming intimately acquainted with the true self. As the saying goes, "If you want to quench thirst, you must lay aside the books that explain thirst, and take a drink!"

That's the point of employing the Daily Examen we've been exploring over the past few days. Let's review the practice. At the close of each day, reflect slowly on these questions:

- What felt life-giving to me today?
- What inspired me today?
- What moved me to smiles or tears today?
- When did I lose track of time?
- What felt depleting or draining to me today?

- What piqued my curiosity today?
- Where did I notice my shadow self today?

As the answers to these questions evolve into a picture of how we're wired, divine grace enables us to accept who and what we are. Armed with that acceptance, we can expect the following things to emerge slowly:

- We no longer have to pretend to be better or worse than we are.
- We sense our divine DNA (made in the image of God).
- We become increasingly honest and humble.
- We cease trying to prove that we're important.
- We have less need for pat answers, embracing mystery and uncertainty.
- We continue to awaken to who we are as "participants of the divine nature" (2 Pet. 1:4).
- We begin to live out of the natural flow of grace coming from our spiritual core.

Reflect: Are you ready to commit to this practice of discovery? Anticipate the adventure of appreciating and loving yourself as God loves you.

MARCH 29 • *Saying Hello to Your Self*

After the digging, the overturning, the confessing, the banishing of barriers, and the discovering, a sense of clarity takes shape about the core of the self—the light and the shadow, the sacred braiding together of the human and the divine.

Paul was correct when he said, "We see in a mirror, dimly" (1 Cor. 13:12). We never get a complete image of ourselves; it's always evolving. However, the light begins to shine through the darkness more often as you come face-to-face with God and the real *you*.

What we see in that mirror actually matters. Our emerging image can be clouded when we beat up on ourselves for our flaws rather than affirm the God-designed wholeness of our essence. If knowledge of our true selves (especially our shadow side) disintegrates into self-condemnation, that negative picture stymies our ability to love ourselves and those around us. The shadow side of low self-esteem, oddly enough, is self-inflation.

We react by pretending to be better than we are or by constantly putting ourselves down. In either case, it's all about us. The ego is in charge!

Clarity about our true nature allows us to be ourselves—works in progress like everyone else. From this place of honesty and vulnerability, we freely choose from love not obligation. *I must* becomes *I will*—not a position of self-centeredness but rather self-awareness.

Reflect: Look in the mirror. Do you have a sense of your own belovedness and uniqueness? Reflect with gratitude on all you are learning about yourself.

MARCH 30 • *Losing and Finding*

Scripture often presents a cryptic puzzle for us: "Those who lose their life for my sake, . . . will save it" (Mark 8:35). Now that we have begun to find ourselves, why does Jesus challenge us to lose ourselves?

This sacred paradox tells us that when we are willing to lose the false, ego-dominated self, the authentic self emerges in neon lights. During the first half of our lives, we establish the ego—the outer self that we build in order to get along in the world, to gain approval, and to prove our worthiness. That becomes who we think we are. But as spiritual maturity deepens, the soul draws us like a magnet to something more.

Building the ego is a natural human process. We must have an ego before we can intentionally let it go for a greater purpose. The ego is a wonderful servant but a terrible master. In connecting with the true self, we bring the ego into service. Stated another way, the loss of ego is not the loss of selfhood; it is the loss of ego-dominance.

It's as if each of us has an imaginary inner "board of directors," with all the many parts of ourselves seated around the boardroom table— the generous self, the compassionate self, the selfish self, the lustful self, the critical self, the loving self—a mighty chorus of voices clamoring for attention. Though the ego begins as chair of the board, we can choose to elevate the authentic self as leader of the pack. This self is connected to God and participates with the divine in creating a more meaningful life, making soul-centered decisions. A self that maintains its connection to the Source is empowered to be more loving, compassionate, and wise. In other words, through the grace of a generous God, this authentic soul-self takes its rightful place.

Reflect: Consider what it means for you to lose your life in order to find it. In prayer, ask God to help you be aware of those times when your ego becomes the board chair.

MARCH 31 • *Paying It Forward*

This process of tilling your inner garden goes beyond simply answering the question "Who am I?" It moves beyond accepting and loving ourselves as God loves us. It leads to the questions: What is the fruit of this knowledge? What's it for?

Abraham received his marching orders in Genesis 12:2: "I will bless you, . . . so that you will be a blessing." Those orders apply to you and me too. By finding the true self we do not escape from the world but come to embrace the world. The blessing of self-knowledge moves outward as part of a dynamic spiritual energy that flows from the soul's core. We learn that love is the essence of who we are and that energy doesn't just sit there. The well of blessing inside us spills over into the lives of others and keeps on blessing, long after it leaves our little garden.

Back in the second century, Irenaeus of Lyons proclaimed that the glory of God is a person fully alive. As we get in touch with our aliveness, we begin to live out of a divine well of love and meaning. Jesus' command to "Love . . . God with all your heart . . . soul . . . mind . . . strength. . . . Love your neighbor as yourself" (Mark 12:30) becomes more accessible to us, more real, more than a nice idea that lies beyond our grasp.

Blessings ripple, much like the rippling of the water when we throw a stone into a pond. The stone sinks out of sight, but its influence radiates to the shore.

Sure, we stumble over problems—rocks and resistance that litter the soil. But I believe deeply in a love "out there" greater than any leap our minds can make, a Mystery that lies beyond us—yet is a part of us—that willingly guides us through all the struggles of life.

Under the gaze and guidance of the Holy Gardener, our inner garden will be beautiful indeed.

Reflect: As you are filled with the blessedness of your own being, consider how that energy can affect the lives of others. As you become more in tune with God and yourself, you encourage others to do the same.

April

APRIL SHOWERS

"Blessed are those who mourn, for they will be comforted."
—MATTHEW 5:4

BREATH PRAYER
Spirit of Comfort, . . . calm my soul.

APRIL 1 • *When the Rain Comes*

You've heard all the clichés. . . .

- Into each life a little rain must fall.
- April showers bring May flowers.
- This too shall pass.
- There's a reason for everything.
- Learn to dance in the rain!
- Suffering builds character.

Pithy phrases don't help much when we're in the middle of a personal downpour. So what are we to do? How do we cope? Is a broader perspective possible? How do we move through the rainstorm to some sort of flowering?

This month's meditations will focus on times when we're feeling deluged by events that throw us into a transition from one way of life to another. The tempest can turn us upside down in a number of settings:

- Loss of a loved one through death or divorce
- Loss of a treasured job
- Moving to a new location
- Dealing with the empty nest
- Issues with retirement
- A sudden illness
- A dear friend moving away
- Dealing with depression
- The onset of old age

Transitions—large or small, temporary or permanent, expected or unexpected—can break our hearts and disrupt our serenity. I hope that, surrounded by grace, rather than being broken down, our souls can be broken open.

Reflect: Are you dealing with an unsettling transition at this time? Know that the Spirit will go with you through the brokenness as you navigate your way.

APRIL 2 • *Rain in Relationships*

One of life's toughest challenges comes in maintaining our equilibrium when we lose a person dear to us through divorce or death, through choice or chance. The pain of loss has countless causes. An adult child may move away to pursue a dream; a friendship may fade as interests diverge; a betrayal may burn the bridges of trust; a misunderstanding severs what was once connected. Regardless of the origin, loss of relationships hurts.

Sometimes we simply yearn for things to be the way they used to be . . . in the past that seems so idyllic in retrospect. I recall the day a wise counselor listened to my longing to get back to "normal" as I tried to deal with a loss of relationship.

"I just want to feel better," I cried. "Please tell me when I'll be able to get over this!"

She replied gently, "Who told you that was possible? The experience becomes a part of who you are—it doesn't disappear."

That possibility horrified me. I saw a life of continual sadness looming before me. Then the counselor began to explain the process of integrating a loss, of allowing it to become part of the fiber of my being, opening myself to the healing that would bring hidden gifts out of the experience.

Believe me, it's possible, but it takes time. Our task is to pick up the shredded pieces of our lives and, by the grace of God, somehow fashion them anew. The fabric won't be exactly the same, but it can still form a beautiful pattern, albeit a different one.

Reflect: Recall a time in your past when you have suffered the loss of a relationship. Remember the healing that occurred. In what ways did it lead you to deeper humility and compassion?

APRIL 3 • *The Circle of Life*

We know that death is part of life. While we acknowledge the concept intellectually, its reality can be devastating.

Though an abundance of helpful literature is available on this subject, I learned of its turbulent variations firsthand from Janie, a friend whose daughter and husband died within a year of each other.

Janie suffered the shocking death of her robust fifty-year-old husband, Harry, from a surprise heart attack. One moment, he was waving good-bye as he left for the office; the next moment she received the call that he was dead. Both she and her husband had been reeling from the accidental death of their twenty-five-year-old daughter a few months before.

I remember Janie's attempt at describing the despair: "There are really no words," she said, "just a feeling of amputation as if living parts of me had been suddenly cut away with no warning and no anesthesia."

Janie has made a painful and slow journey from fragmentation to wholeness—one moment at a time, almost one cell at a time. Praying in any conventional sense seemed impossible. She experienced instead what felt like a dialogue with both her husband and her daughter. This instinctive reaching out into the mystery, however, slowly led her to the Source of all, and she became more deeply rooted in that Source.

Janie's process did not go smoothly. She noticed surprising glimmers of grace, only to plunge back into despair the following day. A new vulnerability enveloped her as she realized that everything in her life was subject to loss. Along with that loss of innocence, however, she became more firmly rooted in a God who would never leave her. She began to grow stronger in her broken places, like a tree whose roots had gained strength in the storm.

Little by little, hints of hope seemed to peek over the horizon.

Reflect: Is someone you know experiencing the fresh pain of the recent death of a loved one? Reach out as a channel of healing, asking the Spirit to reveal an act of kindness and consolation that is possible today. Don't postpone it.

APRIL 4 • *Desolation of Divorce*

Recovery from divorce has some distinct differences from the death of a spouse. The two experiences have been contrasted using the metaphor of the sword. Death makes a final, clean cut; divorce creates a jagged edge. Both result in life-altering transition.

Sometimes two people arrive at a mutual decision to part with no residual rancor. They may have exhausted every effort—from counseling to prayer—before deciding that divorce is the path to follow. Under those circumstances, letting go of the relationship may be less painful than continuing the damage. In most instances, however, divorce produces feelings of profound failure surrounded by anger, resentment, and guilt. Those affected by divorce must let go not only of the relationship itself but also the accompanying feelings of rage, remorse, or rejection. The wrenching experience makes it imperative that those involved extract every lesson possible in order to salvage meaning. Otherwise, the emotional waste feels overwhelming and unbearable. At the least, a broken relationship provides an opportunity to explore honestly what went awry so that each person can grow from that knowledge.

But before partners can uncover and face the lessons, they must stop focusing on the wrongdoing of the other person—quit the blame game. After feeling and acknowledging the pain, they must take a piercing look at the situation and ask, "What can I glean from this?" Blame, while easier and more ego-satisfying, diverts and obscures the lessons.

Our culture sets up some imposing stumbling blocks to the success of marriage, producing a whole range of unrealistic expectations. Many of our ideas of love have been shaped by romance novels, movies, and sentimental love songs. Music like "You're My Everything" formed our relational expectations just as a hymn like "The Old Rugged Cross" formed our theology.

The desperation of divorce makes it hard to deal with negative feelings in a healthy way. Choosing to move on may feel as if legitimate anger and disappointment are being stuffed down a rabbit hole. In reality, the path of forgiveness and acceptance stretches before us as the way to heal the wounds.

Reflect: Prayerfully consider the plight of those—perhaps even yourself—caught in the web of divorce. What are some honest ways to embody compassion in this difficult life transition?

APRIL 5 • *The Empty Nest*

One of the greatest gifts we can give our children is a life of *our* own so that they can pursue a life of *their* own. As young people courageously launch into the big, scary world, the last thing they need is our neediness. We all have empty places inside us that yearn for love. That vacuum draws in the love of a child, which makes it difficult for him or her to move into maturity. Our keen awareness of our parental need allows us to refrain from using our children to fill the gaping hole inside us. We can easily use their devotion to satisfy our unconscious needs without noticing our subtle motives. After all, we want a close relationship with our offspring. However, healthy love senses the difference between a grasping relationship and a freeing one.

Addressing the vacuum in our own lives can be an exhilarating pursuit rather than a dismal one. At this time we can invigorate and strengthen our marriages, resurrect long-delayed dreams, and energize neglected parts of ourselves. We can view this life transition through the lens of gain rather than loss.

We can refrain from calling too much, hovering too much, grieving too much. We confront our need to be needed and take responsibility for our own wholeness. This rich opportunity encourages us to discover who we are beneath the integral role as parent. Grab it with gusto!

Reflect: Using the self-knowledge you gained during March's month of inner exploration, open your heart and follow the Spirit's leading into new ways of bringing love to the ailing world as well as to yourself.

APRIL 6 • *Shedding a Snake Skin*

On a hike through the woods, I stumbled upon a snake skin, recently shed by its owner through the cycle of life. I wondered how that snake must feel without its familiar covering. Vulnerable, I imagine, yet still alive.

We have skins too—necessary and timely roles we play. We are sons, daughters, mothers, fathers, spouses, friends, CEOs, factory workers, orchestra leaders, writers, preachers. When that role disappears, we often feel that we have ceased to exist. That role had become our reason for being.

Though we transition from one role to another all our days, it is always unsettling and a little scary. As we act out the ever-changing roles of our lives, we meet the parts of our true selves that those roles and experiences reveal. We learn to distinguish what is part of the role and what is authentically us. We hold those roles lightly, wearing them like pieces of clothing (or a snake skin!)—items we don temporarily, allowing them to come and go. Otherwise, when the role becomes unnecessary, we may feel emptied of identity.

In our younger years, most of us identify ourselves through the lives and needs of others. As the ground shifts beneath us in transition, we find it frightening to knock at the door of our own hearts and wonder who lives within. Men usually identify with their work roles, women more often with their relational roles. A surgeon friend who kept postponing his retirement remarked to me one day, "Oh, I can't retire! If I did, who would I be then?" He didn't know who he was behind his surgeon's mask. Though work may be part of our identity, it is not our essence.

Through the years, all of us assume masks that serve us and others in the short run. But over the long haul, the true self can become like an orphaned child—unknown, unloved, and unnurtured—hiding beneath our layers of costuming. Part of our life task comes in letting go of who we thought we were so we can discover who we truly are.

Reflect: What masks and roles are you wearing right now? Take time to connect with who you are underneath today's coverings. Imagine yourself without them. What are the attributes of that person? What changes would you need to make to become more authentically *yourself*?

APRIL 7 • *The Moving Van*

My friend's life had been shaped by one move after another—following the upward mobility of a talented corporate husband. Every two or three years, she would pack up the house, comfort the three children, and head to another city. During her brief sojourn in Dallas, I luckily became friends with this wise and wonderful woman. After twenty-five years and countless moves for both of us, we continue to nurture our friendship across the miles.

I asked my friend how she kept her sanity during the frequent relocations. She replied thoughtfully, "Well, I take some time to think what worked for our family in the present locale and get honest about what didn't work. Then I take the positive lessons and "pack" them with us. I learn from the failures and leave them behind. That way, our family unit becomes stronger as we allow our chaotic life to shape us into the best we can be."

Moving to a new city—or even a new neighborhood—unleashes our familiar moorings. No one recognizes us in the grocery store. No one asks for our help or involvement in an interesting project. We must find a new house, a new bank, a new doctor, a new church, make new friends. While it may seem an enviable opportunity to start anew, it rarely feels enviable. Instead, we may feel cast adrift in a sea of puzzling opportunities and hard choices.

Change—even painful, problematic change—holds the potential for growth if we decide to see it that way. In the flow of the Spirit, perhaps we can do what my friend did . . . allow the detours and U-turns of transition to open us to new vistas.

Reflect: Recall times in your past when a change in location presented a challenge. What did you learn about yourself and your relationship to God? How can you take that knowledge forward into the future?

APRIL 8 • *When a Friendship Fades*

We are born into our families, but we choose our friends. Like the proverbial balm in Gilead, friends soothe our souls, often filling in the painful gaps left in other personal attachments. It's the jack-of-all-trades in the relationship category and presents a huge dilemma when something causes it to fade.

It is helpful to affirm the diverse nature of friendships. In friendship one part of ourselves meets with one part of another person. For instance, we have the following:

- Convenience friends (whose lives routinely intersect with ours, like carpooling the children)
- Special-interest friends with whom we share an activity (golf buddies or book club cohorts)
- Historical friends (who knew us way back when)
- Crossroads friends (who shared a life event with us, like a college roommate)
- Cross-generational friends (where the wisdom of one generation enlivens the other)
- Family friends (not friends *of* the family, but friends *in* the family).
- Spiritual friends (who help us along the inner journey)
- Soul friends (with whom we have a mysterious connection for no discernible reason)
- Close friends (whose unique bond transcends time and space—friends we can call at three in the morning)

Sometimes friendships run their course, and the relationship tends to become forced. Perhaps the common thread of interest that once held you together has frayed. Perhaps the tennis game you once enjoyed together now gives you a bum knee!

Friends can't be all things to us, and they can't be perfect. Releasing our illusions about friendships and appreciating them in their diversity can help us through the transition of letting them evolve without blame or rancor when the time comes. Letting go of a friendship often feels like a lack of love and loyalty—that the friendship's demise is someone's fault.

There are times when we prudently honor a friendship for what it was and let it go. If it later offers itself for renewal, we give it a fresh look!

Reflect: Take time to appreciate the diverse friends in your life. Give thanks for the unique way each one enriches your life.

APRIL 9 • *Risks and Rewards in Retirement*

As Howard cut his retirement cake, he echoed a familiar refrain, "So what am I going to do for the next thirty years?" It was a legitimate question for someone still in good health who came from a family with a history of longevity.

Thanks to medical science and healthy lifestyle information, most of us anticipate a span of years not available to our ancestors. Age seventy no longer represents the beginning of a slippery slope toward the cemetery! Here's some miscellaneous advice I gleaned from interviews with more than fifty seniors who had plenty to say on the subject:

- Be a lifelong learner. Enroll in continuing education courses, or find other ways to stretch both mind and spirit.
- Take care of your aging body, but don't make it your main focus.
- Don't let your world shrink. Stay abreast of news and trends.
- Reach out. Do something of significance with the bonus of years now available.
- Renegotiate your close relationships in advance, rather than putting out fires after problems arise.
- Find ways to use the skills you've honed during your work life.
- Nurture your friendships, and develop new ones so you don't become socially isolated.
- Explore at least one new endeavor or interest.
- Deepen your life of faith and your relationship with God.
- Get in touch with your likes, dislikes, gifts and graces so you can live from a place of honesty about yourself.

The transition to this new phase of life produces some mixture of anxiety and anticipation. Viewed with faith and hope, it can be a grand adventure instead of a prison sentence.

Reflect: Mull over the possibilities for your own retirement years. Daydream about your options. How can you grow more genuinely into the person God created you to be?

APRIL 10 • *Father Time*

The transition of aging comes to each of us, though we certainly marshal our forces against it. I've read a shelfful of books telling me how to grow old gracefully—most of them with specific instructions about how to keep the appearance of Father Time at bay. Eat like a bird, work out like an athlete, nip and tuck like a starlet, be incessantly positive, and stay busy, busy, busy.

We can choose to look at the aging process through rose-colored glasses, smiling all the while. But denial provides only a short-term solution. Those glasses start to fog up when our back "goes out" or some other unexpected malady visits us. As one friend in his eighties quipped, "I feel like an automobile whose warranty is running out!"

Merely managing the body's decline can become a full-time job. Days consisting of visits to various doctors and keeping up with medications can lead to a self-centered existence that isolates the elderly person. It takes determination and grit to face the final third of life with joy instead of resignation.

Those who chirp that "age is just a number" haven't told that to the arthritis in my right knee. On any given day, we can feel decades younger than our chronological age; a week later, we may feel even older than we are. Striking a balance between honesty and optimism is a major challenge of the aging process. That balance, when yoked with a hefty dose of humor and grace, can infuse the later years with vibrant meaning.

You are now free to be yourself. Free to move from the tyranny of "I ought to" to "I choose to," intentionally relishing the daily joys that remain available.

Reflect: Explore your own attitude toward aging. Do you dread it? Look forward to it? Pray that God will help you move into this stage of your life purposefully and joyfully.

APRIL 11 • *The Two Doors*

What have you noticed about your aging patients?" I asked with interest. The three doctors of internal medicine paused thoughtfully before responding. Before the interview, I had asked them not to sugarcoat their answers or pull any punches. I wanted the unvarnished truth.

One doctor summed up his experience by saying, "As the years pile on, people tend to move either backward toward nostalgia about the past or forward with hope for the future."

Another chimed in, "Old folks head through one of two doors—the door of resistance or the door of growth. It's as if one group is invested in the status quo and holds on to what's familiar. The members of the other group are ready to let go of what isn't working anymore and gear up for change, even if they don't know exactly what that change will look like."

When I asked the doctors to be more specific, they came up with these signposts:

DOOR OF RESISTANCE
- Those who repeatedly refer to "the good old days."
- Those who are unwilling to consider ideas that differ from their own.
- Those who seem categorically opposed to change, championing the status quo.
- Those who whine and complain, wanting medication to fix whatever ails them—now—without exploring other possibilities.
- Those who are unwilling to examine old patterns of communication and behavior.
- Those who refuse to reconsider their religious beliefs and deal with reasonable doubts.
- Those who tend to take advantage of physical limitation, making it an excuse not to grow.
- Those who are "set in their ways."

DOOR OF GROWTH
- Those who evidence curiosity about learning.
- Those who eagerly choose to discover their true identity, apart from cultural expectations.
- Those who commit to more honesty in relationships.
- Those who challenge old patterns to test their validity for the present.
- Those who accept what is, rather than complain about it.

- Those who can adapt to loss and willingly change their lives in harmony with the change in circumstances, look honestly at what they are holding on to, and identify barriers to their own growth.
- Those who find the courage to tackle the work of letting go.
- Those who ground themselves in a strong faith.

Reflect: Ponder the signs of resistance and the signs of growth. Though you can't be in either camp all the time, which door seems to define you most of the time? Even if you've "entered" one door, always remember your option to choose the other.

APRIL 12 • *Pain Pays a Visit*

Though pain and suffering are inherent in the human condition, they shrink our world to a pinpoint. We don't care about the latest book, a worthy project, or who said what. All we want is relief and a cool glass of water.

Why wouldn't we resist pain? We don't like it; we beg God to get us out of it; it shatters our illusion of control. Troublesome questions come to call: *What did I do to deserve this? Why didn't I take care of myself? If I pray hard enough, will God take it away? Where did I go wrong?*

And, oh, how it messes with our theology. Our old ways of thinking and our sense of entitlement come forth in such statements as "I've tried to be a good person all my life, and this is what I get?" We may take scripture out of context, such as "The LORD watches over the way of the righteous, but the way of the wicked will perish" (Ps. 1:6) or "Do not regard lightly the discipline of the Lord, or lose heart when you are punished by him; for the Lord disciplines those whom he loves" (Heb. 12:5-6).

We reflect this unconscious reasoning even in our bedside comments: "He is such a wonderful man—there's no way he deserved this!" or "I know God will heal her because she's such a loyal Christian."

As we move through the flood of emotions in the midst of pain, it's a good idea to do so slowly and deliberately. This challenging pathway seems to follow a fascinating trajectory of experience, moving from resisting and hating the pain to accepting and "hallowing" the pain, then on to handling the pain.

Often we assume that a true faith response is a stoic, grin-and-bear-it approach to suffering, one in which we try to do without medication or don a mask of bravery. Once again, it's more authentic to face our emotions and admit the pain. At some point, God invites us to move toward what may seem impossible: a hallowing of the pain. To hallow, to make holy, is to open ourselves to the possibility that physical diminishment can eventually reveal some nugget of growth if we can see it.

Perhaps it will resemble the biblical story of Jacob wrestling with the angel. Jacob wouldn't let the angel go until he received its blessing, until the meaning of the encounter was revealed. Remember that Jacob went away from his all-night wrestling match not only with a physical wound—a limp—but also with a new name, a new purpose, a new blessing. (See Genesis 32:24-29.)

Reflect: Think about your last experience of pain. What lessons did you learn? Allow your experience to increase your understanding and compassion for others in pain.

APRIL 13 • *It Isn't Fair*

Whoever coined the cliché that "God never gives us more than we can bear" should be sent to the corner to work on theology and compassion! My friend's response to that trite statement had the ring of honesty, "Well, I wish God didn't think so highly of my coping skills!"

For starters, God doesn't "give" us trouble in order to whip us into spiritual shape. And to follow up, it's a hurtful message to give someone who is in a troublesome transition.

That said, as human beings, we seem to be created with a desire for fairness and balance. From the trivial to the terrible, we want life to make sense—vice is punished and virtue is rewarded. Whether it's chocolate pie or the mythical American Pie, our innate sense of justice demands that everyone have an equal slice.

Most of us grew up with an idea called the "theory of divine retribution": Do good and you will be blessed; obey God's laws and you will prosper. But life has a way of shattering our illusions about everyone's getting a fair shake, especially when our own hearts or bodies have been broken. When life fails to measure up to the logic we yearn for, we feel bewildered, frustrated, and stopped dead in our spiritual tracks. Once again, we must befriend the mystery of it all.

We can take comfort in recalling two stories from scripture. First, consider the life of Jesus. In this world's terms, the events of his life didn't go well. In the midst of the worst that could happen—abandonment, misunderstanding, rejection, pain, humiliating death—he clearly struggled with human emotion. However, Jesus exhibited an acceptance of what was, while reaching for bedrock faith and a determination to be true to himself as a loving and forgiving person.

Another Bible story throws fairness on its ear—that of the prodigal son (Luke 15). He didn't receive the punishment he deserved, and his father welcomed him home with a grand gala! Clearly, the lavish values of the kingdom of God, though incomprehensible to us, draw us into radical trust.

Reflect: Transitions rarely seem fair or peaceful. Take time to feel your rootedness in the soil of the Spirit, where guidance lies waiting.

APRIL 14 • *In Exile*

When we are weathering the rainy days of transition, no matter the type or cause, it's normal to feel isolated, outside the circle, so to speak. Friends don't know how to comfort us; they want to fix our pain and they can't. The rest of the world goes on while our world has stopped. We feel as if we're in exile.

Sometimes *we* do the exiling. We withdraw to some interior safe place where we disconnect from our feelings, protect ourselves from whatever or whoever we think is threatening us. We build a wall around our hearts to keep the pain at bay. We're reluctant to allow ourselves emotional freedom because we might cry or do something embarrassing! Even in a worship setting, we keep a lid on our emotions so that we can behave appropriately. We distance ourselves from spontaneity and exist in a dry, emotionless desert space. A different kind of exile, for sure, but exile nonetheless.

So what word does God speak to us today about our condition, this familiar part of our life experience? How can we reach for the hand of God to guide us through the loneliness of exile—whether interior or exterior, whether self-imposed or other-imposed?

We can choose to hallow the pain without allowing it to paralyze us. Perhaps we can summon the courage to take the next step, however small, toward healing and wholeness. We can pick up our reluctant feet and move toward the next point of light that we can see, remaining open to God's continued grace and guidance.

Reflect: For a moment, sense the next nudge of the Spirit inviting you to keep on keeping on . . . until the larger picture becomes apparent or until the intensity of the crisis lessens.

APRIL 15 • *The Significance of Solitude*

When talking with people about their life challenges, one topic repeatedly arose: learning to be alone. Margie, a new widow, confronted one of the major tasks of widowhood—that of paperwork. "It's not that I'm helpless," she insisted. "But Henry took care of certain things, from changing the auto oil to paying the bills and taxes. I've managed to learn about insurance coverage and financial details, but I can't seem to make peace with the loneliness."

Oddly enough, the best cure for loneliness is solitude. While both solitude and loneliness are experiences of being alone, only through solitude will we make progress in valuing our own companionship. Self-understanding evolves, and we become more comfortable with who we are. When we voluntarily spend time alone, we find interior conversations taking place in an inside "chat room." There we learn to hang out with ourselves, to become friends with ourselves. Someone or something eventually starts to "talk back"—questioning, analyzing, encouraging, chastising, planning, dreaming. Then when we participate in a desperate spell of whining, that Someone puts a hand on our shoulder, saying sternly and compassionately, "Now, now, . . . you're going to be okay; just hang in there."

Becoming a friend to ourselves means that we curb the inner criticism and give support instead. It becomes a dialogue with our own depths— where God communes with our soul—where we are accompanied and empowered by the Spirit. The ability to be comfortably alone eventually heals the spirit and mind. We may discover that we can become fun-loving companions to ourselves! Appreciating our own company is a giant step from loneliness to meaningful solitude.

Reflect: Spend some time today alone, hanging out with yourself. Ask God to guide you toward becoming your own best friend.

APRIL 16 • *Tending the Wound*

An emergency room physician suggested a fascinating metaphor for the healing of the emotional wounds of transition and loss. He explained it this way:

> Suppose you come into the ER with a gash in your arm that needs stitches. My task is to clean out the bacteria, probe the wound to check for other areas of injury, to tend the wound—even though there may be pain involved. But then I can sew it up and allow God's natural healing process to do its remarkable work. Even the scab itself is evidence of automatic healing taking place. I can't make the mistake of taking out the stitches tomorrow to check and see if it is closing properly. The patient must respect the process and accept the scar.

Even in the face of catastrophe and injustice, we sense a benevolent reliability at the heart of things:

- The gash in the arm has the capacity to heal itself.
- The sun rises and sets daily without our intervention.
- Solar energy warms the earth and enlivens the plants.
- Ordinary people make heroic sacrifices for others with no expectation of repayment.

So how can we respect the process and cooperate with God's natural healing? Our part of the process may come in finding ways to tend the wound gently, nurturing it in harmony with the organic flow of healing.

And then, of course, we must accept the scar. We integrate and hallow the experience in a way that deepens our compassion and love for ourselves and others.

Reflect: Think of an emotional wound in your past or in your current experience. Ask God to guide you toward tending the wound in your own unique manner.

APRIL 17 • *Feel It First*

Talking about the pain or the transition or the injustice—whatever storm we're weathering—is not the same as feeling it.

We may think about sadness, but we hold grief in our bodies as a lump in the throat, a knot in the stomach, a hole in the heart. Experts tell us that a healthy approach allows that to happen. We listen to the body and feel the grief welling from that spot, to allow the tears to flow. A growing body of evidence suggests that physical exercise during times of stress and grief is greatly beneficial because it gets the body involved. It affirms the words of the psalmist that we are "fearfully and wonderfully made" (139:14) in an interrelated network of body, mind, and spirit. What we do in one area affects another.

It may not be easy to find a safe place to do this kind of grief work, to feel the feelings. We need to avoid people who say, "Gee, you shouldn't feel that way because. . . . " Or "Just stay busy, and it will pass," or, worse still, "It's time you should be getting over that." Remember that talking about feelings is not the same as feeling them. Though talking can help, it can also keep the grief contained in the head so that it doesn't move to the heart and body.

Okay, so now we've gotten in touch with our feelings and are experiencing them strongly. What happens if tears well up at a time that isn't appropriate or safe? We can borrow the suggestion of a busy woman who tried to honor her grief in the midst of a demanding life. She treated her grief as a living entity inside her, saying in effect, "I hear you; I know you're there, and I'm going to honor you by spending time with you tomorrow afternoon." Then she kept her promise.

Reflect: Think honestly about the ways you have dealt with grief and disappointment in the past. Have you stuffed it inside, combating it with the power of your will? Allow yourself to imagine new ways to feel the feelings and cooperate with the holy healing process.

APRIL 18 • *Seeking Support*

When it's time to express our despair more fully, supportive friends and kindred spirits can form a safe harbor, a rest from the storm.

Remember the familiar story of the little boy who cried out in fear during a thunderstorm? His father rushed into the room to calm and comfort him, saying ,"There, there, Sonny, everything's okay; remember that God loves you!" "But, Daddy," he replied, "sometimes I need someone with skin on!" Surely one of our main purposes in this world is to be "God with skin on" for someone else.

Folks who have shared a similar loss or transition can serve as channels of divine love because they've been there. Support groups abound in churches, community centers, and health care settings and provide not only a community of commiseration but a source of wisdom and hope. As one person said so poignantly, "I can go on when I see someone else who has gone on."

In some instances, people require individual counseling or personal therapy. Thankfully, the stigma that society attached to the need for psychological help is dissipating. Years ago, many churchgoers believed counseling signaled weakness—or worse still, a lack of faith. Enlightenment has changed that notion. Caring professionals certainly fall into the category of "God with skin on"!

Surely the words of Galatians 6:2 can guide and inspire us: "Bear one another's burdens, and in this way you will fulfill the law of Christ."

Reflect: Consider ways you may need support during tumultuous times, and express those needs to another person. At the same time, pray that you can be "God with skin on" to those who need your support.

APRIL 19 • *Honoring the Memories*

Remembering literally helps us to re-member meaningful moments with a loved one, especially at their passing. We attempt to pay tribute to their presence in our lives. We don't want to forget them.

A recent widower shared a poignant comment about the reactions he received following the death of his wife: "No one would talk about her around me. Folks hardly even mentioned her name for fear they would upset me. What actually upset me was that they seemed to be ignoring my loss—urging me to move on, acting as if she never existed—all because of their discomfort! I just wanted them to be with me, that's all."

Though our deceased loved ones may not be physically present day to day, we can take some simple actions to acknowledge their profound impact on our lives:

- Plan a periodic "grief day"—maybe once a month—when you spend some time alone in a quiet setting looking at photographs, having imaginary conversations with the person, laughing, crying . . . just remembering.
- Create a scrapbook with news clippings, photos, and other mementos from the person's life.
- Host a family event on the person's birthday and display the scrapbook, plus sharing any videos and stories within the group. Drink toasts to his or her memory, giving honor with your words.
- Give some of their cherished possessions to people with whom they had a special bond, knowing that it would have given them joy for that recipient to own the item.
- Donate to causes that were important to them.
- Participate in projects that bring healing to your community.
- Send a card on important anniversaries or occasions to show that you have not forgotten their loved one.

Though honoring memories can bring unexpected laughter and tears, these steps can help us re-member the pieces of a broken heart.

Reflect: As you think of someone you have lost, meditate slowly on Philippians 1:3, "I thank my God every time I remember you." Be grateful for the gift of memory and for the gifts that person brought to your life.

APRIL 20 • *Ask for What You Need*

Is there anything I can do to help?" Too often, when we hear these words, we thank our friends for their offer, and that's the last of it. Why do we hesitate to respond honestly? "If you're free, would you give Mary a ride to her doctor's appointment on Tuesday, and I'll take a little break." Or, "I need some help packing the day before the moving van arrives."

An honest response is a gift to those around us who feel helpless and stumped about how to come to our aid. Our directness enables them to put legs on their wishes, saving them the task of trying to read our minds.

Most of us want to project strength and competence—a sort of I-can-handle-this persona, yet we secretly hope people will anticipate our needs. Close friends sincerely want to help us rebuild our lives, and we respect that desire by being as vulnerable as we really are. In other words, why not tell the truth?

On the other hand, sometimes we are so traumatized that we don't even know what we need. I can recall such a time, when two friends cared enough to anticipate my needs when I couldn't do it myself. They came to my house when I was out and cleaned it from top to bottom, leaving me the following message scrawled on the back of a brown grocery sack:

There's a turkey sandwich in the fridge; eat it.
There's a glass of wine also; drink it.
Then go upstairs.

The entire house smelled of furniture polish and cleanser. The laundry was done, and the place was a far cry from the mess I had left that morning. In my bedroom, I found clean sheets on my bed. My nicest nightgown was draped across the bed, accompanied by a long-stemmed rose and squares of delectable chocolate. Beside my bathtub were more pampering supplies, along with instructions about running hot water, pouring in lavender bubble bath, and lighting a scented candle.

Few of us experience that kind of thoughtfulness. After thirty-five years, their actions still ring a tear to my eye.

Reflect: How do you normally respond to offers for help? Spend some time exploring your own needs, as well as how you can respond to others' needs with sensitivity.

APRIL 21 • *Self-Care Is Not Selfish*

I recall a time, many years ago, when my anxiety level was through the roof as I filled my days with frantic busyness, micromanaging my young sons' lives, and fretting over their adjustment to the divorce of their parents. Though all the stress taxed the limits of my sanity, I couldn't stop trying. Then some words broke through the madness. They made sense then and now: "Linda, the best gift you can give your children right now is a sane mother."

The words bounced against a perspective that was firmly entrenched in my psyche, for I had long equated self-care with ego-centeredness and selfishness. As I pursued the path of "dedication till you drop," it became increasingly difficult to give from an empty cup. My nearly bone-dry well of spiritual, physical, and emotional energy brought me to the reality that soon I would have nothing left to give anyone, especially the two sons I loved so dearly.

So, what would enhance my sanity? I wondered. Since I wasn't accustomed to the question, the answers didn't come at first. Then I began to notice little things that nurtured me—a fragrant soak in the tub, settling against a pile of pillows with a great novel, taking prayerful walks, chopping fresh vegetables and cooking a huge pot of soup to share. I also developed an awareness that the company of some people lifted my spirits and others lifted my despair. I had to hold some folks at arms' length for a while because their sympathy for me became toxic to my healing (though it felt supportive in the short run).

During difficult times, we need to proactively secure our own sanity, seizing every comforting moment we can, rejecting the notion that it is selfish. An emotional wound has to be "bandaged" and tended carefully as God's healing process takes over. We must find ways to support our own sanity because tending to our own well-being is the only way we can effectively enhance the lives of others.

Reflect: Think of times when you feel "guilty" for taking care of yourself. Allow the Spirit to replace your guilt with the awareness that you can't give from an empty cup.

APRIL 22 • *Resourcefulness*

Tending our own wounds during messy transitions usually requires some resourcefulness. Here are some suggestions to get us started:

- Rest. Get more rest than you think you need. Stress depletes the body like an invisible poison. Sleep, take naps; treat your body like the valuable vessel it is.
- Read. Read for inspiration, information, and entertainment.
- Exercise. You don't have to drive your body to distraction—just keep it moving.
- Eat good food. Treat yourself to nourishing food you truly like (though not a diet of only fries). And don't forget the chocolate—really great chocolate.
- Look for homespun touches. Music, crisp bed linens, scented candles, a cup of tea, a new pet.
- Find recreation. Theater, movies, hikes, that trip you've always dreamed of.
- See friends. Spend time with those who make you feel more hopeful and vibrant. Be selective for a time, asking yourself after you've been in someone's company, "Do I feel better or worse?"
- Lend a hand. Stay in connection with others who feel needy right now. You don't have to rescue them; just offer a bit of care.
- Worship. Stay in touch with the world of Spirit, preferably in the company of a loving community that supports and cares for you. However, if it feels better to you, become a worshiping nomad for a while, dropping in on services anonymously and sitting on the back row.
- Seek counseling. If you want to talk with someone about what you're going through, find a pastor, counselor, or spiritual director.
- Pray or meditate. Whatever your mode or method, spend time each day connecting with the Spirit of God—who is greater and more loving than you can fathom.

Small steps lead to large leaps in the landscape of grief. Day by day, you will move, whether it feels like it or not, toward the rehabilitation of your wounded heart.

Reflect: Make a list of things that give you a small lift. Today, promise yourself to do at least one of them.

APRIL 23 • *Rituals for Healing*

Mary's relationship with her boyfriend, Sam, was on the rocks. This man to whom she had been engaged for two years had broken the relationship off abruptly, admitting that he had found someone else. Her devastation and anger dominated every waking moment and was on the verge of ruining her health until a good counselor helped her work through her feelings of rejection and rage. In time, she felt ready to move on. As a symbol of that decision, she created a lovely ritual to mark the new beginning.

Mary stood beside a serene lake near her home with a single, long-stemmed rose in her hand. She took a deep breath and conjured up every memory she could about the relationship. As she visualized a life-giving moment, she pulled a rose petal from the blossom to honor the memory and tossed it gently into the lake. When a painful memory came to mind, she plucked a sharp thorn from the rose stem and dropped it into the water. When the memories, as well as the petals and thorns, were exhausted, she tossed what was left of the rose out into the lake in a final gesture of release. Though the ritual didn't erase the situation, it helped her turn the corner in her recovery and come to accept the loss.

Group rituals offer the blessing of mutual support and encouragement. When congregations celebrate the Lord's Supper, the members engage in a remembrance of Christ. When ashes are placed on our foreheads each Ash Wednesday, we mark the beginning of the season of Lent. Advent candles symbolize our anticipation of the coming of Jesus. Symbols and rituals provide a pathway to meaning and acceptance. Likewise, we can gather with caring friends to create ceremonies that mark the troublesome transitions in our lives.

Reflect: Allow the Spirit to spark your imagination as you devise a personal or group ritual to express your intention to move toward healing.

APRIL 24 • *Respect for the Process*

I know I shouldn't feel this way, but...."

"When things get back to normal...."

"When I feel like myself again...."

We hear ourselves repeating these phrases when we're in the midst of grief and transition. When we expect any of these projections to be valid, we set ourselves up for disappointment, confusion, and guilt. Grief has a life of its own, and we must respect its unique process in each of us. Information and charts outlining the stages of grief prove valuable but only as guidelines. They do not set forth absolutes with which we "should" comply. We are likely to drift back and forth between the stages of denial and acceptance. We can't manipulate feelings into a preconceived formula. In other words, in healthy grieving we relinquish control and allow it to be what it is.

When we demand too much of ourselves, thinking we should be over it by now, we simply deny our feelings and dump a load of guilt on top of the grief. We will never be quite the same again. Rather than viewing this experience in a totally negative way, we can listen for a whisper of hope.

In integrating grief and disappointment into our lives, the analogy of a quilt offers a meaningful image. We can take the patches of our lives (old and new) and piece them together into a new pattern, something uniquely ours.

Above all, God invites us to accept the process of healing as a gift. If we run from it, circumvent it, or ignore it, we may miss the growth that lies within it.

Reflect: Meditate quietly on Isaiah 40:31: "Those who wait for the LORD shall renew their strength, they shall mount up with wings like eagles, they shall run and not be weary, they shall walk and not faint." We may not soar every day. We may not run without weariness in every instance. In fact, we may simply put one foot in front of the other without fainting most of the time. God may not keep us from sorrow, but God does keep us!

APRIL 25 • *Relationship with the Holy*

When transition shifts the sands beneath our feet, we need to stand on something solid. Like the steadfastness of God. Like the reliability of the tides and the annual rising of sap in the trees. Like the inhale and exhale of each breath we take.

Staying in touch with the sacred can take many forms; not all need to be overtly "religious." A spiritual practice free of "ought" and "should," can lead us outside the circle of our own despair and create room for grace. Experiment with activities that pique your interest or beckon to you in some way:

- Journal. Buy a new journal, and record your thoughts and feelings—as if you are writing a letter to a God who loves you and wants to hear everything you have to say. Ignore grammar and punctuation, and keep it in a safe, private place where no one else will see it.
- Meditate. Rather than imploring God to free you from your situation, shift your attention to God's nature as forgiving, comforting, and loving. The book of Genesis tells us that God created light and life out of darkness. Trust that you too are a part of this creative journey from darkness to light.
- Get outside. Experiencing nature rather than just thinking about it touches us at the soul level. Visit gardens, parks, mountains, beaches; watch the full moon or the rising sun. Breathe in fresh air; stand in the rain.
- Pray in new ways. Release your desire to pray "right" and affirm the lavish generosity of the Spirit to pray for you. Romans 8:26 says it this way: "The Spirit helps us in our weakness; for we do not know how to pray as we ought, but that very Spirit intercedes with sighs too deep for words."
- Experience the sacredness of music and art. Allow music you love to wash over you; sing along; visit a gallery or a beautiful sanctuary; pick up a paintbrush or crayons and let go of inhibitions.

In times of trouble, faith is not a last resort but an undergirding, a support beneath our feet, a firm foundation. It is not a feeling but an assurance of connection to the Benevolence at the heart of the universe.

Reflect: Consider the experiences that affirm your relationship with God. Choose circumstances and activities that deepen your connectedness.

APRIL 26 • *Gifts of Failure*

The story goes that Sam Snead, the famous golf pro, and Ted Williams, the famous baseball star, had a regular friendly golf game. One day, their game became a little less than friendly when they got into an argument about which sport was the tougher—golf or baseball. And argue, they did!

Ted Williams was about to tee off, still making his case about the greatness of baseball, insisting, "You've got to hit the fast ball; you've got to field the big hitters; you've got to master the double play—it's definitely the hardest game to play," at which point he drew back his driver and hit a powerful tee shot. He hooked the ball, which landed over in the rough.

Sam Snead stepped up to the tee and said smugly, "You've just proved my point, Ted. Golf is obviously the toughest game because in golf, we have to play our foul balls."

And so it is in life. We have to play our foul balls—as well as our home runs, our pop flies, our hits, our runs, and especially our errors. Sometimes in our detours and despair we must face the fact that we held the bat.

But even our mistakes are fodder for our growth. How do we learn to make good choices? Usually by making bad choices and benefiting from the lessons offered by experience. We use the old to help build the new. Plus, bad choices puncture a hole in our self-importance and remind us of our sweet imperfection. Learning from the past and putting it behind us makes us humble and human.

When we focus on the past with hand-wringing and brow-beating, we siphon off our energy into what was or could have been. When we focus on the future, we invest our energy in what might be. When we focus on the present, we concentrate our energy into acceptance of what *is*.

Reflect: Review a few of your past mistakes. Did you make excuses for yourself, or did you learn some significant lessons? Thank God that both wisdom and forgiveness can bloom from the soil of our mistakes.

APRIL 27 • *Sorrows Are Not Wasted*

I received an unexpected and unsolicited call from a stranger. Someone had suggested she contact me, since I "had been through the same thing." As she poured out her story, I found it distressingly familiar. Her husband had left her; she had two young children. Her rage and frustration were about to overwhelm her. Enough years had elapsed for me that I could listen to her without plunging back into my own despair. I sensed God whispering to me, "Use your own painful experiences to help alleviate hers any way you can."

Similar synchronicities have occurred more times than I can count because hurting people seek the credibility of someone who has been there. Seekers will appear in my spiritual guidance office expressing the same faith struggle I've just weathered or voicing the same confusion over a theological issue. I hear achingly recognizable words, and I can almost predict what they will say next. It has strengthened my trust that in God's economy, nothing is wasted.

Encounters such as these may take us back to our own pain but not with the same ferocity. We can revisit our past hurts that seemed devoid of redemption and slowly infuse them with a sense of meaning. Somehow, we know in our souls that no matter the experience, we can use it to comfort and console others. Some seekers want perspective, advice, or a word of hope. Others may need a loving presence to hear their story without judgment.

When the rains come, our own journey into the light can lead those in darkness to trust what lies beyond. The fact that we have survived a story akin to theirs and lived to tell it becomes a priceless gift that is ours to offer.

Reflect: Recall instances in your life when you have used your sorrows to help another. Pray to be alert and open for any opportunity for the Spirit to love and comfort others through you. You don't need to feel competent. You simply need to be available.

APRIL 28 • *The Mystery of Suffering*

When we approach the mystery of suffering, we tread on holy ground. We watch the evening news, appalled at the barbarity of human beings toward one another. We read of a plane crash where five survive and fifty die. We walk through the hospital wards and wonder why the innocent suffer. We face our own disillusionments and bereavements and want to place the blame somewhere. In our rush to answers, we are prone to accept some faulty theories like these:

- *Suffering is caused by God.* I once heard a troubled woman say, "I know God wants me to have this suffering for a reason." God does not send our suffering, though in a mysterious way, God allows it. In his humanity, even Jesus struggled with this understanding. Luke 22:42 records Jesus' words before his crucifixion, "Father, if you are willing, remove this cup from me." God did not enter in, perform a miracle, and keep him from the cross. God does not necessarily deliver us from suffering. Being fully human, Jesus obviously wrestled with the perplexing condition of suffering in which all of us participate.

- *Suffering is punishment for sin.* Scripture points out the fallacy of this reasoning. Jesus' disciples asked, "'Rabbi, who sinned, this man or his parents, that he was born blind?' Jesus answered, 'Neither this man nor his parents sinned'" (John 9:2-3). Further commentary comes from Matthew 5:45, "[God] . . . sends rain on the righteous and on the unrighteous." We only have to look at life to see that many sinners prosper and many good people suffer. Suffering shows no partiality; it visits saints and sinners alike.

- *Suffering is sent to test our faith.* The book of Job reveals the complexity of suffering. Job loses everything, even having to suffer through the flawed theology of his friends who insist that he must have caused his own troubles. However, Job clings to what remains: his relationship with God and God's pervading presence.

- *Suffering is an illusion.* No compassionate person would say to a person who has just lost a loved one, "It's all in your mind; you'll get over it." Though some schools of thought proclaim this heresy, suffering is as real as the blood in our veins.

After today's explorations of faulty assumptions, tomorrow we'll focus on what we *can* know and trust. Like Job, we can cleave to what remains.

Reflect: What remnants of flawed philosophies remain part of your understanding of suffering? Allow trust in God to clear the path toward truth and acceptance of the mystery.

APRIL 29 • *What We Can Count On*

Even when we find ourselves between the now and the not-yet, we can hold on to some verities:

- Suffering grows the soul. An integral part of soulful living lies in receiving and holding what comes our way. Claiming our humanity (which includes suffering) punctures our perfectionism and replaces it with compassion.
- Suffering moves us toward gratitude, a quickening appreciation of small blessings, an awareness of the power of our emotions—even those of sadness and despair.
- God created us with a mysterious core of resilience.
- A holy dependability resides at the heart of the universe. Seasons come and go; blossoms appear; human beings rise to occasions of surprising love and courage.
- Nothing can separate us from the love of God: "neither death, nor life, nor angels, nor rulers, nor things present, nor things to come, nor powers, nor height, nor depth, nor anything else in all creation" (Rom. 8:38-39).
- God's faithfulness to us is real.

I'm unwilling to believe that God engineers the pain in our lives to foster our growth, but I am willing to affirm that "all things work together for good for those who love God" (Rom. 8:28). No matter what the circumstances or how they came about, the Spirit invites us into the task of picking up the broken shards of our lives and, with the power of divine grace, shaping them into a unique mosaic of greater love for God and compassion for God's people.

Reflect: Affirm the truths you can count on and allow them to give you peace, strength, and comfort. Pray that they will guide you on your way.

APRIL 30 • *From Surviving to Thriving*

Rain can create mess, mud, inconvenience, discomfort—usually triggering a detour in the normal order of events. When emotional rains flood our lives, after the human questions of why and what, we move to how. The quagmire of "Why did this happen to me?" can give way to "How will I respond?"

Our first human impulse is that of mere survival—how to endure it, how to stand it. But in the ongoing growth of the soul, something in us desires more than that. Stoicism does not provide a happy approach; we want joy. Some deep yearning in the soul encourages us to move from slogging through the muck to standing in the sunshine. We may be in darkness but still look beyond to the light.

Hope and optimism afford us spiritual stepping-stones to that patch of sunlight. A tricky tension exists between honesty (the reality of things as they are) and hope (things will eventually get more manageable), along with a desire to live faithfully in the midst of it. In the meantime, we take one step at a time. We keep on keeping on.

Rather than regarding that persistence with impatience and resignation, perhaps we can view it as a spiritual practice in itself. After all, isn't "keeping on" an act of progress? It helps to remember that however harrowing the situation, transition has the potential for unfolding transformation. We move to the tempo of our soul's sweet song, even though the present harmonies may be dirges.

So we don't conform to the conventional "I must be strong" mentality, confusing grief with weakness. We take the soulful route; we cry, cherish memories, question, lament, feel our genuine feelings. And we believe that even though the earth may shake beneath our feet, we carry the seeds of new growth within us.

Reflect: Imagine your heart as a holy vessel—holding the riches of the past and a vibrant faith in an unknowable future. Affirm that in the vessel, the Spirit of healing dwells with you.

May

THE GARDEN GROWS

*"So neither the one who plants nor the one who waters is anything,
but only God who gives the growth."*
—1 Corinthians 3:7

Breath Prayer

God of all growth, . . . expand my heart.

MAY 1 • *Spring Has Sprung*

This is the time of the year when trees have that lime glow in their eyes, and the birds can't stop chirping about it! Mother Nature dons her finest attire in blossoms, and the spring spectacular bursts all around us.

Nature offers endless metaphors pointing to spiritual truths, the garden being one of the richest. In the familiar Creation stories in the book of Genesis, we don't focus on a mountaintop, a cave, or an ocean—but on a lush garden, the garden of Eden. Where did Jesus appear to Mary after the resurrection? In a garden. Jesus sprinkled his words of truth in images of vines, branches, weeds, wheat, lilies, sowers, seeds, and contrasts of rich or rocky soil. John's vision recorded in the book of Revelation includes the tree of life. A few centuries later, Saint John of the Cross and Teresa of Ávila would speak of the soul as a garden, a place where seeds are planted, and God provides the miracle of growth.

The Hebrew word for "man" is *adam*, which has close association with "ground" or *adamah*. This wordplay underscores the intimate relationship of humans to the soil and to the interconnectedness of all living things. No wonder our Christian tradition is replete with images of pastoral settings and earthy parables. These metaphors have the power to speak to us.

Since we are part of this grand creative cosmology, spring can be a season for our blossoming as well. Like the gardens abounding throughout the earth, the gardens of our souls have organic rhythms—patient fallow times, laborious seed-planting times, and surprising spurts of growth.

And every green tip holds a promise.

Reflect: As you look outside today, notice the tiny green shoots—formed by a power that is not your own. What might be bursting forth in you?

MAY 2 • *Trusting the Greening*

Artists would have trouble duplicating the hue of leaves as they first sprout. They appear neon in their brightness and vitality. They shout, "We are alive!"

Hildegard of Bingen, a Benedictine nun and mystical writer in the 1100s, related this vibrant color to the spiritual life, calling it *viriditas*, or greening power—God's life-giving, creative energy, evident in all creation. This creative power of God showers us with refreshment and vitality, giving us the impetus to bear fruit. Without it, we shrivel and "wilt."(1)

The same mysterious force that greens the leaves is present in every single one of us—eager to sprout with potential. Greening is never a fixed state of affairs. It may appear to be slow, but atoms and molecules race about in dynamic motion, rushing toward blossoming, fruit-bearing, and abundance.

So how can we recognize its stirrings? This kind of sprouting in the soul doesn't announce itself grandly or appear on a thunderbolt. It whispers, it nudges, it tugs. Be alert for a phrase that quickens your pulse, a thought that won't go away, a habit that continues to cause uneasiness, a special delight, or a recurrent sadness. A host of interior reminders invite us into the extraordinary process of springtime blossoming.

This magnificent greening power can transform everything that is dull and dead in us! We can trust it.

Reflect: Meditate slowly with Isaiah 43:18-19: "Do not remember the former things, or consider the things of old. I am about to do a new thing; now it springs forth, do you not perceive it?" May it be springtime in your own soul as you connect with the greening process of God.

MAY 3 • *Lessons from the Lilies*

We discover some hints at how to move with this greening rather than against it. Jesus' words in Luke 12:27 give us some tips: "Consider the lilies, how they grow: they neither toil nor spin; yet I tell you, even Solomon in all his glory was not clothed like one of these."

Lilies of the field are grace-filled guides in our own blossoming:

- They don't try to be what they aren't—not roses or marigolds or daisies but lilies! They are merely being themselves, what God created them to be.
- They don't try to do all the "toil" themselves but depend on a greater power, turning their faces to the true Light.
- They are connected to the earth. We too must take firm root in our Source of sustenance in order to blossom and stay connected. This doesn't mean draping ourselves in laziness, waiting for the Spirit to rearrange our messy lives. We participate in God's guidance by staying tethered to the Source of life and cooperating with its divine nurture.
- They don't spin in circles! Many of us begin our spiritual journeys swirling and twirling—trying to earn God's favor, to get it "right," and exerting enormous effort in climbing an imaginary ladder to sainthood.
- They make themselves available to God's work in and through them.

The divine power that lives in the greening grass and flowering lilies gives life not only to the lilies but to each one of us. Our very souls can sense springtime renewal.

Reflect: Take a lesson from the lilies and look at your own life through the lenses of creation and scripture. How can you reflect the trusting nature of lilies in the way you live?

MAY 4 • *The Seed of the Soul*

There is an old Hasidic tale in which a Jewish rabbi says, "When you die and go to heaven and meet your Maker, your Maker is not going to ask you, 'Why didn't you discover the cure for such and such? Why weren't you a leader? Why weren't you successful? Why didn't you become more?" The only questions that will be asked of you are, "Why didn't you become you and stay true to yourself? Why were you afraid to step out? Why didn't you become yourself?"

At the heart of spring resides a longing for newness—not just in the forests and gardens but in us as well. After all the digging and tilling offered in March, the soul's ground is stirred up and ready to nourish the seeds of growth that have been gestating in the darkness. After we have received clue after clue about how we're wired, it may be time to cooperate with the greening of our souls by entering some new territory—an interesting project, a class in a fascinating subject, a way to honor the possibilities that may be swimming in our heads.

Change always involves risk. But so what? You can always begin again, try something else, change your mind. Learning from our risks and mistakes need not involve shame and discouragement. In the words of the old song, "Just pick yourself up, dust yourself off, and start all over again!" Failure does not bring about our soul's deadness; it's caused by refusal to try anything new.

Reflect: Is the Spirit inviting you to a develop a new practice or to delve into an unexplored activity? Release your resistance and excuses, and take a chance!

MAY 5 • *The Seed Sprouts*

We easily forget that we plant some seeds that bear fruit in our lives— inside our heads. Sometimes the fruit creates beauty, and sometimes it doesn't!

There is no such thing as an idle thought. Small wonder that the book of Romans contains the message: "Be transformed by the renewing of your minds" (Rom. 12:2). Thoughts produce energy, which is the power that produces action—either positive or negative. Energy produces behavior. Behavior produces events. Events produce experience. So emotions like gratitude and goodwill don't appear out of nowhere. They usually start with the seeding of our thoughts. Likewise, emotions like anger and judgment don't arise by themselves; they are born in the hidden places where resentment and envy dwell—in our thoughts. The thoughts we choose to hold have incredible power.

The following "saying," attributed to ancient Chinese philosopher and poet Lao Tzu, illustrates the process with different wording:

Watch your thoughts; they become words.
Watch your words; they become actions.

Watch your habits; they become character.
Watch your character; it becomes your destiny.

Managing our thoughts is a daring endeavor with far-reaching influence. In many ways, we become what we think. I used to snub my nose at such a simplistic statement, dismissing it as new-age jargon. After all, doesn't the universe hurl comets at us? Doesn't life dole out pain and pleasure at random? Aren't most life events beyond our control? Though I don't hold the answers to such cosmic dilemmas, I'm willing to admit that I've changed my mind about changing my mind! I agree with author Wayne W. Dyer, who noted in his book *The Power of Intention: Learning to Co-Create Your World Your Way*, "*Change the way you look at things, and the things you look at will change.*"[1]

Reflect: As you go about your day, be a monitor of your thoughts. What emotions and feelings do they produce? If you shift to a more grateful or positive thought, how does your interior disposition shift inside you?

MAY 6 • *Nipping It in the Bud*

Scripture points us to the power of our thoughts, particularly in Philippians 4:8: "Whatever is true, whatever is honorable, whatever is just, whatever is pure, whatever is pleasing, whatever is commendable, if there is any excellence and if there is anything worthy of praise, think about these things."

Perennial wisdom from our religious traditions, as well as modern metaphysics, tells us that what we focus our attention on tends to get bigger. Thoughts create our reality from the inside out, not from the outside in. Phrases such as "change your thinking, change your life" may be sweeping generalizations, but they contain fundamental truths that we ignore at our peril. If we desire to move toward "blossoming" into our best selves, our most significant action will take place within us. If we want to release a quality, a habit, a characteristic that we do not want mirrored in our lives, we must find a way not to dwell on it. If we perpetuate, attract, and manifest what we think about, then it behooves us to attend to the workings of our minds.

Does this mean we ignore problems and predicaments or pretend that evil doesn't exist? No. We can acknowledge the presence of evil and heartache but choose not to live there permanently. Simplistic? Maybe. Effective? You bet. Our worry and desperation have no power to solve hardships on a personal or a global level; in fact, our malaise may hinder efforts at compassion. But we can replace the fretting space inside us with infinitely healthier and holier attitudes.

Even our prayers can reflect an intentionally positive mind-set, one that shows more compassion and less self-judgment. For example, we can restate our petition "Dear Lord, please abolish and control my terrible temper" as "Help me to be the loving person who reflects your Spirit of love and compassion." This reframes and redirects the negative energy. It's always an inside job.

Reflect: When a negative thought arises, practice harnessing it—naming it—and replacing it with a more positive thought, thereby "nipping it in the bud." Watch the wording of your prayers, and reframe them with hopeful language when possible.

MAY 7 • *Big Truths and Small Stages*

Most of us do pretty well with the broad-brush approach, such as "I really should be more optimistic" or "I'm much too negative in my thinking." It's a bit like telling a child, "You be a good boy now, Sonny," rather than "Let's talk about what happens when you hit your sister!"

The Greek word *metanoia* appears throughout the Bible. We commonly translate it as "repentance" or "change of mind," implying some sort of alteration that leads us toward a more grace-filled existence. But this divine movement requires our cooperation. God will not haul us kicking and screaming into compassionate behavior or personal wholeness against our wills. What then is our part of the bargain?

I need to get very specific. Change begins with awareness: paying attention to our thoughts, not in an accusatory way but in a gentle, watchful manner; becoming conscious of the seeds that we are unconsciously planting. Learn to recognize the negative lens when you begin to don that familiar pair of dark glasses. For instance, let's suppose you're part of a group discussion when your mind grabs center stage:

- That sure was a stupid remark!
- She's looking at me in a weird way.
- I'll bet everyone thinks I'm an idiot for saying that.

And the automatic evaluating and judgment take off like a runaway train, bound for frustration and grumpiness. Your task is to train yourself, one thought at a time, to spot the process and stop it. *Aha, there it is again . . . the negative lens,* you might say to yourself. When you discover the negativity, rather than a self-deprecating *Oh, no, I've done it again—when will I ever learn?* let your internal dialogue stem from a surge of gratitude for the awareness that gives you an opportunity to change.

We act out big truths on small stages, seeing the eternal only in the now.

Reflect: As you encounter negative thoughts, rather than debate about their goodness or badness, simply acknowledge them: "I hear you, but I'm moving on; you're no longer in charge of me!"

MAY 8 • *Giant Leaps and Tiny Steps*

Your mind doesn't control you; you control your mind. You can expect your mind to prattle on and on—that's what minds are prone to do. However, rather than engaging in a war with your own thoughts, accept the chatter instead of condemning it. Breathe deeply, calming your mind instead of criticizing it, then creatively move on.

To grit our teeth and doggedly replace a negative thought with a positive one feels phony. We often attempt a grand leap from a dismal thought to a happy thought, instead of taking one tiny step forward. How about choosing a thought that's just a *teeny bit* better? Then another and another and another. A progression of incremental steps can move us from feeling horrible to feeling joyous. Here's an imaginary progression:

- This family holiday is going to be a nightmare—Nick and Nora are so disagreeable that the day will be a disaster!
- I think I'll try complimenting Nora on her cake and watch her smile.
- I'll seat Nick next to Aunt Mary, and she'll bring out the best in him.
- The children can do their rollicking rendition of "Jingle Bells."

- We're a family that tries to allow for differences in a spirit of love.
- Love is always stronger than despair.
- This Christmas dinner will be undergirded with love.

This is not hocus-pocus or the power of positive thinking. It is a concrete way of walking step-by-step with our own soul's wisdom where God's voice gently guides us.

Reflect: Select a particular negative situation from your own life. Play with the possibilities as you journey through incremental steps toward a change of mind.

MAY 9 • *Seed of Self-Love*

I put a flower seed in a small pot one day—then forgot all about it. Naturally, when I failed to give it the required care, it died. We neglect the things we don't genuinely care about.

So it goes with the seed of self-love that the Creator planted in each of us—we must nurture it. Jesus obviously understood that when he urged us to love our neighbors as we love ourselves. So self-love and love of others are part of the same sacred package. In fact, our love of others soon withers and dies if we do not love ourselves. As we learn to understand and nurture our own needs, we can extend the same compassion to others. "It is like a mustard seed; . . . it grew and became a tree" (Luke 13:19).

Yet, we often emphasize the virtues of self-denial and self-sacrifice to the extent that we label self-love as narcissistic and selfish, as if it were better to experience deprivation rather than satisfaction. Differences exist between narcissism and love of self. Narcissism insists on a paralyzing preoccupation with our own interests to the exclusion of others; self-love shows a positive regard for the well-being of self while expressing concern for others' welfare. The command, "'You shall love your neighbor as yourself'" (Mark 12:31) is not so much an order as a statement of fact. In actuality, we tend to love our neighbors in the same way that we love ourselves! When we deny our own needs and blindly reject their existence, we are trying to do an impossible task:

- To tell others what we have not learned.
- To lead them where we have not gone.

- To give them what we do not possess.
- To show them what we have not discovered for ourselves.

Intimacy with self makes intimacy with others possible.

Reflect: Make a list of your own needs—personal, physical, spiritual, communal, being as specific as possible. Which needs are most important? Which are the most difficult to fulfill?

MAY 10 • *The Hand That Rocks the Cradle*

It isn't surprising that during this season of seed-planting, our culture celebrates a special holiday to honor mothers—whose wisdom has sown and nurtured much that is deep within the soil of our souls.

Some of us were lucky enough to have the seed of self-esteem started and watered early on, if not by our biological mothers then by other nurturing female "gardeners." Perhaps some good habits and faithful practices grew from those early plantings, becoming hardwired in our developing brains.

It's been said that "the hand that rocks the cradle rules the world," so great is that early influence in our lives—where a love of justice and fairness can later bloom into service to others. One of the most inspiring women in my early life was my best friend's mother—a preacher's wife with a compassionate heart for the poor and an outspoken voice on social issues and racial equality. Her progressive political positions taught many of us that the hand that rocks the cradle must also be willing to rock the boat!

Whether we are fathers, mothers, friends, or mentors, we unwittingly plant seeds in the minds and hearts of those around us—a truth that calls us to be responsible for the ripple of influence that begins with us. When we instill in young minds a yearning for justice and the confidence to speak out, we ignite a passion that can change the world.

Reflect: Breathe a prayer of thanks for the maternal mentors in your life and a prayer of forgiveness for their missteps. Become more keenly aware of your influence on those around you.

MAY 11 • *The Flowers Speak*

The Spirit, more willing to speak than we are to listen, whispers encouragement to us from surprising sources. Something as simple as a flower's uniqueness can move us toward our own blossoming.

Metaphors have traditionally been used to explain the inexplicable, producing a spiritual quickening of awareness in our hearts. For the next few days, we'll look at the individual qualities of familiar flowers for their messages of inspiration.

One of the earliest sights I see every spring is the crocus, which offers its lessons to us. This patient and persistent blossom is usually the first to peek its head through the snow or ice or from underneath a rock. A stubborn little plant, the crocus reminds us of the astonishing power of the human spirit to strive toward life, no matter what hindrances litter the way.

Words from Philippians 3:13 remind us to press on, "forgetting what lies behind and straining forward to what lies ahead." We face the challenge of summoning the courage to push toward life and to grow—even through the obstacles in our path. We get discouraged; we want to grow the easy way. We shrink from pushing through the hard stuff—the pain—to get to the light. We've been told there's a light at the end of the tunnel, but the way through that tunnel is often through darkness. Yet the light beckons.

A common little crocus prompts us to persevere.

Reflect: Find a photo of a crocus, and let it speak to you about your tenacity and tirelessness in tough times.

MAY 12 • *The Gardenia Speaks*

In our growing-up days, my sisters and I always wore corsages for Easter, Mother's Day, piano recitals, and sometimes for no occasion at all. In our modest household, there was no money for store-bought creations. Fortunately, our mother, a prolific gardener, skillfully crafted homemade miniature arrangements of fresh blossoms.

From her giant gardenia bushes, mother fashioned our favorite adornments—a radiant gardenia surrounded by whatever greenery the backyard offered. I still remember the heady aroma that followed my every step, with a fragrant gardenia pinned to my (also homemade) pinafore. Mother treasured and appreciated that velvety flower and unconsciously used it as a tangible symbol of sweetness to her daughters. We got the message.

The gardenia prompts our awareness of life's high moments of sweetness that can sustain us through the not-so-sweet times—the embrace of a loved one, the adoring smile of a child, the strains of great music, the delectability of a piece of chocolate, the smell of rain . . . or a homemade corsage. Those charming delights strengthen our spirits and nourish our souls if we pay attention and say thank-you.

Let the enchanting scent and silky texture of the gardenia speak to you of the sweet moments in your past and present.

Reflect: Take a moment to recall the most satisfying memories in your past. How did they strengthen you? What sweet moments can you create today?

MAY 13 • *The Tulip Speaks*

So few petals, amazingly vivid color, stark simplicity—those are the markings of a tulip. No ruffles and flourishes, no complications—just straightforward, minimal design.

The austere arrangement of the tulip's features reminds us to "keep it simple, silly." We often need to get down to the basics, to quit burdening our lives with meaningless busywork and complicating our faith by obsessing about dogma, antiquated belief systems, and trivial institutional policies.

Jesus boiled it down to "Love . . . God with all your heart, . . . soul, . . . mind, and . . . strength. . . . Love your neighbor as yourself" (Mark 12:30-31). Just as the tulip has only a few strong, vital petals, so our faith has some basic principles.

I experienced this rich lesson at a theological conference more than twenty years ago—a memory that continues to inspire me. I had been listening to complex, well-articulated positions presented by brilliant teachers for three days and had a headache from trying to keep up with the intellectual pace. At the closing service, a famous classically trained contralto was scheduled to perform. Most of us expected her to sing a challenging aria of some sort, but she sat at the piano and sang verse after verse of "Jesus Loves Me," as if to say, "When it's all said and done, it's about the power and reality of love." In that stark contrast between the complex and the simple, many professors in three-piece suits were sniffing and wiping their eyes.

After the passing of years, that's the one moment I recall from that heady conference. It moved me with its stark simplicity. The unadorned tulip can remind us of that.

Reflect: Think of what has become too complicated in your life. How can you move toward the simplicity that the tulip represents?

MAY 14 • *The Tiger Lily Speaks*

The writer of Ecclesiastes noted, "For everything there is a season, and a time for every matter under heaven" (3:1). He continues, "A time to keep silence, and a time to speak" (v. 7).

The tiger lily brashly and boldly wears its bright contrasts of orange and black to proclaim its individuality—hardly a shy, demure member of the floral community. This flower stands tall and lets itself be known.

The time and place for everything includes occasions when we need to mirror the boldness of the tiger lily. Some situations merit a bit of rebelliousness, outrageousness, for the sake of what we believe to be just and fair. Sometimes we risk being different in order to be true to who we are or to be as conspicuous as a tiger lily for the sake of a worthwhile cause.

The inequities and unfairness that plague the world call us to come to the defense of the powerless, to speak for those who have no voice, to disagree with ethnic stereotypes, to befriend the friendless, to love the unlovable, and to give to those who can't repay us—all in the passionate service of love.

It's never easy to chance being criticized or deemed eccentric. We've only to remember the price paid by the Joan of Arcs or the Martin Luther Kings of this world, who stood out from the crowd to champion the rights of others. A tiny elderly woman in our congregation has spent her entire adult life dedicated to the prison population of our city, often standing up to authorities in order to visit, comfort, and attend to the needs of those rejected by most folks. Celeste is my hero—spunky and bright—like a ninety-year-old tiger lily!

Some people considered Jesus a political revolutionary who spoke out against the injustices of the Roman government and the ecclesiastical hierarchy of his day. The tiger lily reminds us to embody that same spirit, to stand up and be counted when situations call for it.

Reflect: Think of the brave souls you know who, by their example, encourage you to stand up and be heard. In what ways are you called to act on behalf of others?

MAY 15 • *The Morning Glory Speaks*

Have you ever awakened at 3 a.m. and been engulfed in darkness and discouragement, ruminating on problems with no apparent solutions, only to sense hope with the dawn's light?

The sparkling morning glory, which opens its fragile arms to receive the day, reminds us of that experience. As the psalmist wrote, "Weeping may linger for the night, but joy comes with the morning" (30:5). These words speak to us of hope—one of the essential life-support systems for the human spirit.

The hope offered by the Spirit of God moves far beyond mere expectation or blind trust. Rather than a hope *for* something, it's a hope *in* something: A trust in God's powerful presence to see us through each moment, despite what those moments may hold.

Hope goes beyond optimism as well. Optimists often claim that "things will be better." That sounds more like wishful thinking to me. Optimism may sound empty when we hear only the sound of our own breath or our own steps on the pavement or feel our own tears rolling down our cheeks. Hope acknowledges that even if we seem to be traveling through a tangle of trouble that threatens to overwhelm us, we are not alone. We're wrapped in the mystery of life, accompanied by a love that will not let us go and from which we cannot be separated.

So, no matter what the mistakes of yesterday might have been or the uncertainty looming in the future, a new day always brims with promise and possibility. It's a fresh, clean slate on which we can write with the hopeful brilliance of the morning glory.

Reflect: Revisit a memory of hopelessness in your past. How did your faith sustain you? Read Isaiah 40:31, and allow it to fill you with hope.

MAY 16 • *The Rose Speaks*

The rose reminds us of how mixed up life is and how complicated we are. Though the term *a perfect rose* has led us to associate a rose with beautiful perfection, the makeup of this flower tells another story. Its velvety texture and vibrant hues are accompanied by prickly thorns that can draw blood.

The Hebrew word for perfection can also be translated as "wholeness" or "seamlessness," which is spot-on for our analogy. Certainly the path to wholeness can be a thorny path. Being in touch with who we are means embracing the whole package of ourselves, including our "thorns." We come to know ourselves not out of a desire for moral perfection but from our yearning to be real. We can face the parts of us that cause pain as well as the parts that spread joy.

Life itself is replete with petals and thorns, is it not? Those glorious days when the heart is full and all's right with the world stand in contrast to the times when we feel as if a dark cloud were following us all day long. Our successes occur along with dismal failures. Bitter fighting rages on the same battlefield as the squad of volunteers with relief supplies and acts of compassion. The rose tells us that all those complex polarities exist together.

If, through honest appraisal and self-acceptance, we can summon the courage to come to grips with the thorny parts of reality, we can eventually open into a beautiful existence—just like the petals of a rose.

Reflect: Make a list of your "petals" and "thorns" and hold them to your heart, believing that the love of God accepts the totality that is you.

MAY 17 • *The Hollyhock Speaks*

The hollyhock has a strong central stalk that sports clusters of blossoms bursting randomly from it. Its message reminds us of Jesus' words, "Just as the branch cannot bear fruit by itself unless it abides in the vine, neither can you unless you abide in me" (John 15:4). The hollyhock's stunning blooms exist only because of the strong stalk that births and sustains them.

The symbolism suggests that we stay connected to the Source of our strength. All our frantic good works, no matter how worthy, will eventually drain life from us unless we remain attached to that which nourishes our spirit. Of course, this reality begs the question: How do we stay connected to the Vine?

We can receive the sustenance and inspiration of the holy through many means: prayer, scripture, art, music, church community, nature, creativity, prayer beads—the pathways of nurture are endless. Even the automatic act of breathing can jog our awareness back to the source of that breath, the *ruach*, the Holy Spirit, that breathes in and through us. Walking through the day with a breath prayer, inhaling "Breathe on me," and exhaling "breath of God" as we go about our day can help us stay attached to the Vine.

The most powerful carriers of connection (and vehicles of grace) are perhaps the people that bring the love of God to us through their embodiment of it. They seem to radiate divine love. It's our privilege as human beings to participate in this miraculous nurturing of the world when we give others a shoulder to lean on.

Reflect: Imagine your soul as a blossom connected to a strong central stalk as you breathe the suggested prayer, or create your own version, such as "God of love, . . . love through me," or "Source of life, . . . you are my strength."

MAY 18 • *The Black-eyed Susan Speaks*

Orange daisy-like petals, which circle a dark center, adorn this common field flower. The arrangement of the petals, emanating from the black "eye," speaks to us of the value of darkness in our lives.

Life gives all of us a black eye now and then. We can find ourselves engulfed in sadness about our situations or the worries of the world around us. Most of us know what it's like to feel as if we're enclosed in a dark dungeon with no exit. Attempting to describe these times covers a broad range from sadness to a "dark night of the soul." Usually, we paint these times with a negative brush.

The black-eyed Susan, with its bright petals, can open us to some of the current theories about the value of dark times. Often these gloomy times can serve as soulful transitions, containing the seeds of deeper growth. The creative potential of such times is not evident until the darkness passes. It comes with the dawn.

Saints have spoken of the "dark night" as a container of holy transformation, a process much broader and richer than a bout with sad feelings. Just as the darkness of the cocoon serves to incubate the growth of the butterfly, so we can use the tough times as rich soil for the growing of our souls. Though we may have to gulp hard to express gratitude for such painful periods, through grace we can be grateful in them, trusting that the holy dark serves as a cocoon rather than a coffin.

Like the butterfly, we can emerge freer and wiser and more beautiful. And, like the black-eyed Susan, we can allow the dark center to unfold in brilliant color.

Reflect: Recall some dark times in your life. What growth did your soul experience? How do you liken that growth to a cocoon?

MAY 19 • *The Hydrangea Speaks*

The whole is greater than the sum of its parts!" shouts the bountiful hydrangea. Upon close inspection, you can see that myriad tiny flowers compose the huge blooms, which together create a showy presence. Because the small blossoms are alike in color (with a little variation in size), they combine around a single stalk that is part of the larger bush.

What a meaningful picture of the power of human community. When kindred spirits of like mind band together, noble results can occur. We can make significant strides as a group that we can't do separately; we need one another to get God's work done. I can't build a hospital in Bangladesh, but together we can; I can't solve the landfill problem, but together our recycling makes a difference. I can't build a church by myself, but as the body of Christ, a congregation can.

I experienced the power of community firsthand a few years ago when a violent storm roared into Memphis at one hundred miles per hour. Thousands of people were without electricity, many for more than two weeks, in the sultry July heat. One-third of our majestic oaks were lost. The straight-line winds drastically altered the face of the city within minutes.

However, the community spirit that arose unbidden carried the mark of a God-given impulse. In a flash, the residents of Memphis became a close-knit tribe; not a community of convenience but a community of caring. Ordinary citizens directed traffic. People emptied their freezers, pushed their barbecue grills into the streets, and shared the bounty with their neighbors. In darkened grocery stores, cashiers made change from cigar boxes, without digital assistance.

When the creature comforts of my community were stripped away, the members seemed to remember who we were—not separate competitive individuals but a cluster of souls banded together for the common good.

The hydrangea's color depends on the nature of the soil it inhabits. So does ours. Perhaps the soil from which we grew provided nutrients that fed our souls, soil that trumped self-interest. But as we blossom out of the soil of the Spirit, we are fed with everlasting love. The hydrangea bursts with reminders of that reality.

Reflect: Think of times when you have been part of a community of people working together. Recommit yourself to joining with those of like mind toward a common purpose.

MAY 20 • *The Daisy Speaks*

The focus of the daisy is a bright yellow center surrounded by white petals, like the sun radiating in all directions. The sturdy yellow bull's-eye clearly dominates the bloom, while the more delicate white petals depend on their attachment to it.

The image is reminiscent of Jesus' words found in Matthew 6:22-23: "The eye is the lamp of the body. So, if your eye is healthy, your whole body will be full of light; but if your eye is unhealthy, your whole body will be full of darkness." Put simply, it matters how we view the world; the lens through which we see determines not only *what* we see but *how* we respond:

- Through the lens of suspicion, we withhold our trust.
- Through the lens of judgment, we see ourselves as superior.

- Through the lens of threat, we see others as dangerous.
- Through the lens of anger, we seek to punish.
- Through the lens of entitlement, we think the world owes us.
- Through the lens of impatience, we see others as inefficient.
- Through the lens of ego, we see everything in terms of ourselves.

On the other hand . . .

- Through the lens of kindness, we bring comfort and joy to others.
- Through the lens of compassion, we share the hurt of others.
- Through the lens of goodwill, we seek to be our brother's/sister's keeper.
- Through the lens of tolerance, we listen to views unlike ours.
- Through the lens of gentleness, we give people second chances.
- Through the lens of joy, we bring smiles to others.
- Through the lens of peace, we diminish violence in the world.
- Through the lens of love, we fulfill our reason for existing.

Reflect: Pretend you are putting on all the sets of glasses mentioned above. How does each lens affect how you treat others and how you respond to your environment? When you finally put on the lens of love, notice the change!

MAY 21 • *The Snowball Speaks*

As I child, I vacationed each summer at my grandparents' home in Sardis, Tennessee, a tiny rural community full of Bible-believing, churchgoing folks. After Sunday school at the little white church on the hill, my grandparents and I always passed a giant snowball bush, bursting with white clusters of blooms resembling, of course, huge snowballs. My grandparents would sometimes point to the plant, saying, "Though your sins are like scarlet, they shall be like snow" (Isa. 1:18).

I always felt cleaner and lighter after that message from the snowball bush. As I child, I only considered God's forgiveness of my bad behavior. However, through the years, the message of the snowball came to represent the whole spectrum of forgiveness—especially as I encountered the demanding task of forgiving those who wronged me. When I managed to do the work of forgiveness, I usually felt that familiar lightness that I associated with the snowball bush.

Nothing about forgiveness is simple or easy, but it's critical to the blossoming of our soul's garden. We must relearn that forgiving someone does not entail saying, "It's okay—it really didn't hurt that much anyway; it's all right." That is usually a lie. When we forgive we do not condone another's misdeeds or cover over the pain involved. Rather, we say, "I choose to lay down the burden of anger and dis-ease that is poisoning my body and spirit." We acknowledge the incomprehensible forgiveness of God toward us and board that holy train.

Reflect: Consider the prolific nature of a big snowball bush with blossoms too numerous to count! Does this remind you of Jesus' command that we are to forgive "seventy- seven times" (Matt. 18:22)? Listen to the message of the snowball bush as you choose a person or a circumstance to forgive this very day.

MAY 22 • *The Field of Flowers*

One final floral image seems appropriate: the sight of a field of random wildflowers, all fed by the same soil and swaying in the same breeze. Their psychedelic garment of brightness forms a dazzling collection.

Though all the flowers flourish independently, common soil feeds their roots. The human family as beloved children of God has root connections that run deeper than belief systems or dogmas. God's "garden" doesn't contain only irises or all azaleas; it's an amazing mixed bouquet. Likewise, it doesn't abound with only tomato plants or pear trees but with a variety of food-producing plants. Imagine a fruit-bearing plant with a voice, saying, "Since I'm not a flower, I don't belong in this garden!" Or, flowers that declare, "I don't bear anything to eat, so I don't have a place here!" We all know that beauty nourishes us as surely as good food does, and both form the bounty of the earth's prolific garden.

No two snowflakes are alike; no two flowers are identical; no two souls carry the same imprint. We can learn much from the diversity of human tribes as we replace our competition with cooperation and hatred with love. In the words of Isaiah 2:4, "They shall beat their swords into plowshares, and their spears into pruning hooks; nation shall not lift up sword against nation, neither shall they learn war any more."

May we all blossom together to make planet Earth the garden of God.

Reflect: Examine your own heart for any fear or judgment of other faiths. Recall Jesus' words, "I have other sheep that do not belong to this fold" (John 10:16). Open your heart to see the world and its inhabitants through God's grand vision rather than a limited human view.

MAY 23 • *Pruning Back*

My husband and I have a shady arbor in our tiny backyard, supporting a green canopy of wisteria vines. Periodically, its profusion threatens to smother the whole garden, and we have to take the shears to it. No matter how radically we chop or how much we sweat, the result is always tidier growth and brighter blossoming.

Sometimes the apparent abundance of our lives needs a little pruning. We are presented with more worthwhile activities than time to do them. We find ourselves governed by what others expect of us or engaging in activities only because we feel we "ought" to. We may continue time-consuming pursuits because we've always done them; we may hold on to hobbies that no longer hold our passions; we may continue our involvement in endeavors out of a sense of guilt. Things that were once interests have now become duties. We need to break out the pruning shears and trim our time-consuming calendars back.

Sometimes we feel that our lives (or our very selves) are being pruned without our consent. Life's unexpected transitions and tragedies can cut us off at the knees without warning. Pain can prune us of innocence and illusion and teach us lessons we often don't learn from pleasure.

Just as in the garden, pruning makes us stronger, not weaker. Both pruning and being pruned spur us to new growth.

Reflect: Enter the garden of your life and your spirit with sharp shears." Consider what needs to be pruned and make the necessary changes. Then watch for new growth.

MAY 24 • *Repotting*

My favorite household plant, reliably green and growing for years, had begun to droop. Its leaves were limp, yellowish, sickly. Its location remained the same; I watered it on schedule. What could be wrong? Upon closer examination, I noticed some tiny white roots trying to escape the bottom of the pot, as if they were looking for a new home. The plant was clearly pot-bound.

Have you ever felt that way? Have you ever sensed the urge to spread your wings, to breathe some fresh air, to have a more spacious existence? Someone has said that most of us live lives that are too limited for us, like shoes that are a size too small or a pot in which the soil has become stale and the confinement too tight—a sure sign that a situation needs to change. We've become pot-bound. Unfortunately, we often miss the signs of restraint and restriction. Consider these pointers:

- You wake up, not looking forward to anything, though the day will be full.
- You haven't laughed in a long time.
- Life seems to be one long string of obligations.
- You have low-level fatigue for no good reason.
- You seem to exist in a world of "same old, same old."

Expanding your "container" or being repotted takes courage and involves risk. It's easier to stay in your familiar pot. Being repotted probably doesn't mean quitting your job (though it may), moving to a new city (takes money), leaving your marriage (I hope not), or firing all your friends (you may miss them and they, you). However, it does mean honestly taking stock of what feels constricting in your life and exploring new outlets for your growing spirit.

And remember that the process of being repotted takes some getting used to. Be patient with yourself. Allow some time to adjust to your new container. The plants do.

Reflect: Pay close attention to any lethargy or "tightness" that you feel over a period of weeks or months. What would it mean for you to move forward into a larger life perspective?

MAY 25 • *Imperfect Blooms*

Sometimes the stems are crooked; the blossoms have black spots; the shape seems out of kilter. But do we judge the plants as worthless and throw them in the trash? No, we work them into a bouquet so that their differentness is honored. Or, at least, we cut them some slack and put up with their defects.

Ah, the beauty of imperfection. We have only to remember the biblical stories of how God used even the most flawed people to accomplish crucial goals—David, Solomon, Moses, Aaron, Samson, Peter, Mary Magdalene. Perfection is not a prerequisite for faithfulness. If it were, we would all be in serious trouble. Often the compulsion toward perfection can be the enemy of the good as we strive to control our spiritual formation, rather than allow the Spirit to guide us.

Sometimes our flaws make us vulnerable enough to allow others to approach us, making them feel less stained and sinful. Think about it— would you feel comfortable pouring out your troubles to someone who didn't seem to have any? Our common humanity, with all our flaws, makes us feel safe with one another. Someone who isn't perfect understands and empathizes with our messed-up lives. They can be real with us because we're real with them.

Reflect: Imagine the totality of who you are (gifts and flaws) residing in God's loving heart. Offer yourself compassion for being a work in progress.

MAY 26 • *Tolerating the Weeds*

The garden of our souls can get choked and crowded. Distractions clutter the way. Gloomy moods cast a pall over everything. Selfishness rears its ugly head—again. Doubts loom like a dark cloud. A gazillion details distract us. Our blossoming gets sidetracked by unsolicited interruptions. Sounds like a flowerbed hosting some unwelcome weeds.

No matter how "together" we may think we are, something always upsets the apple cart: The roof leaks, the car breaks down, the baby gets sick, the company downsizes. All this occurs not because of anything we have done or not done, not to test our faith, not to punish us because we made a wrong move. That's just the way life is.

Right next to my impulse toward generosity resides the weed of insecurity that makes me grab for more. Beside my generally even-tempered demeanor is a bent toward irritability that can chase away friend and foe alike. Right there with my tidbit of courage grows the weed of fear.

Our private weeds spill over into the public domain. Have you looked at the news lately? The world has weeds too. Soldiers go to war; prisons overflow. Even in the church, folks argue and finger-point. God's garden contains few neat rows or planned landscaping. It resembles a wild meadow.

Perhaps the primary weed we need to pull up is that of believing that we can ever be weedless gardens or perfect gardeners. So we must also sow the seeds of humility and honesty.

But don't despair. Pull the weeds that you can, then sow the seeds of faith. Nurture it daily and trust that little seed of faith to the work of the Holy Gardener. The final harvest lies in trustworthy hands.

Reflect: As you accept the "weediness" of your own garden, as well as that of other gardeners, recommit yourself to the Spirit's invitation to cultivate the seeds of faith, love, and justice in the world's garden.

MAY 27 • *Possibility*

A verse in Isaiah raises a pointed question: "I am about to do a new thing; now it springs forth, do you not perceive it?" (Isa. 43:19).

Sometimes seeds grow inside us in the darkness, and we fail to notice them. A multitude of ways to hear the whispered invitations of the Spirit surround us, inviting us to new possibilities—a phrase in a sermon that stirs the soul, the lyrics of a song that lift the heart, a conversation with an inspiring friend, a piercing comment that unsettles us, the vastness of a starlit night, the sight of a rosebud ready to burst into bloom. But we have to be still enough and quiet enough to notice the subtle messages.

So we return again to the need for times of silence and reflection. There's a song in the silence, but its melody is often drowned out by the noise in our houses and in our heads. Dashing hurriedly from one thing to another, we lose the rhythm of the growing garden. We become like singers who have lost the rhythm of the divine song.

I heard someone say recently, "He really seems to be on a spiritual journey." That's a pretty safe statement; the truth is, we're *all* on a spiritual journey. It's who we are. As the saying goes, we're not so much human beings on a spiritual journey as we are spiritual beings on a human journey. What we call the spiritual journey is not a geographic movement; it is an opening of awareness, a deepening appreciation of the One in whom we already abide. It actually goes nowhere; instead, it moves more deeply into the now—here. As we become more conscious of our own gentle flowering, we're more likely to encourage the blossoming of other folks.

One of the miracles of early spring is the bursting forth of the daffodils from bulbs hidden deep under the soil. Remember that bulb of possibility hiding in your own soul, and take time to perceive its sprouting.

Reflect: Contemplate the seeds of potential sprouting inside you. What will your potential sprout—a new direction? the healing of a broken relationship? a healthier way of relating to others? Pay attention to what's there.

MAY 28 • *From Cocoon to Butterfly*

In high school biology class, we learned that a metamorphosis is a common process of slow growth and emergence. In the springtime, one of May's most compelling examples of this miraculous activity is that of the butterfly. Though I mentioned it in January, it's worth a more detailed look because it so clearly parallels our own internal movement.

The caterpillar spins a cocoon around itself, essentially dying to its original form. Then it incubates in the darkness for quite a while, emerging from the potential it carried all the time—life as a butterfly.

In becoming who we really are, we follow much the same process—the art of spiritual cocooning. It involves choice. Sure, the work of transformation is God's work just as it is for the caterpillar, but we're invited to go within to gestate the newness to which the Spirit leads us. We are called to collaborate with grace.

Our collaboration doesn't mean that grace is not a gift. Nor does it mean that the deliberate process of waiting produces grace by itself. But reflective waiting does provide the time and space necessary for change to occur. When significant times of transition came to Jesus, he entered enclosures of waiting—the wilderness, the garden, the tomb. His life had a sacred rhythm, a divine balance, times of waiting on God and expressing the fruits of that waiting.

In our own "cocooning," it may seem that nothing is taking place or that we're trying to escape reality. We want spiritual awakening to respond like a microwave oven. A woman working at a fast food restaurant commented that the people who lined up at her register sometimes reminded her of people lining up in church on Sunday morning. They seemed to be looking for the same thing—a quick and easy way to reduce the hunger inside—"McFaith," she called it.

When it comes to religion, we're long on butterflies and short on cocoons. Deep faith grows layer by layer, moment by moment, emerging at the next stage in its own good time.

Reflect: Think about a specific time in your life that involved patient waiting. How did you change during that time? How did you cooperate or resist the process? Express gratitude for the lessons learned.

MAY 29 • *Emergence*

Like Mother Nature's remarkable chrysalis, some event or action in our lives causes us to separate from old ways of thinking and being—often a crisis of some sort. We enter a time of metamorphosis, or change, and emerge into a new way of being. We could label it growing up, maturing spiritually, or journeying from inward to outward.

The Bible story of Jonah and the "large fish" follows a similar pattern. A voice interrupted Jonah's secure world, and he received a holy summons to go to Nineveh. Like many of us, Jonah resisted God's call. He tried to run away, only to encounter a storm. (Have you ever had crisis winds blow through your life?) Jonah finally relented and found himself cast into the sea—his own moment of descent into his inner depths. We all know what his cocoon was—the belly of a huge fish! The dark waters closed in over him, just as they do in our own cocooning. But the time came at last when Jonah was coughed up into the world again.

As we emerge from a period of "incubation," respecting the transformation process of the chrysalis state, we may be as wobbly as a butterfly with new wings. As new creatures, we have to try out our unfamiliar wings—perhaps a rearrangement of values, a fresh way of viewing the world, a clearing of our sight. Hopefully, divine compassion wakes within us, and we feel compelled to suffer with, wait with, cry with those around us. We give up our game of what's-in-it-for-me and relinquish our need to be thanked properly.

In our May flowering, we can trust the gentle voice that invites us to enter the cocoon of transformation and reenter the world, ready and eager to blossom.

Reflect: Jonah fought against the darkness for all he was worth. Examine your own tendencies to avoid or escape times of introspection and transformation. What tactics or diversions do you employ?

MAY 30 • *Walking and Talking in the Garden*

I rose from my seat in the choir's alto section as we began the strains of the final hymn, "In the Garden," the questions of uncertainty still swirling in my head. Slowly, I closed my hymnal because I knew all the verses from memory. It was a familiar conundrum, one that I faced every Easter season. Did Jesus physically arise from the dead? Was it his actual body or some sort of "resurrection body"? Was that huge stone—weighing probably a ton—actually rolled away? Was it a bona fide miracle or a metaphor?

Unbidden tears began to flow down my cheeks, and the friend next to me passed me a tissue, concern on her caring face. As I sang the refrain, "And he walks with me, and he talks with me, and he tells me I am his own," my misty eyes fell on a stained-glass window depicting Jesus in a garden. From the depths of my soul, a voice whispered in comforting, insistent words, "Don't you see? I walk with you and I talk with you, and I tell you that you belong to me! Don't worry about the details!"

Something huge shifted inside me, and I felt an enormous release. Maybe I didn't need to have all the answers after all. Maybe I could simply pay attention to the presence and voice of the Spirit in my life and live out of that reality. I felt free from my own compulsion to get all the details right and have all my questions answered. Maybe walking and talking with Jesus was enough.

That was more than twenty years ago, and that freedom still accompanies me on my spiritual journey. My quest shifted from the need to believe all the right things to focusing on living the life of love and compassion that Jesus embodied and taught.

And the garden of my own soul felt ready for springtime blossoming.

Reflect: Spend some quiet moments with the refrain of this hymn. How does the Spirit walk and talk with you? Consider ways that you can respond to this gentle, guiding Presence.

MAY 31 • *Spring's Sacred Pattern*

Every year the pattern repeats itself. Bulbs burst into tulips; calves appear in the pasture; tight green buds turn into canopies of green. Life springs from lifelessness. It happens in our lives too:

- New ideas emerge from the dullness.
- The language of flowers stirs the heart.
- We tune up the rusty bike.
- The wind blows through our hair.
- Suddenly, there's a spring in our step!

Spiritual gardening isn't about what we can accomplish for God; it's about what God can do in and through us. Just ask the flowers.

Gardening (whether it's in the yard or in the heart) involves some effort and sweat, but mostly it's about allowing ourselves to be in harmony with the awesome creativity of the universe. We join hands with the Creator to do the tilling and the planting and nurturing together, then watch expectantly for the greening.

As part of this eternal rhythm, the pattern of dying and rising is stamped on our souls. It simmers in the cells of our bodies. Losses have gains hidden inside them. Death and life are part of the same miraculous movement. Because of that blessed assurance, we can take the risk of blossoming.

And if enough of us commit ourselves to this holy dance of love and creativity, maybe it can be springtime everywhere.

Reflect: What in your life is showing the signs of spring awakening? Commit yourself to cooperate with those invitations to blossom.

June

TENDING
THE GROWTH

*"Work out your own salvation with fear and trembling;
for it is God who is at work in you, enabling you both
to will and to work for his good pleasure."*

—PHILIPPIANS 2:12-13

BREATH PRAYER
O Light Divine, . . . shine on my spirit.

JUNE 1 • *Let the Light In*

This growth business is a cooperative endeavor, to be sure. I don't doubt for a moment that God wills us to live a life of love, joy, and compassion. However, it won't be forced upon us. So how do we get in harmony with this holy plan?

For this month, let's switch the metaphor from a garden to a house, as we explore our part in tending our own growth, both within and without. Some people have depicted the spiritual life as a large house with many shaded windows, surrounded by light. It may be somewhat dim inside, but we manage to function. However, if we'll just open a window, the light will pour in and illuminate everything inside.

Those windows represent the spiritual disciplines and practices through which we open ourselves to the light of God—windows like worship, scripture, journaling, hospitality, fasting, and prayer—just to name a few. No matter which window we open, the light comes in. We can crack one window and welcome a little beam of light. We can throw many of them open wide, and light can pour in. We can choose which windows we open and when. These windows to God, the spiritual disciplines, are not holy in themselves. The purpose of any spiritual tool is to move us beyond the discipline itself to the experience of holy Light.

You may groan at the mention of the word *discipline*. Many of us have a built-in resistance to the concept, because it may conjure up the image of a stern schoolmaster ready to wrap our knuckles and label us as slackers if we don't toe the line and complete the assignment! But spiritual practices are ways to give God a chance to work with us, to ground our desire to grow by embodying our intention.

The practices serve another vital function. The inner sanctuary where the Spirit guides and illumines our soul serves as our "center of consent," a type of inner compass. Steady exposure to spiritual practices trains that compass to point increasingly in the direction of love and compassion.

As we explore many of these windows, be alert for the ones that interest you, beckon you, fill you with anticipation rather than dread.

Tending the growth is a happy and creative enterprise!

Reflect: What spiritual disciplines have been part of your life in the past? Notice which ones you enjoyed and those you engaged out of duty. Consider the light they brought into your life.

JUNE 2 • *Worship—Performance or Participation?*

People of all faiths probably participate in the spiritual discipline of worship most routinely. What actually happens as we gather with our religious communities? Do we primarily anticipate a good performance by the clergy and worship leaders, or do we sincerely seek deeper communion with God and others?

Often, we focus on visiting with friends, listening to a well-crafted sermon, and hearing an accomplished choir. When it centers on these aspects, worship can become merely an enterprise of good religious entertainment and diversion. Did the homily inspire us? Did the choir members sing music that we liked, and did they do it well? Were the congregational hymns our familiar favorites? Was Communion served in the style we prefer? Did the service conclude on time? We tend to evaluate the worship service in terms of how all those aspects operate, as if we are passive recipients of a pleasing presentation.

Let's consider how we can engage worship as a spiritual discipline. To begin, we can prepare for worship by reading the appointed scriptures ahead of time, if the church provides this information. We can arrive early to settle down from the morning rush and be in prayer for the worship leaders. We can sink into the presence of the holy.

But, most of all, we can be open to God's word to us during the service by being present to the words in the liturgy, the prayers, and the hymn lyrics in a prayerful posture of listening. We can notice what irritates, moves, or inspires us, allowing the Spirit to enlighten us. We allow compassion rather than judgment to guide our response when the service doesn't flow smoothly or when our expectations are not met. We allow unfamiliar forms of worship to expand the rigid container of our preferences. It may be merely a difference in style, not substance!

Welcome the light that floods in when seekers express together their desire for the divine.

JUNE 3 • *Sacred Scriptures*

The words of Psalm 119:105 lead us toward appropriate use of scripture: "Your word is a lamp to my feet and a light to my path." As with other spiritual disciplines, reading the Bible brings us closer to the heart of God. The Bible is not intended to function as a weapon for beating up on sinners or a way to prove we're right about some moral issue.

Many refer to the Bible as the living word of God. The word *living* implies that the Bible is alive—dynamic, changing, pulsing with growth. Yet, when we approach it, we often view it as material to be mastered, as if we were hoping to pass an exam on its content. Is the right answer *a, b, c,* or *none of the above*? In that sense, we treat it as a dead, static text—good religious information.

A teacher once explained to me that scripture was not intended to be third-class mail marked Occupant but first-class mail marked Personal. It becomes a spiritual discipline when we allow scripture to touch us, speak to us, change us—right here in the midst of our twenty-first-century lives. In doing so, we take the Bible seriously. I don't perceive the Bible as God's story about us but rather our story about our experience of God—our salvation history. Inspired—yes. Dictated from the lips of God—no. It's salvation history, not literal history. From Ezekiel to Isaiah to Mark and Paul, the writers expressed their understanding and yearning for divine truth through their eyes, their culture, their level of understanding. And they did it eloquently and faithfully.

When we allow the Bible to form us, we see the text not as a god to be worshiped but as a window that reveals the Light of truth.

Reflect: Think about how your understanding and approach to scripture has changed during your life. Select a passage from the Bible, and consider how you received it in your youth. How has your approach changed through the years?

JUNE 4 • *Words Come Alive*

In an encounter with the living word of God, we allow the Spirit who inspired those writings to inspire our own understanding. The most powerful discipline for approaching scripture as the living word of God is the centuries-old practice of listening through *lectio divina*, or spiritual reading. Here are the steps:

- *Lectio*—Read the scripture at a slow pace, as if seeing it for the first time.
- *Meditatio*—Reflect on the text with an active mind, open to connections between sacred stories and our own stories.
- *Oratio*—Allow for the natural prayer of the heart that arises in response to the text: pain, frustration, gratitude, praise, joy— whatever arises from deep within.
- *Contemplatio*—Rest in God receptively, not in an attempt to figure out the meaning of the text. Be content in the holy Presence in the context of what you have read, allowing it to "digest."

Writer and teacher Marjorie J. Thompson uses Basil Pennington's pastoral image to summarize the concept of *lectio divina*, which can help us grasp its function.

> First "the cow goes out and eats some good grass (*lectio*), then she sits down under a tree and chews her cud (*meditatio*) until she extracts from her food both milk (*oratio*) and cream (*contemplatio*)."[1] . . . We can all visualize what it looks like: processing and reprocessing food until it is fully digested! . . . It is a matter of taking in the bread of God's Word, chewing on it, and digesting it until it brings forth new life and energy that can be shared with others.[2]

Reflect: Read Psalm 139:1-18 using this method. What phrases stir you? What emotions do these verses evoke: gratitude, awe, bewilderment? Chew on it.

JUNE 5 • *Meaning and Context*

When we regard the Bible as "living," we're admitting that its words can live through us, that we may have more to learn, that we can always allow deeper truth to broaden our understanding. Let's look at one example, using the familiar words of the Lord's Prayer as found in Matthew 6:11, "Give us this day our daily bread. . . . ":

- If I'm in a refugee tent in a war-torn country, this may be a frantic plea for an actual crust of bread to keep me and my family alive.
- If I'm sitting in my own kitchen with my stomach full, I may be praying for the spirit of Jesus as the Bread of Life to become incarnate in my body.
- If I'm on my deathbed, my yearning may be tied to the concept of the heavenly banquet and a hope of being united with others around God's eternal table.
- If my soul feels depleted, I'm in need of spiritual nourishment.

All these interpretations are true and meaningful. Divine texts have a way of speaking to our point of need, conveying the message we need to hear. However, when we approach the words as final and set in stone, we take away their power to bring fresh revelation.

Many have said that one of the greatest barriers to the spiritual life is certainty. It tends to lull us into a kind of complacency that can morph into rigidity and arrogance. Maintaining a "beginner's mind," that is, a mind that never thinks it has arrived at the ultimate truth, gives the Spirit room to speak to us anew—even through scriptures we're hearing for the umpteenth time!

Reflect: Using the sentence "Give us this day our daily bread" or another selection from scripture, apply it to your life right now. Listen for the Spirit's illumination.

JUNE 6 • *Portable Pastors*

Have you experienced the surprise of picking up a book, opening its pages, and feeling that someone was reading your mind and putting your unspoken yearnings into words? What a comfort—a feeling of being companioned by a stranger you wish you could meet. You realize that you are not the only one who feels as you do!

Reading the wisdom and experience of others, sharing their stories by hearing their words, can make us feel "pastored." A pastor is one who shepherds, leads, tends, and cares for the "flock." Good books can serve as portable pastors because they serve essentially the same purpose. Their words can challenge, inform, lead, and inspire, supporting us on the journey. There are countless ways to engage wise words as a spiritual discipline:

- Read a chapter a day; take a walk, and pay attention to the phrases and concepts that stick with you, turning them over in your mind as you stroll.
- Read a section, highlighting the sentences that inspire or challenge you. Take a few moments to journal about what affected you and why.
- Read one page (especially if the writing is rich or dense). Put the book down and close your eyes. Imagine how the insights can change the way you live today.
- Choose a book that seems worthwhile to you. Call two or three like-minded friends, asking them to commit to reading the book at the same time. Meet once a week and discuss it as a shared discipline.

We benefit from reading about the struggles of others because it makes us feel less alone in ours. Hearing others' opinions can stretch us, because it makes us examine our own. We come to fresh understanding through the wisdom of others. So, read, read, and then read some more.

Reflect: Look over your shelves of cherished books. Which ones have been "pastors" to you? Which ones have fostered your faith?

JUNE 7 • *Write It Down*

Sometimes the act of putting pen to paper unleashes unexpected thoughts, unsolicited wisdom—even an encounter with the voice of God. Journaling is a long-established and much-heralded discipline of the spirit.

Let me mention a few caveats. The familiar "diary approach," that is, a surface news report of the happenings of the day, bears little fruit. To prime the pump of keen awareness, we allow the yearnings of our hearts to travel straight from the heart down our arm to the pen and onto the page without passing through the head for evaluation. That ever-present editor in the intellect needs to be fired! In spiritual journaling, we get diverted when we pay too much attention to spelling, punctuation, speed, and grammar. Better to clean out the corners of consciousness—the trash as well as the treasure. A friend of mine confesses that her journaling is mostly whining! Another calls it her free psychiatric couch where she dumps all her emotional garbage. Somehow, consistent journaling can provide legible proof that we want to commune and connect with the Spirit—our sole audience.

In school we learned to figure out what we think before writing it; the opposite method works better in spiritual journaling. We express scattered thoughts, unthinkable questions, heretical doubts, embarrassing confessions. Writing about our confusion invites God to enter the chaos and move us toward clarity. However, rather than revealing answers, sometimes the journal serves as the reservoir for our questions: What am I holding on to? Why am I trying to control this? What is causing this anxiety? What is the light of God trying to show me?

In this quiet discipline, we can develop an ongoing conversation with God if we stick with it. Words start appearing unexpectedly; patterns of thought are revealed; sicknesses of the spirit are offered for healing.

Journaling is not about your writing ability; it's about your availability.

Reflect: Pick up a pen and let your soul breathe and express itself. Give it a voice.

JUNE 8 • *Angels in Disguise*

Do not neglect to show hospitality to strangers, for by doing that some have entertained angels without knowing it" (Heb. 13:2).

The practice of hospitality has a long history as a hallmark virtue in religious traditions. The Rule of Saint Benedict decrees that "all guests to the monastery should be welcomed as Christ." Jesus' teachings explicitly define hospitality: "I was hungry and you gave me food, I was thirsty and you gave me something to drink, I was a stranger and you welcomed me" (Matt. 25:35).

The spirit of hospitality shines its light in a multitude of forms. We provide physical space to someone who needs a room for the night. We provide emotional space when we offer someone the safety of a listening ear. As we open our hearts to minister to others' needs, we inadvertently tend the growth of our own souls. This practice mysteriously links us not only to people but to the God whose nature is hospitable grace.

The hospitality of food resides in a category all its own. Whether it's a family gathering, a church bring-a-dish supper, a community food pantry, or the sharing of recipes, our souls are fed as our bodies are fed. As one woman told me when a church friend brought food during her convalescence, "Sometimes the love of God comes disguised as a casserole!"

Reflect: Remember with gratitude the times when the hospitality of others has nurtured you. Commit to one specific act of hospitality today. A phone call? A meal? An invitation to visit?

JUNE 9 • *Music Matters*

The swell of a symphony, the melody of a song, the whistling of a tune. Hearing the movement of music with our ears wide open puts us in harmony with the music of the spheres. The power of music's influence is too often ignored or taken for granted in our spiritual formation.

We have only to revisit our own past to realize how music shaped us from early on. Even now, when I hear the simple refrain of "Jesus Loves Me, This I Know," or "He's Got the Whole World in His Hands," my heart stirs in response.

People over the centuries have described music as the language of the universe and the song of the soul. Studies show that hymns form our theology, loud metallic music scrambles our brain cells, and rhythms coax our muscles into movement. Music also makes our hearts pound, our eyes fill with tears, and our spirits soar. In more ways than we can count, music matters to body, mind, and spirit.

Take particular notice of how different genres of music affect you. What music memories are embedded in your body and soul? What melodies inspire you? What rhythms spur your energy? What calms your soul? What lyrics bring you hope? By listening more intentionally to the music that moves you, you'll stay in touch with the voice of your own soul and you'll tend its growth as well.

Reflect: Take a short walk, listening to music that inspires and calms you. How does the music change your walk? Or engage in another task, adding musical accompaniment. Notice the enrichment it brings.

JUNE 10 • *Fasting from Our Addictions*

Fasting involves more than abstaining from sweets during Lent. The practice of fasting may seem outdated and old-fashioned to contemporary seekers, but most religious traditions encourage it, which makes fasting worth a closer look.

Refraining from food can remind us of the emptiness of our inner life when not nourished by the Bread of Life. It can remind us of the millions of people around the world who experience empty stomachs every day, while ours are more than full. It moves us toward gratitude for the abundance we take for granted.

Often we trivialize the practice of fasting by using it as a means to satisfy personal goals. Maybe we want to lose a few pounds, and the practice will help us achieve that. And maybe we want to feel a degree of pride that we're able to stick to some tough food rules. As we become aware of our own unspoken agendas and let them go, we can enter the spaciousness that fasting offers, an emptiness that we can fill with divine guidance and growth.

What about other kinds of fasting? We have countless other crutches outside the food category. Here are some potent possibilities:

- Media fast: No newspapers, TV, or radio for a week
- Techno fast: No cellphone, iPad, or e-mail for a time
- Gossip fast: Refrain from repeating titillating information about others
- Shopping fast: No unnecessary shopping for a month
- Fast from words: Go on a chatter-fast, a silent retreat, or a day committed to silence

Whatever its form, the practice of fasting can create unaccustomed openness to hear the still small whisper of the Spirit.

Reflect: Try the practice of fasting by choosing one category that will especially challenge you. Commit to abstinence for a day, and allow the emptiness to enrich your spiritual life.

JUNE 11 • *Spiritual Maintenance*

Most of us wouldn't think of skipping our annual medical checkup or ignoring the need for dental care or failing to give the car a good tune-up. So how do we maintain our spiritual selves?

We all need companions on the journey—those who share a commitment to the reality of the spiritual dimension of life. Seeing a spiritual guide, or to use the traditional term, a *spiritual director*, can provide safe space to ask questions such as "How can I be more aware of the presence of the holy in my life? Where can I see God calling me through the events and emotions I'm experiencing right now?"

A spiritual guide, a person trained in prayerful listening (normally in a lengthy, rigid training regimen), essentially listens to God on your behalf and encourages your growth in noticing spiritual cues. Even though the words *spiritual director* imply a teaching relationship, it more closely resembles a gentle companioning, a shared desire to find meaning and purpose through a more intimate walk with God.

Seeing a spiritual guide once a month can help you . . .

- Identify and trust your own experiences of the divine dimension of your life.
- Hear your own voice, questions, and concerns with no judgment.
- Receive guidance in your discernment in making hard choices.
- Notice signs of spiritual movement in your daily affairs.
- Listen more intently to your soul's voice.
- Discern the voice of God more clearly.

Though spiritual guidance can address pressing concerns and issues, I see it more as spiritual maintenance, a time set aside for the purpose of paying attention to what's cooking on my spiritual stove. In our busy lives, we're swallowed up by the pace of keeping it all together. We rarely stop to examine prayerfully the spiritual meanings and movements. Meeting with a trained companion can flood your spiritual "house" with light.

Reflect: Give yourself the gift of a regular spiritual tune-up session, and note the effect on your inner and outer life.

JUNE 12 • *Confession Cleanses the Soul*

In my growing-up years, I remember a Roman Catholic playmate rolling her eyes as she said with exasperation, "Uh-oh, it's time for me to go to confession!" It didn't strike me as very appealing.

As I began to notice the words of confession sprinkled throughout the liturgy of the Protestant church, my sense of dread and guilt increased. I felt as if the ominous, all-seeing eye of God kept watch and judged me from afar, always finding me wanting—a selfish sinner, to be sure.

Thank goodness, some maturity began to soften my response and resistance. Over time the all-seeing eye of God became more of a friend than an enemy. While we may want to escape the penetrating gaze of Love, being fully known by God can open us to healing as well as embarrassing exposure. Confessing our brokenness and separation invites God's redemptive presence, especially with our awareness that the situation is clothed in forgiveness and unconditional love.

Heartfelt confession has a way of clearing the decks, of acknowledging our humanness. Being honest with ourselves need not lead to self-loathing but to self-awareness instead. Maintaining a mask of goodness slips us straight into arrogance and pride. Besides, it takes a ton of energy to pretend to be better than we really are. Maybe it's more helpful to be real than to be right.

The luminous light of Love brings more to us than the exposure of our shortcomings. It also delivers lavish, unadulterated forgiveness and continuous offers of restoration. Discovering the truth about ourselves and discovering the truth about God form parallel journeys. Through the Spirit's unconditional acceptance, our confessions can lead not to condemnation but to divine invitation.

After all, God has more interest in our growth than in our guilt.

Reflect: Imagine being surrounded by love and light as you make your confession. What gentle invitation to grow do you recognize in the experience?

JUNE 13 • *Sabbath Rest*

There's an interesting paradox hidden in this practice. While "tending the growth" represents an active endeavor, honoring the sabbath means taking our hands off the plow.

Centuries of tradition point to the importance of sabbath. The Creation story in Genesis 2:3 ("God blessed the seventh day and hallowed it, because on it God rested from all the work that he had done in creation") established the ordained rhythm of work and rest. One of the Ten Commandments brings the matter up again: "Remember the sabbath day, and keep it holy."

Keeping the sabbath includes much more than attending church or synagogue, which can often turn into a day of rushed spiritual busyness. It's more than taking a day off from your job, then exhausting yourself with other tasks. Many of us can make hard work out of play! Finding a day filled with genuine rest for the body and replenishment for the spirit is a challenging discipline in this rushed and beleaguered world. It's a radical and intentional commitment to carve out regular sabbath space, not waiting "until I have time for it."

Here are some pointers to guide your commitment to the practice of keeping sabbath:

- Listen for what your body tells you it needs: a walk? a nap? gentle exercise?
- Rest emotionally from worry and stress. "Do not worry about tomorrow, for tomorrow will bring worries of its own" (Matt. 6:34).
- Move slowly. Walk instead of run. Replace shallow breathing with deep cleansing breaths.
- Enjoy the activities that delight you. While cooking, for instance, may be drudgery for some, others consider it a joy to prepare a favorite dish while not looking at the clock.
- Don't think you must be constantly accomplishing something.
- Hold the day lightly, allowing it to flow rather than being tied to a schedule—even a schedule of R and R!

Have the courage to arrange your life to conform to this sacred pattern that honors the limits of your humanness. Watch as your resting turns to joy and then to thanksgiving for the gifts of life and the blessings of down time.

Reflect: Make preparations for a day of sabbath. What do you long to do? What work and worry will you need to set aside to honor this day?

JUNE 14 • *Prayer—The Big Picture Window*

We return to the metaphor of the spiritual life as a house with many windows and spiritual practices that let the Light in.

Not all windows are created equal. Do you remember the fifties' architectural trend of a huge, unpaned window at the front of ranch-style homes called a "picture" window? Well, by far the biggest window in our metaphorical spiritual abode is prayer. In fact, it has no limits. We may begin as children with little more than "Now I lay me down to sleep," but as we mature spiritually, prayer seems to burst out of any box we put it in—even a religious box.

I'm not sure when I began to feel boxed in by my current prayer practice—when the boundaries began to blur and the formulas faded.

My prayer notebook, which had recorded petitions offered and answered, was banished forever to the attic of outworn relics. My mind wandered during church prayers, and my morning rituals were dull as dirt. Though I still valued private prayer time, the traditional prayer liturgies, and grace before meals, I began to yearn for something more.

My feeling of discontent didn't stem from only one cause. It resulted from a slow piling up of inconsistencies toward a tipping point where my carefully constructed understanding of prayer strained at the seams. To be frank, my expectations were rarely met. I prayed for people to get well, and they died. I prayed for marriages to be saved, and they marched off to divorce court. I prayed for peace in the world only to see an escalation of conflict. How could I reconcile these realities?

Thus began my journey from prayer as *results* to prayer as *relationship*.

Reflect: Think of your earliest memories of prayer. What characterized your early childhood "talking to God"? What made you feel heard? Who influenced your attitudes about prayer?

JUNE 15 • *Growing Up in Prayer*

Growing up is a natural phenomenon. Our physical bodies mature. Our emotional intelligence expands. Our social skills become more sophisticated. Yet many stay stuck in juvenile concepts about prayer.

Most of us cut our teeth on "gimme" prayers, telling God our laundry list of wants and needs. We decide what we want to happen and ask God to help us get it. True, we're encouraged through scripture to make our requests known to God, and we do. We ask God to please make the tumor vanish or help find us a job or various forms of *saying* our prayers—and these requests are valid. Often, however, rather than sincerely asking God's guidance, it is we who decide what we want and ask for God's stamp of approval on what we've decided. Though we may start at this point, we need not stop there.

We pray in many significant ways: religious liturgical prayers, private devotions, intercessory prayer groups. But if our prayer life consists only of telling God what we want or only of prayers we recite that others have written, then I believe we miss the height, breadth, and depth of prayer.

Prayer is more about relationship than results. And prayer as relationship can't exist unilaterally—that is, if we do all the talking and none of the listening.

Ponder what we actually do when we want to connect with people and foster friendships. We usually want to *talk* with them, spend time with them, "hang out" in their presence. Yet, when we contemplate strengthening our relationship to God, we find ourselves freezing prayer into a formality. When we care for someone, we speak straight from the heart. But often when we pray, we try to craft a prayer with "good words." As we grow up in prayer, we relate to God more candidly and conversationally.

Reflect: When you pray, do you sense a distance between you and God? As you pray today, imagine the Spirit alongside you as a friend. Then imagine that this presence has made a home in your heart.

JUNE 16 • *Our Native Language*

We were born to pray. It is our primary speech, our native tongue.

The basic instinct to pray runs through the history books and memory banks of every culture on earth. We see it in the Bible, certainly, but the urge to pray seems rooted in human beings everywhere. Think of the Native American rain dances, the Sufi whirling dervishes, the prostration of monks lying face down on the chapel floor, tribal groups beating drums to petition the Great Spirit, and literally millions of us crying out in hundreds of languages when we're in trouble—"Help me, God!"

Before this instinct passes through our intellectual filter (where we judge it and analyze it to death), it springs from a soulful place, the same place that houses the Spirit of God within us. This instinct echoes the essence of the book of Genesis that says we are made in the image and likeness of God. If faith itself is the soul's true country, then prayer is its native language.

In true prayer, we tell the truth. We say who we are—not who we wish we were or would like others to think we are. It affords an opportunity to be one-on-one with God—our most personal and private act of devotion. Our minds are free, our souls are free. We don't need words to do justice to the feelings, images, wishes, terrors, pains, or pleasures that we exchange with God.

I believe we need to trust this instinct to pray far more than we do, because it's clearly natural and therefore valuable and reliable in a fundamental way. Prayer reminds us that we live in two worlds—the world of the senses that we control, our egotistic world, and the world of mystery and timelessness that transcends our abilities and control. Prayer helps connect these two realms. It builds bridges between the two and relates us to the God who is the source of all life.

Reflect: When has prayer felt like a natural expression of who you are? When is it more a matter of rote or duty? For a few moments, release your rules about prayer, and speak as if you are talking to a close confidante.

JUNE 17 • *Answers to Prayer*

I have never cared much for pat answers. For as long as I can remember, I have prayed—sometimes with blind faith, sometimes with great confidence. But then sometimes it all seemed to tumble down like a house of cards. Then my doubts would spiral out of control.

Some years ago, a dear friend's young, athletic husband was dying of an aggressive form of cancer. Prayer groups and devout individuals in our community were praying for him, and his faithful wife felt convinced of God's healing. As his condition continued to worsen, I recall her heartbreaking words, "Linda, he's not getting any better. I must be praying wrong. Somehow I've got to get it right."

My friend's sense of guilt and self-judgment brought me to tears. I realized how we misunderstand the character of God by implying, however innocently, that God waits with arms folded for us to spout the proper prayer formula before releasing divine healing. I have no answer to the secret of healing, but I can't believe in God as a capricious entity we manipulate. Would a loving parent require a child to phrase a request "just so"? Neither does our heavenly Parent, who knows our need before we ask.

It's easier to say what prayer isn't than what prayer is:

- *Not manipulation.* Surely prayer is not a matter of convincing God to take action. When our prayers aren't answered, we are left wondering what went wrong. Were our prayers not fervent enough, our promised changes not sacrificial? Are we not good enough people for God to heed our prayers? Was God not moved by our desperate plight and persistent pleading? Why won't God give us what seems to go to other, less deserving people? We don't need to manipulate God; God is already in our corner.

- *Not measurable.* Some years ago, keeping prayer journals gained popularity in my part of the Bible Belt. In my journal I recorded the content of prayers and then the date and time of that prayer's answer. This subjects the awesome mystery of prayer to a human measuring stick and to the limits of our own reason.

- *Not logical.* We love logic. We want to know how prayer works and why. Two plus two should equal four—except when it doesn't. Sometimes we want to nail down the cause and effect so much that we will accept faulty answers for our intellectual satisfaction. Prayer, a profound mystery beyond our control, creates anxiety in human beings. What's wrong with admitting that some aspects of life lie beyond our comprehension and control?

I hope that the old adage "doubt is the cutting edge of faith" is true, because those times of doubt have usually wrestled me into greater groundedness. The searching and questioning have unsettled the soil of my soul. It's a bit like disturbing the serenity of the garden in the spring by getting a hoe and loosening up the dirt so the natural nutrients of sun and rain can reach the roots. The arena of answered and unanswered prayer presents a spiritual conundrum common to every thinking person.

As we release our need for control of the prayer process, we are free to sink into the depths of mystery and relationship that it offers.

Reflect: Sit in stillness for a while, releasing your arguments about the efficacy of prayer. Imagine plunging into an unknown but loving space where relationship with the Spirit is more crucial than the gifts the Spirit can give us.

JUNE 18 • *Praying with the Body*

We acknowledge that we are a marvelous matrix of mind, spirit, and body. The evidence abounds. Anxiety can produce a tension headache.

Fear causes the heart to race. A scarlet blush reflects our embarrassment. What would happen if we allowed the body to serve as our ally in prayer?

Most of us live our spiritual lives in the prayer box called the intellect: reading, studying, analyzing, concentrating on words and thoughts, all of which may be commendable. But the body can also be a part of our prayers.

Consider the participation of the hands—palms up in openness, hands lifted in praise, fingers touching in a gesture of petition. Think of the effect of a head bowed in reverence, knees bent in adoration, the body dancing in divine delight. Even the experience of praying with the eyes open or closed affects the nature of our prayer.

Here are some suggestions for inviting our bodies to be part of our prayers:

- Exercise. Many runners witness to the fact that their attentiveness to the holy heightens as they engage in the rhythm of running. Cycling, rowing, even repetitive calisthenics can present opportunities for chants, prayers, and simple appreciation for the wonders of the body.

- Rest. Allow your body's need to rest to lead you to resting in God. For instance, run a bathtub full of warm water with scented oil or bath salts. As you sink into the comforting water, do nothing and think nothing. Simply soak in God's unconditional love. God understands and accepts your fatigue after a long day.

- Labyrinth walking. This ancient geometric form has been associated with prayer for centuries. Though strolling in circles along a prescribed path may seem a strange way of praying, this practice serves as a meaningful prayer tool. It has one entrance, one exit, and is devoid of dead ends or tricks. A symbol of wholeness, it represents the spiral nature of the spiritual journey inward then out again into the world—a pathway with a purpose.

- Household chores. As you make the bed, feel gratitude for the person who sleeps there. As you wash the windows, allow your spiritual sight to be cleared. As you set the table, hold those who will be sitting there close in your heart.

Reflect: In what ways do you involve the wisdom of your body in your prayer life? Experiment today with new possibilities.

JUNE 19 • *Praying with the Breath*

Take a deep breath and count to ten," my teacher counseled when we youngsters stood red-faced and angry on the playground. She may not have known it, but she was repeating the wisdom of the ages. One of our most potent prayer partners is literally right under our noses.

To enlist the aid of the breath, we don't have to read anything, buy anything, or perfect a complicated skill. We do what comes naturally and pay close attention to it. The breath reminds us that something outside ourselves, yet miraculously inside us, is working in our lives, breathing in us and through us. It's automatic and always available. No wonder religious traditions around the globe have recognized the power of linking our prayers with our breath, an instant connection to the kingdom within each of us that tethers us to the present moment. We have no way to return to a past breath or fast forward to a future one. We're here now, being breathed by the Source of the universe.

Here's how you can unite your breath and your prayer using a breath prayer. Choose a name or metaphor for the Holy One that feels right for you and attach it to your inhaling breath. Create a brief phrase expressing your petition, desire, or affirmation and attach it to the exhaling breath. For example:

- God of Wisdom, . . . be my guide.
- Loving God, . . . love through me.
- Holy One, . . . my heart is open to you.
- God of Healing, . . . restore my soul.

Or you may use a favorite scripture or meaningful phrase to shape your prayer, such as:

- The Lord is my shepherd. . . . I shall not want.
- Make me a channel . . . of your love and grace.
- I trust you, O God, . . . and all is well.
- Those who wait on the LORD . . . will renew their strength.

The witness of praying people (as well as modern science) is that repetition somehow grooves a neural and muscular pathway in the brain and body, allowing the body to participate in the prayer. When we pray the same breath prayer over a long period of time, simply breathing it whenever it occurs to us, the body seems to learn it. This sweeps us into the unconscious realm where the Spirit prays for us "with sighs too deep for words" (Rom. 8:26).

Reflect: Sit quietly and formulate your personal breath prayer. What name for God feels natural to you? What is your deepest desire? Combine the two, then breathe the prayer repetitively as often as you can, allowing it to sink into your soul.

JUNE 20 • *Praying with the Mind*

Being mindful involves paying attention without judgment, being 100 percent present to what's happening, even if it is scrubbing the floors or mowing the lawn. Mindfulness can transform a humdrum activity into a prayer of the heart. Across the centuries, many teachers have pointed to the witness of Brother Lawrence, a seventeenth-century monk who performed his mundane kitchen duties to the glory of God. His book *The Practice of the Presence of God* has become a spiritual classic. We strengthen our connection to the Holy by performing simple tasks in a mindful manner.

Consider these two practices:

- *Mindful Walk.* Take a walk with no purpose in mind beyond openness to God's presence. Notice what you see, what you feel, what you think—then let the thoughts go, like the bushes and trees you pass. Keep returning to the present moment. You may realize you are deep in thought and haven't been paying attention for the past few minutes. Return and continue to feel your feet in a single step, your breath as it is right now. The point is not to be happy; it is to be present.

- *Mindful Task.* This practice involves taking a specific task and allowing it to trigger your prayer:
  —While dressing each morning, pray to clothe yourself in grace and kindness.
  —When washing your face, pray that all falseness will be washed away and your true self will emerge.
  —As your broom sweeps dirt away, allow your heart to be swept clean of resentment.

—As you tuck your children (or yourself) into bed, express gratitude for life, then release everything to the nurture of the Holy.

—As you pay the bills, remind yourself to be aware of the contribution that others make to your life.

Reflect: Select an activity (driving to work, preparing a meal) or a favorite creative pursuit (gardening, knitting, carpentry, photography). How might you infuse that activity with blessing and meaning?

JUNE 21 • *Praying in the Car*

If we count the hours we spend alone in our cars, it would probably shock us. Given that reality, why not turn our cars into "rolling sanctuaries"? All it takes is a little imagination and intention; it can get our creative juices flowing while enhancing our prayer life at the same time. Of course, some ground rules are necessary:

- Turn the radio off.
- Silence your cellphone.
- Sack up the snacks.
- Continue to watch the road!

With a playful spirit, create your own structure for the drive time. Here are some suggestions:

- Stop sign—pray for those who are ill or in special need.
- Red light—pray for the upcoming activities of the day.
- Green light—pray that love and peace flow freely through your life to those you encounter today.
- Stopped at a train crossing—use each passing railcar to list items for which you are thankful, one blessing per car.
- A distressed person—if you spot someone in a passing car or waiting at a bus stop who appears troubled, pray for his or her well-being.
- Visual cues—let your surroundings prompt your prayers: a field of flowers brings gratitude for beauty, a pond reminds you of your baptism, a billboard nudges you to pray for a worthy cause.

Oddly enough, that hunk of metal that carts you around can become a holy enclosure, an outer rolling sanctuary that unites with your inner sanctuary.

Reflect: Try this creative spiritual discipline as you drive around today. What prayer prompts come to mind? How does it lessen the drudgery of drive time?

JUNE 22 • *Trying It Out*

The following relates my experience as I played with the "rolling sanctuary" concept on a lengthy solo driving trip. I'd spent all day on I-40, returning from a conference . . . long, humdrum hours in familiar terrain. Lately, I've felt as if this stretch of interstate has become my "home away from home." How could I offer this monotonous part of my life to God for enrichment?

Sometimes merely asking a question can become a prayer, an opening to divine leading. Trusting that, I cleared my mind and allowed it to wander freely with no imposed agenda as the miles rolled by.

Soon, I became aware of an invisible companion—the Holy Spirit steering my thoughts through the visible cues around me, forming in the uninterrupted time:

- A bridge reminded me that Christ is my constant "bridge over troubled water."
- The trucks and speeding sports cars represented my world community as I breathed a prayer for their safety.
- Around the bend, a mountain range sprang into view like a startling surprise, a reminder of the free gifts of creation.
- The long, winding road brought to memory the meandering road of relationships threading through my life.
- The white center line on the pavement symbolized the "plumb line," a biblical image that keeps me on track.
- Roadside barriers corresponded with the boundaries that I must observe to stay safe.
- Towering trees stood for the green growth in my spiritual life that needs deep roots.

- Tangled vines prompted memories of the "vine and the branches," a metaphor voiced in Jesus' teachings.

We've been told to pray as we can, not as we can't. So the open road can become a visual buffet of images at times when we can't close our eyes or kneel at the altar. In these expansive ways, we can allow our lives to become prayers, prompting us toward a relationship with God in the midst of life, not in spite of life.

So what constitutes my life today? Eight hours on I-40. I quell all the noises and open myself to wordless communication with God, gazing into the sun that sustains all life, including mine. Maybe, with the guidance of grace and a little imagination, I can make driving a discipline and the interstate an altar.

Reflect: What are your set times for prayer? Consider other times, including road trips, that can become occasions for prayer.

JUNE 23 • *Driving Out the Demons*

We all have our Dr.-Jekyll-and-Mr.-Hyde moments—times when a hidden part of us jumps up unbidden and makes itself known. Sometimes this happens when we're behind the wheel of a car!

I know a kind, sensitive, compassionate man, the model of benevolent behavior. But put him in heavy traffic, saddle him with unexpected construction delays, or keep him stalled at a railroad crossing, and another self emerges. He revs the engine and stops inches from someone's bumper; he makes a game of switching lanes to "beat the competition"; he complains that the street is too crowded, the drivers too reckless, the lane too slow. Eventually, his commitment to spiritual growth made him aware of the disconnect between his driving behavior and his normal behavior. To his credit, he decided to use driving as a spiritual discipline.

Breathing deeply each time his anxiety escalated, he intentionally allowed other drivers ahead of him in the lane; he slowed down to accommodate fellow travelers; he ceased his judgmental diatribes; he waited patiently for the long train to pass; he quit slapping the steering wheel in frustration. What a transformation!

Our positive response to the Spirit's invitation to wholeness exposes our little demons. We can learn to recognize them, take responsibility for them, and gracefully move them out of the driver's seat of our lives.

Reflect: Recall a time when one of your own "demons" became obvious to you. Did you withdraw blame from others and take responsibility? What demons (great or small) is the Spirit trying to reveal to you at this point in your spiritual journey?

JUNE 24 • *Praying with the Senses*

Since I was already in a stew, I decided to cook a stew. Upset by some sort of squabble, I was soon chopping, dicing, sniffing, mixing, simmering, stirring my way back to sanity. Losing myself in the colors, aromas, taste, textures, and the chop of the knife became a sensate prayer that brought me to my senses.

Cooking often serves as a vehicle for prayer for me. As I sort out flavors, adding leftover vegetables, I try to blend them into a tasty combination by using what I already have. In a surprising alchemy of attention, my thoughts are led to explore how I can blend my life into balance and harmony, what belongs and what doesn't belong, what adds spice and what ingredients bring a balance of flavors. The kitchen becomes a portal to prayer.

The life-giving properties of our five senses are astounding gifts of the Creator. Why not engage their potential to enhance our relationship with that Creator? Try this "Stroll for Your Soul" walk to sharpen your awareness, focusing solely on one sense at a time:

- Go to a quiet, natural environment, if possible. Walk tall, lifting your head and chest, noticing how your body feels in motion and allowing your spirits to lift along with your body.
- Hear—for several minutes, restrict your focus to your ears: the birds, the rushing of the wind, the crackle of leaves beneath your feet.

- Touch—stop to feel the silkiness of a blade of grass, the roughness of tree bark, or to sift a handful of dirt through your fingers.
- Smell—sniff deeply as you become aware of the assortment of smells surrounding you: wet grass, flowering trees, fresh soil.
- See—cast your eyes on the sights in every direction: the blue of the sky, the bright color of flowers, the squirming caterpillar on the path.
- Taste—lastly, open your mouth and drink in the taste of the air that you share with all living things. Their emissions into the atmosphere enter your cellular cycle just as your breath enters their environment.
- Allow a burst of gratitude to bubble up for your body's capacity to see, hear, touch, smell, and taste all these wonders!

Reflect: Take a few moments today to sharpen your sensory awareness. Take a nature walk if possible. Or simply stroll around your house or sit in a chair in front of a window and intentionally engage the wonderful gift of your senses in a prayerful way.

JUNE 25 • *Praying with the Circumstances*

A sprained ankle, a shift in work hours, a sick child, a knock at the door—circumstances can wreak havoc with our meditative times. Yet, rather than look for creative ways to integrate our prayers into our sometimes chaotic lives, we often sink into the guilty space, "I don't seem to have time to pray anymore!"

Here are some examples of prayer practices that can help us pray *with* the circumstances, rather than *in spite of* them.

- What's Happening Prayer—A group of noisy workers leading a house renovation and installing new carpet sabotaged Kathy's morning devotional time. Spiritually speaking, her relationship with God was undergoing "renovation" also. So she decided to integrate the two efforts, sorting her interior "stuff" as she sorted her exterior belongings to make room for the new carpet. In her soul work, her image of a judgmental God expanded to encompass one of grace and peace. As the workers laid new carpet, she looked forward to a new way of "walking" in her spiritual life. The act of stepping on new carpet put a new spring in her step, both physically and spiritually.

- It-Is-as-It-Is Prayer—After taking appropriate time to work through painful feelings and events, this prayer invites us to break a pattern of victim talk that may have gone on too long. By inserting the phrase, "It is as it is," into our thoughts when we find ourselves revisiting the blame-game, we are plunged back into the present moment with acceptance.

- Hospital Prayer—Whether we're occupying a bed or standing beside it, imagining the light of the Spirit pervading the whole room can be a prayer of healing. Such prayers spur us to action, focusing on what the sick person needs—someone to make phone calls, to screen visitors, to write thank-you notes, to bring a cup of cold water. We offer ourselves as part of the healing that can come to us and through us.

Praying in and through whatever circumstances surround us help break down the barriers and separation we imagine. Truthfully there is not a spiritual life and a secular life—there's just life.

Reflect: What circumstance in your life right now challenges your prayer practices? Allow grace to lead you to bring your prayers into the situation.

JUNE 26 • *Praying with the Imagination*

The power of the imagination has captured the fancy of everyone from business leaders to athletes to health providers. "Imagine the ball going into the hole," say the golfers. "Imagine the cancer cells being defeated," urge the healers.

However, the concept is not new. In Mark 11:24, we read, "So I tell you, whatever you ask for in prayer, believe that you have received it, and it will be yours." Many prayer leaders emphasize the need for affirmative prayers rather than those that signal our lack of something. Though we cannot prove it or explain it, power resides in imagining something as already completed, already given.

Here are some examples of reframing our prayers in the affirmative:

- God is my light and my salvation (rather than "Be my light").
- The Lord of life walks with me (rather than "Please walk with me").
- Healing Presence, you are my strength (rather than "Please bring me strength").
- I am a channel of God's loving-kindness (rather than "Help me be a channel of. . . . ").
- It is well with my soul (rather than "Calm my soul").

Since a great deal of our praying focuses on making requests, affirmative prayer offers a challenging change. Praying positively is a practice worth exploring.

Reflect: Notice the nature of your prayers today. What are some affirmative thoughts that can build new patterns in your mind?

JUNE 27 • *Praying with the Silence*

If I want to hear classical music on my radio, I know the frequency is 91.1. I must tune in to that particular wavelength to hear what I want to hear.

Centuries of spiritual wisdom have affirmed that silence is the language of God—the frequency, if you will. Remember that old hymn "Come, Thou Fount of Every Blessing"? The second line of that song states, "Tune my heart to sing thy grace." So, connecting with the grace and guidance of the Spirit requires that we tune in to the silence.

I once believed in silent prayer as one of many offerings on the "prayer buffet": corporate prayer, healing prayer, petitionary prayer, praise, adoration—to name just a few. I've changed my mind. I now believe silence to be the foundation of all prayer—truly the language of God. Only in the silence are we stripped of control, of ego needs, of our own attempts at micromanaging our spiritual lives. Our openness and vulnerability offers us a better chance that we can learn to listen.

Though we explored the value of silence in our January meditations, I cannot overstate its use as a steady, repetitive spiritual discipline. Only in the silence are we reduced (perhaps elevated) to what we genuinely are—an integral part of the loving web of life, united to the Source that formed us and sustains us.

Reflect: Consider again your own relationship to and commitment to the discipline of silence. What challenges does silence present? joys? lessons?

JUNE 28 • *Praying for Others*

Please pray for me," a friend asks. "Our thoughts and prayers are with them," we say in response to tragedy. Much of our praying involves intercession for others. It carries our compassion.

Though any sincere prayer of the heart seems valid to me, I must admit that my own practice of intercessory prayer has changed over the years. One day I received a disturbing phone call about a friend's illness; my heart twisted in concern and love. At the same time my head raised the question, "How should I pray for her?" From somewhere deep inside me, I heard "You just did."

Maybe the quickening of compassion formed the heart of the prayer. Maybe the actual words were for me, not God. Maybe God hears the soul's sincere desire, not only our carefully crafted words. We pray more unspoken prayers than we realize.

Sometimes our words don't match our hearts. Perhaps we're mouthing sentiments that don't reflect our honest feelings. Congruence between intention and prayer is vital. God hears the prayer of the heart. As Gandhi wisely reminded us, it's better to have a heart without words than words without a heart.

I'm praying more thy-will-be-done prayers these days. I often wonder if I have any business telling God what ought to happen. While petition and intercession are important, there's a difference between asking as a part of our relationship with God and directing God on how to run things. Surely God's wisdom and providence exceed our own.

As we pray for others, it's essential to trust the mystery of prayer without judgment or evaluation. Intercessory prayer isn't about manipulating God's will; it's about placing ourselves and those for whom we pray in the loving hands of the Presence who hears our prayers, even if the words are simply, "Lord, have mercy on Jane."

Reflect: As you pray for others today, allow your heartfelt compassion to pour forth, trusting that an outburst of love is prayer in itself.

JUNE 29 • *Praying in Community*

We need one another. Relationships feed us, challenge us, enlighten us, and bless us—especially in the growth of our spirits. Praying with a faith community and encouraging one another along the path of the soul can tend our growth in significant ways:

- Corporate worship enriches our individual worship.
- Small groups—prayer groups, covenant groups, study groups help keep us accountable for personal disciplines.
- Group prayer, whether in worship, sharing a meal, or gathered in a hospital room, ignites our own prayer.
- Sharing with others makes us aware of the community's needs.
- Hearing the prayers of others prompts us to pray.
- Communication with others in their struggles helps us deal with our own.
- Involvement with a faith community offers specific ways to put our prayers into action.
- Joining in the journey with kindred spirits encourages us along the path.

Returning from church one day, my husband (a retired minister) remarked that the spoken prayer of the youth minister had almost moved him to tears. "Her words really blessed me," he reflected. The sharing of our faith in community is one way we can live out the words of Genesis 12:2, "I will bless you . . . so that you will be a blessing."

Reflect: Think of the meetings, groups, and projects your faith community offers. In what ways does your engagement with others "tend your growth"?

JUNE 30 • *Trusting the Tending*

When all is said and done, we must remember the true source of growth. In our backyard gardens, no matter how much we till, plant, water, and fertilize, we do not bring about the miracle of actual growth. The garden of our souls is no different. We can read, study, journal, fast, pray, and serve, but we can't cause the heart to bloom into love and compassion.

Our efforts to measure such improvement will be frustrating at best. I recall the lament of a spiritual directee while describing an incident with her own recurring demon—judgmentalism. "Here it is again," she exclaimed. "We've been working on this problem for years, Linda! And I'm still the same old judgmental *me*. Have I not grown at all?"

As her observer and spiritual companion, I could easily acknowledge her growth. "Look how quickly you spotted it this time, Marie! You were aware of it; you named it; you owned it as your behavior, not someone else's. Plus, you made the conscious choice to offer it for healing and move beyond it. The meticulous, exacting part of you is never going to die. That's what makes you an efficient and competent person. But you now recognize when the shadow side—judgmentalism—sneaks into the driver's seat. You noticed it immediately this time and made a healing choice. The process is slow and sure." The transformation of the spirit occurs mysteriously as we cooperate in the process. Sometimes it appears to move at a snail's pace.

Spiritual practice is a bit like putting ourselves through an exercise regimen. Of course, we want the muscles to tone up overnight. We must commit ourselves to a process that is ultimately beyond our control and takes time. That's where trust enters the picture. We plant and tend, trusting that the tomato seeds will yield tomatoes to feed us and others. In like manner, through the spiritual disciplines, we allow Light to shine on our souls, trusting that slowly the fruits of love, joy, and compassion will appear through a power greater than our own. It's a Spirit-driven process that we can trust.

Reflect: Review all the spiritual disciplines mentioned this month. Which ones call to you? Which ones seem the most challenging? Spend some quiet time in prayer, following the Spirit's leading, and commit to trying a new practice that has potential to help "tend your growth."

July

THE FRUIT FORMS

*"The fruit of the Spirit is love, joy, peace, patience, kindness,
generosity, faithfulness, gentleness, and self-control."*
—GALATIANS 5:22-23

BREATH PRAYER
You are the Potter. . . . I am the clay.

JULY 1 • *The Miracle of Fruitfulness*

The first time I saw a bright orange hanging from a tree—juicy and ripe—it struck me as a dazzling miracle. It seemed to offer its nourishment to the world, to be shared and savored with abandon.

This same powerful creative force works within us, believe it or not. As we listen to the movement of the Spirit in our lives and sharpen our ears, we can trust that the fruit will form—ever so slowly.

The litmus test of all our listening and tending is this: What evidence do we see that the fruit of the Spirit is beginning to bud within us—organically and naturally? This is not a matter of forced behavior to meet a set of moral standards, not a disciplined ladder to sainthood but an outgrowth from the core seed of the possibility planted deep in the soil of our souls. We tend this process faithfully through spiritual practice.

Unfortunately, we don't graduate one day into full-fledged loving, kind, generous, faithful, joyful, patient people. Our fruit remains flecked with impurities and imperfections. But the question remains: Are we gradually maturing in the direction of fruit bearing? Sometimes our growth is so minute that we cannot perceive it. We may feel that our progress is stymied, that we make no progress whatsoever. Usually, we can detect it only in retrospect. That's what validates times of spiritual reflection.

This holy process doesn't stop in our little garden patch. Spiritual fruit enriches not only ourselves but all those whom our lives touch. How will we share it in service? How can our fruit feed those around us? How can these virtues nourish the common good?

Reflect: Write down the fruit of the Spirit listed in Galatians 5. Imagine each one growing in your own soul. How are they beginning to reveal themselves in your day-to-day life? in your relationships? Which are growing more robustly than others?

JULY 2 • *The Greatest of These Is Love*

All fruit springs from the rich soil of love. Without it, they will eventually wither from lack of power and purpose. This life-giving love provides the nutrients that energize the other virtues.

Love, as viewed through a spiritual lens, moves beyond feeling, admiration, and a racing heartbeat. It's a whole-body, whole-being experience—involving the muscles and the mind as well as the heart. Its meaning escapes all definitions and spills over the edges of any verbal box we put it in. It is pervasive, yet elusive.

Other languages express the nuances of love much better than our English vocabulary, though their attempts don't fully capture the meaning either. It's a gigantic umbrella that shelters erotic love, familial love, brotherly/sisterly love, love of friends, God's love. We say we love chocolate; we love that new movie; we love to dance. The concept seems to overflow endless boundaries, often diluting and obscuring its spiritual significance. So what do we mean when we speak of love as a spiritual fruit?

First Corinthians 13 makes a poetic stab at it, telling us what it is and what it isn't, what attributes fit the holy pattern and which ones fall short.

- Love is more than flowery words.
- Love is more than intellectual understanding.
- Love is more than faith.
- Love is more than generosity.
- Love endures.
- Love believes.
- Love never fails.
- "Love never gives up."
- "Love cares more for others than for self."
- "Love doesn't want what it doesn't have."
- "Love doesn't strut."
- Love "doesn't have a swelled head."
- Love "doesn't force itself on others."
- Love "doesn't fly off the handle."
- Love "doesn't keep score of the sins of others."
- Love "doesn't revel when others grovel."
- Love "looks for the best."
- "Love never dies" (THE MESSAGE).

We might add that love is a choice, a perspective, a persistent goodwill toward all creatures and creation. It seeks the highest good for everyone we know, even those we find hard to love. It reflects a reverence for life that unites being and doing; it is the rock upon which life rests.

Reflect: Read 1 Corinthians 13 slowly from several translations, especially Eugene Peterson's paraphrase, *The Message*. Use it as a measuring stick for everything you think, say, and do today.

JULY 3 • *A Wellspring of Joy*

I vividly recall standing with a group of my first-grade friends at the front of the church, arms linked and faces beaming, singing, "I've got the joy, joy, joy, joy down in my heart—down in my heart to stay!"

No wonder the Bible prompts us to "become like children" (Matt. 18:3) in order to be in touch with the kingdom of God. That innocent, uncomplicated sense of wonder opens the doorway to joy. It's a shame that life's cares cloud that purity of spirit with pain, worry, and heartache. How can we regain that sense of delight when the realities of existence seem to squelch it? Yet, joy is one fruit that hangs from the tree of a growing spirit.

Though joy has childlike qualities, it takes a certain degree of maturity to unearth its mysterious meaning. We learn that true joy differs from pleasure and happiness. It does not depend on good fortune and success. It involves the following:

- The capacity to savor beauty, even when it's engulfed in sadness.
- The ability to reach for meaning when it seems that there is none.
- A profound appreciation of the totality of the human story—both the light and the dark.
- The capacity to revel in foolishness, to laugh till our sides ache.
- The awareness that a smile lurks beneath buckets of tears.
- An unswerving trust that all will be well within the unbroken circle of God's grace.

We find it hard to define joy accurately. It's more of a condition than an emotion, more about something hidden than something visible. It's a robust relishing of life—a gleeful, cosmic Yes!

Reflect: As you go about your day, notice the ways that joy manifests itself in your life. How do you observe it in others? What dampens your joy? What releases it?

JULY 4 • *The Peace That Passes All Understanding*

Peace is in short supply in our twenty-first century culture. The melancholy evidence surrounds us—nations at war, political factions sniping at each other, families in disarray, and our bodies protesting with stress reactions. No wonder our souls and spirits cry out for "the peace of God which surpasses all understanding" (Phil. 4:7), a priceless fruit of the Spirit.

Like love and joy, its meaning is elusive and multifaceted. We express our desire for inner peace through statements such as, "I need a feeling of peace about our decision to move to Florida." Another yearning is expressed by "I'm praying for peace in the Middle East." What do we mean when we speak of peace as a fruit of the spiritual life, as an outgrowth of our relationship to God?

The following attitudes and feelings point to peace:

- Becoming clear about what we can control and what we can't.
- Lessening of struggle within ourselves.
- Disappearance of the need to win or to extract revenge.
- Relaxing of tension in the body and soul.
- A feeling of calm in the midst of chaos.
- A declining of complaint.
- A decrease in resistance.
- Unguarded acceptance of what is.

The more we intentionally go to the calm place inside, the more easily we get there. Peace stems from a core connection with divine harmony, resulting in a spiritual confidence that we are held and loved by a boundless Love. We join a greater peace—a sense of rest in a sea of unrest.

The peace that we long for in the world starts with the peace of God within us. From that place creative approaches to resolving conflict and achieving justice can begin to flow.

Reflect: Make a breath prayer part of your existence today. As you inhale, imagine that you are breathing in divine peace; as you exhale, imagine that you are breathing out anxiety. Give thanks that in doing so you're strengthening the "peace of God which surpasses all understanding."

JULY 5 • *Practicing Patience*

Someone once told me that you get the chicken by hatching an egg, not by smashing it! But most of us find the virtue of waiting in short supply. After all, we're accustomed to power and productivity at our fingertips. Strike a match and a fire erupts; turn a key and a two-ton automobile springs into motion; erase a thousand words by hitting "delete." We even become exasperated if someone doesn't have an answering device because we don't have time to call back!

Patience seems almost countercultural in our speedy society. We want to get the job done, respond with an instant solution, find the answer right this minute. Our bodies often register our impatience. We tap our fingers on the table, swing a leg in rhythm, or pace the floor because quiet waiting feels too uncomfortable. All these actions herald impatience.

Synonyms for patience include "forbearance" or "long-suffering." Anyone who has waited for a broken bone to heal or an illness to run its course knows about forced lessons in patience. Never mind the patience required to stick to a diet! Our intellect tells us that impatience doesn't speed healing any more than it makes a long line at the supermarket move faster. The ability to hang in there is an attribute worth honing.

Though patience may appear passive, it's actually a form of concentrated strength. It respects the reality of process—whether we're waiting for the crops to grow or for our spirits to bear fruit. Once again, the garden can teach us. Sure the fertilizer and the watering help, but without the essential quality of patience, the process is incomplete.

In the formation of spiritual fruit, toil and trying come as part of the package. But so does patience. It's usually harder to wait than to work.

Reflect: Once again, the breath can be our ally in ushering us into the presence of patience. Today when you feel a rush of impatience, take three deep breaths and intentionally slow down, tasting the fruit of patience.

JULY 6 • *Random Acts of Kindness*

I wanted to teach my young sons an object lesson in kindness. I thought I could orchestrate the controlled experiment in Christmas kindness all the way to its thankful finale.

As part of our church's holiday service project, I secured the name of a needy family, complete with the names and ages of the children. The boys and I combed the mall and the grocery shelves for toys and turkeys and all the trimmings. When all was festively wrapped and loaded into the station wagon, we headed off with hearts full of a holiday spirit of kindness and generosity.

When we arrived at the apartment, my timid knock at the door was answered by a disheveled woman, who eyed me suspiciously through a crack in the door. I eagerly told her why we had come and, with obvious reluctance, opened the door. Cheerfully, we introduced ourselves to the children and unloaded all the packages and parcels of food. Almost immediately, she mumbled a hasty thank-you and ushered us out the door. Hardly the display of gratitude that I expected.

As my sons and I were leaving the porch, we encountered another unexpected surprise. "Hey, you!" a man shouted from next door. "Didn't you bring me anything? I need some Christmas too, ya know!" Taken aback and frightened by his anger, we hurried to the car and drove back home. So much for controlling my children's formation in compassion.

The greater lesson had yet to be learned—not by my children but by me. As the days passed, my righteous indignation finally turned to prayerful consideration, and I saw my hubris clearly. I hadn't even given a thought to the embarrassment the woman must have felt in seeing strangers give her children the Christmas she herself must have wanted to provide. I hadn't considered the shame she may have experienced in being a charity case. For a moment, I forgot the separation between us and my heart felt her despair. We were both mothers. Not only did I feel her shame; I felt my shame too.

The act of kindness was as much about my needs as hers. Genuine kindness comes from a reservoir of goodwill that does not depend on how others receive it or respond to it. It is born of heartfelt compassion, not choreographed behavior. Kindness doesn't focus on benevolence but on willingness to be channels of love—along with sensitivity to the dignity of others.

Reflect: Imagine that an angel within you wants to use your hands for the work of loving the world. In what specific ways can you respond?

JULY 7 • *A Generous Heart*

Generosity embraces an open heart more than an open wallet. Whether it's a widow's mite or a rich man's charity, it involves motivation more than money.

Subtle attitudes compromise this virtue of expansive goodwill.

- "I never received a thank-you note."
- "I had them to dinner, but they never reciprocated."
- "I gave lots of time to that project, but I didn't get any credit."
- "I sent them a contribution, but they didn't spend it like I thought they should."

Sincerely generous people don't give from a sense of obligation or a need to obey a religious code (even tithing). They don't give out of guilt or a need to control others. Miserly measurement and calculated fairness do not enter the spiritual nature of generosity.

Even in the case of great riches, true philanthropists give out of a need to share their bounty—a living out of the knowledge that one is "blessed to be a blessing." Understandably, good stewardship often calls for some accountability, as in a loan to an adult child or a gift to a charitable cause. But the underlying motivation is not one of power and control. Genuine altruism stems from an unselfish regard for the welfare of others.

Time is a precious gift too. Ask any child about the value of an hour of playing-catch-with-Daddy time versus a ten-dollar bill. A generous spirit tends toward second chances and forgiveness. Spiritual generosity comes from a love that spills over, not an obligation to pay accounts.

Reflect: Spend a few moments thinking about your own relationship to generosity. Be honest with yourself about your motives and actions. From what source does your generosity spring? from a spirit of sharing? a sense of duty?

JULY 8 • *Fearless Faithfulness*

Faith is the assurance of things hoped for, the conviction of things not seen" (Heb. 11:1). Life is filled with challenges that tax the human spirit. We may want to cut and run, to abandon ship, to renege on our commitments. Not so for a person steeped in the fruit called faithfulness.

My small congregation includes many faithful servants, but I'm continually inspired by the woman who keeps our food pantry ministry in motion. She's on the job, rain or shine. She perseveres when the shelves get bare, relentlessly reminding us to bring a canned ham or a box of diapers. If church renovation alters her storage space, she finds different shelves for her supplies. She champions the needs of the poor, even when they disappoint her. Her unswerving commitment exemplifies walkin', talkin' faithfulness!

When we think of faithful friends, we realize we can count on them when the chips are down. They don't keep score of our neediness to ensure that the friendship stays on "equal ground." We can call on them at three in the morning. There's no such thing as imposing on them. They remain loyal in their love for us.

If we think of faithfulness in terms of our loyalty to God, what qualities do we consider? A life of compassion, forgiveness, inclusiveness, and unconditional love affirms a trust we cannot prove and an assurance of a love we cannot see.

Faithfulness is about dedicated deeds of love, about staying the course. Like a farmer facing unpredictable weather, a faithful person keeps on planting.

Reflect: Think of the lives of people you would consider "faithful." What actions point to their faithfulness? In what ways does your life reflect faithfulness?

JULY 9 • *Gentle Giants*

In the world of the Spirit, gentle persons do not act like doormats but exhibit a powerful combination of strength and softness. Think of a compassionate physician who, even when called upon to administer a painful procedure, does the work gently and skillfully. Consider a caring counselor whose tender words invite vulnerability and healing. Call to mind practitioners of other healing ministries whose gentle touch aids in recovery. Reflect on loving parents who embody a blend of firmness and sensitivity when guiding a child. Remember Mother Teresa, Mahatma Gandhi, Nelson Mandela, Rosa Parks—all gentle giants.

In the Christian tradition, Jesus comes to my mind. Though many folks carry an image of Jesus as meek and mild, it's an incomplete picture. As a political revolutionary, an outspoken champion of the poor, and a challenger of established authority, his example is hardly meek and mild. Yet, his gentle spirit led him to death on a cross. History abounds with giants whose fusion of strength and gentleness changed the world.

A gentle person . . .

- Gives advice delicately and only when asked.
- Doesn't grab the spotlight.
- Is sensitive to the wounds and needs of others.
- Listens readily and is open to learning from others.
- Doesn't need to win the argument.
- Knows it's not all about them.
- Has self-knowledge without self-consciousness.

Reflect: Remember people who have influenced your life through their gentleness. Remember their soothing presence. Identify ways that the fruit of gentleness is growing in you.

JULY 10 • *Hold Your Horses*

Misunderstandings can erupt in angry words. Disagreements can rile us up. Conflict can blaze into violence. We know the process well; we've all been there. The spiritual fruit of self-control can deter some of our baser instincts.

As human beings, we naturally react to get even, to exact revenge in the name of fairness, to retaliate verbally or physically. The spiritual fruit called self-control runs counter to that impulse. It tells us, "You are the boss of that impulse; don't let it be the boss of you!"

The Bible has plenty to say about this matter. It urges us to turn the other cheek and to love the unlovable. It counsels us not to seek an eye for an eye. (See Matthew 5:38-39.) These are difficult precepts to follow and a daunting challenge to our human nature.

Self-control does not demand that we stomp on our feelings in hopes that they'll disappear. That allows them to fester out of sight. However, when we honestly face the emotions and courageously acknowledge them—feel them—then we can freely choose our response from a place inside us where the Spirit guides us to grace.

We can short-circuit the reactive process early on by monitoring our mental mutterings and thoughts of revenge. We can harness the power of the breath by inhaling deeply and letting some time pass instead of leaping to an angry reaction.

No one can bridle our passions for us. The fruit of self-control reminds us that we hold the reins of restraint.

Reflect: Notice when you feel upset. Pause to remember that you have the power to choose your response and that the Spirit supports your self-control.

JULY 11 • *Getting from Sunday to Monday*

As spiritual fruit form, we may come to a crucial realization. In all likelihood, we'll become aware of the gap that exists between what we espouse on Sunday and how we live on Monday; that is, the disconnect between belief and experience, between intention and execution. It's as if we live with a split between what we profess and how we behave. Wrestling with this reality and closing that gap between information and transformation is the demanding part of the fruit-bearing process.

A simple travel analogy may be appropriate here. Suppose I'm planning a trip from Memphis to Manhattan. I would buy a map, a travel guide, and google all sorts of data on the Internet. But no matter how well I study the material or glean information from others who have made the trip before me, no matter how well I prepare myself for the journey, I will still be right here in Memphis unless I experience the journey for myself.

Even if this analogy oversimplifies the case, it conveys a truth about our spiritual paths. Whether we identify the "map" as the Bible or church doctrine or the American way—any map is just a guide to the trip. Some-times in our religious fervor, we mistake the map for the journey and end up worshiping the map! It's possible to be a diligent student of the Bible as a map for our lives, quoting verses right and left, and still not have a transformed heart. The concepts must move from the head, lodge in the heart, and travel to the hands and feet in actual fruit-bearing.

Faith as belief has little power. We can believe all the right things and still be mean-spirited. We can believe and remain miserable. We can believe and stay in bondage. True faith comes through our experience *of* God not our knowledge *about* God. We have the divine gift of free will, and that means we can refuse to change, to explore, to "take the trip." God's love surrounds us and invites us forward but full healing waits for our longing and consent—for the inner yes necessary to integrate our beliefs into our ordinary, day-to-day living.

Reflect: Look honestly at the gaps between your Sunday beliefs and your Monday behavior. Know that divine love and forgiveness will follow you as you explore the disconnects and commit to closing the gaps.

JULY 12 • *Inner to Outer*

Authentic fruit-bearing starts from the inside, deep in the orchard, deep in our souls. It's about genuine integrity—so that what a person is on the inside determines what her or she does on the outside.

Simply altering our exterior actions—focusing only on "doing the right thing"—is like putting a Band-Aid™ on something that requires surgery. As we commit ourselves to soulful living, our deeds increasingly evolve out of the fruitfulness that the Spirit is forming within us. This means having the courage to shine a laser beam on our motives. Am I doing this in order to feel proud of myself? to elicit the admiration of others? to enhance my standing in the community? to satisfy what I think God wants? Why am I doing what I'm doing? The why is more important than the what.

Paul describes the way a spirit-filled person lives:

> What happens when we live God's way? He brings gifts into our lives, much the same way that fruit appears in an orchard—things like affection for others, exuberance about life, serenity. We develop a willingness to

stick with things, a sense of compassion in the heart, and a conviction that a basic holiness permeates things and people. We find ourselves involved in loyal commitments, not needing to force our way in life, able to marshal and direct our energies wisely (Gal. 5:22-23, THE MESSAGE).

Directing our energies wisely depends on a strong link to our inner compass—our center of consent where the divine Voice dwells. As we become increasingly familiar with this God-given internal guidance system, our confidence that God can actually guide us from the inside grows stronger. Then we can blend those inner promptings with outside cues—a both/and kind of guidance rather than either/or. We view this sense of ultimate authority as not only the wind of God's Spirit that blows through all creation but also the breath that animates our bodies and guides our souls.

Reflect: What are the primary ways that you receive guidance? Think of your times of listening to the Spirit both inside and outside. What kind of "blended" guidance do you sense in your life?

JULY 13 • *The Sacred Intersection*

It's easy to make a narcissistic career out of spiritual growth. After all, theology is fascinating. Kindred spirits are usually wonderful folks to be with; retreats are relaxing; books are compelling. However, the beautiful process of spiritual growth moves in a cycle of blessing that doesn't stop with me, mine, and my development. It moves outward in a dynamic flow.

As lofty as that sounds, we know from experience that sometimes decisions about where to invest our time, money, and energy can vex and overwhelm us. Ideally, our inner work energizes our outer work, and we become less attached to what others think, what they expect of us, and whether they approve of us. We become less chameleon-like in allowing others to dictate and define who we are.

Our decisions about intentional service need to emerge from a thoughtful, reflective place where we weigh the needs around us and see where they intersect with our gifts, graces, and passions. That sacred intersection points to our place of service at any given time. To be sure, this is a moving target throughout our lives. Our own interests and the world's needs change constantly. What I physically could do at age thirty is not what I'm capable of in my seventies! On the other hand, we have wisdom to share in our later years that we have garnered over time.

In assessing our own gifts, there's no need for false modesty. That is not true humility. Humility involves clarity and honesty, not belittling ourselves. In a spirit of gratitude, we look at the activities we feel passionate about and those we have talent and energy for. How have folks around us affirmed our gifts? When have our efforts borne fruit in the past? Above all, we remain clear about what we truly want to do as opposed to those things we think we ought to do.

Once we have taken a thoughtful inventory of what we have to offer, then it's time to look outward to focus on the needs around us.

Reflect: Think honestly about how you make decisions concerning your time and energy. When needs in the community arise, how do you decide if and how to respond?

JULY 14 • *Sensing the Needs*

Sometimes the needs around us get lumped into ambiguous concepts, such as "there needs to be peace in the world," and we miss our call to be bearers of peace right this minute—in our relationships, our families, our immediate communities. Bearing the fruit of the Spirit means developing a keen sensitivity to the needs directly in front of us.

It isn't always easy to walk in someone else's shoes, to imagine what he or she might need. Does our troubled sister or brother need a word of encouragement? a ride to the doctor's office? a hot meal? a babysitter for the kids? a few hours' packing help before the moving van arrives?

Rather than rush to satisfy our desire to mark items off our to-do lists, we can instead take time to consider what it's like to be in other persons' situations. Consider their limitations of money, energy, and time. Prayerfully ask for the Spirit's guidance in your desire to help. Use your compassionate insight to intuit what actions would meet their needs.

Our interior posture in sensing the needs of others can be one of "kind alertness," allowing the fruit of kindness that is growing within us to find its most useful target. Being a channel of love to others requires some sensitive discernment on our part.

Reflect: As you consider someone who may need your help, take the time to put yourself in his or her shoes. Mull over the possibilities. Make a prayerful choice, and act on it.

JULY 15 • *Now, Rather Than Later*

We've been told from childhood to "strike while the iron is hot." When someone's need confronts us, it's better to meet that need now rather than later. Procrastination can turn our best desires into sad regrets:

- "I was going to visit him, but now it's too late."
- "I intended to make that phone call; I wish I had."
- "I meant to offer help, but I never got around to it."

I'm not saying that rushing to a decision is better than thinking it through. Prudence about our use of time differs from procrastination. Stating that we'll do something next Tuesday is not the same as deferring action to some vague "later."

This goes for words that need to be spoken now as well as deeds that need to be done now. Though some signs on church marquees are more pithy than profound, I spotted one recently that applies here. "Aspire to inspire before you expire!" Don't put it off. We often think rather than utter words of affection and compassion. Say it now.

A hospice volunteer once told me, "I've had the privilege of sitting with quite a number of dying folks, and none of them wished he or she had spent more time at the office. Sometimes they regret that they lived the life others expected of them, rather than the life they wanted to live. They talk about words they wished they had said and assistance they wish they had given when they had the chance."

We always have time to lighten the burden of someone who's toting a heavy load—with our words and our deeds—right now.

Reflect: Whom do you know who needs the fruit of the Spirit that are growing in you? Review the list again—love, joy, peace, patience, kindness, generosity, faithfulness, gentleness, self-control. Take a long look around you, and consider where your spiritual fruit might feed another.

JULY 16 • *From Idea to Action*

The familiar verse from Luke 12 counsels us to "consider the lilies, how they grow" (v. 7). But it seems to me that there's one significant difference between us and the lilies. Lilies have no choice but to blossom; as human beings, we do. The wonderful (terrible?) gift of free will gives us a choice not only about our blossoming but about the nature of our fruit-bearing.

Service begins with good intentions, and we often stall right there at the starting gate. Compassionate ideas need to propel us into compassionate action.

To illustrate, here is a list of ways to help a grieving person. It provides a thought-provoking example of how to put legs on your desire to serve:

- Be there for your friends—by listening, laughing, and crying—even when you don't understand what they are going through.
- Defend their right to grieve in their own way, even if it differs from the way you might grieve.
- Send flowers to remind them of beauty.
- Send money if you know it will help.
- Send cards often to let them know you haven't forgotten them.
- Leave a voice mail or send an e-mail, allowing them to respond when they feel up to it.
- Try to anticipate their needs; they may not know what to ask for.
- Avoid offering easy answers and platitudes that may make them feel "rushed" through their grief.
- Give them permission to grieve in front of you; don't change the subject or tell them not to cry or act uncomfortable if they do.
- Ask questions; don't tell them how they should or shouldn't feel.
- Invite them to events, allowing them to decide yes or no.
- Be especially mindful of holidays, birthdays, and anniversaries. Put appropriate reminders on your calendar.

As you reach out beyond your own front door, fruit-bearing realizes its purpose for existence. God created you with a natural compassion for other human beings. Think of your own visceral response when you witness a child's finger being pricked for a blood test—your insides probably contract and you wince in shared pain.

That's an accurate illustration of our proper place in the human family. When one person suffers injury, we all bleed.

Reflect: Ponder your own process of turning your intention into action. What usually keeps you from taking the next step?

JULY 17 • *A Call to Fruit-Bearing*

On a solo trip out West, I was hoping to gain some guidance for my future. However, it came in an unexpected way.

I was walking alone along a path in the Sonoran Desert of Arizona, accompanied only by hundreds of saguaro cacti that dotted the landscape. As I rounded a bend in the path, I found myself face-to-face with an old, beat-up cactus about fifty feet tall. Up close and personal, these stately plants are anything but beautiful. This one bore ragged holes where birds had nested, ugly gashes cut by years of weather and wear. Unexpectedly, I burst into tears. My silent thoughts said clearly, *Look how tall she stands. See how proudly she wears her scars; she is unashamed.*

As I gathered my emotions, my eyes fell on the open desert, sparsely covered with hundreds of tall cactus plants, looking like fingers pointing to the sky. After a long silence, the gentle inner voice whispered again: *Just be a "pointer." . . . I have scores of them. You don't have to be the smartest, the prettiest, the best-educated, or the most engaging. Just be one . . . always point up.*

Turning once again to face the cactus that provoked my tears, I noticed that the gigantic plant was situated in the center of a small rise, surrounded by smaller desert plants. Another thought emerged: *Be a pointer in your small area of influence. Don't try to do everything; just point the way ahead to those on your little hill.* And then the most surprising suggestion of all arose: *Allow people to build nests in your wounds.*

I felt stunned, confused, full of self-doubt. Was I imagining all this? Had I been in the desert heat too long? I began to chastise myself for having such a crazy, vivid imagination!

But the experience has not faded over the weeks, months, and years since that day in the desert. I keep a photo of a saguaro cactus on my desk to remind me of the purpose she shared with me that day—to stand tall in the dry, desolate landscapes of life and to allow people to build nests in my wounds. I'm only beginning to understand what that means.

Reflect: When have you had a surprising or confusing sense of call? Share your experience with someone you trust. Be willing to honor your own times of unexpected guidance, even if you don't understand the details.

JULY 18 • *Imperfect Fruit*

The fruit we bear is rarely flawless and perfect. We all carry the scars of mistakes, inadequacies, and times when we've messed up. That need not make us unworthy of bearing fruit.

In fact, awareness of our own imperfections usually enables us to be more compassionate toward others who have messed up. We cut folks some slack; we're generous with second chances; we understand their vulnerability. When we are familiar with our flaws and foibles, it somehow creates a safe space for others to deal with theirs.

We have only to look around us at the success of Alcoholics Anonymous and other support groups to see the power of one struggling seeker helping another. Widows bring understanding to other widows; storm victims champion the needs of others dealing with the same losses. Being a wounded healer extends a mission to every human being.

Oddly enough, our acknowledgment of our errors creates an integral piece of the path to wholeness. Unless we see clearly both the light and the dark of ourselves, we're looking at a distorted picture of who we are. Remember, goodness always has self-righteousness as its shadow side. Piety can lapse into judgment if we aren't careful. Self-confidence can easily turn into arrogance if we aren't mindful of the tendency.

Mistakes and imperfections supply the building blocks to wisdom. Our human nature is such that we usually learn how to set things right by first getting things wrong. So, even though our fruit may be flawed, it can still provide nourishment for those around us.

Reflect: Recall a time when you've played the role of a "wounded healer" by ministering to someone whose situation mirrors an incident in your life. Be grateful that grace flowed through you to another person.

JULY 19 · *As Time Goes By*

Many people experience a sense of uselessness as they age, as if their fruit-bearing time has ended. The words of Psalm 92:14 tell a different story: "In old age they still produce fruit; they are always green and full of sap."

In doing research interviews for a book on aging, I encountered quite a number of elders who extolled the virtues of giving back. "If we don't," one person warned, "we risk becoming both bored and boring!"

Burt had been a busy business professor all his life and was still full of vigor when he retired. Rather than doing contract work for a business consulting firm, he made a surprising decision to devote all available time and energy toward being a positive part of his five grandchildren's lives. He babysat often; he took them on trips; he attended ball games and recitals; he spent one-on-one "slow time" with each child to affirm his or her uniqueness. Instead of lavishing gifts on them, he lavished time. "After all," he offered with a smile, "I've discovered how children spell the word *love*. It's T-I-M-E."

Reaching out also includes addressing the primary causes of the world's distress by involvement in peace and justice issues. Claire decided to put her passion for the poor to work by volunteering for an organization called Bread for the World, while her husband, Henry, used his carpentry skills to build houses for Habitat for Humanity. Many worthwhile organizations depend on the energy and commitment of older adults to give voice and vigor to their causes.

I noticed a special vibrancy in those seniors who were bearing fruit in their communities. They used less "us-and-them" language, as if they no longer needed an enemy to rail against. Their sense of separation dissolved. Their preoccupation with their own problems diminished. They began to build bridges instead of borders. They moved from hubris to humanity, from isolation to involvement.

Reflect: Think about the older adults you admire. How are they making a difference in their families and in the world around them? Make a commitment to continue to bear fruit as long as you have breath.

JULY 20 • *Fruits of Your Labor*

In God's economy, nothing is ever wasted. Even after retirement, the skills honed over a lifetime can find their way into the fruit-bearing process. To avoid outliving our usefulness, we can create ways to use what we already know or to pick up a discarded dream.

My sister had never owned a loom in her life—that is, until she plunged into her well of creativity after she retired. Now her creations find their way into people's wardrobes, adorn their walls, and grace their tables. Well past her midseventies, she still actively engages in learning new techniques and teaching them to others—including her eager granddaughters!

George's lifetime of practicing law found new life in his volunteer work in legal aid for the poor. A physician friend works with the Church Health Center. A former fashion model shares her advice in a program called "Dress for Success," helping job applicants prepare for interviews.

However, we need not wait until retirement to weave our vocational skills into the process of fruit-bearing. During a move a few years ago, I remember the meaningful offers made by friends who shared their expertise. A bookstore owner offered to come over and alphabetize my books as I unpacked them. A woman who was an organizational whiz helped turn my office files from chaos to order. One friend with many demands on her time offered to fill the back of her pickup truck with lamps and plants and make a one-time delivery to the new residence. You can imagine my gratitude as their kindness bore fruit during a difficult time.

Some folks find a way to spread sunshine even with formidable health issues. Tiny and wrinkled as a prune at ninety-seven, Rose had a spinal curvature that formed a noticeable arc. But her spunk and spirit were still ramrod straight. In response to a question about her health, she remarked emphatically, "My dear, you can't let limitations limit you!"

No matter what, no matter when, we always have something to give—even if it's as simple as a smile.

Reflect: Ponder your unique set of skills and talents. How can you employ them to bear fruit? Play with the possibilities.

JULY 21 • *The Invisible Sign*

When my sons were small, a friend suggested a playful and creative method for teaching children basic kindness. Though it seemed like child's play at the time, I realize now that it made a difference in my adult life as well. Sometimes a simple image can yield greater results than an hour's lecture on the value of kindness.

As I sent my children off for the first day of school one September, I cautioned them to be aware of any newcomers to their class and to be particularly friendly and helpful. "Every person you know is wearing an invisible sign. Did you know that?" I asked them. "You can't see it with your eyes, but it hangs around each person's neck by a silver thread, and it has four words on it: *MAKE ME FEEL SPECIAL*. Everyone in your class is wearing the sign—even your teacher! I have the sign on too, and so do you!"

As part of a magical story, the sign's invisibility increased their fascination. The challenge to imagine something like a secret code made it a game worth playing. For a long time, I could send them off to any gathering with the words, "Remember the invisible sign!" They eventually outgrew the game, but somewhere inside them the message registered. Now, as men in their forties, they've forgotten most of what I said or thought I taught in those young years. But they still remember the invisible sign.

Reflect: As you go about your day, playfully imagine MAKE ME FEEL SPECIAL displayed across the chest of every person you meet—young and old. Notice how it affects the way you relate to them.

JULY 22 • *The Fruit of Words*

Words matter. We can use them to bully or to bless. They become a weapon or a consolation, symbols of love or harbingers of hate. In powerful ways, they convey the fruit of the Spirit.

Words from Proverbs 25:11 state the message in poetic language: "A word fitly spoken is like apples of gold in a setting of silver." Words are sounds uttered, but the setting matters significantly. The tone and the body language that accompany the sounds affect the meaning. Consider the power of a raised eyebrow versus a serene countenance. Or the difference between a scowl and a smile.

As children, most of us were told, "If you can't say something nice about a person, don't say anything at all!" That's sound advice. Blessing others means saying a good word about them. In doing that, we affirm their essential belovedness, their intrinsic worth as children of God. We convey a resounding yes to their true self.

We can experience our interior speech as a blessing or a curse as well. If we live with a sense of being loved and blessed by God, we will more likely extend that affirmation to others. Conversely, if we harbor a feeling of divine judgment and constant criticism, it will find its way into our spoken words. Messages of complaint, criticism, blaming, and gossip all manifest a curse, not a blessing.

The fruit of the Spirit spring to life when our words bring blessing to everyone we meet.

Reflect: Today, claim your own blessedness by noticing every grace that comes to you. Let those affirmations find their way into the words you speak.

JULY 23 • *Stunting the Growth*

Most of us sincerely want the fruit of the Spirit to ripen within us. We aspire to be loving, peaceful, kind, generous, patient, faithful, gentle people. So why aren't we? Maybe we're blind to the inadvertent ways we stunt our own growth. Here are some common ways we do that:

- Automatic pessimism—Pessimists see the problem in every opportunity; optimists see the opportunity in every problem. If your automatic response is "What's wrong with this?" or "Here are the reasons that won't work," then you're probably throwing a wet blanket on your joy and peace.
- Disconnect of deeds—These are occasions when what we do runs counter to the virtues we're trying to develop. Even though we aspire to gentleness, we may continue our bossy ways—sticking our nose in others' business or telling others the "right" way to

do things. We may want to be patient but continue to huff and puff around, indulging in short-tempered behaviors.

- Word poisoning—Just as food poisoning can wreak physical havoc, word poisoning is toxic to the fruit of the Spirit. Words like *should, ought,* and *must* serve as harbingers of resistance, signaling a sense of duty instead of devotion. (They imply, "I'd rather not, but I guess I will. . . . "). Gossip that demeans others chokes out kindness; hateful expressions stamp out love; hoarding possessions hinders generosity.

As the Spirit works within us, it's our task to work with the Spirit, not against it. This requires an increasing awareness of our own complicity in curbing the growth that yearns to be nourished, not negated.

Reflect: Ask the Spirit to guide you in monitoring your part in the ripening of the fruit, both within you and in your outward behavior. Without blaming anyone else, take responsibility for change.

JULY 24 • *Suffering from Drought*

Like a field withering from lack of water, our spirits may also feel parched with thirst. Centuries ago, monks had a handy word for this kind of spiritual inertia: *acedia*. *Acedia* is not spiritual laziness. It's a kind of blah-ness, a sense of being stuck, a lack of motivation. The monks did not equate this dullness with sadness, which is an outgrowth of heartbreak, making sadness a natural part of the life cycle. Nor is *acedia* clinical depression, which is treatable with medication and counseling.

Bleak feelings of emptiness, an inability to care or even to care that you don't care characterize this spiritual malady. You tell yourself you must "get a grip," but you can't. Others may say, "Snap out of it," but you don't have the energy. It manifests itself in a variety of ways: restlessness, boredom, distractibility, even workaholism—as if additional effort will break its hold. *Acedia* rarely responds to our usual methods of trying harder or talking ourselves out of it. It seems to escape any attempt to corral it or control it. Even talking about it is like trying to grab a shadow, and trying to explain it seemingly increases its power.

So what are we to do when this profound indifference envelops us? when a drought settles over our spirit? when the well runs dry? Getting up off the sofa is a start, a way to begin moving out of the closed circle of our misery. Sing and chant with others; engage in corporate worship; have lunch with a group of fun-loving friends. We can help someone with a problem unrelated to our own malaise or join others in a worthwhile project. We engage our creativity and stretch our minds outside the confines of our condition.

At the same time, repeated spiritual practice can remind us of the Spirit's steadfast presence, even when we can't sense it. Reciting a psalm, praying the daily office, reading uplifting stories, saying affirming breath prayers that state the reality of God's love—all acknowledge the Divine and our relationship to our Creator.

Then we claim the fruit of patience as we wait for the fog to lift. Breaking the bonds of *acedia* takes courage and commitment. Just ask the desert mothers and fathers of old—they coined the word.

Reflect: If you are experiencing *acedia*, what would help you feel understood and accepted? What specific action might help? Think of one definite step to take.

JULY 25 • *Spurring the Growth*

Just as certain things *stunt* the growth of spiritual fruit, some things *spur* the growth. Feeding the fruit is often a matter of paying attention. Notice how the Spirit bears fruit in your heart through your unique personality in your one-of-a-kind life. As the old saying goes, energy flows where attention goes. What we focus on tends to escalate:

- If being around babies and children increases love in your heart, spend more time in their company.
- If silence nourishes your peace, intentionally carve out quiet moments.
- If petting your dog expands your gentleness, focus on that gesture.
- If musical theater sparks your joy, then buy a ticket.
- If family meals feed your faithfulness to your loved ones, then make your presence a priority.

- If working with the homeless enlarges your kindness, then volunteer.

The negative aspect is also true. If watching the evening news dulls your compassion, then limit your exposure. If constant noise disrupts your peace, turn the volume down on everything you can. Whatever diminishes your kindness or curbs your generosity, let it go.

Practicing the little things that feed the fruit can produce a bountiful harvest.

Reflect: Return to the list of the fruit of the Spirit you listed July 1. Think of one action or situation that increases and decreases the growth of each fruit.

JULY 26 • *Spark the Senses*

Each time we heighten our senses, we heighten our aliveness. That, in turn, brings us into harmony with the fruit growing in our souls. Here are some spiritual practices that focus on our awareness of smell, taste, touch, sight, and hearing:

- Aromas—From scented candles to fragrant oils to kitchen aromas, sharpening the sense of smell can stir the soul. Experiment with aromas that lead you more deeply into relaxation and open you to the Spirit. Breathe deeply to engage a variety of scents.
- Mindful meal—Eat a meal alone and in silence. Focus on the taste and texture of the food: the silkiness of a sauce or the crunchiness of fresh vegetables. As you relish each bite, chew slowly with prayerful attention and gratitude for the pungent tastes.
- Prayer beads—The practice of touching beads as you pray has a long tradition in most major religious groups. Adding the sense of touch to the structure of prayers has enriched the experience of the sacred for scores of seekers through the centuries. *A Bead and a Prayer: A Beginner's Guide to Protestant Prayer Beads* by Kristen E. Vincent contains valuable suggestions for the use of this practice for Christians.
- Camera as a prayer tool—Even an amateur photographer is awestruck at the sight of a child's face through a zoom lens or the

singular focus on a purple iris in bloom. A camera lens can reveal a microcosm of the world's wonder as it witnesses intricate design, human emotion, or a lush landscape. Bask in the beauty that reaches the soul through your eyes.

- Birdsong—In a grove of trees (with little extraneous noise) tune your ears to the chatter and twitter of birds. Listen intently to the variety of tones, cadences, and melodies. Allow their music to warm your heart.

Whether you're feeling the warmth of a cozy fire or biting into a delicious piece of chocolate, the celebration of the senses can be a potent reminder that we are indeed "fearfully and wonderfully made" (Ps. 139:14).

Reflect: Which of your senses seems to be sharpest? dullest? Try a spiritual practice that emphasizes the sense that most needs enhancing.

JULY 27 • *Talk to the Trees*

Nature offers many compelling metaphors for encouraging the growth of the spiritual fruit. From words of poetry to the parables of Jesus, fields and flowers offer their images to inspire us. These three practices single out the power of the trees as potent teachers:

- Stand under a large tree. Be aware of your feet solidly planted on the ground and then slowly look up through the leaves and branches. Be silent for several minutes, staying receptive to what the tree has to teach you. Does it speak of the value of deep roots? Does it remind you of the patience required to wait for the budding of leaves? Does it offer juicy fruit or nuts to share with both friend and foe?
- Sit on the ground, leaning against the trunk of a tree. Feel its sturdiness. Let it speak to you of standing firm in the storm of life, of allowing the wind to blow through its branches and move on while the tree remains.
- Find a tree with a visible bird nest in it. Notice how the tree, faithful to its purpose, offers safety and shelter to the creatures it welcomes. Listen to the joyful sounds of chirping birds and rustling leaves.

Sometimes the novelty of allowing the creation to serve as a teacher can add zest and novelty to our spiritual regimen. Try it!

Reflect: The psalmist uses images of trees to speak of God's glory: "Then shall all the trees of the forest sing for joy" (Ps. 96:12). Journal about the messages the trees have whispered to you.

JULY 28 • *Walk It Out*

Most of us stand on two incomparable aids to connection with the Spirit— our feet. We can deepen the work of our souls by harnessing the power of our soles! Just as walking gives our physical health a boost, so engaging in walking meditation can freshen our growth in the Spirit.

- Syncopated steps—Using your feet as a metronome, create a rhythmic beat to your walking while the mind recites an evocative phrase or song. As the body participates in this practice, the repetition provides a psychic tattoo in the spirit. For instance, chant "Love, joy, and peace are mine!" to the beat of four steps. Or, if you are musically inclined, sing "How Firm a Foundation" as you plant your feet firmly on solid ground.

- Companion walk—Picture a silent companion who strolls alongside you, perhaps Jesus or an angel or the spirit of a loved one—whatever feels natural or comforting to you. Imagine a holy conversation in which you talk about the fruit of the Spirit that grow in your life. Discuss doubts and difficulties as well as thanksgiving for the manifestations you have noticed. (Try to refrain from self-judgment if you attempt this imaginative exercise and it falls flat. The first time I called on a silent companion to "walk with me," I felt like a kindergartner playing pretend. Hold the experience lightly and playfully.)

- Revelation walk—As you walk at a leisurely pace, focus intently on your surroundings. Be open to whatever might draw your attention—a spiderweb, a falling leaf, a puddle of raindrops, a dandelion. Stop and spend time with it, letting your imagination flow. For instance, you might notice a tiny green shoot growing proudly through a crack in the sidewalk, reminding you that life finds a way to push through hard times with remarkable resilience. Or, you may pause to notice how a watery puddle mirrors the earth and sky. Allow the detail to create a personal parable for you.

If you walk regularly, you can add spice and meaning to your exercise regimen by converting your strolls into spiritual practices. When circumstances make it impossible to walk outdoors, try a slow stroll around your home and see what happens!

Reflect: Today, as the soles of your feet meet solid ground, may it remind you that you can trust the Spirit of God as the ground of all being. Feel the solidarity and trust contained in that affirmation.

JULY 29 • *The Quest for Questions*

Our questions are more consequential than the answers we seek. Questions carry the concerns that lurk in the soul's corners. Holding a question in the heart without judgment and softening it with gentle patience can help us live into answers or at least into a more spacious perspective.

If we don't express doubts about the status quo, why would we ever change anything? If we don't question hardened habits and set patterns, we can't grow more fully into what we might become. If we can't confront our brokenness, how can we heal toward wholeness?

One spiritual tool for facilitating the quest for questions I call the Pause Practice. The process begins by noticing an emotional surge—a rush of impatience, the tightening of the jaw, an exasperated sigh, a frown of frustration. Before rushing to blame or judgment, take a deep breath and accept the fact that we are human beings with human responses. Summon the courage to ask: *What is happening here? What in me is so reactive and why? What fear is being triggered? Do I need to express my feelings with proper boundaries and a generous dose of kindness? Or, can I smile with thanks that I've just been given a sterling opportunity to learn something about myself?*

Our reliable inner compass provides all manner of emotional responses and physical cues to what happens around us if we'll stop to notice. This practice helps us pause long enough to ask questions that can lead us toward wisdom and awareness.

Reflect: The next time you feel an emotional surge, stop and question its origin. If it's negative, ask the questions above. If it's a surge of positive delight, ask what place of joy it touched inside you. Either way, you learn something.

JULY 30 • *Fruits and Fellowship*

The fruits of the Spirit don't grow in a vacuum. Though we may plant the seeds in moments of quiet contemplation with God, we work out the growth in the tussle of daily living—especially as we bump up against other human beings!

Our impatience with a trying person can make us aware of our need to develop patience. Being in a loving relationship teaches us what it means to love. A person's kindness to us will more likely infect us with his or her "disease," and the contagion spreads in a ripple effect of thoughtfulness.

Interaction with others is the arena where we test and hone our fruits. One of the greatest spiritual disciplines in life comes in marriage. Living with another person 24/7 offers a proving ground for the validity of the fruit. So does parenting. So does friendship. So does being in an office or a church or a fellowship group. In the give and take with other strugglers, the fruits reveal their juiciness. Without that interaction, those admirable virtues are simply a list of ideals.

So move fearlessly into the fray of human contact. Take the risk of relationship. That's where the fruits of the Spirit grow nourishing food for others and for ourselves.

Reflect: Think about the presence of spiritual fruit in your personal relationships, in your interaction in groups, and with strangers.

JULY 31 • *By Their Fruits You Shall Know Them*

It's been said that service is the rent we pay for the space we occupy on this planet. These words remind us that the fruits of the Spirit do not exist for our solitary satisfaction only. By their very nature, those virtues reach out to bless those around us. They are meant to enrich the common good.

Though love, joy, peace, patience, kindness, generosity, faithfulness, gentleness, and self-control start as seeds in the soul, their fruit is scattered along our spiritual path in every act of mercy, every comforting gesture, and every sacrificial deed. They also bear witness in our politics and our religious attitudes. We live them out, not only in the way we treat the person in front of us, but in the perspectives we hold toward the entire world, including those who differ greatly from us:

- Those of other religious faiths
- Those whose culture is foreign to us
- Those who don't seem to deserve our goodwill
- Those who are difficult to love
- Those who have wronged us

When the fruits extend to the least of these—to the unlovable and to the stranger—we then will know that the harvest is near.

Reflect: Resolve to be a blessing to all around you—near and far—in everything you do, say, and are!

August

A CHANGE OF PACE

"'Martha, Martha, you are worried and distracted by many things; there is need of only one thing. Mary has chosen the better part.'"
—LUKE 10:41-42

BREATH PRAYER
God of the sabbath, . . . I rest in you.

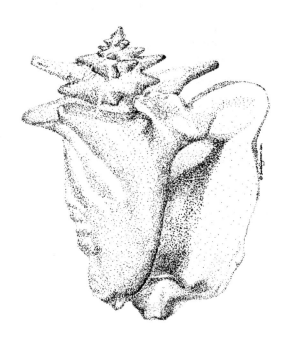

AUGUST 1 • *The One Thing Necessary*

A beach umbrella . . . a hiking stick . . . a good book. Sometimes we need a stoplight to bring our personal traffic to a halt—a respite from the bustle of productivity and packed agendas. Like Martha, our distractions are particular and plentiful: work demands, family dramas, daily chores, or just plain old weariness. It's time to take a breather from the treadmill we're running on. A change of pace can reset the clock and renew the spirit.

August is that special vacation time for many people. Like children in a calendar countdown to Christmas, grown-ups tick off the days to the magic moment when the regular grind stops grinding. Whether on a luxury cruise or cuddled in a cozy log cabin, strolling the surf or hiking the desert, every vacationer dreams of his or her own personal version of R & R. As we head to the beach or the mountains, or wherever we can afford to go, our need for spiritual nurture travels with us.

This month we'll visit a number of venues—in imagination, if not in actuality. We will allow those getaway places to spark some spiritual significance. Rather than get caught in a merry-go-round of tours and theme parks, taking time apart with family and friends in natural settings can give us an opportunity to *be* instead of *do*. We can revitalize important relationships, pausing for honest-to-goodness eye contact and shoulder squeezes. Slow, rambling conversations can bubble up. We can bask in the joy of sitting silently side by side and reading an entertaining novel. Or simply sitting, noticing, breathing, being.

Solo vacationers often retreat from life's tempo to renew their relationship with the Creator. In extended sabbath time, they—like Mary—can focus on the "need of only one thing," sitting at the feet of Jesus, remembering that we are loved simply because we exist. We don't have to prove anything or produce anything to receive that gift beyond all measure.

Whether you go around the corner or around the world, allow a change of pace to give you the spiritual surge you seek.

Reflect: Think long and hard about what a vacation signifies for you. Increased activity? Sports? Educational opportunities? Plan a time apart that might serve as spiritual renewal as well as fun.

AUGUST 2 • *Sea Salt*

I was standing waist deep in the surf, relishing my first moment at the seashore, when a giant wave somersaulted me. Sputtering and gulping for air, I surfaced with a briny taste in my mouth—a salty reminder of other kinds of saltiness. "He's the salt of the earth." "She's really worth her salt." "Take it with a grain of salt!" "I need to salt something away for my retirement." Jesus called his followers "the salt of the earth" (Matt. 5:13). What is it about this ordinary, basic element that could be significant enough to warrant so many meaningful metaphors?

- Value—In ancient times, salt played multiple roles. People used it as a trading commodity in the marketplace, a unit of exchange. Roman soldiers received a salt allowance as part of their pay. For reasons of health and commercial value, salt mining was vital to the life of the community.
- Preservative—Salt has long been used to preserve food, preventing decay.
- Healing agent—Do you ever gargle with salt water to soothe a sore throat? Salt has disinfectant properties and healing effects.
- Balancing properties—As a dietary mineral, salt regulates the fluid balance in our bodies.
- Seasoning—Salt brings out the inherent flavor of foods, adding zest and enhancing taste.

But what is its spiritual significance? When we describe a person as the salt of the earth, we usually mean someone who is unpretentious, uncomplicated, loyal—a "what you see is what you get" kind of person. Certainly those folks add value to the lives of others. They preserve virtues like kindness and honesty. Their straightforward qualities have a cleansing, healing effect in their relationships. They bring a balance between pride and humility. And for sure they add seasoning to society, not only by their own zestiness but by enhancing the flavor of others.

Reflect: Ponder what it might mean for you to be "the salt of the earth." How can you add value, prevent degradation, and lend balance and flavor to the lives of others? Find ways to retain the flavor and fervor of your own "saltiness."

AUGUST 3 • *Sand in My Shoes*

It was a windy day at the beach. Gusts blew tiny grains of sand every-where—between the pages of the book, into the fresh lemonade, around the tangles of my hair. Sand is messy.

Strange as it may seem, the grittiness of it provoked a disturbing thought in the corners of my soul. It bumped up against the orderli-ness—the "cleanliness" if you will—of my life at the time. The days were pretty predictable and uncluttered. I spent hours in solitude, writing a book, preparing lectures for presentation, studying, researching. Sure I attended church, cooked meals, and took care of business, but was I living too much in an ivory tower, aloof from the disorderly needs in the world around me?

Sometimes we maintain a comfortable distance from the distress of others, immersing ourselves in our little world, preoccupied with our own pursuits and demands. We hear the cries of the lonely, the disadvantaged, the hungry and hurting souls, but we remain safe in our surroundings, somewhat protected from the chaotic existence of others.

The sand in my shoes chafed against my skin and my conscience, reminding me of the untidiness, the scruffiness, the nastiness portrayed on the evening news and the morning paper. Maybe I needed to get my hands dirty in the messy lives of those around me—in my relation-ships, in my community, in the cares of the needy. Maybe I was avoiding something. Sometimes God sends a message. Sometimes God uses sand.

Reflect: Consider the balance in your life between maintaining your personal responsibilities and being engaged in service to others. What, if any, changes do you feel called to make? What messiness do you choose to hold at arm's length?

AUGUST 4 • *Treasures of the Tide*

Even though I strolled along the same stretch of beach every morning, it was never the same. One day the sea emptied up a scattering of starfish, the next offered fresh sand dollars, then tangled masses of seaweed—all from unknown origins.

An ordinary day can resemble my beach experience. It begins as a predictable expanse of time, only to be punctuated by the unexpected—a phone call from a frantic friend, a forgotten five-dollar bill in my coat pocket, a tumble down the front porch steps. We rarely know what's coming next. Like the sea offering up its daily treasures, life unfolds with startling surprises, twists, and turns that demand the pliability of our spirits, an ability to bend without breaking.

Perhaps the key to living one day at a time is to keep our eyes on the horizon, our souls in touch with a mysterious perspective, a bigger picture. We often see life as a series of setbacks to be overcome rather than an erratic adventure that evokes laughter as well as woe. Thank God, we are not alone in this fluctuating journey. The same unseen force that scatters shells on the seashore undergirds our spirits to deal with what flows onto our personal stretch of beach. That loving Source enables us to notice each bit of trash or treasure, accept it for what it is, and decide what to do with it. Rather than an endless lesson in endurance, life can be a meaningful quest toward seeing the face of the holy in everything that comes our way—not in the sense of causing each event but in companioning each moment.

Reflect: What will surface in your life today? Take a brave, deep breath, and plan to greet it with grace. Like the surf, flow with the tide.

AUGUST 5 • *The Oyster's Opinion*

Ask the lowly oyster for some advice, and he would probably say, "Just hang in there." When a tiny, uninvited object—a parasite, a chip of shell, a grainy bit of sand enters the shell of an oyster, it becomes part of the oyster's life from that moment forward, causing pain and irritation. Sort of like the gritty things in our lives—from minor annoyances to life-altering tragedies—they come to stay and become a part of who we are. But nature tells us that oysters simply keep on keeping on, continuing to be who they are. They integrate the unbidden irritation. They don't become hard and leathery in order not to feel. They continue to trust themselves to the ocean, to open and breathe in life so that a miraculous kind of growth can occur. But it doesn't end there.

The oyster patiently wraps the provocative irritant in thin layers of pearl, and over time the miracle happens. In the spot where the oyster became most vulnerable to its pain, a valuable creation develops—a pearl. Not all oysters respond to suffering in this way; not every oyster produces this treasure. But those that do fulfill part of the purpose for their existence.

Everything that happens to us can become grist for the mill of our spiritual growth, a potential pearl. The pain can become a catalyst for awakening our values and vitality. Of course we don't wish suffering on ourselves or anyone else, but we can ultimately find gratitude for the pearl, if not for the event that produced it. Transforming suffering into wisdom is a painstaking process. But if we offer ourselves to that amazing work, we will be left with a deeper sense of life's value and a greater capacity to live it. Now that's a pearl of great price.

Reflect: Think of times in your life when you experienced the oyster's pearl-forming process. What were your grains of sand? What pearls did they eventually produce?

AUGUST 6 • *Song of the Seashell*

She had always done as she was told, even though her soul was silently screaming. He followed in his father's footsteps, even though he had no knack for business. For them and for us, finding our voice can be brave business indeed.

The first time I held a giant conch shell to my ear, the roar astounded me. It seemed as if the shell joined a song of the sea much grander than itself, yet uniquely its own—a powerful and potent natural expression. It brought to my mind the authentic voice that honors the truth within us. That is, if we will summon the courage to put our ear close enough to hear it.

How does the valid voice become muffled over the years? What silences or distorts it so that we learn to ignore its pleas? Throughout our development, we unconsciously erect barriers to its honesty. Usually, in mid to later life, however, its whispers turn to shouts, and we can no longer suppress it. That persistent voice challenges our status-quo thoughts:

- If I say that, my friends will disapprove.
- If I tell the truth about my feelings, my spouse will leave.
- If I talk about my faith, people will think I'm a religious fanatic.
- If I don't agree, they'll regard me as belligerent.
- If I say this or do that, I'll end up alone.
- If I'm afraid of failure, I say "I can't" to mask my unwillingness to act.

We want our discourse to be acceptable to others, our prayers well-crafted and pious, our responses conventional. We ignore our inner voice so often that it becomes an unconscious habit. Of course, we are not to use the authentic voice to badger others with our opinions or to demean them with criticism. Tempering our words with kindness presents itself as an ongoing balancing act. But eventually, muffling or misrepresenting our deep truth becomes too high a price to pay.

It takes courage to speak as boldly as the sound of the seashell.

Reflect: Explore the gap between what you say and what you actually feel. What truth is God inviting you to speak? Take a risk with honesty and integrity.

AUGUST 7 • *The Naked Crab*

Crab shells reveal a multitude of stories about their owners—and about us. Hermit crabs borrow the shelters of others. Some simply discard their shells because the dwelling is too small for its growing occupant. That's how crabs grow bigger. When their shells get too tight, their shell splits open and they grow a new one.

I imagine the process of splitting open a shell must be scary and painful. I'll bet that until they grow a new shell, crabs feel defenseless and vulnerable. That's how we humans feel when we crack open our shells.

While our shells aren't visible like those of crabs, they exist: shells formed by years of habit, shells that protect us from other people, shells of the roles we play. Every now and then, we crack our shells open and emerge into a new stage of life, quivering and defenseless.

Teenagers do this as they become adults. (No wonder they get crabby sometimes!) Adults do it as they learn to quit running their kids' lives or when they get laid off from work, a spouse leaves, an investment fails, a dream disappears. In all these life experiences, we undergo the breaking of a shell and the birth of a new vulnerable life.

Like a crab, the longer that shell has been growing around us, the harder it is to break open, to start again; and the more painful the breaking becomes.

Some of our shells we have worn for generations. Our Christian faith can be a shell handed down by our ancestors. Some faith shells are worth keeping. Others may have become prisons, shells so encrusted with the barnacles of the past, so burdened with trailing weeds, so constricting, that we can no longer move when God calls us to a new venture.

No one looks for painful experiences in life or in faith. To avoid vulnerability, we may prefer to stay in shells that no longer fit rather than risk the vulnerability of leaving them behind.

When a crab's shell becomes too thick, too restrictive, too tough to crack open and start again, then the crab can't grow anymore. And that's when it dies.

And so do we. . . .

Reflect: Recall an event in your life that caused you to break open your shell to risk new ideas or behavior. What growth emerged? Do you feel your present shell beginning to crack?

AUGUST 8 • *Following Footprints*

A grandfather took a leisurely beach walk with a bevy of grandchildren frolicking hither and yon behind him. As he turned to check on their whereabouts, he noticed one four-year-old stepping carefully into each of his footprints, oblivious to everything but putting her foot precisely into the trail he had left behind. Not surprisingly, it set him thinking, about the footprints he was leaving in her life.

To some degree, we step in the footprints of all who have gone before us, not only in our close relational orbits but in the large family of humanity itself. We leave imprints on those we intentionally mentor—like our own children—and those we inadvertently affect, like the server who just placed our dinner before us. Many scientists posit that everything we think, say, and do alters the energy field around us and is shared in ways we can scarcely fathom. The influence of who we are can take our breath away!

An approving look, an encouraging word, a spontaneous smile, can brighten someone's spirit in ways we rarely consider. Recently, our local newspaper carried the uplifting story of a man who stands every morning on a busy street corner for an hour, waving joyously to everyone who passes by. Some drivers deliberately take the lane nearest him to receive his daily blessing! By the same token, a sullen scowl, a sharp retort, or a dismissive glance casts a pall over everyone within the range of its gloominess. We forget the power of our own presence to bless and to curse.

Lest we become giddy with our potential to affect others, here's an fundamental caveat: Though we certainly have influence, we never have control!

Reflect: Remember with gratitude those who have left loving footprints in the sand of your life. Now think of people whose presence makes you feel blessed, even if they don't utter a word. Be mindful today of the footprints you are leaving behind.

AUGUST 9 • *The Water and the Wave*

Few experiences expand my heart like standing at the ocean's edge. I can imagine myself as a dancing wave—individual and unique, cresting and falling—yet a part of the vastness that supports it all. It feels like living at the edge of what I know, yet don't know. My feet are planted solidly, but everything else is in motion.

Even the vista of the horizon has a steadying impact. I remember being told during a bout of seasickness to go on deck and stare quietly at the farthest point I could see in order to recover my equilibrium. Sound advice for the soul, as well as the body. As I gazed at the distant horizon, I felt I could trust in a mystery beyond my comprehension and control.

If we believe we are made in God's image, then some part of God's self is also part of us—like a wave in relationship to the ocean from which it arises. Perhaps, like the wave, we emerge and return to that which birthed us. Though we may sense our individuality, we know we are not the sea itself. Yet spiritually, we are made of some of the same stuff. That said, we realize that in the vast ocean of God's unconditional love, we have a connection not only to the deep but to all the other "waves" that share our humanity. Grace floods our hearts when we know that we are made of love, for love, and will return to love.

So the lessons of the ocean will continue to teach us. The tides ebb and flow in predictable reliability. The horizon remains constant and trustworthy. The depth beneath the surface turmoil retains its calm. Somehow, it all speaks of God.

Reflect: Imagine yourself standing on the beach. Sense the vastness of the ocean, and allow its messages to soothe your soul.

AUGUST 10 • *Desert Drought*

Make straight in the desert a highway for our God" (Isa. 40:3). Time in a desert environment can awaken a broad spectrum of spiritual experiences—barren times, oasis moments, loneliness, sudden beauty—a host of paradoxes reflected by the landscape itself with its burning days and cool nights, its bursts of green against palettes of brown. But most of all, it speaks to us of dryness.

Spiritual dehydration creates a desolate feeling. "I felt an emotional flatness, a disconnection from God," the minister remembered. "I couldn't sense any inspiration for my sermons. My prayers—that is, when I could make myself pray—seemed to bounce off the ceiling. I questioned my vocation. Why was I doing what I was doing? It was terrible. . . . I was as dry as a parched desert."

Most of us can describe our own version of desert drought—when doubts assail us, when dark thoughts chase away all cheer, when we feel separated from the Holy One. It feels as if loneliness invades every dimension of our lives, and we wonder what to do. So what can we do?

There are no easy answers, of course, and no quick fixes. We can begin by acknowledging the feelings without blame, especially the blaming of ourselves. We can accept the drought as part of the journey that reminds us of the precious sense of connection and forces us to admit our inability to sustain it. Though no formula will make the dryness immediately disappear, here are some pointers that will pave a path back to the Living Water:

- Stay spiritually hydrated. Keep showing up for times of prayer, meditation, spiritual reading, worship. Continue to engage in the disciplines that have borne fruit in the past.
- Try at least one new spiritual practice to stir the spirit a bit—prayer beads, walking meditations, some new approach.
- Memorize a helpful verse of scripture or meaningful affirmation and repeat it to yourself throughout the day.
- Seek out those who care about you, and be honest with them about your feelings. Find a reliable spiritual companion or director to accompany you through the desert drought so that the feelings don't fester.
- Be willing to examine beliefs that may no longer hold truth for you. Bravely seek new revelation that resonates in your soul.
- Be of help daily to someone who needs your presence or service.

Remember that God created us as relational beings, and our willingness to be real with one another is more crucial than appearing holy. That includes being real with the God from whom we feel separated.

Reflect: Slowly read Psalm 139:1-18. How does that passage speak to you in a period of desert drought?

AUGUST 11 • *Drenching Monsoons*

On the rare occasions when rain visits the desert, it often comes in abrupt downpours—soaking monsoons. We can have the same experience in our lives as grace soaks our parched souls.

Crises surrounded Dorothy like circled wagons as her husband battled cancer. Even though he was in home hospice care, he still required her constant attention. She was sleep deprived, financially strapped, and suffering her own health decline. Then the monsoons brought life to her barren desert.

I noticed a difference in her countenance when she opened the door. I had come by to bring an encouraging word and a bowl of chicken salad, expecting to find her in the throes of despair. Instead, she exclaimed, "I've never experienced such an outpouring of love!" The congregational care group at her parish had arranged a steady delivery of meals. Old friends from far and near were showing up to visit and share memories with her husband. A caring professional was helping her sift through the web of insurance entanglements. Someone came forth with surprise cash. A priest came to serve the Eucharist on a regular basis. Prayer groups were calling her name. She felt saturated with support of every kind.

When love drenches a dry spirit, even the most desperate person can burst into bloom. Though our small acts of support may seem like a drop in the bucket, together they can form a monsoon of grace. In situations like Dorothy's, communities of faith can become streams of living water.

Sometimes we can feel grace flooding over us for no apparent reason. At a time when Alice was coming to grips with her life as a single woman, despairing that she would probably never find a mate in her seventies, she described the moment when an incredible peace swept over her. "I was sitting on my porch with a cup of coffee, when suddenly the light on the trees outside brightened, and the sun poured on my face. With it came an assurance that everything would be okay, that my life would still be worthwhile and meaningful. It was as if the same Light that warmed the trees was warming my heart. What a gift it was!"

No matter how the monsoons come to us, they swell the spirit with overwhelming gratitude.

Reflect: When have you felt drenched with love? In what specific ways did it come to you? Think of someone to whom you can provide a measure of comfort this day.

AUGUST 12 • *Alone in the Desert*

In interviewing folks about their greatest life challenges, the recurrent problem of loneliness occupied center stage. Many people experience being alone as a kind of desert, like being abandoned in dry, desolate terrain. However, being alone and feeling lonely are not necessarily the same thing. We can feel lonely in the middle of a crowded party, but sometimes solitude can surround the soul like a cozy blanket. It depends on our perception and reception of it.

Learning to receive aloneness in a healthy way includes the perception that ultimately each of us is alone. Every married couple knows that inevitably one of them will be left standing. Embracing that condition without resentment or resistance takes considerable courage and a lot of intentional action. Thoughtful people told me it was necessary to focus on the up side of living alone rather than the down side (which normally grabs the lion's share of attention.) One person shared a list she had begun about the joys of flying solo:

- Eating what you want when you want to
- Listening to the music you really like and turning up the volume
- Having a choice between cuddling up with a good book or mingling with the concert crowd
- Turning on the light at 2 a.m. and watching an old movie
- Learning to value privacy over loneliness
- Learning to appreciate your own company

The best cure for loneliness is solitude. While loneliness defines the *pain* of being alone, solitude defines the *richness* of being alone. Intentional solitude invites us to be real about ourselves to ourselves and to face the dismantling of our self-delusions. In a strange and glorious way, the desert journey of solitude introduces us to ourselves and makes us more keenly aware of our connection to God.

Reflect: Ponder the ways you deal with your alone times. Do you run from them in panic mode? Do you turn on the TV for company? Plan a time, even if it's brief, to be alone and quiet. What inner chatter do you hear?

AUGUST 13 • *Bursts of Beauty*

After growing up in the lush greenery of the Southeast, my first trip west stunned me. The landscape looked like an endless expanse of brown hues. Of course, that was before I saw the red rocks of Sedona or the purple sunsets in the Big Bend country. Desert territory produces its own palette of colors.

No matter what barren landscape of life we might be traveling, bursts of beauty can coax our gratitude out of hiding. The desert taught me that lesson as I floated on my back through the Santa Elena Canyon section of the Rio Grande River in southwest Texas. It had become so sweltering during our raft ride that the guide suggested we rafters float in the river alongside the raft to cool off a bit. Even though the muddy water seemed uninviting, its wetness tempted us overboard. So, over the side I went.

Up until that moment, the vistas had been interesting—pretty in a desert sort of way—but hardly spectacular. Layered rock formations formed an array of angles and textures against a bright blue sky as we snapped the predictable photos. But when we started through the canyon floating on our backs, the scenery changed. We saw a whole panorama of life and color underneath the massive monoliths up to fifteen hundred feet high. On the underside of the rocks, birds swooped from their nests, iguanas slithered across the stones, plants somehow found life from the evaporating water beneath them. Through some botanic miracle, cacti burst into blossom. I wept at the sheer glory of it.

It may seem quite a leap from that scene of heart-stopping beauty to the twinkling lights in my own darkness, but my heart made that connection. It reminded me to notice, notice, notice the bits of brightness resting underneath the surface "browns" of my life, to be grateful for that light, to cling to it like a blooming cactus to the canyon wall. It all existed together in one scenic, psychic, spiritual whole.

Thank you, Santa Elena Canyon, for your lesson in the beauty beneath the barrenness.

Reflect: Recall the last time you felt barren and colorless. What bits of beauty were hiding underneath?

AUGUST 14 • *Desert Details*

From the air, the desert can look lifeless, like a sea of bland nothingness. However, if you crouch down on the sandy ground and pay close attention (as if you were holding a magnifying glass), you discover a world teeming with life. Ants march in motion, leathery lizards slink toward a cool hole in the ground, petite pink blossoms perch on a spiny stalk. Tiny things make up the whole.

Someone told me once that God is in the details. It's worth pondering. Maybe it says to us that we can't really love humankind without loving the person next door to us. It does little good to fantasize about being rich if you can't pay this month's rent. There's no integrity in preaching against injustice in the Congo while ignoring it in your community. It isn't likely that we'll develop a heart of wisdom without paying attention to the daily lessons in our lives. We won't build a strong spiritual center without devotion to spiritual disciplines. We form a gracious soul by walking the soul's path in small steps.

Desert details point to the beauty of simplicity—a waxy yellow bloom on a scraggly cactus, a welcome spot of shade to buffer the sun's heat, a cool cup of water on a scorching trail. But so often, we overlook the simple in search of the spectacular. A person on the path to spiritual maturity may take interest in big things but finds joy in small ones.

Reflect: Focus on the seemingly insignificant aspects and occurrences of your life today. Value them. Vow to perform the tiny tasks in your day with great love.

AUGUST 15 • *A Burning Bush in the Desert*

There the angel of the Lord appeared to [Moses] in a flame of fire out of a bush; he looked, and the bush was blazing, yet it was not consumed" (Exod. 3:2). Moses wasn't doing anything particularly spiritual or special. It was an ordinary day on his ordinary desert path going about his ordinary business of tending sheep. Then something unusual grabbed his attention—a burning bush. To his credit, he stopped. He noticed. He wondered about what it meant. Then he heard a voice calling to him, saying, "Moses, Moses! . . . Remove the sandals from your feet, for the place on which you are standing is holy ground" (Exod. 3:4-5).

I was emptying the dishwasher when a burning-bush moment stopped me in my tracks. The phone rang, and it was a book editor inviting me to write a book for them. My response was much like that of Moses: "But I'm not a writer! Besides, I'm sixty-four years old, and it's too late to start down a new path. Plus, I don't have what it takes!" During the weeks of discernment that followed, I knew I had to trust that the One who provided this opportunity was the One who would enable me to do it. In my kitchen that day, I had indeed been standing on holy ground. It changed the course of my life.

Not every burning-bush moment is that dramatic, of course. Sometimes the Voice calls in a whisper, we feel it in a nudge, or words continue to enter our thoughts with the same persistent message (the bush keeps burning). We probably pass by many a burning bush every single day and don't stop to feel the heat. Or, even if we do, our list of excuses and reasonable resistance force us to keep walking.

We tend to expect these communication flashes when we're in worship or on retreat or deep in prayer. But for most of us, most of the time, it happens during the course of daily living when we least expect it. We are invited to turn from our busyness to notice the nudges. They may be calling us to a fresh insight, to a higher calling, or simply to an awareness that the ground on which we stand is steeped in holiness.

When the Spirit nudges you, it's a good idea to pay attention.

Reflect: In what settings do you usually hear the voice of the Holy? Remember the burning-bush moments in your life and resolve to open your heart to more burning invitations from God.

AUGUST 16 • *Riding the River*

There is a river whose streams make glad the city of God, the holy habitation of the Most High" (Ps. 46:4). During years of vacation time on the Spring River in Arkansas, I found that the river had much to teach me. It began with a simple canoe.

Canoes and currents need to work in tandem; it's a both/and situation. You recognize the power of what's moving beneath you, and you ride with it, not against it. However, you still have to do your part—paddling to steer clear of logs and rocks and keeping within the banks—but you cooperate with the dynamic force that already exists. Riding the divine currents of life is a lot like that. When we put our "canoe" into the flow of God's purposes, we still have to participate by paddling, but we're supported by a force much greater than our little boat. And there's an extra bonus. When we make a miscue and tip over (and we usually do), we can bravely climb back in and that same reliable current will continue to carry us—mistakes and all.

Our obsession with where we are going and how fast we can get there often hampers our going with the flow. We're eager to reach a preplanned destination, to meet a particular goal—determined to get somewhere through our own dogged efforts. When we ignore the current beneath us, we can impede the progress instead of participating in its power. I know someone who came face-to-face with a health problem that would surely change the course of his life. He fought it angrily, railed against the things he could no longer do, failing to see that the flow could take him down other worthwhile "streams." His journey finally became peaceful when he decided to ride the current with acceptance rather than resistance.

It can be a joyful journey when we flow with the divine current, the power that carries and sustains our life.

Reflect: Examine your times of resistance today, those moments when your spirit is fighting something inevitable or you are complaining about circumstances you can't change. What would it look like to ride the river?

AUGUST 17 • *River Banks and Boundaries*

When a raging river overflows its banks, it usually means trouble. The water can spread anywhere it wishes, rushing harum-scarum onto other people's property. Doesn't that remind you of the havoc we wreak when we do not set and respect the boundaries in our lives? When we become swamped in business that is not our own?

Setting proper boundaries follows some basics that can guide the flow of our lives:

- Decide where the boundaries are. This need not mean we are rigid or fail to grant leeway to others; it simply indicates an awareness of when lines get crossed that compromise our honesty or genuine feelings.
- Refuse to accept recurring poor behavior. When we continually make allowances for unhealthy behavior or tolerate toxic communication, we're not helping ourselves or the other person.
- Be responsibly assertive. Assertiveness implies clear communication, not verbal assault. For instance, if someone repeatedly shouts at us or demeans us, there comes a time to state our concern calmly and seek an agreeable solution.

- Learn to say no. If we'd rather not, if we're exhausted, if it goes against the grain, say no. No need for a lengthy explanation or for engaging in self-blame because we think we let someone down.
- Learn to say yes. If someone volunteers his or her help, and we need it, say yes.

Just as the banks of a river keep the water flowing smoothly, so our own boundaries can help control the chaos in our lives. Setting limits is an honest undertaking that results not only in more respect from others but in more respect for ourselves.

Reflect: Examine the boundaries you have at home and at work. Notice ways that you succumb to requests that are incongruent with your feelings or somehow compromise your values.

AUGUST 18 • *Fishing in the Spirit*

I remember sitting with my father, rod and reel in hand, while we fished under a Tennessee River bridge where we could be sure of deep water. Daddy was convinced that a giant catfish awaited us if we cast our bait far beneath the river's surface.

Jesus' disciples liked to fish together too. A story in Luke 5:4-7 describes a frustrating state of affairs in which the group's fishing nets kept coming up empty. Jesus suggested that they cast their nets out into deep water, which resulted in a huge bounty of fish. What a meaningful metaphor for our own "spiritual fishing!"

We rarely catch any worthwhile insights by dipping into the surface water of our lives; we need to plunge into deep waters to snag something significant. In the depths of the unconscious lie the hidden things that can tell us the truth about ourselves. Secret feelings often don't want to be caught. Genuine motives may not be eager to surface. Even heartfelt longings may be buried at the bottom. Dreams may be dying for lack of discovery and attention.

Diving into the deep end of our life experiences gives us the chance to fish for gems of wisdom. As we reflect on our mistakes, triumphs, failures, successes, doubts, and beliefs with courageous honesty, sifting them through the Spirit's net of forgiveness and acceptance, we have a chance to "catch" the lessons lurking there. Who knows—fresh revelations may be swimming toward the surface. We may also bring in one of the biggest prizes in all spiritual fishing—awareness of our God-given nature.

So don't be afraid of what you might find in the mysterious murkiness below the surface. Love awaits you—ready to help you cast your net into the deep.

Reflect: Imagine yourself on a quiet river bank, casting your net into the water of your life. What do you catch? Ask the Spirit to help you filter out your challenges, your gifts, your blessings, your wisdom and integrity.

AUGUST 19 • *Bridges*

I've walked across the Spring River bridge countless times. It takes me from the cluster of rustic cabins on one side to the town's grocery store on the other. As it conveys me across the expanse of water, I recall the role bridges play in our lives—both the ones we build and the ones we hope to be. Bridges take us across a chasm, some kind of divide—whether it's between cities and farms, between them and us, between the secular and the sacred, or between where we are spiritually and where we want to be:

- Bridges to the Holy: We usually begin our spiritual journeys with a perception of a yawning chasm between us and God. However, as the relationship deepens, our sensibility of God as "Other" softens to include God as "Inner." Spiritual disciplines, especially prayers of silence and receptivity, increase our awareness of the Spirit that permeates everything, including human beings. Meditating on Jesus' promise that he and the Father will "make [their] home" in us (John 14:23) or that "the kingdom of God is among [us]" (Luke 17:21) can help shrink the divide until it disappears.
- Bridges to ourselves: In the life of the soul, we need bridges to span the gap between what we desire and what we actually do. It's one thing to affirm an idea, to believe in it; it's quite another to embody it. (Paul talked about willing one action and performing another in Romans 7:15). Prayerful self-monitoring can be the bridge that shows us when we're sabotaging ourselves; when our

thoughts, words, and actions are deepening the divide, and when they align with the law of love.

- Bridges to others: As disciples of Jesus, we are called to be bridges. Polarization is a reality, not only in our politics but in our personal relationships. Bridging gaps between people requires accepting the existence of another's point of view and crossing the divide with communication and compromise. This acknowledges the reality of you and me, while affirming the hope that can be us.

With grace as our partner, let us take on the task of building bridges and being bridges.

Reflect: Consider specific ways you can embody the concept of bridging the gap within yourself, in your relationships, in your community, and with God.

AUGUST 20 • *A Path of Light*

I woke up early that morning with a heavy heart. A dear friend was facing a life-threatening illness, a personal relationship had some serious kinks to work out, a vocational crisis was looming, and more violence had erupted in the Middle East. Not a peaceful way to start the day.

Walking the path to the river's edge, I wanted to pray but felt stuck for the right words. As I sat down, the sun rose through a soft mist, and I watched it slowly form a path of light across the water. In my imagination, I traveled the path from my bench on the bank into the strip of sunlight till it ended in the blazing sun. A prayer pattern presented itself.

I imagined a glowing white chair at the end of the path, bathed in shimmering light. Some mysterious inner whisper encouraged me to place each person, each concern—one at a time—into the radiant chair for healing. No words, no instructions, no pleading to the Spirit—just trust that a Presence wiser than myself was hearing my prayer. It felt powerful and peaceful and trustworthy.

For weeks, I followed that pattern of intercession, each time experiencing a calm release of my anxiety. Then, another surprising prompting bubbled up from somewhere, "Don't forget to place yourself in the gleaming chair too." I had overlooked the obvious—that I too needed healing love to light up my life.

In the years since that moment of grace, I have returned to the path of light many times. It continues to shed its calm warmth and to free me from having to pray "right."

Reflect: Sit in quiet for a few moments, and allow a prayer image to arise from your heart.

AUGUST 21 • *Muddy Water*

A middle-of-the-night downpour had pounded the river, stirring up the silt, shifting the bottom, muddying the once-clear water. It reminded me of the muddiness of spirit that sometimes envelops us—times when thoughts jumble, decisions become clouded, and we feel as if we're living on a sea of sludge. Ugh. It isn't as if life stops—no, we keep rushing from task to task, functioning reasonably well. But we approach our tasks with a sluggishness that takes its toll on soul and body. The only way to still the swirling is to stop.

Stop and ask what the muddiness is about, why its tiny specks of dirt have added up to this confusion. Am I moving so fast that my feet are creating this mixed-up mess? Am I pursuing too many worthy projects? too few? Are unresolved conflicts churning around? Free-floating anxiety about something unnamed? Have I lost touch with life-enhancing values? Is there a feeling of separation from the sacred that shifted my solid ground, as if my feet could no longer touch the bottom?

Sometimes we have to remain very still in a muddy puddle for a long time before the silt settles; only then can we see the bottom again. In like manner, our being still in spirit places our feet on a firm foundation. Practically speaking, a time-out is called for—an hour, a day, a week—when time can be unclocked and undisturbed. Just as river particles slowly drift to the bottom, so our cares and concerns can drift through our spirits until they make themselves known. Solitude, slow breaths, journaling, listening prayers, perhaps a conversation with a caring counselor or friend can help to unclutter the consciousness until the water of our spirits clears once again.

But most of all, standing still until the mud settles provides the key.

Reflect: If your spirit feels cloudy and muddy, take some time today to breathe deeply into grace and see what settles.

AUGUST 22 • *At a Child's Pace*

Out of the mouths of babes and infants. . . . " (Ps. 8:2). One misty morning as I was taking an early stroll beside a lazy river with my two-year-old grandson Andrew, I heard him gasp. Had he stumbled upon a frog or a snake? No, he saw a spider web stretched from one bush to the other across the path. His eyes riveted in wonder on the intricate creation, its precision outlined in sparkling dewdrops.

I stooped down to his eye level as we examined the spider's daily offering of "Victorian lace." We sat there on the ground, oohing and aahing over the skill and persistence of the spider, awestruck at such perfection and artistry. It seemed ironic that the creator of this masterpiece was a creature regarded as ugly and repulsive! Beauty often has surprising origins.

As we talked about the specifics of the spider's tasks, I began to see that the learning opportunity was not for Andrew's ears only. Spiders' yearning to do what they are meant to do is literally programmed into their being. It urges them to climb the branch, release the silk from their body, and cast it into space with utter abandon, confident that it will "catch" somewhere so that they can begin their work. After the leap of faith, they connect one silk thread to another, trusting that a beautiful pattern will emerge.

How amazingly the life of the spirit echoes that process! We risk opening our lives to the Creator in trust, and we too take a leap of faith. We willingly enter a complex process, one spiritual step at a time, and trust that new patterns will form in our lives. And when that task is done, we, like the spider, must let it go and risk ourselves again in the assurance of God's grace, weaving the next pattern of meaning into the web of our days.

As Andrew and I meandered back to the cabin that morning, a final aha stung me where it hurt. I faced the sobering realization that I had walked that same path countless times before and had never stopped to notice the wonder that surrounded me. I had been moving too fast. That leisurely stroll with a two-year-old—an ordinary moment in an ordinary day—had been replete with extraordinary epiphanies.

Reflect: Take a slow stroll with a magnifying glass in hand. Stop, as you are led, and examine the intricate life of a single object—a leaf, a rock, an anthill, a flower. Marvel at the exquisite detail of creation and breathe a heartfelt thank-you that you are part of this astounding web of life.

AUGUST 23 • *Floating in the Spirit*

Remember learning to float in the water? At first, it was hard to trust that the water would really hold us up. We usually would struggle and flap our arms wildly in an effort to keep our noses dry. Finally, at some point of exhaustion, we relaxed our rigidity and—bingo—some magic buoyancy took over and we began to trust the power of the deep.

The same process operates in many of our life struggles. When we let go of our frantic efforts to find joy or happiness, we discover that it visits us unbidden when we immerse ourselves in love and compassion. When we let go of our efforts to please God or earn divine favor, we find that we are loved as we are, where we are. When we feel distant from God, rather than redouble our attempts to deserve connection, we must float in the love of God, trusting that it exists and will buoy us up. Physical or spiritual floating demands skill, but its difficulty lies in its demand that we let go! When we try to make it happen through our own efforts, we soon wear out and find ourselves sinking.

We seem to float fairly well when things are going swimmingly; but when the water gets rough, we frantically try to scramble to the safety of the familiar. We want everything to be normal and predictable. As human beings, we long for a sense of control and manageability. Unfortunately, the currents of human existence don't flow that smoothly. Negotiating the river of our lives involves keeping our relationship with the Living Water alive and allowing the powerful current of God's buoyancy to carry us.

Divine love surrounds us all the time, but we forget it. Like a fish in the river looking for water, we are swimming in God, looking for God.

So simply float in that love.

Reflect: Remember how it feels physically to float in the water with complete trust in its buoyancy. How do you experience those feelings in your spiritual life?

AUGUST 24 • *Mountain Majesty*

The first time I saw a mountain sunset sheathed in every shade of purple, I finally understood the songwriter's lyrics. The strains of the familiar patriotic hymn filled my senses. "For purple mountain majesties above the fruited plain...." I sang along, just like a school girl on the Fourth of July.

Since then, mountain metaphors have continued to swell with meaning in my life. Power and grandeur, peaks and valleys, distant horizons and mountaintops—all burn with spiritual energy and unspeakable beauty. A single mountain can reveal a host of seasons and weather shifts that mirror our lives—patches of lush green, rocky crags, rushing streams, arid plateaus topped with a snowy crown. No wonder mountains have inspired artists to paint masterpieces, poets to pen phrases, and photographers to widen their lenses.

When I gaze at a massive monolith in the distance, it sometimes makes me wonder about my own place in the universe. On one hand, I feel small and fragile—like a tiny speck, a mere wisp in one galaxy, a blink of God's eye. On the other hand, the gracious dominion of a huge mountain makes me feel like I matter, like maybe the hairs on my head are indeed counted! (See Matthew 10:30.) I can feel insignificant in the world, yet supremely significant as a child of God at the same time. Quite a paradox.

As we focus on mountain settings for spiritual revelation, let's receive the gifts of the heights with open hearts and vivid imaginations. From serene summits to plunging valleys, mountains stand tall with inspiration cascading as surely as their waterfalls.

Reflect: If a mountain is not visible from where you are, gaze at a picture that shines with grandeur. Write down the first images, lessons, or questions that occur to you.

AUGUST 25 • *Mountaintop Moments*

Why wouldn't we all love *mountaintop moments?* Just saying the phrase brings a smile to our lips and a lift to our spirits. They are times when vision clears, when life makes sense, when inspiration oozes from every pore. We may feel a flash of loving and being loved, of gifting and being gifted, of being a cherished part of the grand scheme of things.

We need not be actually standing on a summit. We may be . . .

- Filled with a rush of devotion as we watch a sleeping loved one.
- Overcome with gratitude at landing a new job.
- Witnessing the birth of a child or the death of a parent.
- Moved to tears while singing a familiar hymn.
- Inspired by a rash of colors on a canvas.
- Surprised by a sense of holy presence.

Whether it's a dramatic event or an ordinary experience in an ordinary day, mountaintop moments bring gifts of grace. We honor those instances by noticing them with our entire being. We also honor them by writing them down so that we won't forget them. They represent treasured times atop some spiritual summit, where we stand lost in the vista of wonder around us. Though we won't remain at that altitude, the inspiration can invigorate us during more mundane moments.

Reflect: Purchase a journal to contain your highest moments. Record as much detail as you can to rekindle their electric energy over and over again.

AUGUST 26 • *Down in the Valley*

The old folk song describes the condition well, "Down in the valley, valley so low; hang your head over, hear the wind blow." There can be no mountaintops without the valleys that surround them.

Of course, we would prefer to stay on the top, where the vision of wholeness is visceral, where we perceive that life makes sense. But we eventually leave the rarified atmosphere of mystical moments, and our feet hit the ground of everyday existence. This low-lying terrain winds its way through our days as we walk, sometimes trudge, from problem to problem.

We may enter a valley of illness—a dangerous surgery or a season of chronic pain. The life limitations we discover in these transitions turn into unexpected detours that threaten to derail even the most upbeat spirits.

We may enter a valley of loss—containing everything from death or divorce to the loss of waistlines or wages. Losses of every kind multiply in the valley, especially as we age.

We may enter a valley of deep disappointment—where we face our lives as they are instead of how we hoped they would be. "I wanted to marry, but the right person never came along." "I wanted children, but it wasn't in the cards." "I wanted to travel the world, but I was never able to wander far from home."

When we are dwelling in the "valley so low," sometimes we wonder if the mountaintop even exists. The cloud of despair temporarily obscures the peaks above. Though we cannot see the summit, faith in the unseen keeps hope alive. The continued affirmation that God is indeed with us points the way to gratitude and optimism, even from a distance.

Reflect: Think about what sustains you in the valley times. Refer to your journal of mountaintop moments for reassurance.

AUGUST 27 • *Plateaus*

Plateaus punctuate most mountain climbs. They may seem to eat up valuable time, serving as useless interruptions to our progress. After all, the purpose of the climb (we reason) is to get steadily higher.

In the spiritual life, we may experience a plateau as a condition of being stuck. One spiritual direction client, a devout and committed woman, expressed it like this: "I'm not making any progress at all! I'm stuck in the same old place—the same old me. Have I quit growing? Has God abandoned me?" Her anxiety was palpable.

Plateaus can remind us that we are not in charge. Even though we usually operate under the illusion that we control the process, growth doesn't respond to our management skills or herculean efforts. It doesn't obey our commands to speed up or slow down. We think that if we double down on disciplines, read the Bible more, try harder, we can regain a semblance of control over our own progress. Certainly, blame for the lack of it seems to fall squarely at our feet. Ah, that it were that simple and manageable!

So how do we greet a plateau? How do we engage the apparent blandness of it? First, we acknowledge that our faulty reasoning will land us in a ditch. To label these times the result of God's displeasure or our own laziness follows our compulsion to find an answer—any answer, please! Here are some suggestions:

- We can relinquish ourselves in radical trust to a Power greater than ourselves.
- We can make friends with uncertainty.
- We can continue to have faith in that which we cannot see or explain or control.
- We can look back down the mountain at where we've been and glance with hope at where we're going. (An important caveat here: Don't let yesterday or tomorrow use up too much of today!)
- We can regain a perspective that escapes us when we're striving.

Slow down and relish the present for the precious gift that it is. Plateaus serve a purpose, even if they don't fit our expert analysis or our determined efforts to "figure it out." Our lack of understanding doesn't strip events of their sacred meaning; it affirms the recurrent need to trust a process that we can't control.

Reflect: How does a spiritual plateau feel in your life? Examine the anxiety or doubt that may result. While occupying a plateau, sink into a profound trust in the mystery we call God.

AUGUST 28 • *Switchbacks*

On a mountain hike with my grandchildren, I was oh-so-grateful for the switchbacks—those zig-zag interludes where I could regain my stamina and steadiness. I knew they made for a longer climb, but those moments of respite allowed me to continue the climb. Switchbacks give us a chance to regroup.

The terrain of spiritual growth sports its own switchbacks: The journey is never a steady climb. It's more like three steps forward and two back—the spiritual equivalent of a switchback, I suppose. For instance, the sneaky demon called "sharp tongue" is never banished forever. That trait just returns in more subtle ways, switching back to us. Our tendency to judgmentalism doesn't die a permanent death. True growth just introduces us to those varmints so we can see them coming the next time (and the next and the next), each time a little sooner. It's as if we return to where we were but find ourselves better equipped to deal with the demons.

A switchback slowly brings us back to the same place on the climb, only a little higher. The point of view, if you will, becomes a wee bit clearer. We know where we are and what's happening. I have a similar experience when my nemesis—impatience—revisits (usually wearing a new mask). Maybe instead of my customary lane-switching (trying to reach the intersection before the light turns yellow), the impatience appears as my difficulty in waiting for the pot to boil or an irrational surge of irritation when a person is five minutes late. In situations both large and small, I see her coming more readily than I used to. It gives me a choice. I can say, "Sweetie, I know you're part of my natural wiring, but you're no longer in charge of me. I'm going to settle down with my new friend Patience!"

The switchbacks on our paths give us an opportunity to see not only where we've been but where we are headed.

Reflect: Try to pinpoint the switchbacks on your personal journey. Let them give you a chance to respond instead of react.

AUGUST 29 • *Soaring in the Spirit*

I was clearly out of breath. Sweating and puffing, I stopped on a rocky precipice to regain my strength for the rest of the climb, and then I saw him. A huge hawk calmly rode a gust of wind at my eye level, totally relaxed in his element. He seemed at one with the current of air, allowing it to carry him with abandon.

As a young adult I decided to take flying lessons, and I was a naïve novice. The patient instructor tried to teach me to fly a single-engine aircraft, which I assumed would be a matter of pushing the right controls in the right order. Not so. He insisted that first I understand the basics of aerodynamics, quite a challenge for someone with no background in physics. His recurrent admonishment came back to me, "Don't you see, Linda? The plane is built to fly!" Only after tedious hours of ground flight school did the principle finally click into my consciousness. Just like the hawk, the plane was created to engage the dynamics that already existed, to ride the wind.

I watched the hawk flap his wings occasionally, but for the most part, the wind beneath his wings supported him. How often are we called to quell our frantic flapping and rest on the current that carries us, allowing it to guide our path. We don't create that current; we simply cooperate with it. Sometimes that vital "air support" comes to us through other people when they allow the breath of God to move through them. Sometimes powerfully written words provide the buoyancy. Sometimes a surprising moment of inspiration fuels the resilience we need.

Maybe we too are made to fly. When we are at one with the power of the Spirit, we can relax into that relationship and begin to soar. Just like the hawk. Just like the single-engine Cessna.

Reflect: Go outside and quietly watch a bird in flight. Let the bird provide a lesson in how to ride the wind and soar.

AUGUST 30 • *A Homespun Holiday*

Sometimes a leisurely vacation is impossible when we're surrounded by a world of domestic demands and limited dollars. Besides, a week isn't enough time to provide spiritual nourishment for a year. The spiritual journey is not a sprint; it's a marathon. And we need intermittent "vacations" to sustain us for the long haul.

With a little thought, time, and creativity, we can create our own holiday havens—inspirational environments that provide regular mini-retreats. Find a space in your home to christen as your special space, hopefully where there's a modicum of privacy. If you don't have a room, find a corner. If you have no corner, designate a chair. If you have no indoor space, find a space outside—a bench, a hammock, a folding chair.

Choose a small table, if possible, to hold objects that carry particular meaning for you—a rock, a photo, a seashell, a feather, a child's artwork. If a table isn't available, cover a cutting board with cloth on which to arrange your treasures, and put it on a surface or in your lap. Keep it simple; don't clutter the objects in a jumble; rotate them periodically according to your desire or mood. Give them room to shine. Of course, a lighted candle can remind you of the unspoken prayer that invites the light of the Divine to flood your soul.

Have a journal and pen handy to record questions or insights that drift through your mind as you sit relaxed. The simple act of honoring time and space for communion with God creates an atmosphere of openness and receptivity.

Avoid having a fixed agenda to fill your sacred time. Too much planning may obstruct the free flow of the Spirit. Just show up regularly. Whether it's a minute or an hour or a whole day, God can use it to nurture and shape your soul. Suspend judgment—quelling evaluations such as "Nothing happened; this must not be working" or "I didn't receive any messages or insights, so I've wasted my time." The offering of yourself as a willing vessel is a gift of trust. It can also become an island of inspiration!

Reflect: Whether you're in an exotic setting or in your own backyard, let a change of pace spark your renewal. As you sink into a deeper part of yourself and reconnect to the Spirit, you can express gratitude, offer up struggles, seek wisdom, or simply be available. Will you make that commitment?

AUGUST 31 • *The Thin Times*

Occasionally, we encounter moments that induce a change of pace within us. At these times an awareness that defies explanation visits us, an inner knowing of the existence of something larger than what we see with our eyes. Through the centuries, some have referred to these bursts of perception as thin times or thin places. It's as if the veil between the visible world and the invisible world becomes particularly "thin."

We may experience these highly charged moments in a variety of settings:

- An instance of supreme joy or pathos, perhaps while witnessing a birth or a death.
- Visiting a favorite place of refreshment or renewal, where the soul is uplifted.
- Being surprised by natural beauty.

- Feeling a sudden rush of tears, origin or reason unknown.
- Hearing a piece of music or viewing an exquisite work of art, causing goose bumps.
- Having a nighttime dream where we waken and know that something or someone came through the curtain while our conscious guard was down.
- Feeling the movement of a yet-to-be-born child.
- Experiencing an unexpected depression, a sense of plunging into inner depths that may eventually transform us.
- Standing on a holy site or strolling a mountain path.

No matter what occasion prompts these unannounced epiphanies—whether exhilarating or disturbing—they invite us to attune ourselves to God, to honor the grace of our relationship to the divine dimension of life. We suddenly realize that the invisible is as real as the visible and that our highest human achievement is not reason but reverence.

Reflect: When have you experienced something that you might call a thin time or place? Revisit that feeling of awe and honor it with an interior bow.

September

LETTING GO WITH THE LEAVES

"This one thing I do: forgetting what lies behind and straining forward to what lies ahead. . . . "
—Philippians 3:13

Breath Prayer
Loving Spirit, . . . I release my burden.

SEPTEMBER 1 • *The Lesson of the Leaves*

As the leaves flutter toward the earth during this season, they release their grasp on the branches. It prompts us to wonder what needs to fall away from our own lives. What do we cling to? How can we let it go?

We usually think of loss in terms of the tangible: persons when they die or leave, places when we relocate, or endeavors when we attempt to simplify our lives. But the layers of letting go are much more pervasive than that. We're engulfed in a myriad of intangibles that need releasing. What about our attachment to being right, our illusion that life should be fair, our unspoken requirement that people agree with us? Unless we learn the art of these necessary good-byes and hellos, we will remain stuck in patterns that retard our growth and make us miserable.

All the noted spiritual traditions endorse a key piece of wisdom: Our awareness of unhealthy attachments allows us to travel the road to wholeness. However, as human beings, our spirits buckle under the burden of unrealistic expectations, outworn beliefs, unresolved conflicts, harmful patterns—baggage that weighs us down. Society's expectations packed many of these "bags" for us. Our culture demands success; our churches demand perfection; our egos demand approval. We find ourselves lost in a chorus of competing voices.

It's time to lighten that load by examining and eliminating some of the burdensome baggage. Just as the vista becomes clearer when we gaze through empty branches, so our spiritual sight clears as we release the objects that obscure our vision of the holy. It's more a process than a project, more a way of living our lives than a one-time action. Simple, maybe—but not easy. We must first become aware of what needs letting go—admit it and own it—then release it. It's the portal to spiritual freedom and profound contentment.

The time has come to listen to the leaves and let go.

Reflect: As you move through this day, notice times when you feel burdened, agitated, impatient, fearful. Pray for growing awareness of the things that weigh you down.

SEPTEMBER 2 • *The Clenched Fist*

As soon as we decide to let go, resistance mounts a counterattack and we clench our fists to hold on. Unfortunately, the longer we hold that tight grasp, the more our hands ache.

What creatures of habit we are—so much so that we hold on to the familiar even when it serves us poorly, even when it keeps us stuck. After all, if we let go of what we know and how we habitually react, what would take its place? It's a bit like the flight of the trapeze artist. He lets go of his flying partner and faces a terrifying transition before the next pair of hands appears and he can actually see what's coming. He learns to trust what he cannot yet touch.

This fearful resistance can wear many disguises and deceptions. Excuses spew forth; procrastination comes to visit; we cling to the familiar patterns and stiffen ourselves against change. In an amazing way, when we name the resistance and face it squarely, the door to dismantling it swings open.

A friend's example taught me the power of bringing such inner fears to consciousness. Her resistance manifested itself physically through constricted neck muscles, debilitating back spasms, teeth clenched with tension. Chaos reigned in her home, and she felt powerless to control it. Her desperately ill husband was waging a battle of defiance against doctor's orders—refusing to cooperate with medical advice. Her persistent attempts to cajole, coax, shame, and even beg him to take better care of himself had been soundly rebuffed. Though the implications of his behavior were dire, the situation clearly lay beyond her control. She could support and suggest but not dominate.

As my friend named her own fear and resistance, owning and feeling it, she let go of her illusion of control. The naming that started in her head began to send its healing messages to her body, releasing the constricted muscles. Though the ongoing difficulties remained, her repetitive exercise of "unclenching her fists" made her more available to support her husband in loving ways that he could accept.

Reflect: Tighten your fist, then allow it to slowly open. As you do so, imagine relinquishing the things you can't control. Look at your open hands, ready to receive the grace that God offers.

SEPTEMBER 3 • *Lightening the Load*

My friend's remark was full of frustration, "My life feels so heavy, . . . so burdened all the time. I just want my spirit to feel free!"

Is that sense of a springy step, an uncluttered mind, and a soaring spirit really within the bounds of reality? The wisdom teachings through the ages, as well as the comforting words of Jesus—"my yoke is easy, and my burden is light" (Matt. 11:30)—assure us that it is. As we enter the land of letting go, we can expect surprising detours, emotional land mines, and spiritual challenges. We never seem to run out of things to let go:

- Sometimes we need to let go of a person in order to move on.
- Sometimes we cling to a role that no longer has validity in our lives.
- Sometimes a point of view blocks our growth.
- Sometimes the volume of our own mental and physical clutter threatens to engulf us.
- Sometimes we must release an idea about God so that a fuller faith connection can emerge.
- Sometimes an unrealistic expectation sabotages our joy.
- Sometimes hurts and resentments keep us from experiencing God's forgiveness.
- Sometimes fear of failure and disapproval keeps us from answering the call of our soul.
- Sometimes our limited dreams keep us from joining God's grander dream for us.
- Sometimes we must let go of who we think we are to discover who we really are.

Before we lay down our burdens, we begin by naming them.

Reflect: Imagine you are walking down a road dragging a heavy suitcase. You meet Jesus, who asks if you would like to lighten your load. Stop, open the luggage, and allow him to lovingly go through its contents with you.

SEPTEMBER 4 • *Rhythm of Loss and Gain*

Look around you. The pattern of loss and gain is everywhere! Winter is followed by spring; night is followed by day; death is followed by resurrection.

Consider this same rhythm in life as it follows us from the cradle to the grave. We enter this world by letting go of the symbiosis in the womb. Then, as toddlers, we let go of the safety of a parent's hand to launch out on our own two feet. As adolescents we leave home to experience independence in the outside world. Middle age finds us saying farewell to our younger selves and moving into a new stage of identity. Ultimately, we encounter the final letting go in the experience of death.

Our psychological and spiritual selves get into the act too. We discover that peace of mind comes with letting go of perfectionism, fairness, approval, and a host of other perceived psychic needs that create anxiety. Growth in the spirit requires us to move into God's cycles of revelation and transformation, dying and rising over and over again.

God created everything—from galaxies to trees to human beings—with inherent cycles of loss and gain. But unlike trees, we humans have the wonderful (and terrible!) gift of free will. We can choose to cooperate with this natural divine process, or we can fight against it. We can spend our whole lives refusing to loosen our grasp, or we can open to the future. No matter how fervently we pray, God will not arbitrarily take away what we refuse to release.

If the Creator fashioned the world with these patterns of losing and finding, doesn't it make sense to get in sync with that intrinsic design?

- We have to let go of one breath before we can breathe in another one. Our physical health depends on it.
- We have to let go of a negative thought before a positive thought can take its place. Our mental health depends on it.
- We have to let go of our spiritual barriers before God can help us grow into the fullness of love. Our spiritual health depends on it.

When we live in harmony with divine rhythms, we—and everyone around us—benefit from healing grace.

Reflect: Think of examples in your own life of physical letting go, psychological letting go, and spiritual letting go. Identify any instances of resistance, as well as instances of growth.

SEPTEMBER 5 • *Complexity and Courage*

The letting-go process is not for the faint of heart. As we wade into this complex territory, full of spiritual and emotional conundrums, we will have to confront some of our unhealed wounds and manipulative behavior patterns. In other words, we have to assume responsibility for our own stuff—and that takes courage.

We not only let go of "what they did to me" but honestly delve into our reasons for holding on to the resentment. When we enter spiritual territory, we may uncover prejudices, faulty ideas, phony ways of relating to others—a host of barriers to our wholeness and ability to serve others. We may feel appalled and discouraged by this kind of self-knowledge. However, each tiny step forward brings the satisfaction of shedding baggage, creating a spiritual buoyancy that rewards us for staying the course.

Letting go is also multilayered. We may let go of a particular behavior only to discover the need to let go of the attitude underlying the behavior! For instance, if I'm attempting to release my need for the approval of others, I'm apt to find that underneath lies a lack of self-confidence in who I am as a beloved child of God. I may not be in touch with the inner certainty that I am valued, forgiven, and unconditionally loved by the Creator. Too often our belief in our belovedness is a matter of lip service, not profound knowing. Others may hurt us, disappoint us, or disapprove of us, but they can't dislodge our core identity as children of God.

Sounds like hard work, doesn't it? A natural question arises: Is this our work for God or God's work in us? The answer is yes, yes. We must enter the dance of being both active and passive, willing to do our part,while maintaining receptivity to the Spirit's work in and through us—a delicate balance indeed.

So, letting go is not denial or condoning hurtful behavior. Letting go moves beyond behavior modification or being above it all. Letting go loosens our grip on attachments—a profound spiritual process that removes barriers to our communication with God. We make ourselves available to serve a marginalized and hurting world. We enter the inherent process of loss and gain that shapes our entire lives.

Reflect: Spend some time in prayer as you contemplate this complex process of letting go, and open yourself to new awareness about what you're clinging to. As you randomly encounter moments of grasping, begin to write them down.

SEPTEMBER 6 • *Letting Go—Chance or Choice?*

Many letting-go circumstances are thrust upon us. A dear one dies; someone asks for a divorce; work requires relocation to another city; an adult child moves across the country; a medical emergency sidelines us. No matter what the situation, it may lie beyond our control.

But we can control one aspect—our response. Once our system has absorbed the shock and we have owned the feelings, we stand at a cross-roads. What now? How do we begin to embrace gratitude and growth?

For example, letting go of attachment to a significant person in our lives usually involves a great deal of anguish. But some simple steps can move us toward healing. It helps to affirm every positive aspect we can recall about the person and the relationship, returning to those thoughts repeatedly as we move forward. Even if a marriage has failed, there may be children to cherish and memories to hold dear. We must separate the flowers from the weeds, pressing the flowers into a mental scrapbook and allowing the weeds to wither away.

However, another huge category in the letting-go process entails the things we choose to let go. This requires a different kind of courage, one that calls for intention as well as response. First, we must notice the symptoms of bondage and follow those threads of awareness to their origin.

Sandra came into my spiritual guidance office in a state of anxiety. She exhibited numerous signs: a swinging foot, darting eyes, clasping and unclasping of her hands. She showed less obvious clues too—a sluggish hesitation in her speech, long sighs before replying, a dismissive shrug of the shoulders, a vague sadness underlying her clever comments.

"I'm sure I need to 'let go and let God,'" she sighed, "but I just can't seem to get on with it." She was wound as tightly as a brand new ball of yarn. Part of Sandra's difficulty—and our own—involved coming to the process of letting go in strokes writ large, generalities with no specifics, idealistic goals with no flesh-and-blood connection. In short, few of us can let go unless we get real about exactly what we're clutching. And we have to unravel that ball of yarn one thread at a time.

During the upcoming days, I will suggest some sample threads that you may wish to unravel.

Reflect: Explore your particular signs and symptoms of anxiety—nervous energy, lethargy, physical tics, altered speech patterns, insomnia. Be grateful that your body gives you clues that you may need to choose to release something specific.

SEPTEMBER 7 • *Letting Go of Our Personas*

Someone once asked Michelangelo how he created his incredible sculptures, teeming with soulful beauty. He replied that the statue already existed within the marble; he simply chipped away the excess stone and revealed God's creation. So it is with us. In the process of letting go, we chip away the bits of our false, adaptive selves that obscure the human work of art at the heart of us, miraculously crafted in God's image.

And how do these false layers accumulate? One insidious, unconscious chip at a time. We learn how to survive in our culture, repeating behaviors that get us what we want, that garner approval from others, that fit into conventional society. Through years of adaptation, we identify ourselves with those behaviors and begin to believe that's who we are.

So the masks and roles accumulate, layer upon layer. Some roles may honestly express our true selves; others may simply be familiar. For instance, we legitimately undertake many roles—daughter, son, mother, husband, community leader, caretaker—personas that we consciously acknowledge. Masks, on the other hand, typically involve ways we present ourselves that may be inauthentic to our nature. We've adapted to what works.

People have written volumes about the personas women wear. We're the "steel magnolias" who can cushion everyone's feelings; we can unravel emotional entanglements within the family; we'll take the chicken wing instead of the breast. We say yes when we need to say no and persevere when we need to rest. We may do good things, but if we don the "martyr mask," we make sure that everyone knows how hard we've worked and how much we've sacrificed and how tired we are!

Our culture encourages certain personas for men too. There's the stoic cowboy image marching into the frontiers of life, slaying the outlaws, and rescuing damsels in distress. Society applauds those who pull themselves up by their own bootstraps, work tirelessly, and provide lavishly. Men are encouraged never to doubt themselves, never give up, never cry. The man with the most toys wins. And the real self, including the vulnerable side, often stays hidden behind a tough-guy façade.

Our task involves thoughtful discernment about what fits us and what doesn't. Only then can we decide whether to let it go. Awareness precedes action.

Reflect: How do you project yourself to the world around you? Notice the prevalent personas that have become an unconscious part of you: the good girl? the competent businessman? superwoman? perfect father or mother?

SEPTEMBER 8 • *Releasing the Personas of Others*

Sometimes we won't allow our perception of people to change. We cling to our past judgments, our old ideas of who they are. We recite their misdeeds once more. We set their character in concrete. We brand them with indelible labels such as *slacker, stupid, sinner,* and countless other negative name tags. Conversely, our positive labels—*perfect, brilliant, holy, beautiful*—can be equally insidious. All pigeonholing limits authentic personhood.

The stories of Jesus, on the other hand, abound with second chances. Jesus invited the woman at the well to new life when he urged her to let go of the community's stigma of a loose woman (John 4). Jesus astounded Nicodemus by telling him that he must "be born from above" (John 3:7). Throughout the Gospels, Jesus invited those who were lame and blind to let go of the past and move forward in the newness of God's grace. Can we offer others any less and continue to call ourselves disciples?

Jesus accepted people as they were, where they were. Who among us hasn't wished, "I just want others to accept me as I am"? Surprisingly, we often fail to give others the acceptance that we desire for ourselves. In theory, letting go of our opinions of others may seem easy. In practice, however, we slip into old patterns like "He always does that" or "She'll never change" or "They're lazy and always will be." We must examine our limited idea of who people are in the light of God's view of their potential.

While most of the time we cleave to negative personas of others, an overly positive view can distort as well. We may idealize folks in ways that blind us to the truth of their flaws, putting them on such a pedestal that we don't allow them their humanity. Affirming others is one thing; idealizing them is quite another. It can make them feel boxed in, constricted by our expectations—a kind of psychological hyperbole. Affirmation of good qualities encourages folks. Expecting the best raises the behavioral bar. But we must also give others the freedom to be themselves, to make their own mistakes, with the assurance that we still care about them.

Reflect: Consider honestly your evaluation of those around you. Hold those opinions lightly, and give them the room to grow and change without being bound by your projections.

SEPTEMBER 9 • *Letting Go of Perspectives*

Sages have reminded us that it matters how we see things. There's a clever fable about the man who fell asleep with Limburger cheese on his mustache. It seems that he woke from a nap, sniffed suspiciously, and began complaining about the unpleasant odor in his bedroom. He stalked to the living room, exclaiming, "It smells awful in here too!" In a huff, he burst into the open air of the front porch, concluding, "Gee, the whole world stinks!"

We too take our perspectives with us. We look at life through our own unique lenses, which affects everything we see. Rarely do we have the courage to examine those lenses—those ingrained ways of thinking—to see if we need to clean or adjust them. Doing so can potentially challenge our beliefs and raise questions about long-held opinions. Our perspectives need to open to God's ongoing revelation.

This openness to change requires a certain amount of humor and humility. A mentor of mine, Dr. Herb Smith, former professor of psychology at Rhodes College in Memphis, often amused students with a tattered note he tucked into his shirt pocket and boldly brought to class.

With a twinkle in his eye, he read it to us: "What I'm saying today reflects my current understanding and is not to be confused with the ultimate truth." He embodied a rare willingness to change his mind if and when greater wisdom was revealed to him.

A crucial layer of the letting-go process involves a close examination of the perspectives that filter our view of the world at large and our lives in particular. Our need to have things cut-and-dried, right or wrong, perfect or flawed, can serve as chains that limit our freedom to grow. If we're serious about spiritual growth, then the dynamic movement of the Holy Spirit will continue to expand our understanding of life.

Reflect: What do you cling to as "absolutes" or inflexible ideas? Consider loosening your grip on some perspectives so you can embrace growth as an ongoing adventure.

SEPTEMBER 10 • *The Perspective of Certainty*

Not only do we want to be right about ideas and thoughts, to win the argument, to be on the side of the real truth, but we desperately want to be certain of our stand.

Someone once told me that one of the greatest deterrents to spiritual growth is certainty. Being sure about too many things makes us rigid and unteachable, when we need to be pliable and open to the Spirit's ongoing revelations. We're like the man who answered the preacher's altar call, marched down to the front of the church, fell to his knees, and pledged, "O God, I'm giving my life to you. And to show my sincerity, I've made a long list of all that I'm going to accomplish for you." Immediately, a booming voice answered, "Is that all?" The embarrassed man returned to his pew, got out his pencil, and expanded his list. Returning to the altar, he implored God again, "O God, I've added more to our contract." Again the voice replied, "Is that all?" After a third attempt to improve his list of intentions, the voice says in exasperation, "Look, just sign it, and let me fill it in!"

Most of us derive a sense of security from the illusion that we know what the future will hold. Letting go of this illusion leaves a hollowed-out space into which the Spirit can blow fresh air. In this posture of releasing we do not sit in an imaginary "spiritual recliner" and wait for God to speak decisively like the voice in our whimsical story. Instead, our posture indicates participation; we wait and watch in prayerful anticipation, ready to act in concert with divine guidance.

In my experience, God's guidance usually evolves one step at a time. Rather than wait for God to lay out the entire agenda, we're called to take the next step without attempting to control the outcome. We launch out in trust. If we insist on certainty, then why would we need faith? Authentic faith and trust involve the willingness to risk.

Reflect: Think of ways that the perspectives of safety and certainty keep you from growing. God's ongoing forgiveness surrounds you every time you take a brave step forward. Be grateful for divine acceptance and see it for the astounding gift that it is.

SEPTEMBER 11 • *Letting Go of Approval*

I have a friend whose motto is this: "What other people think of me is none of my business." A lofty ideal and cleverly stated, but most of us crave the approval of others. In fact, we want that approval so desperately that it's easy to fall into the trap of deciding what we think others think about us. Then we suppose what they want and expect from us. It's a deadly spiral of projection that leads away from the authenticity we yearn for.

In *The Clear and Simple Way: The Angel Lessons*, author Judith Ann Parsons puts it in plain language: "*It is better to be disliked for who you are than to be liked for who you are not.*" As we let go of our tendency to please, it doesn't take long to discover that the driving force behind such behavior is an insatiable need for approval. We deplete our centeredness by giving away our power in tiny bits and pieces. Before we know it, we have adapted to this or agreed to that and have placed our sense of worth in the hands of others. We find ourselves in the precarious place of allowing others to tell us who we are and believing it. It makes chameleons of us.

At what point does flexibility become adaptation? It's a matter of sensing that fine line where we are not being true to ourselves, where we are betraying our honest feelings. Unfortunately, many of us habitually say yes when our silent souls are urging no. We don't want to disappoint others or incur their disfavor. The word *no* is a complete sentence and need not be followed by excuses, manufactured or real, unless we genuinely want to explain.

This need for approval spreads its grasping hands into every part of our lives. Often we don't realize how it subconsciously drives our actions. One serious barrier to being authentic is the psychic presence of questions such as: How am I coming across? Do I look okay? Do they like me?

When we no longer need others to define our worth, we find ourselves in a better position to learn from their opinions. Of course, applause feels better than criticism, but we can benefit from both if we remain centered in who we are. Viewed objectively, affirmation can tell us what we're good at, and criticism may tell us ways we can improve.

As we release our need for others' approval, we can then freely enjoy it when it shows up. Strangely enough, that freedom enables us to love others with greater abandon.

Reflect: Imagine a broad spectrum of opinion, ranging from criticism on one end to flattery on the other. As you stand anchored in the center of the spectrum as a beloved child of God, let go of your vulnerability to either end of the scale.

SEPTEMBER 12 • *I Must Believe It. . . .*

Does the church require that I sacrifice my intellectual integrity? I'm not willing to check my brain at the church door anymore," Richard remarked. He expressed the frustration felt by many genuine seekers of God who want an open and accepting environment in which to explore their spiritual yearning, even if it includes doubt. They agree with the clever analogy that likens the mind to a parachute. It functions only when open.

In the practice of spiritual guidance, I encounter people along all points of the faith continuum—those who are devout, churchgoing disciples and those who are, for one reason or another, alienated from the church. Since part of my task as a spiritual guide is to help folks listen to God's voice in their everyday experience, I am privileged to witness the nature of honest spiritual struggle. And I'm convinced that God does not frown upon honest doubt. It can be the cutting edge of genuine faith.

Some churches welcome a searching spirit of questioning, and some don't. Some perpetuate the idea that merely repeating a series of words or assenting to a creed buys a ticket to heaven. However, mastering the rules, so to speak, is often a far cry from the process of developing a compassionate heart. Jesus gives a more graphic illustration of compassion in action in his parable of the sheep and the goats:

> I was hungry and you gave me food, I was thirsty and you gave me something to drink, I was a stranger and you welcomed me, I was naked and you gave me clothing, I was sick and you took care of me, I was in prison and you visited me. . . . Just as you did it to one of the least of these . . . you did it to me (Matt. 25:35-36, 40).

Beliefs, though they may help us articulate our faith, have little transformative value in and of themselves. We often box ourselves in with doctrine and dogma, some that expand our spirits and some that contract our spirits. Only with testing in the arena of experience can we infuse our creeds with a beating heart. Beliefs must be lived and breathed, not merely spoken.

If you're a member of a church where you are becoming narrower instead of wider, smaller instead of larger, you may want to find another faith community.

Reflect: Slowly repeat a familiar creed from your religious tradition. If you have areas of doubt, find persons in your faith community with whom you feel comfortable exploring your questions. If there is no one, you may want to search for a more open religious environment.

SEPTEMBER 13 • *Salvation and Security*

Sometimes our desire for salvation masquerades as thinly disguised narcissism. At its root, it is often about getting what we want. How can I avoid hell and get to heaven? How many stars will be in my crown? How can I get my prayers answered? How can I garner more blessings? This ego-centered approach is a far cry from the selfless love that Jesus embodied and proclaimed. Beware of self-interest disguised as piety and goodness.

This perspective, a wolf in sheep's clothing, appeals to our basic neediness—to be rewarded and protected from harm. When the psalmist sang praises to God as "my light and my salvation" (27:1) or when the writer of Philippians urged Christians to "work out your own salvation with fear and trembling" (2:12), the authors imply more than securing a spot in Paradise or an invisible buffer against pain and suffering. Salvation calls us to a process of drawing closer to the Source of all, a God whose very character is love. We can grow toward loving and honoring God for God's self rather than for what we can get out of it. We spend a lifetime living out the implications of salvation's meaning—a process designed to save us from our ego-dominated selves.

Think about it. When we turn to God, we often seek peace or healing or faith or heaven or whatever. But when we love God truly, we do not seek God's devotion; we offer our own.

Reflect: Ask the illuminating light of the Spirit to shine on your deepest motives as you pursue your faith journey. Know that the Spirit understands your human needs but desires a deeper relationship of reciprocal love.

SEPTEMBER 14 • *Letting Go of Patterns*

Psychologists have long told us that a definition of insanity is repeating the same behavior and expecting the results to change. Yet we are often slaves to our own repetitive patterns of living.

Throughout our lives, we develop ways of acting and reacting that become entrenched—grooved into our psyches and spirits in ways that put our behavior on automatic pilot. Unless we uncover our particular pathways and summon the courage to let the harmful patterns go, we will repeat the same cycles that prevent our progress. Most patterns start out innocently and unconsciously in the service of our emotional survival as children. Usually we did the best we could, behaving in ways that we hoped would protect us from pain and gain us love. Unless we challenge the patterns, we will regress into those immature sequences.

Years ago, a skilled spiritual director made me aware of a pattern I had never acknowledged. As she attempted to explore my feelings during a discussion of a difficult time in my life, she noticed that I went straight into my cognitive function—analyzing the problem and masking it with words. It had become my vehicle for avoiding pain.

I had no idea that an unconscious pattern had me in its grip. But the director's confrontation cracked open the protective shell around my locked-away wounds, leading the way to some serious healing work. To tell the truth, this natural wiring is still a part of me. I continue to prefer making a list, getting cranked up, and going straight to problem-solving. I remain an extroverted wordsmith who likes to figure something out and nail it with words. However, she taught me to break that automatic pattern, to use the behaviors consciously rather than letting them use me.

To discover the patterns in place in your life, listen to the voices in your head. What recurrent phrases do you use? How do you talk to yourself? What behaviors seem to jump in the driver's seat for no justifiable reason?

Reflect: Pray that the Spirit will nudge you along your personal path of unhealthy patterns. Give thanks that this awareness can lead to letting them go.

SEPTEMBER 15 • *A Perpetual Victim*

We all know the searing pain of being hurt by someone—in body or spirit, with weapons or with words. A sense of victimization can result from many sources—abuse, workplace downsizing, a devastating storm, random crime, plain old meanness. We find ourselves engulfed in anger, blame, helplessness, or a righteous desire for revenge. So why should we let it go if the truth justifies our feelings?

I'm not talking about suppression of legitimate suffering or condoning bad behavior. When we've been hurt by others' actions, we experience visceral pain that requires an outlet. The hurt may demand reparations and action.

However, a subtle seduction of the role of victim can stop our growth dead in its tracks. Over time, we may begin to identify ourselves as perpetual victims, so that a gray cloud of suspicion and blame colors all we do and say. We unconsciously cling to that ID tag called "sufferer" because it engenders sympathy or procures aid. In a perverse way, we can develop over time an ego investment in suffering.

Men and women alike can unknowingly slip into the subtle patterns of behavior that victims exhibit. I know a man with good health, a successful business, money and the time to spend it, plenty of friends—in short, an enviable life. Yet, when asked how he's doing, he recites a litany of complaints about every aspect of his life, as if he were searching every hidden corner for negative material: "Receipts are down at work." "I'm tired all the time." "No one seems to have time to talk anymore." His identity as a victim has become so habitual that he lacks awareness of the gray aura that surrounds him. No matter what happens, he seems caught in a pattern of victimization.

Shedding this perception means accepting what has happened to us as true and ceasing to chew on it over and over again, stirring the feelings into yet another cauldron of emotion. No matter how shattered our lives may be or how they got that way, God's grace works with us to pick up the broken pieces and refashion a future. Through this kind of letting go, we can move from that rigid measuring stick called "fairness" to the flexible one called "forgiveness."

Reflect: Recall a situation in which you have felt victimized. How did you address the situation? Did you bury the feelings? Are you still wearing that badge of a victim? Letting it go can open the door to joy once again.

SEPTEMBER 16 • *Letting Go of Blaming*

The blame game wears a host of clever disguises. "The devil made me do it." "If he helped in the house more, I wouldn't be so exhausted." "Her addiction must be my fault." We want to hold someone accountable for our miseries. If we can't nab a person, we can always invent a mythical man in a red suit, carrying a pitchfork!

Blaming is usually a smokescreen that obscures deeper issues. If I blame someone for mistreating me, I can escape my responsibility for speaking up for myself. If I feel propelled by an evil force outside myself, then I don't have to face the potential for evil inside myself. If I blame myself for all the wrongs around me, I may miss my insecure pattern of assuming "It must be about me."

Self-blaming's insidious nature often wears a mask of humility. It assumes that we can control events that lie beyond our influence. If a loved one is upset or despondent, we wonder what we did wrong, why we didn't fix it, or why we weren't perfect enough or competent enough or loving enough to set matters right. Though we often associate self-centeredness with being self-inflated, it can also be reflected in our deflation—an exaggerated assumption that we cause things to go amiss. When we imagine that other people's moods or madness hinge on our actions, we mire ourselves in codependence and misplaced guilt. We don't possess that kind of power!

Confronting our patterns of blame requires looking situations squarely in the eye and recognizing these patterns in ourselves and others. The illuminating light of the Spirit can enable us to step back, release the automatic rush to blaming, and look at ourselves and others through the lens of grace.

Reflect: Today, be aware of your thoughts and words that carry blame—either to others or yourself, and let go of this pattern of distortion.

SEPTEMBER 17 • *When This Is Over...*

I heard myself muttering again, "In a few more days, this will be over." I eagerly wanted to put the week behind me, even though I was knee-deep in a project I supposedly enjoyed. And I wasn't alone in occasionally feeling this way. I heard my friends' recurrent comments, "When I lose weight.... when I find the right person.... when the kids are grown. ... when the loan is paid.... when I finally retire.... "

Then a recent memory poked me in the psychological ribs. At the theater a few weeks before, I recalled my customary antsyness as I repeatedly checked the playbook to see when the curtain would come down and how I could sneak to the nearest exit before the aisles crowded. Never mind that I had relished the review and paid big bucks for the orchestra seats. My mental pattern involved standing in an imaginary queue, tapping my foot.

My dependable defenses marched forward. My schedule was too full; I had to learn to say no; I needed to slow down. But I sensed something deeper, a familiar recording playing in my head—a pattern of impatient projection that permeated my days. I would often get up in the morning, already looking forward to the evening letdown that I associated with the six-o-clock news, which signaled day's end. That edgy pattern would weave itself through the entire day. I found myself mentally ticking off the minutes, my days cluttered both with what I must do and what I wanted to do. Even though I told myself to focus on what lay in front of me, I had to admit that 75% of me was already moving on to the next thing.

Given my wiring, I will always be a recovering multitasker. I may continue to empty the dishwasher and water the plants while I'm talking on the phone, but my pattern of perpetual busyness deserves a withering look. In fact, I'm beginning to sense that my devotion to productivity is counterproductive to my soul's serenity—a habitual pattern that needs to be let go. I don't want the beauty of life to race past me because my mind has gone somewhere else.

Reflect: As you go about your day, notice each time your mind veers away from the present moment. Bring it back with a smile, not a slap . . . after all, you're a beloved, though flawed, human being.

SEPTEMBER 18 • *Letting Go of Worry*

Can any of you by worrying add a single hour to your span of life?" (Matt. 6:27). In her wise, homespun way, my grandmother offered a sterling comment about worry: Worry is like a rocking chair; it gives you something to do, but it doesn't get you anywhere.

Worry is shrouded in fear, a dark projection of what might or might not happen. It robs us of sleep, of serenity, of hope. I wonder why we usually paint it with a brush of virtue?

It's hard to make a good case for the practice of worrying, though in my family of origin, everybody tried. The women had a way of equating worry with love, and I soon learned to translate their peculiar language of affection. "I've been lying awake all night worrying about you," which actually meant, "I love you enough to worry." In their minds, the greater the worry, the greater the love.

Not only does worry obscure the language of love, not only is it unscriptural, but it's bad for our health. Studies show that people age more by worry than by work. Worry fatigues the brain and sabotages creative thought. It constricts the muscles and inhibits blood flow. It seems to develop a life of its own, repeating the toxic mental pictures that continue to cause consternation. In other words, it can make you sick. Besides, it doesn't do any good.

Part of our problem comes from our failure to distinguish between fruitless worry and appropriate concern. Much of the time, failure to worry feels irresponsible, irrational, even neglectful. I remember my parental fears of my child running into the street, falling from a tree limb, getting behind the wheel of a car. Prudence dictates some preventive action—

safety rules, driving lessons—but hand-wringing anticipation of disaster accomplishes nothing but ulcers. And it absolutely, positively robs us of joy, peppering our thoughts and speech with those telltale words, "What if," and "Watch out—you might hurt yourself!"

A healthy tension will always exist between trust and responsibility. But we know that scripturally speaking, worry and faith are incompatible. In practical terms, we attempt to trust that children will be safe, but we don't leave a three-year-old at home unattended.

Reflect: Notice your own preoccupation with worry today. When does appropriate concern bleed over into paralyzing worry? Read Matthew 6:27, and allow the words to enter your prayers today.

SEPTEMBER 19 • *Letting Go of Pessimism*

The pattern of looking on the bleak side of things slips into our speech, often camouflaged as rationality and intellect. We reveal its subtle signs when we use phrases such as, "Yes, but . . . " and "What if . . . " as we habitually highlight the negative side of people and situations. We hedge our bets in an effort to protect ourselves against the unknown:

- Yes, but they might get mad at me.
- What if it doesn't work?
- What if we get rained out?

Such remarks sprinkled through our communications are like putting the brakes on a moving car, slowing its momentum, keeping it from reaching its destination. Though our "yes, buts" sometimes introduce important exceptions or warnings, most of the time they represent excuses not to move ahead into uncharted territory. In other words, we use "yes, but" in the service of our fear and timidity to avoid taking a risk.

The old adage warns us, "All the water in the world cannot sink a ship unless it gets inside." When negative voices—someone else's or our own—get inside our psychic ships and take over the helm, we can count on a shipwreck.

Every time Greg reaches the edge of much-needed change, he lapses into "Yes, but that's just the way I am, the way Mom and Dad made me." Celeste bemoans her relationship failures, automatically assuming that others will reject her, saying, "What if I visit that church, and no one talks to me?"

This kind of pessimism spreads its toxicity into every aspect of life. It engages the familiar metaphor of the half-empty cup, ignoring the reality that the cup is also half-full. If we truly want to change our "yes, buts" to a resounding yes, we must connect the dots to the inner core of wounding, then choose to let the negativity go. We can say compassionately to that wounded inner child, "I know why you're feeling this fearful outburst, this recurrent pain. I know how you ended up like this, but I'm choosing not to live this pattern again."

Reflect: Notice how your own "yes, buts" put the brakes on your momentum. As you catch yourself in limiting language or fearful doubts, ask the Spirit to help you release any negativity that is stunting your freedom to embrace life.

SEPTEMBER 20 • *The Illusion of Control*

The need to control—to plan and implement outcomes—is a cultural bias. We grow up with the illusion that we are, can be, and should be in control of our lives. The illusion of control is an idol, requiring that we devote our time and energy, our hearts and souls, to keeping this illusion alive—and we do. Of course, when things don't conform to our projection, we feel as if we've failed.

Most of the time we don't recognize our compulsion to control because it's cloaked with good intentions and justified by worthwhile goals. We seek to control others to get them to "do the right thing"; we seek to control the Spirit of God through our prayers; we want our country to be in control of world affairs. The possibility of losing control of our lives through sickness terrifies us. Dying looms as the final challenge to our control; we see death as an enemy to defeat. We believe medical science should be able to control illness and suffering.

As human beings, we can't resist the urge to pursue the outcomes we desire through whatever control techniques are at our disposal. Though that tendency is a natural response, it keeps us enthralled with a distorted sense of our own power. From early childhood, our culture encourages us to acquire, compete, deserve, and win. It connects success with getting more and building bigger. We buy the notion that "new" is automatically "better."

Letting go of this overblown notion of power sets forth an ongoing challenge. A degree of personal power does not translate into ultimate domination. To repeat, we may have influence but not control.

Reflect: Examine the illusions of control that form part of your life. Pray for the balance that comes from being responsible while not assuming that you determine the outcome.

SEPTEMBER 21 • *Letting Go of Plans*

Set goals and stick to them." "Take charge of your life." "Design a plan and follow it."

Sound familiar? We've all probably heard and repeated these statements. It's good advice if you're opening a new business. But in the business of life, making plans may be part of the problem, not the solution. The act of letting go calls for relinquishing some of our plans—the rigid agendas and unspoken dreams that can prevent us from being open to God's best for us. Our attempts to micromanage extend even to our own process of spiritual growth and formation in a life of love and compassion.

One day Maria arrived for her monthly spiritual direction appointment without her day planner. Usually she had a neat page of "spiritual issues" to discuss and a pen in hand, poised to make necessary notes. A successful businesswoman, she was prepared, prompt, and proactive. But this day she seemed a bit disconnected and unsure of herself. Being without her trusty agenda obviously made her feel like a ship without a rudder.

Maria's first words tipped me off, "Well, I don't really know what to talk about today . . . no real plan for our session. Maybe I shouldn't even have come." I suggested a brief period of silent, receptive prayer in the hope that we could both get out of the way and allow the Spirit to lead our time together. After the silence had settled over us, we began to chat companionably with no goal in mind.

Before long, tidbits of conversation yielded some clues about issues that lurked beneath the surface. Maria began to voice some unexplored tension with a coworker, wondering out loud about her own feelings of envy and competition toward the woman. Then other submerged concerns bubbled into consciousness—financial worries, signs of stress, time constraints. In each instance, she expressed a vulnerable willingness to tackle the question of her own motives, rather than focusing on others' behavior. As she searched for the Spirit's movement through her current life events, we began to connect the dots that emerged through the "aimless" conversation.

God seemed to be inviting her toward a more integrated spiritual life—not one that split along the lines of corporate life, family life, and religious life. Maria was clearly tired of being fragmented. She wanted to be the same person with the same values on Monday at the office, on Sunday at the altar, and at home having dinner with her family. Her soul yearned for a unity of self.

Letting go of her plan for the day opened her to letting go of the tight grasp on her life that stifled her freedom to soar with the Spirit. She still keeps the day planner. But nowadays, she tries to manage it rather than allowing it to manage her.

Reflect: How do you react when you encounter a change of plans? Rather than redouble your management efforts, consider leaning into the unexpected shift in agenda to explore what could be in store.

SEPTEMBER 22 • *If Only That Hadn't Happened*

If only that hadn't happened to me. . . . It wasn't in my plan." These words give voice to the recurring motif in our litany of poor choices and missed opportunities. At 3 a.m. on a restless night, stubborn second-guesses—the "why-did-Is" and "what-ifs" that plague us all—can bombard us with regrets that seem impossible to release. *How could I have made such a mistake? Why did I say those hurtful words? Why did I have such dysfunctional parents? If only she hadn't left me. . . .*

Renewed remorse can sabotage our intentions to let go and move on, and a pity-party can shift into high gear before we know it. Releasing regrets is one of the most daunting challenges in the letting-go process.

Nina had a checkered past that kept invading her present. In her family of origin, anger formed the chief currency of human exchange. Her horrific domestic atmosphere pushed her to leave her Midwestern home at age eighteen, vowing never to return. But she couldn't break the ties that easily. They wove themselves through her adult years as she began to establish her own family. She found herself in a familiar pattern of angry overreaction, lashing out indiscriminately at her children—a copycat of her parents' behavior. She had vowed not to do it, but she did it anyway.

The turbulence of Nina's anger increased with her husband's escalating alcoholism and her son's drug and criminal involvement. The family spiraled downward into violent outbursts, separations, and prison sentences. Even as she desperately reached for a lifeline—through Al-Anon and a church counselor—she maintained an ongoing conversation with God. She lamented with the Psalms, found inspiration in the Sermon on the Mount, and persisted in her prayers. Her openness allowed God to use many instruments for her healing—therapy, the lay renewal movement, and the loyal support of her church community. Slowly, slowly, she let go of the enormous burden of guilt and shame, and peace began to replace rage. It was a long, painful process.

Nina's life had been one of continued dysfunction, living out the faulty blueprint that she inherited. By releasing the pain of the past, she opened the door to God's guidance in her future. She now serves as an instrument of healing in the lives of her church congregation.

Clinging to past mistakes is a form of sabotage. "If only I had done it a different way," we say remorsefully. Well, we didn't. We can't do it over. And once we've faced the truth and extracted the lessons from the situation, the time comes to walk forward into new life.

Reflect: Carefully examine the ways that you revisit your past. Take a breath of release, and let go of any resentment and shame that clings to you.

SEPTEMBER 23 • *Letting Go of the Dream*

Once upon a time I had a dream for my life. Schooled in the standards of Proverbs 31, describing a woman whose value was "far more precious than jewels," I dreamed of becoming that woman. I would be treasured by an adoring husband, delight in my obedient children, and host Christmas celebrations straight out of Currier and Ives. Love and laughter would fill the house, friends would come to call, and the needy would not be forgotten.

The few inevitable bumps and bruises along the way would be handled bravely, and the family bond would strengthen with every passing year.

I believed that if I tried hard enough, I could make it happen. I poured my energies into the effort, stumbling blindly but continuing to believe in my idyllic world. When my husband asked for a divorce, my dream crumbled. My rose-colored glasses left me ill-prepared to deal with the ensuing feelings of rejection and loss. I resembled an immigrant entering a strange land of letting go; I didn't speak the language and didn't know the customs.

Very slowly I learned to let go of a husband I idealized, a luxurious lifestyle, and—most jarring of all—my identity as a married woman. But I never let go of that original dream. A clenched fist inside me still held tightly to the ideal of wife and mother as the definition of feminine success and happiness. Anything else felt like a second-best existence, an inferior way of life that I might have to "settle for." Through many years, I had wounds to heal, guilt to confront, and failure to face. At first my religious piety wouldn't allow me to shake my fist at God, but the sense of abandonment was there nonetheless. Something inside me wanted to shout that I had done my level best to be a good person, and I was anything but "blessed." The well-meaning words of friends who said "everything happens for a reason" did little to comfort me. It took literally years of spiritual struggle for me to face a truth that had eluded me: My dream was hampering God's dream for me. I needed to let it go.

The dream slowly ceased to be the underlying yearning of my life, the unspoken idol that I worshiped. As I let it go, I felt ready to release my death grip on my own agenda for happiness. I realized that I might be clutching a limited definition of who I was and who I could become.

Reflect: Revisit the dreams of your earlier years, of what you wanted your life to hold. In what areas have you had to let go of your own dreams and allow God's dream for you to unfold?

SEPTEMBER 24 • *Whatever . . .*

Mary said, 'Here am I, the servant of the Lord; let it be with me according to your word'" (Luke 1:38).

"Whatever . . . " the apathetic teenager says with a toss of the head. We've come to associate the word with a cavalier lack of concern, an attitude of dismissal, even a sense of irresponsibility. But Mary's "whatever" response expresses a profound trust, a resounding "Yes, . . . let it be."

I had heard that part of Mary's story and read Luke's account hundreds of times. However, as often happens with scripture, one day the words leapt from the page like a personal letter from God. They grabbed me with fresh meaning. The angel visited Mary, informed her that she would conceive a son, and she said yes. As I reread the story, I suddenly realized the extent to which she had to release the dream of her life! Certainly, as a young woman, it wouldn't have been her plan to become pregnant out of wedlock in a society that would shun her for it. Nor would she have dreamed of living a life of uncertainty and sadness and to have her son cruelly killed.

I doubt she intended to give birth to her first child in a smelly, unsanitary stable with barn animals as helpless onlookers. I'll bet it was far from a happy evening. Mary—probably cold, hungry, scared, and in pain—somehow let it be. Knowing nothing of what lay ahead of her, she signed on to her life with God. In some small way, we follow in her faithful footsteps when we let go of our narrow dreams and trust God's dream for us.

What would happen if we made *whatever* a code word for surrender to God? Suppose we dropped all resistance to grace? Suppose we flowed with it, one step at a time, without attempting to control the outcome. Taking that approach doesn't signal weakness but strength. Spiritual surrender also demands that we pay attention to opportunities and take action on what we know so far. If we believe that God wills wholeness for us, then we allow that wholeness and well-being to develop—rather than trying to make it happen.

When we release control of our lives, it may seem frightening at first. But surprisingly, the relinquishment loosens fear's grip and opens our soul into a passionate and hopeful freedom—a kind of contentment that does not depend on circumstances. We stand ready to encounter "whatever . . . ," knowing that a loving God walks into the unknown with us.

Reflect: Read the story of Mary's visitation by the angel in Luke 1. Imagine what it might look like in your life to say, "Whatever. . . . "

SEPTEMBER 25 • *How to Let Go*

After exploring the ins and outs of the letting-go process, after naming the people, personas, perspectives, patterns, and plans that we need to release, we get to the nitty-gritty of it. How can we actually implement these intentions in our flesh-and-blood lives?

In broad terms, the process is more about . . .

- Letting go than trying harder
- Yielding instead of controlling
- Subtraction rather than addition
- Allowing rather than managing
- Loosening instead of grasping
- Participating rather than directing

When we break the process down, it seems that no matter what we're trying to release, it involves five basic movements. The framework for understanding this is dynamic rather than rigid. The spiritual energy merges, moves back and forth, and occupies permeable boundaries, while still adhering to this fundamental flow:

First, we have to become *aware* that something has to change.
Second, we make ourselves *available* to new wisdom.
Third, we *act* responsibly on the insights we receive.
Fourth, we *allow* the healing process to begin.
Fifth, we *accept* the realities of life as they are.

Life offers many tools that can pave the way through these vital stages—from prayer to play, from counseling to creativity, from inner work to outer work—a virtual buffet of choices. You don't have to eat them all. Experiment with the suggestions, chew on them, and swallow the ones that suit your unique palate. Some of these spiritual "foods" will facilitate your letting-go process more than others. Take a bite here and there, and see what satisfies your hunger.

Reflect: Recall a time when you experienced letting go of a person, persona, perspective, pattern, or plan. What evidence do you see of the five stages of letting go? Consider how they will apply to your present process.

SEPTEMBER 26 • *Awareness*

When the Spirit of truth comes, he will guide you into all the truth" (John 16:13).

Sometimes we have no idea what we're holding on to or why. Sometimes we're afraid to find out. Sometimes we'd prefer just to leave things as they are, even though our soul is nudging us out of our complacency. Though we tend to cling to the familiar, our deepest growth comes through what I call "the taffy pull"—that is, the spiritual push and pull that yields something sweet.

We can easily spot some barriers to growth—traits or habits that we can immediately identify. But what about the ones that hide in the unconscious? What about the motivating forces that direct our decisions without our conscious knowledge? How do we discover the names of those powerful forces? Remember, we cannot let go of something we don't know we're clutching. We must know ourselves intimately and honestly—both the good and the bad—and tell ourselves the truth. Befriending our shadow stuff—the stuff hidden in the unconscious—opens the door to transformation.

As serious seekers have shared their struggles with me in spiritual guidance sessions, I have noticed the practices that time and time again seem to bring people to awareness, help them face their lethargy, and wake them up to life. Here are some avenues to that awareness:

- Prayer and meditation—Most of us give prayer a functional meaning, defining it as a well-intentioned effort to get something—health, peace of mind, good fortune. To be sure, petitionary prayer has its place, but that's a type of prayer we can control. In more contemplative kinds of prayer, listening prayers, we open ourselves to a transformative energy that we can't predict or direct. (See January 6, 7, 8.) The contemplative mind doesn't judge or decide but offers the heart and soul to God as is, trusting that the Spirit can help us wake up to the aspects we need to release.

- Journaling—When we write down our random thoughts daily we become aware of issues that arise repeatedly, questions that continue to puzzle us, sorrows that still weigh us down.
- Mindfulness—This is a matter of noticing what nags at us: the recurrent irritations, the chronic frustrations, the unmet expectations, the persistent pebbles in our shoes—the causes of anxiety that plague us. These signposts beckon us to let go.
- Insightful support—Whether a friend, a skilled counselor, a spiritual director, or a trusted pastor, those who are willing to be caring yet candid with us can lead us toward deeper awareness—that is, if we're ready to put aside our defensiveness and listen.

Reflect: Think of times when you've experienced aha moments, when you've been able to sense the inner nudge of new insight. Choose at least two practices that are congruent with your natural ways of being open to awareness.

SEPTEMBER 27 • *Availability*

As we took a companionable walk around the neighborhood, I glanced at Nancy's tight-lipped profile—eyes ahead, jaw clenched in consternation. I could tell she was chewing on a disturbing thought. A devout woman of intellect and integrity, she obviously had a bee in her bonnet that wouldn't stop buzzing. Something was out of sync, churning inside. She knew her emotions were out of kilter, fueled by exasperation at her ex-husband. She had that awareness, but she couldn't budge any farther.

As a counselor herself, Nancy knew all about letting go. She knew full well she needed to get rid of her anger, but—try as she might—her rage refused to respond to her well-intentioned commands. Knowing what needed doing and actually doing it were two different things. One part of her told the anger to go away; the other part held on stubbornly, wanting to experience her righteous indignation just a little longer. After all, she had clearly been wronged and didn't want to release her sense of victimization. Yet the burden of it was weighing her down.

Finally Nancy sighed and shook her head in frustration, "I can't do this forgiveness thing by myself. My feelings are too bruised, too tender. I know I need divine power to assist me, but my prayers for help are not really sincere. I'm not sure I'm honestly ready to let go. The best I can say right now is that I'm willing to be willing."

That courageous, honest admission kept her in the game. She made herself available for the next healing step, even if it was a baby step. Sometimes we can manage only a tiny opening in the heart, so it makes sense to begin where we are, as we are. No need to wait until we feel like it or until we have it figured out or until we're good enough.

Scripture tells us to "knock, and the door will be opened" (Matt. 7:7). Making ourselves available comes in the rapping of our knuckles on the door. It's our way of moving from readiness to willingness.

Reflect: How do you usually avail yourself of inspiration and wisdom? Imagine yourself standing before the mighty river of divine forgiveness. Even if you aren't ready to jump in, will you stick a toe in the water?

SEPTEMBER 28 • *Action*

It's easy to become discouraged in the process of letting go when we envision it as climbing Mount Everest. Simply taking the next step can propel us along the path.

Some of those steps are external—a phone call that needs to be made, a conversation that needs to take place, an addiction that needs to be addressed. We may find it necessary to change the way we spend our time and with whom. It may involve a financial decision, a change in location or vocation, exploring new friendships or church environments. Any number of choices put legs on our intention to let go. Even though most actions contain some element of risk, power and grace undergird us when we're moving toward wholeness.

Most actions, however, are internal ones that eventually feed external circumstances. For instance, in the case of resentment, we must let go of interior grumbling before it results in gossip. We must deal with interior contempt before it erupts in angry outbursts. Thoughts of worry become words of worry. Negative self-talk finds its way into outer embodiments of low self-esteem.

If we yearn to release an aspect or quality that we don't want mirrored in our lives, then we must find a way not to dwell on it. What we think about repeatedly infuses what we say and do. The complex nature of the mind/body/spirit connection is an astonishing system. If we perpetuate, attract, and manifest what we think about, then it behooves us to become attentive to the workings of our own minds.

Once feelings have been vented and given the expression they warrant and we're sincerely ready to move ahead, nothing is a more powerful ally than the discipline of our thoughts. Rather than deepening the neural "grooves" of negativity, we intercept the thoughts. We confront them and tell them to leave!

Reflect: Today, commit to taking one external action in your letting-go process and one internal action. Be as specific as possible, and do the next loving thing.

SEPTEMBER 29 • *Allowing*

At some point in the journey of letting go, it's time to stop striving. After leaning forward into awareness, availability, and action, the time comes to allow the process to work. Nature abounds with rich reminders of this patient relinquishment. The caterpillar waits in the chrysalis of the cocoon, staying in the shadowy stillness until its transformation into a butterfly is complete. Seedlings must be allowed to sprout; bulbs take time to bloom.

Though allowing the process to work may appear to be a passive activity, it entails our ongoing participation. An imaginative essay titled *Bicycling with God* captures the heart of the process.

> At first I saw God as my observer, my judge, keeping track of the things I did wrong, so as to know whether I merited heaven or hell when I die. God was out there sort of like the President. I recognized the picture, but I didn't really know God.
>
> But later on, it seemed as though life was rather like a bike ride, but it was a tandem bike, and I noticed that God was in the back helping me pedal. I don't know just when it was that God suggested we change places, but life has not been the same since. It's much more exciting. When I had control, I knew the way. It was rather boring but predictable. It was the shortest distance between two points. But when God took the lead, God knew delightful long cuts, up mountains, and through

rocky places and at breakneck speeds; it was all I could do to hang on. Even though it looked like madness, God said, "Pedal."

I worried and was anxious and asked, "Where are you taking me?" God laughed and didn't answer, but I started to trust. I forgot my boring life and entered into the new adventure. And when I'd say, "I'm scared," God would reach back and touch my hand. God took me to people with gifts that I needed, gifts of healing, acceptance and joy. They gave me their gifts to take on my journey . . . my journey with God.

And we were off again. God said, "Give the gifts away; they're extra baggage . . . too much weight." So I did—to the people we met. I found that in giving I received, and still our burden was light. I did not trust God at first, in control of my life. I thought we would wreck. But God knows "bike secrets"—how to make it bend to take sharp corners, jump to clear rocks, fly to shorten scary passages. I am learning to be quiet and pedal in the strangest places, and I'm beginning to enjoy the view and the cool breeze on my face with my constant companion, the Spirit of God.

And when I'm sure I just can't do any more, God just smiles and says, "*Pedal*."

Reflect: Imagine yourself on the front seat of a tandem bike, then moving slowly into the second seat. How would that switch change the way you live your life? What would you need to let go of to enter that trust and freedom?

SEPTEMBER 30 • *Acceptance*

But I have calmed and quieted my soul, like a weaned child with its mother" (Ps. 131:2). I wonder why the psalmist mentioned a *weaned* child? Why not an adoring child, a happy child, an obedient child? Perhaps because the weaned child asks for nothing, needs nothing, demands nothing. The child accepts what is—satisfied, content in the loving arms of the mother.

This kind of serenity is neither placid nor passive. It exists as a baseline to life—a peace that passes all understanding, a feeling of rest in a sea of unrest. Circumstances lived on top of this peace may be chaotic, tragic, exciting, dull, euphoric, happy, sad. But the foundation of meaning undergirds everything with a dependable weight of blessing. It's a place that we quietly enter when we don't need to change anything in the present, regret anything in the past, or dread anything in the future. That kind of acceptance brings joy.

Saint Teresa of Avila, a sixteenth-century Spanish nun, imagined a concept of the spiritual journey that speaks to this kind of joy. As I incorporated her images into the flow of my own life, they took on special significance in the letting-go process. She invites us to think of God planting a garden within us, asking us to water it and tend its growth. The experiential stages seem to follow this outline:

- Hauling water. At first, it feels as if we're dipping a heavy wooden bucket in the well, hauling the water to the garden, bucket by bucket.
- Pumping water. Next, we discover a water wheel nearby, and we continue to water but now with a little assistance.
- Stream of water. Then we notice a stream flowing through the garden, perhaps providing an irrigation system—if we open the gates, it will flow in.
- But in the final stage, we merely stand in the rain, accepting the gifts of grace as they wash over us.

When I first imagined myself standing in the rain, I could feel the relief flood over me in a state of effortless joy. Was it really possible to live that way? To continue to till and tend the garden but to depend on a greater love to shower me like rain soaking my upturned face? Just as each stage of the spiritual life involves less and less effort on our part, the journey of letting go employs a similar dynamic. It moves through awareness, availability, action, allowing, and ends in acceptance—a "standing in the rain."

Reflect: Focus on a situation in your life that is hard for you to accept. See yourself standing in the rain of God's grace with your face uplifted and your arms raised to the sky.

October

LIVING IN
FULL COLOR

*"From this time forward I make you hear new things, hidden things that
you have not known. They are created now, not long ago."*
—Isaiah 48:6-7

BREATH PRAYER
Creator God, . . . fill my life with color.

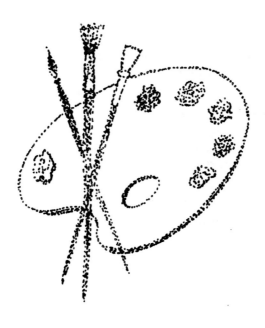

OCTOBER 1 • *Splashes of Color*

As the days grow shorter, what once was a panorama of green erupts in a riot of color, as if some happy-go-lucky artist has thrown a palette into the wind. Strokes of crimson, violet, tangerine—even chartreuse—offer their brilliance to the landscape. Each leaf is unlike any other. Neighboring trees mix their concoctions of beauty to fashion a collage of color. Drinking in this annual delight brings a smile to our lips and a thank-you to our hearts.

Nature is an inspired artist. Think for a moment about the profound truths hidden in this autumn event. Each leaf dons its own cloak of color in a dashing display of nonconformity—refusing to hide its gift. The leaves don't compete or judge or withhold their beauty; they simply reflect the exuberance of the great Creator. Collaborating with this divine creative force of the universe can color our existence as well. As we tap into the creative juices embedded in our nature, we engage in a transformative spiritual practice that brightens the dullness in our lives and produces healing effects.

Making room in our lives for art doesn't mean a revamping of our days so much as an enhancement of them. We need not rush to abandon our "day jobs." However, a shift in priorities occurs when we honor our essential nature as creative human beings. Connecting with the artistic parts of ourselves means learning the language of the soul—lilting music, colors on canvas, a messy potter's wheel, rows of radishes— earthy evidence of the generative force of the universe itself.

The fire of creativity can melt our frozen souls.

Reflect: Visualize yourself being grounded in God's creative power. Imagine roots reaching from your body into the earth as you allow the creativity of the Holy One to awaken your own.

OCTOBER 2 • *Our Divine DNA*

Creativity, the natural order of the universe, flows into and out of everything that spells life. It's no surprise that as children of a Creator God we are hardwired to be channels of that powerful flow of energy. We participate in our own transformation every time we respond to the creative urge that is encoded in our DNA.

"But I'm not artistic!" we protest, always pointing to painters, sculptors, musicians, and writers as the "talented" ones. But we can't let ourselves off the hook that easily. Just because we neglect or ignore the creative child within us doesn't mean that child doesn't exist. Life offers us a limitless array of choices to honor that basic instinct to shape, to sing, to design, to express. As Auntie Mame so cleverly phrased it in a memorable scene from the musical comedy, "Life is a banquet, and most poor [souls] are *starving* to death!"[1]

The domain of dullness is locked from the inside—our side. We diminish our God-given potential with self-negating statements like, "I don't have a creative bone in my body" or "If only I could turn a phrase like he can," or "I'm sure I'll have to hide this painting in the closet!" We tattoo these self-imposed limits in our minds, becoming inner skeptics that sabotage the reality of who we are. We must shush those degrading voices by digging into the creative soil that provides the seedbed of liveliness, refusing to allow those inner judges to affirm our self-doubts.

If this instinctive need to create is a part of how God made us, how can we honor its potential? Whether we're rearranging furniture, playing a game of "Pretend" with the children, shaping a business plan, concocting a vegetable stew, or splashing a canvas with paint, we're exercising a life-giving part of ourselves. So during this month, we'll explore ways to dismantle the resistance to our own artistic impulses. As we do so, we will release a healing and renewing power that will bring color to every area of our lives.

Reflect: What stories have you told yourself about your own creativity? Resolve to change the plot lines of those stories, and open yourself to a fresh exploration of the unique expression of the creative DNA within you.

OCTOBER 3 • *Your Inner Child at Play*

In my memory bank, it's the first day of first grade, and my parents have armed me with a giant box of crayons—with a new-fangled sharpener built into the box. Though no one had ever applauded my lopsided stick figures, I still believed those stunning colors could change my artistic future! Such was the power of that box of multihued possibility.

That hopeful schoolchild got sidelined somewhere in a barrage of numbers and grammar rules and historical facts. But she would temporarily come out of hiding during playtime. My sisters and I played dress-up, "cooked" mud pies, and staged musical productions in the garage behind the house. Our tools were free-flowing imaginations and unguarded time. When we occupied a land of whimsy and magic, no one labeled us as silly little girls who were wasting their time.

Without the interference of digital electronics, children at play are spontaneous, innovative, and, yes, remarkably creative. Ever watch a couple of toddlers on the beach? Undeterred by judgment of their "art," they grab what's there—shells, seaweed, stones, and sand—to fashion a castle fit for the finest monarch. How can we as adults recapture the vibrant energy that brings such refreshment for the soul and spirit?

We all have creative gifts, but some of us feel reluctant to open the package. We think we're too busy, too loaded with work, too burdened with "more important things to do." If we do take time to play, we often make work of it, reducing its healing power by coating it in competition and productivity. We call it play but in practice it becomes one more way to win, to excel, to prove something. Many of us, myself included, forgot how to play as we poured ourselves in the process of constructing a life of productivity and keeping up with our peers.

Through the years, the innovative child within us becomes a lonely orphan—shrinking from lack of attention and nurture. As seekers of the spirit, we need to awaken that child. What would it mean for us to reacquaint ourselves with that neglected part? Let's invite our inner spirited child to come out and play.

Reflect: Revisit your childhood memories of play. What were your favorite toys and games? Who was your favorite playmate, and what did you enjoy doing together? Consider ways to recapture some of those deep-seated fascinations.

OCTOBER 4 • *Being a Beginner*

When I walked into a watercolor class for the first time, I felt insecure, inept, unprepared and afraid. I imagined that the other participants knew what they were doing, and many of them did. They were all smiles, lugging their well-worn portfolios of supplies, eager to wet their brushes and dip them in color.

Frankly, I had not even understood the list of supplies—vermilion, cerulean, cadmium, #2 brushes—I didn't have a clue. As a rank beginner, I had a keen sense of my place at the bottom of the class ladder. Ready for step-by-step instructions, I was startled when our enthusiastic teacher produced a small vase of common thistle—loaded with lavender blossoms—and said simply, "Paint it."

Asking for assistance again and again, I haltingly mixed purple and white while wondering about my use of the proper brush. The teacher continued to insist, "Just begin. Just paint." My random swirls of color differed from the precise reproductions being created around me, but I swallowed the lump in my throat and kept at it. I found it hard to set aside my competitive nature; I wanted to be as good as they were. My aha moment came with my realization that my inhibitions were stifling the creative urge inside me that was struggling for expression.

Oddly enough, abandoning my desire for proficiency made it possible to abandon the anxiety that blocked me. I had to get past the idea that if I couldn't produce a Rembrandt, then I couldn't pick up a brush! It was okay to stumble, to make a mess of it, to turn out a piece of art that the local art gallery would never display. Just for a moment, it was enough to experience the joy of being lost in an explosion of color on canvas.

Most of us don't relish being beginners at anything. We prefer competence, capability, perfection—certainly not the humility of a beginner. Deflation won't destroy us but suppressed creativity will. We must be willing to risk mediocrity and forgo stardom. Self-compassion will help us suspend our inner judgments and be gentler with ourselves.

The paint has long since dried on my brushes. I never painted again, ignoring that amateur artist and getting caught up in other pursuits. But one day soon, I'll become a beginner again. This time, however, I'll know that producing a spectacular work of art is unnecessary. I can return to being that wide-eyed first-grader with a new box of crayons.

Reflect: Recall a time when you've felt the anxiety of being a beginner. What did you learn from the experience? Recover your own teachable spirit, and choose a creative endeavor to enter as a beginner.

OCTOBER 5 • *Artistic Alchemy*

Just as persons rumored that the alchemists of ancient times could turn base metals into gold, I believe creativity in our lives can turn the common into the special. Art has a spiritual alchemy of its own.

Because the creative impulse plays a central role in God's nature and our own, it has the power to heal and alter us in ways that seem as magical as the old stories of alchemy. Far from being a self-centered pursuit, this expansion of our soul spills into the world around us in all its curative dimensions. It kindles our energy and makes us more available to the needs of others:

- Creative words can soothe a strained relationship.
- Creative presence provides an instrument of healing.
- Creative cooking feeds body and soul alike.
- Creative thinking can bring new solutions to old problems.
- Creative hospitality surrounds the stranger with welcome.
- Creative arts inspire and comfort the spirit.

Made in the image of the Creator God, we share a heritage to honor as creative beings. That effervescence yearns to spring to life and be set free to do its inspiring work. The combination of spirituality and creativity set a magnificent force loose in the cosmos. It's up to us to be thoughtful stewards of this gift that lives in our core.

Unearthing our creativity in all its diversity brings us into an alchemical process that can spin the dross of our lives into threads of gold.

Reflect: Embrace the truth that the God of the universe invites you to serve as a cocreator. How can you be a good steward of this dazzling gift?

OCTOBER 6 • *Creative Companions*

Though reviving our sleeping artist offers a satisfying solo pilgrimage, teaming up with kindred souls can enhance the experience. When someone says, "C'mon, you can do it!" or "That's an exquisite thing you created with your own hands," the support spurs us to flourish even more.

Surrounding ourselves with creative companions produces encouragement rather than competition. I witnessed this phenomenon firsthand in an experiential group study titled *The Artist's Way: A Spiritual Path to Higher Creativity*, a book written by Julia Cameron. A twelve-week study in spirituality and creativity, the book explores the artistic urge as a part of our God-given nature with supportive companions on the same journey. While stimulating a variety of creative possibilities, a powerful part of the book's potency unfolds in group interaction.

In my group, participants learned to play together as a piece of the process. One ongoing assignment consisted of scheduling a weekly "artist's date" with one's inner artist—just the two of you. Some of us wrestled with what to do on those weekly excursions; others had innovative and fun-loving ideas. While one person visited an art exhibit, another visited a yarn shop. While one embarked on an hour of solo roller skating, another flew a kite. One walked in the woods, another ambled through a nursery of potted flowers. A cross-pollination of ideas invigorated all the activities.

We read one another's poems and short stories and listened to others' piano compositions—all in cheerleader mode. We laughed at our amateurish efforts and lifted one another out of discouragement. All the while, we prayed for one another.

And even though we shared our broken places, we didn't try to fix them. We listened compassionately, supporting each person's individuality and unique journey. We became a band of brothers and sisters dedicated to lighting a spark of sizzling creativity.

Reflect: As you think of people who might accompany you on this adventure of creative recovery, start a list. When it grows to five or ten people, call them together to form a group of companions who are eager to collaborate with the great Creator.

OCTOBER 7 • *The Courage of Creativity*

I entered the gallery where my artist friend was featured in a one-woman show. Her vivid oil paintings enlivened every wall, showcasing her immense talent. But that wasn't the only thing on exhibition. Her breathtaking bravery was also on display.

Until that moment, I hadn't imagined the courage it required for my artist friend to expose herself to dozens of people who stroll by and scrutinize the work. What if she overheard comments like "Wonder why she used those colors?" "Would that work over our sofa or should we shop for something better?" or "I'm not fond of that style, are you?" I wanted to wrap her in a hug and protect her, along with her defenseless inner artist.

Fear of criticism and a driving compulsion to please others can cripple even the keenest artistic impulse. Budding artists often wilt under the glare of the spotlight that exposes their passionate work to the opinions of others. An awareness of this vulnerability can remind us to support those brave souls who venture out of the studio and into the public arena. If we aspire to be channels of love and compassion, let's reserve a special corner of our hearts for those who have the courage to fill our lives with color and drama and music.

That evening in the gallery I saw more evidence of art's divine alchemy at work when I looked at my friend's face. Its magic had turned timidity into bravery and a private artist into a public one.

Reflect: Pray a prayer of thanksgiving for the creative courage of others who color your life through painting, music, poetry, books, and other art forms. Contact at least one of them today, and express your gratitude for the gift he or she shares so bravely.

OCTOBER 8 • *The Painter and the Prodigal*

When I consider examples of the alchemy of art, I always think of writer Henri J. M. Nouwen's life-changing encounter with Rembrandt's famous painting *The Return of the Prodigal Son*. In fact, Nouwen's powerful experience generated a book about the painting's impact on his life. Inspired by the sight of the prodigal in the arms of the loving Father, he willingly released years of addiction to the approval of others and his control over his own spiritual journey. The book chronicles this movement toward a freer spirit.[2]

Have you ever felt the ground shift beneath you when you gazed at a work of art? It's as if the Holy Spirit enters the space and calls your name through the colors and images, and you experience a fundamental change. I witnessed that kind of holy encounter years ago in Florence, Italy, as a group of us stood before Michelangelo's magnificent sculpture of David. Our travel-weary and art-saturated tour group entered the museum. Of all the travelers, my friend Gayle was the epitome of composure and control—not given to emotional outbursts. In fact, I had never seen her "lose it." But as we stood in a circle around Michelangelo's massive sculpture, she slowly and silently sank to the cold marble floor on her knees and began to sob in reverent appreciation.

Gayle's emotional response was a gift—a reminder of unexpected and involuntary artistic power. As I observed Gayle that day, her reliable composure reduced to rubble, I knew I was witnessing a holy moment. In some mysterious way, art and music have the capacity to touch our souls in places that words may not reach.

So take up creative pursuits. Attend a concert. Spend quality time at an art museum. Those might not seem like obvious tools for spiritual growth, but they have the potential to touch our hearts and expand our souls.

Reflect: Recall a heart-stopping moment when a work of art moved you. What did it feel like? How did you feel spiritually stirred?

OCTOBER 9 • *The Potential of Pilgrimage*

In each of us, there dwells a pilgrim—eager to walk the path to the holy center, to connect with the Source of life, to wander with a purpose. In the sentiments of Saint Augustine, our hearts are restless until they find their rest in God. We were created as meaning-seeking creatures, and the experience of pilgrimage symbolizes that part of us.

Pilgrimage has a rich history that spans centuries of travelers seeking this deeper connection to the sacred and to the self. It symbolizes an interior journey to the depths of the soul where genuine change takes place—a simultaneous movement of the feet and the soul toward intimate meaning.

The Bible mentions pilgrimage as part of Hebrew tradition from the book of Exodus (23:17) to the familiar story of Jesus attending the festival of the Passover with his parents in Jerusalem (Luke 2:41-42). Pilgrimage is rooted in the spiritual practices of religious groups all over the world, drawing thousands of visitors each year to holy sites and shrines.

As a link to the creative expression of the soul's journey, pilgrimage has three main parts:

- External Separation—leaving home to travel to a specific sacred site; Internal Separation—leaving the status quo of the soul to plunge deeper.
- External Journey—traveling a path, often by foot, to a hallowed destination; Internal Journey—traveling to the soul's center where transformation of the heart takes place.
- External Homecoming—returning home with renewed purpose and strength; Internal Homecoming—returning to life with a new sense of relationship with God and a desire to bless others.

It can be a life-changing experience to travel to the Holy Land or to a Celtic Christian site such as Iona, Scotland. However, as you read these words, you are already on the holy pilgrimage to the sacred center of yourself where the Spirit welcomes you.

Reflect: If you know of a labyrinth in your community, walk it as a symbol of pilgrimage. Stop in the center for prayer and guidance from God, then slowly exit to bless the world around you. If a labyrinth is unavailable, travel the Stations of the Cross at a church nearby. Or, simply take a walk to and from an inspirational site to create a symbol of your inner journey.

OCTOBER 10 • *Room by Room*

Walking into a room with harmonious colors settles us with a sense of serenity. Sitting down to a table centered with fresh flowers and vibrant place mats makes us smile with anticipation. Entering a doorway circled in fresh pine and bearing a wreath wraps us in holiday welcome before we even cross the threshold. From the dishes we use to the fabrics that cover our chairs, creativity abounds in our homes. They not only provide safety and shelter but a daily dose of beauty as well.

Even the art of decorating our homes can connect us to the Spirit. If renovation is taking place, we can use it as a metaphor for renovation in our lives. Discarding items we no longer need helps us practice the art of letting go. Rather than obsess about what colors are in vogue, we can give free rein to our own imaginations and preferences. We can release our inhibitions about what others think and focus on the desires and needs of our families. We can build domestic togetherness by asking for input from everyone in the household so that the project can unify rather than disrupt.

And we can intentionally bless our homes through the ancient tradition of a house blessing. Walking from room to room, we ask God to bless each new space with a mantle of love and kindness. It reminds families (especially children) that God doesn't live at the church! If your tradition doesn't contain appropriate liturgy, you might use these simple words to hallow your home:

> Gracious God, please bless this place
> as it becomes a sacred space.
> May it be a home to soften sorrow,
> to cushion cares, and from beauty borrow.
> May hospitality hallow each room,
> encouraging truth and discouraging gloom.
> May conflicts be measured in feelings so fair
> that discord dissolves in understanding air.
> May kindness be a treasured token
> where harmony hails and sincerity is spoken.
> May the lilt of laughter in symphony sound;
> may friendship flourish on grace-filled ground.
> And may all who enter and rest from their roam
> find your loving Spirit here. . . . ever at home.

Reflect: Gather your family members this evening and ask if they have an interest in joining you in a house blessing. Whether clergy-led or family-led, such a ceremony can be a source of blessing to everyone who lives there. Follow the blessing with your family's favorite meal!

OCTOBER 11 • *The Magic of Music*

Whether through performing, composing, or simply listening, music soothes the soul with its healing balm. As harmonies surround us, they stir the heart in enchanting ways.

As I noted in the meditation for May 13, I witnessed music working its magic. The occasion, a stimulating theological think-tank event, brought the best and the brightest together to discuss the fine points of theology in a rarified seminary atmosphere. The challenge pushed me to the brink of my brainpower, so I felt weary and word-saturated by the week's end.

As I slid into the pew at the closing worship service, I expected to hear a little Handel and Bach with a formal high-church liturgy. Special music was provided by a classically trained African-American contralto, and I hoped she would sing something familiar from the *Messiah*. My overtaxed brain didn't want a musical challenge on top of everything else. To everyone's surprise, the musical offering took an unexpected turn. The singer sat at the piano and hit one chord of introduction. Then her voice filled the room. "Jesus *loves* me, this I know, for the Bible tells me so. . . ." Then with a change of key and tempo, she began again, "Jesus loves *me*, this I know. . . ." With yet another rhythm change and range, she ended with "Jesus loves me, this I *know!*"

We could have heard a pin drop in that sanctuary. It seemed that all the theological posturing had been suspended in the face of the loving power that united all of us. After the dogma had been debated and the ink had dried on all the presentation papers, the chorus of a children's song reminded us that "the greatest of these is love."

Reflect: Slowly sing or listen to "Jesus Loves Me," repeating it as you emphasize the words, one at a time. Let its message fill your heart with gratitude and joy.

OCTOBER 12 • *Tuned-in Therapy*

The scientific evidence that supports the idea of music's healing properties is growing. Patients in physical therapy move their muscles more energetically with rhythmic music prodding them along. Soft melodies are piped into MRI machines. Dialysis patients experience reduced anxiety when songs fill the air. We can employ music therapy to manage stress, alleviate pain, express feelings, enhance memory, and improve communication—and certainly, to nurture spiritual connections.

A few years ago, while sitting with my ninety-eight-year-old aunt during her final few days, I witnessed the power of old gospel hymns to soothe the spirit. Just past midnight my aunt's agitation failed to respond to the medicines provided by the hospice nurse. Though she could no longer communicate, her body signaled distress and disquiet. She couldn't seem to settle down with any degree of comfort. Finally—in desperation, really—I began to sing songs from the old *Cokesbury Hymnal,* memorized from long-ago church services. The more I sang, the more tranquil she became. Her body stopped its restless movements; the lines in her face relaxed; her demeanor became peaceful. Though she never opened her eyes or moved her lips, I knew the music awakened memories of worship and prayer somewhere in her spirit.

Even those of us who aren't great musicians have experienced the salutary effects of singing in a choir, playing with an orchestra, or simply strumming a guitar at home. Music is an immeasurable miracle, but we can observe its effects and feel its healing balm.

Reflect: When you are upset or in pain, find ways to allow music to minister to you. In what ways can you offer this ministry to those who could benefit from its power?

OCTOBER 13 • *Soil and Spirit*

No wonder the parables of Jesus abound with earthy images of fields and flowers, planting and plowing, rich soil and fertile plains. All silently remind us of the creative force around us and inside us. Even if we simply water the pot of ivy on the desk or grow tiny tomatoes in a city apartment, we participate in this rich humus of the Spirit.

My friend Anthony loves to putter in his garden and finds countless metaphors that feed his spiritual life:

- He can till the soil of his soul through prayerful meditation as he turns each spade of dirt to prepare it for new growth.

- He can pull up the weeds of resistance that could choke the progress of his plants and his spirit.
- He can plant seeds of hope and resurrection.
- He can rake away old hurts and habits.
- He can water the green sprouts with gratitude and let the rain of grace shower them.
- He can celebrate the emergence of fruits of the vine and fruits of his own spirit.
- He can share the bounty of his garden and his spirit with others.
- He can sense the garden's reminders that life is changing every minute; as the vegetables mature, so does his soul.

Anthony inspires and instructs novice gardeners in our inner-city community garden. Not only does his gardening grow his own spirit, but he's helping God feed the world.

Reflect: As you grow things in a small pot or on an enormous farm, borrow some of Anthony's thoughtful metaphors. Focus on ways gardening can give you a sense of cocreating with the Holy Gardener.

OCTOBER 14 • *Wisdom in the Workshop*

I will put in the wilderness the cedar, the acacia, the myrtle, and the olive; I will set in the desert the cypress, the plane and the pine together, so that all may . . . consider and understand, that the hand of the LORD has done this" (Isa. 41:19–20).

Cradling the raw wood in his hands, the woodworker, a retired minister, mused thoughtfully, "It's as if I'm holding a piece of God's creation and being invited to enter into partnership with a divine creative process—building something beautiful and useful from scratch."

The retired minister's hobby served other functions as well. It transported him into another realm—one in which sermons and studies played no role. In addition to that, woodworking harmoniously integrated itself with his natural wiring. As a lover of things clear-cut and purposeful, he took great satisfaction in measuring, cutting, splicing, and making the joints fit. His appreciation of meticulous planning found expression in figuring out the particular wood and carpentry products for purchase, the shades of stain to select. While his penchant for predictability and precision could sometimes be problematic in his daily world, in the world of woodworking those qualities proved to be assets! In the sanctuary of his workshop, he could be himself.

Being authentic with ourselves opens the way to authenticity with God. As the woodworker planed and refined the wood, he felt his soul going through the same sacred shaping. The wood became his teacher. Even engaging the grain in the wood reminded him to "go with the grain" of his own life, to get in the natural flow. He cast cares and concerns aside with the wood chips and the shavings. A sense of peace prevailed.

Each project sparked some dream time also . . . time to envision the finished product, to anticipate its purpose and function. "It's not altogether different from giving birth to a sermon," he said with a smile. "When the inspiration strikes, you get to work!"

Reflect: Think about the discoveries you've made about your natural wiring. What creative outlets seem to dovetail with your innate desires and talents?

OCTOBER 15 • *The Passion of Poetry*

Some of us have an inferiority complex when it comes to poetry. We mistakenly assume it's the purview only of the literate, the educated, the smart folks—or that it's too obscure for us to figure out. My mind takes me back to high school English class when the teacher assigned a poem and commanded me to write an essay unraveling its meaning, which was for her to know and me to find out.

To open ourselves to the power of poetry, we must set those self-doubts on a shelf and allow the words and images to enter our vulnerable souls. We know that has happened when we read a line and gasp in recognition. Or unbidden tears splash onto the page. Or neon thunderbolts brighten our vision of who we are and what life is about.

Life-changing words can sometimes visit us without announcing their arrival. As I sat in the cool grass of an ancient cemetery on the island of Iona, Scotland, I read Mary Oliver's famous poem, "When Death Comes." The lyrical lines sang in my ears, while a haunting phrase awakened something sleeping in my soul. She wrote that at the end of her life, she wanted to say that she was "a bride married to amazement." My whole being was shot through with energy, shouting silently, *Me too!* The words carved themselves on my spirit, exacting a promise from me that I would never take ordinary life for granted, that I wouldn't waste it. At that moment, I pledged to live life to the fullest, savoring every experience—even those that tasted bitter.

Let poetry surprise you with its power and passion. Let it make your head spin and your heart swell.

Reflect: Read a favorite poem slowly, allowing its images to sink into your soul. Then pick up a pen and write a few lines of your own.

OCTOBER 16 • *The Potter and the Clay*

We are the clay, and you are our potter; we are all the work of your hand" (Isa. 64:8). Forming a piece of pottery is messy—a painstaking work of trial and error, molding and making, refining and reshaping, carving and coloring. It's no wonder that scriptural texts liken this creativity to the process of spiritual formation. Scores of potters today find this tactile art form a symbol of cocreating with God, of seeing something useful and beautiful emerge from a formless lump of clay.

The prophet Jeremiah reminds us that this divine molding can take an imperfect vessel and fashion it anew, "The vessel he was making of clay was spoiled in the potter's hand, and he reworked it into another vessel, as seemed good to him" (Jer. 18:4). Isn't that what happens to us as our own souls and spirits are shaped? We make mistakes; our motivations are muddy; our flaws spoil the process over and over again. Yet the merciful hands of the Holy transform our blemishes into teachers and contours the vessels of our humanness with compassion.

While it seems that the events in our lives form and de-form us, our response to those events molds us most deeply. We participate with the divine Potter, more concerned with what we can still become than what we used to be. In this act of cocreating, we let go of our frantic attempts to shape ourselves and trust God's hands of love and gentleness, trust and respect, hope and delight.

Perhaps "throwing a pot" can remind us of that.

Reflect: Imagine yourself as a formless lump of muddiness that contains a spark of the divine. See yourself molded into the unique work of art that you are, and be grateful.

OCTOBER 17 • *Running with the Spirit*

As the priest of a large inner-city parish, my friend faced needs from all directions. He oversaw meetings, funerals, weddings, illnesses, meetings, sermons, meetings, remembering newcomers' names, and still more meetings. Add to that the crying needs of the poor who lived in the shadow of the church. Add to that the demands of a growing family who filled his heart with joy but were bursting with activities and energy. Add to that the reality that though wired as an introvert, his life bustled with extroversion. He had precious little time to feed the hunger of his soul.

So the priest ran. When he laced up his running shoes at 4:30 a.m. and entered the darkness before dawn, he greeted a still, silent world where the breath that filled his lungs was the breath of God. The path he jogged became holy ground. The minutes that ticked by morphed into eternal moments.

The priest described the experience haltingly, as if he couldn't completely capture it in a web of words. "To tell the truth, it hurts a lot," he said with a smile. "It pushes me beyond my limits; it disciplines me; it refines me. But at some point, I cross the threshold of another realm—a spiritual space of freedom and inspiration where God's presence is very real."

The man could also feel the cross currents between body and spirit doing their holy work. As the running shaped and toned his muscles, he experienced a simultaneous shaping of the soul—a refining of himself as a father, husband, priest, encourager, friend, compassionate human being. Sermon ideas were planted; words for an upcoming article lit up his mind. He could sense the creative "muse" running in step with him. Breaking through the barriers of pain and exhaustion awakened his longing to break through barriers in the world around him. And with each cleansing breath, he felt closer to the blessed rhythm of the earth itself.

"Running balances me; it calms my soul," he reflected. "It equalizes the external busyness in my life by providing a quiet internal place . . . just me and my hound dog. After a long run, I'm tired; but I feel restored too. And sometimes when I least expect it, I'm wrapped in a strange afterglow—now that's pure gift."

Reflect: What physical activity or creative pursuit brings the balance and inspiration described by the runner? Examine the content of your day, and try to include an experience that can evoke the unity of body and spirit he expressed.

OCTOBER 18 • *Creative Cooking*

Depending on the need of the moment, Susan's kitchen serves as a cathedral, a psychiatrist's couch, an art gallery, a party venue, or a retreat space. But above all, it explodes with creative energy:

- When lonely, she gathers friends and feeds them royally.
- When angry, her sharp chef's knife chops and dices in a fury.
- When craving beauty, she marvels at the blazing colors of red and yellow peppers.
- When sad, she lets onions prod her tears.
- When overworked, she balances flavors in the stew while she figures out a better balance of her life's ingredients.
- When she is doubting her growth, a salad bowl overflowing with brilliant lettuce reminds her of the greening of her soul.
- When she is sick, a bubbling pot of chicken soup provides healing medicine.
- When fragmented, she mixes seasonings into a harmonious blend.
- When longing to serve others, she bakes fresh bread to give away.
- When yearning for the Holy, she honors the miracle of nature's bounty.

Every whiff of culinary creativity carries an appreciation for the work in progress—on the stove and in her soul.

Reflect: Pay special attention to the creative possibilities in your kitchen today. Which of Susan's pointers can enhance your own slicing and stirring?

OCTOBER 19 • *Weaving the Warp and Weft*

Weaving has its own rich language, and my sister, a devotee of the loom, speaks it well. She has taught me that the basic terminology of weaver-speak centers around the warp (the vertical strands of yarn on the loom) and the weft (the horizontal strands). Weavers can't always be sure of the outcome as they interlace yarns and threads together. As the colors interact with one another, their combined characteristics change the hues and emerge as a creative surprise. She says that at some point, good weavers let go of their original concept to some degree and allow the threads to weave their own magic. What a meaningful metaphor for the spiritual life!

Think of the vertical warp as our relationship with God, born out of our innate hunger and God's saving grace offered to us. Those threads receive vitality through holy encounters with the Spirit, and the faithful practice of spiritual disciplines strengthens them. The horizontal weft represents the experiences of everyday living—the mundane chores of working, rearing children, mowing the grass. The mystical "warp" shapes the "weft" of our ordinary days.

However, sometimes the weft of daily life can crowd the warp of the Spirit. Maybe our personal weaving process contains flaws. Maybe we need to unravel some threads. Maybe we need to add some new yarn for texture. The loom of our lives contains unfinished fabric. The warp and weft are woven from our colorful basket of yarn, the diverse experiences that thread their way through every waking minute.

If we intertwine our regular moments with the guiding hand of the Spirit, what a lovely tapestry emerges!

Reflect: Imagine this ordinary day, the weft, mingling with the grace of God, the warp, as the loom of your life is formed with color and texture.

OCTOBER 20 • *Looking through the Lens*

Whether you're taking a snapshot with a smart phone or a portrait with a fancy professional camera, you hold in your hands a powerful creative tool for deepening the spirit. The eye is truly "the lamp of your body" and can flood our souls with images of color and beauty. It can record the ordinary and extraordinary events of our lives, as well as honor the relationships so dear to our hearts.

A zoom lens can transform a butterfly's wing into a microscopic masterpiece, reminding us that holiness dwells in tiny details. A wide-angle lens can expand our vision and our hearts at the same time. What matters is that we look and how we look.

A signature scene in the movie *The Color Purple* captures our tendency to waltz by the beauty of the world in a cloud of blindness. One of the main characters Shug imagines that it irritates God when we walk by the color purple in a field and fail to notice it. Splendor should not go unwitnessed. A camera lens allows us to feast our eyes on blazing colors, unusual designs, and the smiles in a family photo. It not only focuses our vision on a budding rose but also on the lace of a bridal gown. It reveals the tragedy of a killing field, as well as the treasure of a child's laughing face. The lens captures both tears and joy in vivid contrast.

As a spiritual practice, picture taking becomes an avenue of awareness, prompting us to appreciate the presence of the Holy that animates everything. Grandeur enfolds both the minuscule and the gigantic.

Reflect: Take a few moments today to pick up your camera or phone and zoom in on an object that catches your attention or stirs your heart. Without hurrying, notice its details and take a photo of it (making it your "wallpaper" for the day, if you wish). Thank God for the mysterious infusion of the Spirit in everything you see.

OCTOBER 21 • *Words from the Heart*

There are moments when a fresh sheet of paper (or a blank computer screen) becomes a reservoir for emotions and insights that spill from the heart like summer rain.

In its most potent form, the creative tool of writing connects a passionate heart with the grander passion of God, almost as if the writer is composing a personal letter to the Holy Mystery. By allowing words to tumble out with abandon, the writer gives expression to feelings and emotions from within. If the writing doesn't connect with heart-stirring feelings—leaving us breathless or disgusted or wildly curious—then it's little more than a news report.

Writing and journaling provide an effective form of therapy. They afford an escape from the madness and melancholia of life. They grab joy and wonder in a luminous web of words. When we write, we dig for memories; we turn sentences around and upside down; we try to recall what the world is really like and tell the truth about it. Whether it's a simple journal entry or a great novel, we set the same remarkable process in motion when we put pen to paper or boot up the computer.

With this particular channel of creativity, there is no such thing as a nonwriter. The words need not be eloquent or publishable. They don't even need to be grammatically correct. They just need to express life. As we empty ourselves onto a page, we somehow become fuller and richer and more in touch with the Mysterious Other who welcomes our words.

Reflect: Today, find a time to write something—a poem, a letter to a friend, a thank-you note, a page in your journal. Don't judge the words as worthy or unworthy; simply let them flow unimpeded from your heart and soul.

OCTOBER 22 • *Housecleaning and Harmony*

A broom may not look like a spiritual tool. When we're sweeping leaves from the front porch or sorting clutter in the garage, creativity may be the farthest thing from our minds. However, prayer and housekeeping are natural partners. As we clean our homes and keep things in order, our thoughts can move seamlessly to the cleaning and ordering of our internal "house." Savoring the inherent blessedness of daily life becomes a way we can "pray without ceasing," linking humdrum tasks to the holiness that infuses them. For example:

- Taking out trash—What can I learn from my messy overflow? What qualifies as necessary letting go and what represents waste?
- Dusting—As I polish the antique bureau that belonged to Mom or the new dining table that gathers my family, I am grateful for the furniture that links the past and present of my life.

- Sweeping—May I briskly brush away the lingering resentments that cling to my mind.
- Washing the dishes—As I clean each plate, may I remember with love the person who ate from it.
- Mending—What is torn that can be stitched together in love? What is beyond repair and must be accepted as it is?
- Ironing—What is wrinkled in my relationships and requires ironing out with grace into a smoother situation?
- Sorting the laundry—As I divide the lights and the darks into separate piles, may I remember to accept both the light and dark of my life as valuable parts of daily existence.
- Shoveling snow—Remind me, O God, of the feelings I shovel aside into a heap, refusing to deal with them.
- Straightening the pantry—May I be thankful for the abundance in our household and the security of being able to feed my family.

Our home chores, though repetitive and unglamorous, can move us toward a clean house and a clean heart!

Reflect: Be attentive to your humdrum chores today. Allow them to be a hallowed ground for creative prayer and grateful awareness.

OCTOBER 23 • *Painting Away the Pain*

Pain arrives in all our lives, dressed in a myriad of shapes, sizes, and shades of color. Broken relationships, dashed dreams, crushing depression, chronic pain—the list is long and laborious.

Hosts of hurting people experience a gentle healing through a box of colored pencils or a paintbrush and palette. These amateur artists emerge from all age groups—emotionally disturbed children, troubled teens, addicted adults, grieving seniors. In hospital settings around the world, art therapy is emerging as a valid means of enabling patients to express their feelings emotionally as well as physically. They portray their pain on canvas or on a piece of paper.

For instance, children who have limited ability to communicate their feelings in words can demonstrate clearly what is happening to them through the use of stick figures or dabs of paint. A child suffering from migraine headaches might draw a circle to represent his head with a black X across it or with arrows piercing it.

The benefits derived from picturing pain through artwork cannot be measured or quantified. However, some interesting positives are emerging:

- Art gives people a nonverbal way to express the problem without being judged or having others get fed up with their complaints. Loved ones are often more responsive when they see the person's suffering on paper.
- Art provides information to doctors and other health care workers who may be puzzled by the person's pain. Under- or overmedicated patients can use imagery to portray the intensity or type of pain.
- Art reveals how the person perceives the pain, which can lead to greater understanding for both patient and health team.
- Art helps the person take ownership of the pain, providing some sense of control over the confusing situation.

And, unlike some other forms of pain therapy, art does no harm. One physician likened it to chicken soup because he saw no downside. Art has a potent way of painting away the pain with ribbons of color.

Reflect: If you are experiencing pain of some kind, take a few moments to draw it or paint it. You may want to create a collage, using materials or items relevant to your pain—bits of fabric, a prescription label, a picture of a hammer. Imagine the Spirit of healing covering you with comfort and relief.

OCTOBER 24 • *Walk Humbly with God*

What does the LORD require of you but to do justice, and to love kindness, and to walk humbly with your God?" (Micah 6:8).

Ambling along in the company of these words from the prophet Micah can produce "exercise" for the spirit as well as for the body.

Living a life of justice involves pursuing equality for all people, seeking fairness in dealing with others, and championing the rights of the powerless. When we take Micah's directive seriously, we engage in relationships and projects that promote matters of justice in the intimate world of the home, the communal world of a nation, and the global world of the planet.

A life of kindness involves not merely doing good deeds but of thinking good thoughts, giving folks a second chance, caring enough to walk in their shoes and imagine their needs. A kind heart views all situations and people through a lens of goodwill and mercy.

Abiding with these lofty goals requires creative living on our part. In tandem with the Creator's inspiration, we can help craft legislation to ensure equal rights. We can find creative solutions to the problems of the homeless. We can build a ramp for a neighbor who is wheelchair bound. We can cook a pot of Brunswick stew for a sick friend. We can recycle our waste and reduce our carbon footprint.

Walking humbly with God requires keeping in touch through worship, study, and prayer in a spirit of vulnerable surrender. While we are made in the image of God, cradling the divine spark placed within us, we also acknowledge that we are not God. We don't know it all; we don't understand it all; we live in faithful openness to continuous revelation. We need a holy nudge now and then to prod us toward acts of justice, mercy, and kindness.

And when we feel that nudge or sense that creative solution or have an idea about someone's needs, we take a step to act, to walk humbly with our God.

Reflect: Take a brief, slow walk, imagining the spirit of God walking with you. What acts of love, justice, and mercy is God inviting you to consider? Hear those divine whispers with humility and openness.

OCTOBER 25 • *The Shepherd and the Sheep*

My friends Harrison and Eleanor live close to the earth, tending their animals and tilling their land on a small farm. It's a cherished haven—not only for them but for their dogs, cats, cattle, chickens, rabbits, and most of all, their beloved sheep.

Every time I watch my friends interact with their livestock—sheep Dixie, Isabella, Ellie, Millie and two alpacas, Jeremiah and Gabriel, the scripture from John 10:27 comes alive for me: "My sheep hear my voice. I know them, and they follow me." As my farmer friends call them by name, the sheep unmistakably know the sound of their voices and will follow them anywhere!

I'm told that sheep are among the simplest of livestock and are quite vulnerable without a shepherd to tend, feed, and guard them from harm. But the shepherding doesn't stop there. We employ and value the natural gifts of the sheep. Year after year, at shearing time, Harrison and Eleanor harvest the sheep's shaggy coats with care. The wool eventually finds its way to Eleanor's spinning wheel. There she spins the shaggy bounty—voluminous piles of wool—into lustrous yarn, weeding out the impurities, refining the sheep's inherent gifts, and fashioning them into stunning sweaters and blankets.

How like the divine Shepherd's process with our souls, spirits, and bodies! Tuning our ears to the Voice and following its call transforms our inborn gifts into useful and meaningful service. That which contaminates us is lovingly removed, and our inherent beauty is brought forth to find its place in the world.

Throughout scripture, the image of the sheep and shepherd teaches us about the relationship offered by a loving Creator and the gentle, guiding wisdom that is a part of that connection. In the familiar and comforting words of Psalm 23, "The LORD is my shepherd, I shall not want" (v. 1).

Reflect: Read Psalm 23 slowly, using several translations, if possible. Allow that ancient image to enrich your own relationship with your Shepherd. What new thoughts span the centuries and connect biblical times to your life today?

OCTOBER 26 • *Dancing in the Dark*

I remember the day that Tilden Edwards introduced the possibility of "dancing prayer" to my class at the Shalem Institute for Spiritual Formation. The group of twenty-six adults was as scared and skittish as a group of first-graders. Through the Institute's two-year program, we participants had been exposed to many challenging spiritual disciplines—from icons to meditative practice to praying the Bible—but this one clearly fell outside our comfort zone. In his gracious way, Edwards explained the traditions and potential of engaging the body in prayer, giving those who felt massive resistance permission to excuse themselves if they wished. Several folks quietly slipped out of the room.

Edwards invited those of us who nervously stayed put to spend some time in silence, allowing our bodies to move freely to the music in any way that felt authentic to us as an expression of our prayer. The lights were dimmed; restful, melodic music filled the room. After quite some time, one person got up, then another and another, each moving independently and prayerfully. Each of us avoided eye contact to help create a feeling of complete safety and acceptance. It was probably the most daring of any of the disciplines we attempted but one that embodied the relinquishment and abandonment to God we sought.

We became keenly aware of the enormous barrier most of us live with—that of timidity and embarrassment about our bodies. This awkwardness causes a host of unspoken questions to bubble up: "What will everyone think?" "Can I really let go in my body as well as my spirit?" "Can my body teach my stubborn heart to do this?"

As participants danced that evening, we learned a freeing lesson about the power of creative dance to move us toward our private prayer of release and relinquishment. It offered a small taste of what it might feel like to dance—rather than plod—through life.

Reflect: Put on some instrumental music and courageously dance your prayer. Allow your body to speak nonverbally, letting go of words and letting your muscles express your heart's longing for God.

OCTOBER 27 • *A Conversation with the Cosmos*

Drowned out by the drone of airplanes and the din of traffic, the whispers of the earth often fail to reach our noisy minds. This old earth has supported humankind for millennia, yet we fall deaf to her wisdom. Mother Earth has fed us, supported our steps, and carried us through the day, but our mechanistic and bustling world largely takes her for granted or ignores her. She takes care of us, but we forget our responsibility to take care of her. And we forget to thank her.

When we take time to commune with the aliveness of God's universal energy, we rekindle our own aliveness. We need to pause in places where we hear a bird's call, feel the wind in our faces, and become aware of the animation that surrounds us and infuses us. The forest, the mountaintops, the seaside and other quiet refuges can invite us into holy conversations with the cosmos. Nature speaks a unique language, conveying thoughts and concerns that fail to reach us in other ways.

As children, most of us had experiences of lying in the grass or on a rooftop and gazing at the vastness of the sky—identifying stars, sensing our littleness, wondering about how and why it all came about. Part of our creative awakening rests in reviving those moments of wonder and opening ourselves to the unity and interconnection of reality. Underneath the wonder lie the relentless questions of "Why am I here?" "What is my place in the universe?" Asking those questions in hopeful anticipation can help us live faithfully into the answers.

After times of silent communion with the cosmos and its Creator, we can make our way back into our earthbound lives, whole creatures connected to heaven and to earth.

Reflect: Recapture the wonder of lying down with eyes gazing at the stars, imagining your place in the grand scheme of things. Let the darkness make you aware of the Light that shines into your life.

OCTOBER 28 • *Knitting It All Together*

It was you who formed my inward parts; you knit me together in my mother's womb" (Ps. 139:13).

Knitting has been credited with turning out beautiful souls as well as sweaters. It's slow, it's process-oriented, it's meditative. Each stitch gathers separate yarns into a colorful blend of order and design—an ideal activity for bringing together the disparate threads of our lives. Many have discovered that this craft brings new dimensions and depth to their spiritual journey.

This method of handwork, though traditionally the province of women, is being embraced by men also. Exploring the loops and patterns of life while creating loops and patterns with the hands is not gender specific. It's more than knit one, purl one. Sorting and blending yarn resembles sorting and blending our inner "loose threads." Like any meditative practice, it engages the body, mind, and spirit in a rhythmic movement that invites contemplative thought and deep prayer.

In recent years, knitting has blossomed into meaningful ministry through hundreds of Prayer Shawl groups. These knitters weave love and prayer into comforting coverings for those who are ill, bereaved, or distressed. Recipients report that they feel covered in kindness and enfolded by prayerful support. Shawls can also be given as gifts of appreciation, wrapping those who receive them in grateful affirmation. No matter what the occasion, prayer shawls express the love of their creators as well as the love of the great Creator. The experience feels like a cuddly, comforting, cosmic hug!

This creative pursuit sets up a win-win situation by enriching our spiritual lives as it brings solace to the lives of others.

Reflect: Consider taking up some form of handwork—knitting, crocheting, carving, whittling—as a creative contemplative process. You may want to join with others to support your efforts or to serve the community through your craft. Remember that busy hands give your mind a chance to rest in God's grace and guidance.

OCTOBER 29 • *Dreaming in Color*

I once thought that dreams were just neurons firing in the head—the flotsam and jetsam of the brain's overcrowding. Not anymore. When I learned a bit about dream language and experienced some dreams that clearly pointed my way toward wholeness, I began to take them more seriously.

Certainly the biblical writers did. Consider the respected status of dreams in both the Old and New Testaments—from the vivid dreams of the Joseph story in Genesis to the spectacular symbolism of the Revelation to John on the island of Patmos. Many groups today are reclaiming this ancient tradition of paying attention to dream content, some even referring to dreams as "personal letters from God."

Some schools of thought assert that dreams are unconscious material seeking to be made conscious, thereby making it hard for us to find the meaning in our own dreams. It's more productive to work with a person trained in dream work or in a group setting where the participants have studied reliable texts on dreams. The dream always belongs to the dreamer, and any suggestions about the meaning must resonate with the dreamer.

Most of us consider our dreams too bizarre or embarrassing to have any significance. But the craziest dreams can often yield the most fruit. Even those that seem nightmarish can contain positive, encouraging information when viewed by those familiar with dream language. The symbols are often graphic and earthy—therefore natural.

Here's an example of a horrific dream that carried a healing message:

> I enter a classroom with a guide beside me. There are bloody, dismembered limbs and body parts of the children and teachers scattered everywhere. However, each dismembered head has a faint smile on it. We are aghast but strangely calm. I tell the guide unemotionally that I'm glad my children are in another classroom. We step carefully through the carnage, and the guide says, "I'll show you a better way." We leave the room and enter a long hall, simple and uncluttered, with clean, blank walls on each side. I can't see the end of the hallway, but it dissolves into pure light.

The dreamer's association of the scene was with the school her children attended when they were young. Her counselor wisely asked her, "What was your life like then?" The reply brought her to tears. "I was trying to be everything to everybody—a good wife, mother, church leader, and caretaker for my parents." Obviously, the woman recalled a period of intense fragmentation, where she felt emotionally torn apart. She always kept a smile on her face no matter what chaos reigned inside her, rarely displaying emotion. Her dream was inviting her to simplify her life, establish clear boundaries, and move toward the Light.

Sometimes, nighttime scenarios that emerge during unguarded sleep can carry powerful pointers toward deeper growth.

Reflect: Make a practice of writing down your dreams as soon as you awaken. Pray with the images, being open to the symbolic spiritual messages. If possible, find a person trained in dream work to help you sort out the clues. God works in mysterious ways—even in the depths of darkness.

OCTOBER 30 • *Strolling with Soul Mates*

A walk in a fall forest of blazing yellow and bright orange wraps us in coats of color. But these vivid hues gather intensity in the company of fascinating friends.

This happens every time I march along with a diverse group of women who walk regularly in a botanic garden near my neighborhood. We don't merely share the path; we share our lives. No matter if it's winter, summer, spring, or fall, our forty-five-minute hikes add "color" to our days:

- Their thoughtful solutions to family dilemmas inform my own challenges.
- Their book suggestions fill my library with stimulating reading.
- Their movie reviews guide me in trips to the cinema.
- Their discussion of medical issues leads me to make healthy choices.
- Their honesty about spiritual struggles makes me feel less lonely on my soul's path.
- Their courage and compassion contagiously spur my own.
- Their encouragement supports my creative leaps.
- Their perspective on global matters brings intelligence to my worldview.
- Their sizzling conversations light up my brain cells.

In other words, their creativity feeds my own. Together we walk our way out of a problem and into a solution: out of anger and into acceptance, out of chaos into calm. As we meander our way through the troubles and triumphs of everyday existence, an unspoken common purpose carries us along—a yearning to live with purpose and faith. With that silent goal to unite us, each step tightens our bonds of friendship and adds bold color to our lives.

Reflect: Call a few like-minded friends today, and take a walk together. Share your soul journey as you share the path.

OCTOBER 31 • *Artists of Life*

Creativity is not limited to the arts. Beyond the painting, the sculpting, the singing, the running, a fundamental creativity calls to us all. We are charged with the challenge to be artists of life.

Since our "medium" is life itself, how do we express this inexpressible gift—the art of being human? Whatever our vocation or artistic pursuit, we can infuse each day with creative thought and action:

- Embrace possibility. Leave the doors of your life slightly ajar— always open to unknown possibilities. Like the weaver, allow the yarn to take over.

- Embrace diversity. Broaden your scope; suspend your fear of "differentness." Be willing to color outside the lines.

- Embrace your uniqueness. When you inhabit your authentic self, everything you touch will have increased life.

- Embrace abundance. Abundance creates overflow, which spills into the lives of others.

- Embrace the holy. Join the flow of God's boundless love and compassion, soaking everything you do and are in the unquenchable Living Water.

As we tune our hearts in harmony with the divine heart and allow God to weave the threads of our experience, God will fashion our lives into one glorious work of art. And don't forget to notice the purple.

Reflect: Pick up a colorful leaf; trace its veins with your fingers and sense its uniqueness. Claim your own particular endowment of creative energy, silencing the negative murmurs within you.

November

ASPECTS OF
APPRECIATION

"Rejoice always, pray without ceasing, give thanks in all circumstances."
—1 Thessalonians 5:16-18

Breath Prayer
Source of all blessing, . . . I give you thanks.

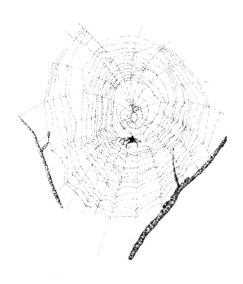

NOVEMBER 1 • *The Grammar of Gratitude*

Gracias, Merci beaucoup, Danke schoen. From every area of the globe, we hear expressions of the same basic impulse. Every language and culture registers a response that is embedded in our human nature, the urge to say "thank you." Grin at a baby, and he grins right back. Tickle a toddler under the chin and a chuckle erupts. Hand a child a Christmas package, and she wraps you in a bear hug. I believe God implants an innate inclination toward thanksgiving in our very souls.

That is, until something snuffs it out. Somewhere along the road, the trials of life begin to erode our feeling of blessedness. Tragedy and discontent derail thanksgiving, and we get caught in a downward spiral of negativity and worst-case scenarios. So how do we hang on to this gracious gift of gratitude that springs from our core? How can we cultivate and nurture it so that feelings of appreciation can outlast the assaults of life? Isn't thankfulness more than measuring our blessings against the calamities and seeing which list is longer?

My own attitude about gratitude has come full circle. As a young girl, my parents encouraged me to take a positive approach no matter what. Adulthood introduced me to a healthy cynicism in which psychologists urged folks toward radical honesty about their feelings. Psychologists urged us to face our feelings and "get them out." They dismissed the power of positive thinking as pie-in-the-sky theology—harmful at worst and naïve at best—a kind of behavioral Band-Aid™ that was out of sync with the real world. Surely authentic thanksgiving had to involve more than warm, fuzzy feelings or getting what we want. Much more.

Scripture charges us to live in the tension between distress and hope. It calls us to deal honestly with not only the big losses but also with the daily doses of disappointment and irritation, the aches and pains, the rocky relationships, the unpaid bills—while retaining a sense of gratitude for life and all it holds. The overriding message of the Christian tradition as expressed by Paul is to give thanks, give thanks, give thanks—not *for* all circumstances but *in* all circumstances.

As we explore the aspects of appreciation in this special season, we'll discover many choices we can make that cooperate with the divine dynamic that beckons us to say thank you.

Reflect: What is your earliest memory of feeling grateful, of saying thank you? What seems to spark your gratitude on a daily basis? Read Psalm 100 prayerfully, allowing it to awaken your God-given impulse to praise.

NOVEMBER 2 • *More Than a Thank-You Note*

Many of us start out learning the attitude of gratitude. We learn to say thank you for gifts, to recite a grace before meals, and later to express gratitude in print—all of which build the "gratitude muscle," which is certainly a beginning. But the journey to true thanksgiving requires a process of embodiment rather than a list of specific actions.

For years, I accepted the popular definition of gratitude as the "recurrent affirmation of what's working in our lives." This notion leads us to limit our idea of blessing to times when events or ideas please us or make us feel good. Eventually, however, that simplistic idea bumps up against the scriptural injunction to "give thanks in all circumstances." So what are we to do with all that isn't working in our lives? Renowned writer Henri J. M. Nouwen expressed our common dilemma this way:

> How often we tend to divide our past into good things to remember with gratitude and painful things to accept or forget. . . . We quickly develop a mentality in which we hope to collect more good memories than bad. . . . Gratitude in its deepest sense means to live life as a gift to be received gratefully. But gratitude as the gospel speaks about it embraces *all* of life: the good and the bad, the joyful and the painful, the holy and the not so holy. . . . It is so easy for me to put the bad memories under the rug of my life and to think only about the good things that please me. By doing so, however, I prevent myself from discovering the joy beneath my sorrow, the peace hidden in the midst of my conflicts, and the strength that becomes visible in the midst of my weakness. . . . As long as we remain resentful about things that we wish had not happened, about relationships that we wish had turned out differently, about mistakes we wish we had not made, part of our heart remains isolated, unable to bear fruit in the new life ahead of us.[1]

This kind of gratitude encompasses life as it is—in its ups and downs—knowing that all of it, all of it, is enclosed in an incomprehensible love. This is gratitude infused with hope—not just hope for something but hope in something.

Reflect: What portions of your life experience seem devoid of gratitude? Bring them into the circle of God's sustaining love so that you can be grateful *in* them if not *for* them.

NOVEMBER 3 • *Praise the Lord!*

Most of us cut our religious teeth on praise scriptures such as "I will give thanks to the LORD with my whole heart" (Ps. 111:1), "Enter his gates with thanksgiving, and his courts with praise" (Ps. 100:4). We praise God in our worship liturgy and our prayers. We sing hymns of adoration and devotion. How do we move from praising God with our lips to praising God with our lives?

Perhaps we need to begin at the beginning by affirming that, indeed, a grand and mysterious goodness lies at the heart of creation. Genesis 1 affirms its goodness (vv. 4, 10, 12, 18, 25, 31). That means us too!

Affirming this basic goodness colors the way we talk and walk. We dare to believe there's a kernel of goodness in every person, a ray of hope in every circumstance. To be sure, that divine spark within each of us flickers weakly sometimes. The pain of life seems to drown out the hope. Yet, we are never to lose sight of the benevolence that undergirds it all.

So a good starting point for our journey to authentic gratitude comes when we speak praise with our lips, trusting that some of the profound truth will seep into our hearts and eventually wind up in our actions toward self and neighbor. Continuous words of praise tend to expose the disparity between what we say and what we do. Our repeated acknowledgment of the goodness of the Creator and creation permits us to see the complaining, judging parts of ourselves for what they are—a disharmony in the symphony of glory at the heart of things.

Reflect: Spend some time with these words from Psalm 103:1: "Bless the LORD, O my soul, and all that is within me, bless his holy name." Consider how your thoughts, words, and actions can live in harmony with this decree.

NOVEMBER 4 • *Gratitude Is Good for Us*

There is something primal, mysterious ,and holy in the way we are created. Medical research confirms a reliable link between generosity and health. Scientific studies measure the degree to which attitudes of thankfulness and acts of gratitude actually release positive hormones in the body and strengthen the immune system. Research reports that optimism is good for the brain, that it can reduce the risk of dementia, improve focus, build resistance to depression—even contribute to faster recovery from illness. Former scientist Gregg Braden makes these points: "Life-affirming emotions such as gratitude, compassion, and love are now documented as being triggers for life-promoting conditions such as lower blood pressure, release of good hormones, and enhanced immune responses.[2] Laboratories are producing quantifiable results that confirm what religious traditions have been teaching for centuries.

The field of psychology is weighing in as well. Grateful people experience higher levels of joy, enthusiasm, love, and happiness. The disciplined practice of generosity and thankfulness can protect us from the destructive impulses of envy, resentment, greed, and bitterness. Benefits include the ability to cope more effectively with stress, combat frustration, increase resilience, and improve relationships. Ungrateful folks remain chronically discontent, always wanting something more and bigger.

These findings grab our selfish attention and spur our natural desire for self-preservation. We may find ourselves wrapped in an ego-centered gratitude in which the motivating factor is our own well-being, that is, "I'll be thankful because, after all, it's to my benefit." Even if truthful, surely we can view this reality in a more loving and expansive way, and it's this: When we align ourselves with the precepts of the Spirit and bring ourselves into harmony with the way God created us—getting in the sacred flow—everything works together for good, not only for ourselves but for the world around us. This sphere of influence includes our bodies, our emotions, our relationships, our vocations, our ministries, our communities.

Gratitude produces a divine ripple effect that fills us with wonder and, yes, even more gratitude!

Reflect: Ponder how your body feels when you are immersed in feelings of thanksgiving or in acts of generosity. Celebrate this holy interaction between spirit and flesh.

NOVEMBER 5 • *. . . And Good for the World*

When Paul spoke of the divine reality as that in which "we live and move and have our being" (Acts 17:28), his words echoed the name God revealed to Moses, "I AM WHO I AM" (Exod. 3:14). The Mystery addressed by contemporary science sounds strangely reminiscent of both those attempts to express the magnitude of the Divine.

The terrain that once divided the spiritual and the scientific is being spanned by a multitude of crossovers. Theologians now venture into the realm of science; scientists sense spiritual elements in their discoveries of creation's complexity. In other words, science and theology are beginning to affirm each other and engage in meaningful discussion. Studies from both quantum physics and the behavioral sciences offer empirical evidence that not only is gratitude of benefit to us as individuals, but its invisible properties seep into the world in a wondrous way.

I am no scientist, but I can no longer avoid considering the exciting implications presented by the quantum world.[3] Layers of existence containing electromagnetic energy and vibrational frequencies form part of the world we live in every day. Though I may be unable to see those "force fields" or understand the science of them, I can't deny the fact that I can pick up my cellphone in Memphis and in seconds be chatting with someone in Tokyo! Science tells us that these fields of pulsating energy affect and influence one another in a miraculous manner.

Here's where it gets personal. Studies show the measured effects of human emotions on this electromagnetic field. Our emotions emit certain vibrations. Emotions such as compassion, peace, love, and appreciation emit a higher vibration than those of resentment, jealousy, anger, and negativity. Because of this, we influence (and are influenced by) this unified field that we share with others. The invisible effect extends to other systems in the created order. Singing to your plants, petting your cat, and smiling at the baby are far from trivial notions.

Think of how primal this impulse is, so much so that we take it for granted. When we observe someone else's finger jabbed with a needle, our own cells react. When we help someone, we sometimes experience a "helper's high," which refers to a phenomenon in which both the helper and the helped feel a pleasurable vibration. The awesome idea that all life is connected in this web of feeling affirms our faith in the One who fashioned this elegant existence.

Gratitude is one key that unlocks our willingness to participate in this amazing pattern of blessing.

Reflect: Imagine for a moment that your emotions and actions affect the world in ways that are beyond your comprehension. Allow that notion to spark your resolve to foster feelings of appreciation and love.

NOVEMBER 6 • *The Disconnect*

My friends and I had just attended a meaningful workshop on the importance of gratitude. The thoughtful, convincing, and inspiring presentations encouraged all participants to believe that a thankful heart is a worthwhile goal, that appreciation is a climate of the soul in which our spirits thrive.

But then, in a matter of minutes, life began to intrude. During the car ride home, the conversation slowly deteriorated into nit-picking comments about the inferior chicken salad at the workshop luncheon, exasperation at the stalled traffic, anticipation of an upcoming Sunday jammed with too many demands, chronic fatigue, the kids' messy rooms, the last three rotten things that happened at the office, the sorry state of the world—you get the idea. Even though our brains had bought into the concept of gratitude, our wills and bodies stubbornly resisted. Like rubber bands, we unconsciously bounced back to business-as-usual, inhabiting our same surly selves.

When I returned home, I thought to myself, *There is something seriously wrong with this picture!* I could sense the vast distance between the head and the heart, between the words of thanksgiving we spoke on Sunday and the ingratitude we expressed on Monday, between who we thought we were and who we actually were. As I reviewed the conversation, I had to own my complicity in the toxic game of "ain't it awful." When the complaining began, I had automatically joined the fray. The truth is—whining can be a heap of fun, especially in a jovial group.

Change begins with heightened awareness. A lightbulb comes on in the "room" of our unconscious behavior, and we make a choice. In that moment, I knew that healing the disconnect between advocating thankfulness and becoming a thankful person would take more than the snap of a finger. However, I felt the grace of the Spirit inviting me, egging me on, and promising to walk with me on the journey to a more grateful heart.

Reflect: Explore the disconnect you sense in your own life between talking about gratitude and walking in gratitude. As you become conscious of the disconnects, deal with them one at a time without self-judgment. After all, you're an imperfect human creation of a forgiving Creator.

NOVEMBER 7 • *Belief in Gratitude*

I believe that I shall see the goodness of the LORD in the land of the living" (Ps. 27:13). We have to start somewhere, so perhaps clarifying our values is the place to begin. Beliefs are a bit like the blinker signal on a car: They indicate the direction toward which we're moving. They point us toward a path and give impetus to the journey we're on. Beliefs—those tenets we hold to be true—don't transform our hearts in and of themselves, but they certainly open the way for spiritual energy to take root.

Despite all experiential evidence to the contrary, traditional wisdom and scripture urge us to steer our spiritual growth toward thankfulness. But sometimes the meanness of humankind and the messiness of Mother Nature seem more visible than the "goodness of the LORD" for which the writer of Psalm 27 yearns. As daily reports of murder and mayhem bombard us, it's difficult to remember, much less believe, that we are wired for gratitude. However, the medical, scientific, and psychological evidence affirms that our bodies (as well as our spirits and emotions) respond positively to feelings of thanksgiving. Thankful people live longer, have lower blood pressure, more active immune systems, and (not surprisingly) more friends. Books and studies assert the value of this virtue, telling us that we not only need gratitude but that we are made to be grateful. It is a state of the soul that enhances both health and happiness.

So we can begin this journey toward a thankful heart by believing that it's in harmony with the way creation is put together; that's it's a journey worth taking, an attitude worth practicing, a way of life worth living.

Reflect: Affirm your own belief in the power of gratitude, in its ability to align you more closely with God's dream for your life. Make that a grounded starting point for becoming an authentically thankful person.

NOVEMBER 8 • *Gratitude and Guilt*

Gratitude and guilt are strange bedfellows, but they cuddle together just the same. The guilt trips start early in life, and we keep on taking them.

"Eat all your vegetables. Be thankful for your food because there are starving children in the world." My parents said this with unquestionable authority, though I never quite understood what that had to do with canned peas. I ate them anyway, choking down a generous portion of guilt along with the peas.

"Thank goodness God 'spared me' in the auto accident, but my buddy didn't make it," reflects the guilty survivor. "Just look at all my blessings. . . . I really should be more grateful," my friend remarked shamefully. We don't become more thankful simply by thinking that we should be.

Our memory banks are full of such statements that attest to the fact that gratitude is often tinged with guilt. Those statements imply that despite the genuine nature of the gratitude, it comes to us at someone else's expense—the person with no food, no home, no life. When we say, "There but for the grace of God go I," what do we mean? That we received God's grace, and "they" didn't?

These judgments may seem harsh, but they contain a kernel of truth that bears scrutiny. True, awareness of another's plight sparks our compassion and can serve a formative purpose. We often begin our journey to a thankful heart with this kind of reasoning. Hopefully, we don't end there. Even when a vague sense of guilt motivates our appreciation, we are invited to move from gratitude-as-an-ought to a purer sense of thanksgiving. Otherwise, we'll settle for a gratitude that breeds arrogance.

Reflect: Ponder the relationship of guilt and gratitude in your own life. Do you feel gratitude mixed with a measure of guilt? Pray that your thankfulness will be expansive enough to embrace the mystery of abundance and insufficiency, which does not depend on fairness or explanation.

NOVEMBER 9 • *Gratitude and Privilege*

God gave us a cloudless day for the patio party." "Our company has been blessed with huge profits this quarter!" "God protected our plane on that stormy flight to Chicago."

These all-too-human statements mask a tinge of entitlement. What are we saying? That the nearby farmer in desperate need of rain was not blessed while those at the party were? Are the owners of failing companies somehow out of favor with God? Was the plane that crashed while mine stayed aloft full of folks who were outside the realm of divine protection? The unspoken implications of some of our thankful words hint at a hidden arrogance, that somehow we deserved favor or that God must have thought we deserved it.

Scripture tells us that God "makes his sun rise on the evil and on the good, and sends rain on the righteous and on the unrighteous" (Matt. 5:45). Bad things happen to good people, and good things happen to bad people. Being righteous doesn't necessarily protect us from anything but allows us to hold whatever happens in a faithful and spiritual way.

One glimpse into the complexity of the problem will remind us that any glib talk about the mystery of suffering is too simplistic. (Scholars and layfolk alike have debated the points made in the book of Job!) As much as we yearn for clear answers, we must inevitably bow to that mystery and admit that we just don't know why some things happen. In our privileged culture, we tend to confine blessing to what gets good results, producing happiness and prosperity—favors we can catalog and count. However, as we move toward a more profound understanding of the nature of true gratitude, we will learn to include the wholeness of life's journey, the good and the not-so-good—and the holy potential in each. When we struggle with those things we don't understand, we often experience the birth of a deeper faith.

Being thankful for our blessings does not mean that we are entitled to them. We can express our gratitude, free of any notion that we were favored over others.

Reflect: Spend some time pondering the mixed messages in some of your thoughts and words about divine blessing. Pray for loving motives rather than complete understanding.

NOVEMBER 10 • *Gratitude in the Dark*

Not all growth happens in the light-filled moments. Sometimes gratefulness twinkles in the darkness.

I had contracted to write a book manuscript. The deadline loomed, and I was almost ready to throw in the towel. I had sabotaged my writing with uncharacteristic procrastination, and my disciplined schedule lay in the ditch. Each time I sat in front of the word processor, the sense of urgency felt like a dam that blocked the creative flow. I felt like a dictionary with the pages ripped out, leaving no words.

So, although I knew I should be writing, I escaped my office and went to the monthly meeting of our writers' club. I had sent the members the first chapters of the book for feedback, but I had yet to receive any comments on the content. As the meeting began, our facilitator (a gifted young creative writing instructor) invited their responses, "So what did you think about Linda's opening chapters?" There was dead silence.

Finally, someone spoke up, "Linda, chapter 1 sounds like a school report, an academic exercise—not like you." Then another chimed in, "Yeah, like you were taking an exam or something and wanted to make an *A*!" Other gentle comments came tumbling out. People affirmed my research and citing of sources, but they perceived a shortage of my own opinions and overreliance on those I considered experts. The consensus was that they didn't hear the "heartbeat" they had come to expect in my writing. They cited examples, and I took notes. At last, someone summed up the discussion with this question, "Where is your own voice in this writing?"

The comments devastated me, and I limped home in a deeper hole than ever. How could I take time for major rewrites and still meet the deadline? In my misery and frustration, I anesthetized myself with a TV movie and sank into sadness for a while.

By the next morning, unexpected emotions surfaced. As I sat prayerfully with my disappointment and discouragement, feelings of hope—even gratitude—came bubbling up out of nowhere. Was hearing the criticism of my work a pleasant experience? Did it feel good? Absolutely not. Applause definitely feels better. So what was this unbidden burst of thankfulness all about?

Suddenly, I knew. A profound sense of being valued, not only as a writer but also as a human being lay beneath the crush of criticism. The members had cared enough about my work to examine it with a fine-tooth comb. They had cared enough about me to be candid. They had graciously spoken the truth in love—surely a cause for thanksgiving. So I returned to page one, heeding their prudent advice.

The gratitude I felt resulted from their gift of being real with me. The process of genuine thanksgiving often gets worked out in the rough and tumble of everyday life.

Reflect: Remember a time when you have had a difficult heart-to-heart talk with another person in which each of you suspended your defenses and truly listened. Even with contentious topics, what gratitude did you feel in the honest exchange?

NOVEMBER 11 • *Blessedness*

May God be gracious to us and bless us and make his face to shine upon us" (Ps. 67:1).

The concept of blessing is mysteriously elusive. We use it casually, as in "Bless her heart, she spilled tea on her new dress." We say it seriously as we pray, "Bless this home, O Lord." We utter it often as we sit down to dinner, asking God to "bless this food to the nourishment of our bodies." The idea of blessedness can't be captured by our words, no matter how eloquent they might be.

Most of us think of blessing in positive terms—a grace, a gift—and it is that. We recall this definition when we "count our blessings" or when we list them in the season of Thanksgiving. However, Jesus paints a different picture in his Sermon on the Mount (Matthew 5; Luke 6). When we read the Beatitudes—blessed are the meek, the mourning, the persecuted, the poor— it sounds like tough duty to me. Our net of meaning has to expand to those times when the proverbial ox is in the ditch, when we encounter the inevitable setbacks and heartbreaks of life. Then blessedness gets bigger. Rather than receiving the bag of heavenly goodies that we secretly hope for, we'll become aware of God's presence in all things.

We do not limit places of blessing to times of favor. Rather, it is a cloud of wonder that we can live in. We inch closer to this divine concept when we express deep appreciation of the blessing that is the cosmic Yes! of God—a holy Presence in both the light and the dark.

Reflect: Imagine yourself surrounded by and enmeshed in the web of blessedness that is the presence of the Holy. Say yes to God's Yes, so you can be blessed to be a blessing.

NOVEMBER 12 • *Gratitude Grows*

Jesus "took the seven loaves and the fish; and after giving thanks he broke them and gave them to the disciples, and the disciples gave them to the crowds" (Matt: 15:36).

Just like the loaves and fishes, gratitude grows. The more you say thank you, the more you see things for which to give thanks. Thanksgiving is contagious. Being around grateful people makes us more likely to catch this delightful "disease."

I remember a friend from my past whom I'll call Cindy. She lived in the throes of the pattern called "yes-but." She inevitably second-guessed any positive happening in her world. If she had had a pleasant visit with her grandchildren, she focused on the backache she suffered as a result. If I complimented one of her accomplishments, she would cite everything that was wrong with her achievement and tell me why I shouldn't have praised her. In an effort to appear humble, she had forgotten to be grateful. When we deny ourselves and others the mutual experience of gratitude, we suck the positive energy out of the atmosphere!

On the other hand, it encourages my own journey to a thankful heart when I'm in the presence of my friend Harold. Though up in years and enduring significant health challenges, he reaches for a thankful thought in every circumstance. When I visited him during his recovery from knee-replacement surgery, he didn't deny the discomfort. However, after briefly acknowledging the problems, he went straight for the silver lining—his beloved golf game. With a twinkle in his eye, he said, "I should be back on the golf course in a matter of weeks—good as new!"

It's inspiring to be around folks who don't skirt reality but automatically move to a positive place without the irritating chirpiness of a Pollyanna. With a mysterious contagion, their appreciative attitude spreads like a wonderful wildfire because genuine gratitude feeds itself exponentially. If someone helps us with directions and we thank them, they are more likely to assist others in the future. Studies show that waitstaff who write "thanks" on the bottom of the restaurant receipt are rewarded with larger tips!

Gratitude begets gratitude begets gratitude. The more we see with eyes of appreciation, the more our sight is shaped by the seeing.

Reflect: Think of someone you know who exhibits a thankful heart. Does it encourage you toward appreciation? Commit to participate in this happy contagion by filling the atmosphere around you with thanksgiving.

NOVEMBER 13 • *Barriers to a Thankful Heart*

Spiritual wisdom tells us that gratitude matters. I daresay that most of us believe that wholeheartedly. Then how do we slip offtrack? How do we stifle that natural impulse and sabotage our progress to thanksgiving?

The barriers usually hide in our familiar responses, and we fail to notice the ways they deflate the bubble of gratitude. Many of our normal responses to compliments represent what I call discounted thinking. Someone thanks us for a favor done, and we promptly devalue their gift by saying something like, "It was really nothing." Without intending to do so, we throw cold water on their spontaneous expression of thanks. Many of us grew up with the notion that acknowledging a compliment or another's thank-you to us carries a hint of boastfulness on our part. Instead, it acknowledges the person's gratitude and affirms their thoughtfulness.

Another subtle barrier accompanies our frequent reply to "How are you?" Even when things are pretty awful, we often say, "Everything's just great!" On the surface it appears to make everyone feel better. Sometimes, fake-it-till-you-make-it behavior does serve to coax our minds to fall in line with our upbeat words. But often, it acts as a cover-up for unexpressed feelings. False gratitude fails the test of authenticity.

It helps to think of thanksgiving as a kind of continuum with whiners on one end and over-the-top gushers on the other. The whiners thrive on a chaotic existence where nothing is ever okay; the gushers, on the other hand, are likely to lose touch with their honest feelings by habitually forcing a plastic smile.

Striking a balance between honesty and hope will always resemble walking an emotional tightrope. Perhaps the steadiness we seek involves sitting honestly *with* our feelings rather than *on* them. We can acknowledge difficulty without choosing to live in its icy grip, without feeding the growing gloominess so that it becomes a pattern of behavior, a part of our identity.

Reflect: Think about how you personally find the balance between seeing the harrowing parts of life and affirming hope and happiness as well. Reflect on the model of Jesus as one who openly stared evil in the face and experienced despair while choosing to live in authenticity and hope.

NOVEMBER 14 • *Anticipating the Worst*

We also take the steam out of thankfulness by allowing cynicism to seep in. "Of course, I'm thankful," we may say, "but this can't last." This familiar form of discounted thinking assumes that the present fortune is a fluke, the calm before the inevitable storm of misfortune. After all, "Isn't that how life is?" whispers our inner cynic. We feel more prudent and somehow smarter to hedge our bets, steeling ourselves for the disappointment that surely lurks around the next corner. So we willingly move the negative energy ahead in anticipation of the joy falling apart so that we won't be caught off guard. In doing so, we make it impossible to be present to the wonder of the moment. In an insidious way, we project a somber reality that we actually live into.

The power of pessimism wears many disguises. Often, it shows up as comparative thinking. "I'd better be grateful because it could always be worse." "I'm looking forward to our week of vacation, but then it'll be back to the same old grindstone." "We're thankful for our new home, but I really wanted to live on Elm Street." We even point to the maladies and misfortunes of others in an attempt to alleviate our own. No matter what form the negativity takes, it pricks the balloon of appreciation and allows the joy to escape.

As in other areas of spiritual growth, awareness of our subtle pessimism creates an opening to let go of the negativity and replace it with expressions of gratitude for life's abundance, being present to the joy and leaning toward hope and love.

Reflect: Notice today any vestiges of pessimism that sneak into your thoughts and words. While acknowledging the reality they may represent, reframe your attitude with feelings of thankfulness.

NOVEMBER 15 • *Questioning Our Blessings*

Sometimes when I'm lying snug and warm, covered by a down comforter on a cold winter night, I can't help wondering, *How did I happen to be here instead of shivering in some windy refugee tent halfway across the globe?* Surely this conundrum occurs to many of us who are privileged to have a full stomach and a roof over our heads. It may not carry the clear label of "guilty thinking," but it can form a barrier to gratitude nonetheless.

I was reminded of this inconsistency during a recent conversation with a friend. Mildred had begun a redecorating project in her spacious home. The sofa had become threadbare and the draperies faded by the sun's rays—the living room needed a face-lift. She voiced a concern that, though seemingly trivial, hinted at an underlying tension that confronts all serious seekers. She wondered how she could justify spending thousands of dollars putting frills on her elegant existence when some folks didn't have a home at all. How could she delight in the colorful fabrics and rich textures that made her happy when some couldn't taste such beauty?

The short answer is, I don't know. Perhaps this dilemma is not meant to be resolved. Perhaps this paradox should plague any sensitive spirit. It seems appropriate and honest to live with some measure of this anxiety, always searching for ways to affirm both the reality of abundance as well as the world's need.

Mildred will probably always struggle, under God's grace and mercy, to delight in her lovely home while not forgetting the homelessness of others. And all of us will struggle as well.

Reflect: For a moment, stretch out your hands—holding gratitude for your own abundance in one hand and the pressing needs of the world in the other. Bring your palms together slowly as you pray for ways to act responsibly and lovingly in the face of both realities. How might your gratitude be converted into good works for the less fortunate?

NOVEMBER 16 • *Busyness and Blessing*

Appreciation takes time. And focus. And an ability to live in the moment. In our hectic lives, we often become immune to the truth of clichés like

"Stop and smell the roses" or "There is more to life than increasing its speed," while we continue our addictions to multitasking and busyness.

We even paint positive activities with a negative brush. For instance, I hear folks complain about how tired they are because "business is booming," so that gratitude for prosperity is swallowed up in protest. Our own busyness is often the culprit in these situations, crowding out appreciation. When we make choices that require an exhausting pace, fatigue can rob us of joy. Most of the time, we choose how we allocate our time. We automatically say yes to activities without passing the decision through a filter of discernment by asking, "Is this something I truly want to do?" "Am I called to do this—at this time, in this place?" "Do I have the energy to devote to this?"

Even though I know better, I recently found myself experiencing the consequences of overscheduling—again. I heard myself grumbling to friends about being away from home too frequently and suffering the exhaustion of airport travel and long hours on my aging feet. A warning bell sounded in my head: I needed to have a serious talk with myself.

I loved my work. I had prayed for and longed for a way to share the fruitful process of spiritual growth with others. In many ways, I was living the life of my dreams. But my thankfulness had become buried in the ashes of burnout. Rather than focusing on what I wished I could do, I had to deal honestly with what I actually could accomplish without sacrificing my health and passion for the work.

When we attempt to thrive on chaos, we can lose our grip on gratitude.

Reflect: Once again, take stock of your attachment to busyness. What simple changes can you make to settle into a more peaceful and thankful place?

NOVEMBER 17 • *Thankful for Suffering?*

Suffering and gratitude seem like an abrasive duo, as if they don't belong in the same sentence; yet scripture often links them. For many, it is an uncomfortable combination.

Maybe rigid interpretations of scripture set the tone for some of us: "We also boast in our sufferings, knowing that suffering produces endurance, and endurance produces character, and character produces hope, and hope does not disappoint us" (Rom. 5:3-5) or "Give thanks in all circumstances; for this is the will of God in Christ Jesus for you" (1 Thess. 5:18). Cultural maxims underscore these interpretations: "What doesn't kill you makes you stronger."

We cannot deny the enormous growth potential that comes with suffering; the fruits often do include endurance and character. Even in that cruel crucible, we prudently reach for some measure of thanksgiving, even if merely acknowledging those latent fruits. But a critical difference can open the door for us: We are called to be thankful *in all* circumstances, but not necessarily *for all* circumstances. We need to view the passages about suffering in light of Romans 8:28, "All things work together for good for those who love God." Notice it asserts that all things work together *for* good, not that all things *are* good.

Gratitude springs from trust that the Holy Spirit waits in the wings of any suffering that befalls us, helping us repair the brokenness. I don't believe God intends that we suffer; but when we do, we can claim the blessed assurance that the divine Presence never deserts us. This restorative power brings healing (on some level) and forms in us the fruits of resilience and wholeness.

Reflect: Remember a time of suffering in your life. Without being grateful for the experience itself, try to identify the nuggets of growth that ultimately surfaced. Give thanks for them.

NOVEMBER 18 • *Bridges to a Thankful Heart*

Believing in gratitude is not enough. Even our removing the barriers to gratitude won't automatically reward us with a thankful heart. Like going to the gym to build healthy muscles, we tone our spiritual muscles by building bridges of discipline. Ultimately, we can transform good intentions into reality through exercise and repetition. How can we tone the gratitude muscle?

Our beginning bridge engages the power of words, the potency of appreciative prayers. The words of Meister Eckhart provide impetus for our intentions: "If the only prayer you ever say in your whole life is 'thank you,' that would suffice."

It can be as simple as beginning the day with the affirmation from the Psalms, "This is the day that the LORD has made; let us rejoice and be glad in it" (Ps. 118:24). Then as you envision the day's happenings, surround each event and opportunity in a cloak of thanksgiving. Imagine each task, each encounter, each challenge, and each appointment wrapped in hopeful anticipation. Take a deep cleansing breath, say "thank you" out loud, and greet the day with a smile.

When worry and dread become chronic companions during our waking moments, they cast a pall over the day before our feet ever hit the floor. In negotiating the pathway from belief in gratitude to being a grateful person, our first words and steps set the mood for everything that follows.

Unless an idea (thankfulness) moves from the intellect to experience, from the abstract to the practical, it remains a nice idea. Admirable maybe, but without a heartbeat and dynamic movement. When we start our daily round by opening ourselves to the divine flow of thanksgiving, we build an invisible bridge from the *idea* of gratitude to the *practice* of gratitude.

Reflect: Think of ways you can tone your inner "gratitude muscle" today. Begin with words of praise and thanksgiving that support your day with appreciation.

NOVEMBER 19 • *The "Write" Thing*

The mail on that March morning contained an unusual note, penned on lovely pink stationery in purple ink. The message was short and simple—a brief acknowledgment of a small favor, which I had forgotten long ago. The writer had taken up the Lenten practice of sending a note of thanks to one person each day for forty days. I found her gesture touching, and it made my day.

As I went on about my business, I couldn't quite forget about that note. Thoughts drifted in and out, such as *Writing forty notes would be such a drag. How could she do that?* But the idea wouldn't go away. It returned with the persistence I had come to recognize as the Spirit nudging me. But my excuses were equally persistent. I had no note paper; I didn't have time; I couldn't think of forty people to thank. Besides, I would feel guilty when I failed at such a demanding task. But the hound of heaven kept sniffing at my resistant heels.

Finally a reluctant yes whispered deep inside. I first had to anticipate all the pitfalls that I knew would sabotage me. My supplies had to be handy—new note cards with matching pen, a fresh book of stamps, my complete address book—all placed on the table where I drank a leisurely cup of coffee each morning. As for the forty recipients, I vowed not to panic about that, trusting that the names would drop each day like manna from heaven.

And the names did. Obvious choices came first—friends and family—then that writing practice began to mess with my mind in surprising ways. The name of the high school English teacher who inspired me with her love of words, the nurse in my doctor's office with her unhurried manner, the youth minister at a church who shepherded me through teenage doubts and dilemmas—all were part of the long-buried memories that surfaced. With each passing day, I remembered and noticed more and more people whose kindness I had taken for granted.

I had begun the note-writing practice hoping to generate the same warm feelings that I experienced when I originally opened my friend's note. Little did I realize that God could use it to jolt me out of my own complacency. While I thought I was doing a good deed and obediently "paying it forward," God was using the experience to strengthen my flabby gratitude muscle.

Reflect: Pick up a pen and write one note of appreciation today. Let the Spirit guide your imagination.

NOVEMBER 20 • *Gratitude Journal*

Keeping a gratitude journal has the power to change our perspective. At the end of the day, list five things for which you are thankful—the more precise, the better. For instance, instead of noting that the weather was lovely, express thanks for the warmth of the sun as it fell on your face or the cool breeze that filled the house when you opened the windows. Record how you felt when a friend showered you with affirming words over lunch (recalling the exact words, if possible). Remember the enchanting aroma of the bread baking in the oven or the spontaneous squeeze your child gave you for no reason.

People who keep a gratitude journal develop a stronger sense of connectedness as they remind themselves of God's grace—expressed through the kindness of others or the simple pleasures that drift through the day. They report higher levels of alertness, enthusiasm, determination, and joy. With the regular practice of listing thanksgivings, we tend to anticipate the experience of gratitude, to notice things that normally pass by without appreciation. When we focus on blessing, it crowds out the focus on the hassles in our lives.

No matter the circumstances, we can usually find something for which to be thankful—to our neighbor for driving the carpool, to Mother Nature for the rainbow, to our spouse for clearing the table. Or, if the day has been really rotten, we can express gratitude that we made it through without punching somebody and that it's finally over!

Reflect: Commit to the keeping of a gratitude journal for a week. Notice how, as the days pass, your perspective begins to shift, making you more aware of your blessings.

NOVEMBER 21 • *Noticing Name Tags*

This pleasant practice can make a surprising difference in someone's life. A friend's experience bears this out. After a grocery store worker spent an unusual amount of time assisting him in locating a particular item, my friend made a note of the person's name. Later, he went to the store's website and posted a report of the employee's helpfulness and competence, asking that the information be relayed to his supervisor. The ripple effect was astounding.

My friend's note of thanks got printed out and posted on the employee bulletin board to inspire other workers. The employee received recognition and honor at a subsequent meeting. The employer filed the comments in the employee's permanent record, which eventually led to a promotion and a raise. Not only did the expression of gratitude make a difference in the atmosphere around the store, it made a difference in dollars to the employee!

Actions like this put legs on our casual feelings of gratitude; they extend our spoken words of thanks in unpredictable ways. Besides, it's a win-win-win—a win for management, a win for the employee, and a win for the cause of spreading thankfulness in our world.

Reflect: Take time to thank someone in a tangible way today. It not only makes a significant difference in his or her life, but through grace it strengthens your own "gratitude muscle."

NOVEMBER 22 • *Sacred Seeds*

Whatever you ask for in prayer, believe that you have received it, and it will be yours" (Mark 11:24). Planting seeds of gratitude in the heart yields an ongoing harvest of thanksgiving. Studies increasingly show that interior thoughts and images create corresponding effects in our bodies and beyond—all the way down to the molecular level. When belief and fervent feeling accompany positive thoughts (good seeds), it spurs growth. Anticipating the gratitude helps to build a sturdy bridge of intention.

I've heard stories of Mother Teresa's belief in the power of positive seed planting. Even as a person greatly committed to the cause of peace in the world, she refused to join an antiwar group. She preferred to be part of a pro-peace movement instead. Her rationale: Asking for something reflects a lack of it, asserting that one doesn't have it. On the other hand, the method of positive prayer (in harmony with Mark 11:24) recommends that we visualize the abundance and feel the exhilaration and gratitude as if it were already accomplished—not in the future but now.

There is a distinction between saying prayers and praying. In the first we merely recite the words, while focus and feeling accompany the second. Sit in a serene place, imagining your heart as a fertile field ready for planting. Introduce feelings of appreciation and thanksgiving and affirm the spiritual flourishing. Tomato vines don't sprout from carrot seeds, nor do apple trees bear lemons. The intentional planting of seeds of gratitude and watering them with faith yields the bounty and beauty of a thankful heart.

Reflect: Take a quiet moment to practice this seed planting in your soul. Trust that blessings will abound and that you will bless others.

NOVEMBER 23 • *Thank You—What's Next?*

Simple words and breathing can carry our grateful intention. Praise and an openness to guidance can ride on a single inhale and exhale. The Thank You—What's Next? prayer serves as such a vehicle of growth.

This brief phrase lends itself well to the breath-prayer format because it attaches so seamlessly to the natural pattern of breathing. We breathe in a deep sigh of gratitude—thank you—followed by the prayerful request for guidance—what's next? Blending body, mind, and spirit, it establishes a stance of thanksgiving in the present and opens us to the future.

This bridge to gratitude requires no books, no pencil and paper, no special environment. We can practice it as we look out the window at a lush landscape, as we watch our children sleeping, as we pay the bills or fire up the grill. Even as we walk down the street, we can attach the words to our pace, creating a syncopated rhythm of thankfulness. And sometimes, as we repeat thank you with our lips or in our hearts, we may hear the faint whisper that says, "You're welcome."

Reflect: Incorporate the Thank You—What's Next? prayer into your day. Play with it. Sing it. Say it out loud, then silently. Let it open you to God's intention of generosity.

NOVEMBER 24 • *Group Gratitude*

It's not surprising that words of praise and thanksgiving fill the liturgies of many faith traditions. The thread of gratitude weaves its way from Genesis to Revelation as an appropriate response to God's gifts. Our spirits soar when we join our voices in praise with others.

And the power of praise doesn't stop there. Group gratitude grows into meaningful ministry and spreads outside the walls of the church. Movements such as Appreciative Inquiry, an innovative group committed to community improvement, are making giant strides in companies and schools across the country. The method focuses on the strengths of an organization rather than its weaknesses, spotlighting the strong points instead of pinpointing the problems. At one school, the leadership team posed a core question, "What makes your school special?" That question served as both a springboard and an invitation that united the students, administration, and faculty in creating the future they desired. In an atmosphere of appreciation, they could target specific areas for improvement without conflict.

When thankful hearts come together for the common good, recrimination and competition can take a backseat, even in situations with diverse approaches and solutions. Positive power bursts forth when people pursue life-giving attitudes in good company.

Reflect: Recall a time when you've felt the force of a group united in gratitude. The next time you sing the words *Praise God from whom all blessings flow . . .*, wrap your heart around them and be grateful for those who sing praise with you.

NOVEMBER 25 • *Thanks for the Memories . . .*

To some extent, we choose our memories. We can feed the ones that we want to survive through the years and starve the ones we want to forget. Because of this freedom of choice, however, memory and gratitude form an uneasy partnership.

Memories remind us of who we are and where we came from—they form our identity and our self-image. Family gatherings where stories are told and photos are snapped fill our memory banks with glowing appreciation for those who have formed us. For those who may have de-formed us, however, it's a different matter. Memories of neglect or turmoil often need healing to permit some semblance of gratitude to emerge. The cleansing work of forgiveness helps the wounds fade over time.

No one has a catalog of perfect memories. At some point, taking steps to frame past events as positively as possible is worth the effort. Usually we can find something to be affirmed—even in the most disagreeable people—and remember some vestige of joy from dire circumstances. Making that choice flexes the gratitude muscle and builds its strength.

Herman's wife died. He had bitter memories of their rocky relationship and stormy marriage. Residual anger and resentment clouded his ability to deal with her death in a healthy way. When he finally pulled out of his inevitable feelings of loss, I asked him how he did it.

"I didn't want to exist any longer in that dismal place," he told me," so I shifted my focus. Rather than repeatedly recalling the troubles, I started thinking about the positive aspects of our relationship—our three children and eight grandchildren, the beautiful sofa she chose for the living room, her willingness to stand by me during financial woes. I decided that 'grateful and sad' felt better to me than 'bitter and sad.'" He didn't lie to himself about the realities of his life; he simply chose to honor the good memories more intentionally than the bad ones.

Reflect: Get out some photo albums and affirm the memories, one by one. Be grateful for the people and events that made you who you are. Thank God for the lessons learned.

NOVEMBER 26 • *Bridges for the Family*

Train children in the right way, and when old, they will not stray" (Prov. 22:6). Young minds are like sponges. They soak up environmental cues that shape their psyches at an early age. So why not plant the seeds of a thankful heart?

- Dinner dialogue—Try these conversation starters to steer children's minds (and yours) toward appreciation: What's the best thing that happened to you today? What do you like most about your teacher? What's the most fun piece of equipment on the playground? What makes you smile when you think of your favorite friends?
- Helping hands—Involve the entire family in shopping, preparing, and delivering a Thanksgiving basket to someone in need.
- Art appreciation—Children respond to visual triggers, so try these suggestions: Make a Thanksgiving Tree, starting with a tree trunk with lots of bare branches. Cut leaves out of colored paper and invite your family to write their thanksgivings on them and attach them with colored yarn. As a Thanksgiving-week project, make a "Praise Poster" or "Gratitude Collage" by inviting family members to cut out or draw objects of their thanksgiving. Old magazines and photos will stimulate plenty of ideas.

- Personal touch—Writing thank-you notes may be a tough sell but personalizing the process draws children like a magnet. Have fanciful note cards printed with the child's name; add unusual stamps and brightly colored pens, and they'll be hooked. Ask them to write one person a day during Thanksgiving week, encouraging them with "Whom would you like to honor today?"

Get in touch with your own childlike imagination and infuse thankful activities with a dash of fun instead of dread and duty. The actions of one appreciative person can influence future generations! Plus, you can depend on the domino-effect promised by the Spirit whose very nature radiates generosity and gratitude.

Reflect: Plan a specific activity for your family (or just yourself) to honor the season of Thanksgiving. As you do so, give thanks for the season itself and allow it to awaken the gratitude implanted in your soul.

NOVEMBER 27 • *Aging and Appreciation*

And now to the other end of the life spectrum—the cultivation of appreciation among the aging. As we grow older, the losses multiply at an astounding rate. Gratitude can easily get lost in a sea of despair. Along with the obvious proliferation of funerals and illnesses, the ebbing away of independence eats away at the reservoir of gratitude.

One family came up with a highly creative scheme to address one of the dreaded losses of aging—handing over the car keys. Since Carl had been a car lover all his life, his children decided to give this loss the attention it deserved by making a party out of it. Friends and family gathered old photos of Carl and his beloved cars and fashioned a scrapbook, listing each car and its years of service. They regaled one another (and Carl) with hilarious stories of road trips with Carl behind the wheel. One person made a clever poster listing the advantages of being carless—no insurance premiums, no costly repairs, no frosty windshield to scrape. Then each of them gifted him with IOU coupons that he could redeem at his pleasure—a trip to the grocery store each Tuesday, ten visits to the doctor's office, valet service to his favorite restaurant, three "taxi" rides to the destination of his choice—you get the idea. Carl's children topped the evening off with a cake in the shape of a car. Needless to say, their gestures of kindness and understanding eased the painful transition for him, and he was surprisingly grateful for the occasion!

Many folks report feeling irrelevant and unappreciated during their later years, making it increasingly difficult to connect with their own feelings of gratitude. With ever-evolving technology, thoughtful families honor their elderly members by filming or recording their reminiscences and respecting the wisdom distilled from years of experience. Tokens of love and respect move everyone involved in the direction of gratitude for the person's life and legacy.

Reflect: Put yourself in the shoes of the older folks in your circle of friends and family. What can you do to foster their feelings of thanksgiving, as well as your own?

NOVEMBER 28 • *Reach for the Grateful Thought*

On an ordinary day in our ordinary lives in the midst of ordinary ups and downs, we can develop the discipline of extending our hearts toward thankfulness. This simple prayer reflects the movement of gently reaching for a grateful thought:

Just this once, O God, I'd like to come to you with no mention
of problems but simply to say "Thank you. . . . "
for your forgiveness when I fail to do the loving thing;
for the sheer joy of sleep when I'm terribly tired;
for the silent strength of humility when pride overtakes me;
for the growing remedies that lead to good health when I am ill;
for the nurture of new knowledge when I make a mistake;
for the simplicity of orderliness when I face confusion;
for the joy of helping others when I see people in need;
for the assurance that you have made a place for each of us when I
feel inadequate among my peers;
for the earthly evidences of your will when I am trying to find out
what life is all about;
for the reality of your world when I stray too far into fantasy;
for the rightness of reason when I panic too quickly;

for the fun that refreshes when everything gets too serious;

for the renewal in moments of silence when I am dizzy being busy in a bustling world;

for the confidence of friends when loved ones do not understand;

for the healing love of family when friends hurt me;

for your presence when I am lonely;

and, above all, God, I thank you for the meaning and fullness you have given this world of yours.

Amen.

Reflect: Read the prayer slowly, and let it sink into your soul. Make your own personal additions to the list as you feel the spiritual rhythm of embodied thanksgiving.

NOVEMBER 29 • *Becoming Gratitude*

When we affirm belief in gratitude, deal with the barriers blocking the way, and build bridges to its unfolding, we can hope to become a human vessel of genuine thankfulness one day.

This process of becoming involves . . .

- Accepting what was—releasing it in a shroud of forgiveness.
- Accepting what is—standing squarely in the present with thanks and love.
- Accepting what will be—trusting in the steadfastness of divine grace.

Another aspect of this spiritual awakening is an understanding of the difference between expectation and hope. Expectation is tied to results—our gratitude gets trapped when things don't turn out as we expected. Hope, on the other hand, is tied to faith—a softness of the soul that welcomes grace, no matter what happens.

It's difficult to experience gratitude as a constant condition, but it can be consistent. Over time thanksgiving can seep into our bones and become a part of who we are. We don't need to force it, manipulate it, or summon its presence; it's simply there. We evolve from merely making grateful noises to becoming grateful people. Another way to express this dynamic shift is that we move from listing our blessings to being a blessing.

The embodiment of gratitude is not a cookie-cutter condition, nor does it follow a predictable formula. The generosity of God flows through us where we are, as we are—unimpeded.

Reflect: Think of a time when you reacted with automatic thankfulness, as if you were in the divine flow of gratitude. Remember how your body and your spirit felt the exhilaration of Yes! Open yourself to that experience throughout this day.

NOVEMBER 30 • *A Thankful Heart*

So what does a flesh-and-blood human life look like when a thankful heart is on "automatic pilot"? This pastor's story paints a poignant picture of a plucky senior whose gratitude had become natural and effortless—even humorous!

During his regular hospital rounds, pastor John Claypool visited two women in their eighties, both facing significant health challenges. The first visit contained an understandable litany of woes: complaints about the food, the sandpaper-feeling sheets, the constant interruption of her sleep, and the lonely, miserable state of affairs as a hospital patient. With a heavy heart, he moved to the next room and found an entirely different atmosphere.

> When I told her how sorry I was that she had to come to the hospital, she said, "Well, I'm sorry too that I have this problem, but you know, there are things that the people here can do for me that my family at home could not do. I'm grateful that places like this exist." I asked: "Do you find the commotion of the hospital disturbing to your rest?" She said, "You know, the truth is, my family at home is wonderful to me, but they have their work to do, which means I often get quite lonely. Here, every time the door opens, I find myself wondering what fresh young thing is coming in now!"
>
> "Do you find the bed difficult to sleep on?" I asked. With that her eyes brightened. "We only change our sheets at home once a week. They change them here every day! I call that real luxury, don't you?" I remember making one last effort at consolation. "Do you find the food here hard to eat?" Again she said, "You know, my daughter-in-law is a

wonderful cook, but she tends to fix things the same way all the time, and it gets a little boring. I really enjoy the variety of the menu here." And then she added: "Eating for me under any circumstances is not easy, because I only have two teeth left. But I thank the Lord, they hit!" When she made that last statement, I felt like stepping back and giving her a full military salute. All the heroism in the world is not confined to the battlefield.[4]

Reflect: Imagine your own heart as a home for the natural flow of thanksgiving echoed throughout this story. How can you react to the events in your life today with this kind of gratitude?

December

NEW BIRTH

"We know that the whole creation has been groaning in labor pains until now; and not only the creation, but we ourselves, who have the first fruits of the Spirit. . . . if we hope for what we do not see, we wait for it with patience."
—ROMANS 8:22-23, 25

BREATH PRAYER
Giver of life, . . . I am born anew.

DECEMBER 1 • *Perpetual Pregnancy*

We're always pregnant with something. Whether we are male or female, rich or poor, religious or nonreligious, the Spirit is always stirring new life within us. A fresh insight, a more loving attitude, a broader vision—whatever we need for our greening and growth.

During this season when we celebrate Jesus' birth, we can celebrate also the seeds that the Spirit is planting in our souls—growing ever so slowly. As we gain awareness of the link between our spirits and the divine Spirit, we will begin to notice subtle signs of change. In the coming days of December, we'll explore signposts that have marked the lives of spiritual journeyers for centuries.

We're all wired differently, and it isn't a matter of "one size fits all." I may hear the Holy more clearly through working with the disadvantaged; you may respond to solitude and silence. One person's heart may be moved by Handel's *Messiah*, another through praise music. Our formation comes through pain, pleasure, confusion, mistakes. God uses anything and everything to awaken us to our true identity as beloved children of the Divine and is always planting seeds of growth in our individual lives and distinct personalities.

However, while we are equipped in unique ways, certain spiritual shifts in the faith journey seem to transcend time, space, gender, denomination, education, and vocation. We can read centuries-old texts such as *The Cloud of Unknowing* or Teresa of Avila's *Interior Castle* and recognize the same spiritual dynamics at work in our own lives. The words may be expressed in Castilian Spanish or archaic English, but the experiences are familiar. The dates, the times, the culture, the clothes may differ, but that which is "sprouting" in our soul has similarities to those that have stood the test of time.

People who are growing in the Spirit begin to manifest certain characteristics—like plants in a well-tended garden as they bud and blossom.

Reflect: Think of yourself a year ago—or several years ago. Begin to notice (and note in your journal) any changes in thought or behavior that are slowly developing.

DECEMBER 2 • *Spiritual Shifts*

Spiritual growth is like watching the grass grow. It doesn't happen in a flash. Nor does it happen completely. In fact, if you totally embody all the attitudes described in the following days, you will be a candidate for sainthood! Birthing new ways of being does not come by clicking off one switch and flipping on another. It's more like childbirth—often laborious and tedious but moving toward new life.

I'll illustrate the point with the experience of Marsha, a spiritual direction client who had been seriously committed to her spiritual journey for years—chipping away at her behavioral blocks and looking them straight in the face. Many of her barriers presented themselves as wolves in sheep's clothing, qualities that society would view as good traits: dogged determination to succeed, commitment to meaningful work, a sense of super-responsibility, and a ton of self-esteem. Then the shadowy sides of those traits began to show themselves to her—perfectionism, self-criticism, feelings of competitiveness, overwork.

Marsha continued to believe in God's invitation to wholeness and authenticity, so she kept at it. Though an energetic extrovert, she embarked on the practice of Centering Prayer in an effort to release control in the silence. She trusted the prayerful process, even when she detected no results whatsoever. And she kept showing up for her monthly spiritual guidance appointment, even though she feared she "wasn't making any progress."

For months Marsha had experienced great anxiety about a particularly difficult relationship with a colleague, clinging to resentments and wounded feelings. One day I casually asked her, "How's it going with your friend? Is it still tense and stressful?" Her response was casual as well. "Oh, I don't worry about that much anymore, I guess. She has a right to her feelings. It's not really about me, anyway; oddly enough, I don't take it personally anymore. I just want to love and accept her and our friendship for what it is now, not what it was." Her gradual change of heart was so subtle that it had escaped her notice.

Scripture tells us, "You will know them by their fruits" (Matt. 7:16). Many of us can talk a good game. We can recite the creeds, state what we believe unequivocally (and, by extension, what any "good Christian" ought to believe), and perform worthy works. However, the integration of true growth means that our external acts embody what lies inside us, that the gap between who we are inside and what we project outside begins to narrow.

The topics in the following meditations are not a checklist to see if we're passing muster in Spirituality 101. However, they suggest a behavioral barometer that provides a loose measure of how the fruits of the Spirit are lived out in practical terms.

Reflect: Consider a relationship or situation that has caused stress and anxiety for you in the past. Revisit it in light of the Spirit's effect on your life. Be alert for subtle changes in attitudes, words, and actions.

DECEMBER 3 • *It's an Inside Job*

A major dynamic in this series of spiritual shifts is a decrease in the dominance of outer authority and an increase in inner authority. Most of us begin the spiritual journey by relying on others to define our worth and provide direction. We seek the approval of parents and authority figures. We try to please our friends, to gain the approval of others. We value obedience to exterior rules and cultural norms, a good place to start.

However, as we grow in the Spirit and become more aware of the voice of God within us, our inner compass becomes clearer. We realize that the Spirit guides us from the inside as well as from the outside. Communication and wisdom from our holy center slowly assume more weight than what others think, what they expect of us, and whether they approve of us. Understandably, we like to bring joy to those around us, and we may choose acts of self-sacrifice and kindness out of a loving heart. But we become less chameleon-like in allowing others to dictate and define who we are. Our identity becomes increasingly grounded in our relationship as sons and daughters of the Holy One.

It's an ongoing balancing act. We don't behave as robots, immune to others' feelings, insisting on having our own way. Neither do we suppress our own desires and opinions in order to please or be popular. An inner integrity flows into our outward behavior. A dependable bond between the invisible world (thoughts, feelings, spiritual values) and the visible world (actions and responses) becomes stronger.

Reflect: How do you perceive God's guidance? Consider the sources of exterior leading—scripture, the wisdom of others, the expectations of those around you. How do you experience the interior leading of the voice of God within you?

DECEMBER 4 • *Being Real Instead of Being Right*

Somewhere along the deeper journey, we find that the competitive drive begins to lose its steam. We no longer feel compelled to win the argument. Convincing someone else of our point of view decreases in significance. Winning loses its allure.

Correspondingly, we experience a burning desire to act out of a sense of integrity. This means that we'll probably listen to others more intently rather than rushing to a rebuttal in our heads. Our need to feel superior—to be right—loses its hold on us. We sincerely want to hear others, understand them, try to experience the world through their eyes. After all, they may have something to teach us if we listen with full attention.

We do not become so wavering in our opinions and convictions that we stand for nothing. In fact, considering the viewpoints of others can often clarify our own beliefs and refine our evaluation of an issue. Clearer discernment can arise when we have the grace to ponder diverse outlooks in an atmosphere of mutual respect.

Being real means we may have to utter those dreaded words, "I'm not sure" or "I don't know" or "You have a point there." As we grow, our competitiveness morphs into cooperation and often into compromise. Our ego need to be the best, the brightest, and the "rightest" says a reluctant good-bye! A pithy prayer from Kenya captures this spiritual movement:

> From the cowardice that dares not face new truth,
> From the laziness that is contented with half-truth,
> From the arrogance that thinks it knows all truth,
> Good Lord, deliver me.[1]

Reflect: As you pray this brief prayer, think through your spiritual posture in situations where opinions differ. Affirm your desire to be real rather than right.

DECEMBER 5 • *Prayer without Boundaries*

You may find yourself breaking out of your traditional prayer box. Familiar forms of prayer—confession, praise, petition, intercession—continue to hold meaning, but prayer will call you to less and less, yet more and more.

Less effort to "pray right." Less compulsion for prayer to work (however you define that). Less attachment to getting the result you seek. Less need to accomplish something with your prayers. Less praying in order to please God. Less reliance on words. Less time in giving God instructions in prayers.

More exploration of different forms of prayer. More involvement of the body in prayer. More silence and listening. More "Thy will be done" prayers. More trust that God sees your needs even before you ask. More feeling that your prayers join the Spirit's prayers. More confidence that anything that draws you into the holy presence can be a prayer.

As our prayer lives deepen, we may experience prayer as returning God's loving gaze, whether we're kneeling, dancing, resting, working, running, sitting still, planting a rosebush, or stirring a soup. It slowly becomes much more about relationship than results, more about how we walk than how we talk, more about who we are in God than what we do for God. And our prayers become more candid and real, not as much about holiness as about authenticity.

Our preconceived ideas about prayer begin to fade away, replaced by the awareness that prayer possibilities have no limits, no religious fences surrounding our relationship with the Spirit. We begin to sense the wonder when we "pray without ceasing" (1 Thess. 5:17) and to trust that our immersion in God can transform our lives into prayers of love and compassion.

So rather than trying to figure out the whys and wherefores of prayer or read another book on prayer, we simply pray.

Reflect: Take a deep breath, releasing all your notions and constrictions about what prayer is. As you breathe in, realize that anything that allows you to express honest feelings, especially love, or that gives fire to your relationship with God is prayer.

DECEMBER 6 • *Scripture Comes Alive*

A passage of scripture that you've read a hundred times lights up in bright neon. The hearing of a familiar text on a Sunday morning brings tears to your eyes. A biblical message meant for Abraham now seems like a memo addressed to you. A verse whose meaning seemed crystal clear suddenly leaps with new relevance. An ancient prophetic challenge dumps itself on your doorstep with a call to action. Words of wisdom from other faith traditions grab your heart with truth.

We can expect it to happen. Along with a heartfelt connection to the Holy One comes a barrage of truth and inspiration from all directions and from surprising sources. It isn't about learning more or mastering material or making an *A* in Bible 101. Sacred scripture becomes soul-stirring stuff—loaded with nudges to act, knocking at the door of self-centeredness with an invitation to a love and compassion greater than we have ever imagined.

Reading holy writings becomes not a search for answers but a search for meaning; not a rulebook for behavior but a place to encounter the living God who has a thing or two to teach us about unconditional love.

We're invited to read with a beginner's mind and to allow each word to expand our souls.

Reflect: Read a familiar passage of scripture, such as the Beatitudes in Matthew 5 or the poignant words of Paul in Romans 8. Be open to new applications of scripture to your life as it is right now.

DECEMBER 7 • *Who Is God?*

Like children playing with a pile of building blocks, we begin by constructing our image of God using a variety of names—King, Judge, Creator, Redeemer, Higher Power, Healer, Sustainer, The Man Upstairs—partial pictures of God, to be sure. We may add blocks bearing words like *obedience, sin, shame, duty, love, compassion, hope, salvation, damnation*—and the tower gets taller. At some point, however, the stack begins to tilt and teeter, finally tumbling into a heap of inadequate words.

As we grow in faith, our God-image evolves from these concrete limitations into concepts more complex and mysterious. Specific definitions fade into a non-image image—an understanding closer to the revelation expressed in Exodus 3:14, "I AM WHO I AM." We may desire a more easily grasped definition to wrap our finite minds around, but we are left with a mind-boggling Mystery that somehow exudes love and compassion. Far from being a powerful spectator in the universe, the great "I AM" is a gentle, abiding presence. In a strange and glorious way, we become less interested in defining God and more interested in relating *to* God.

Creeds and dogma and definitions can point the way, but they can't substitute for an encounter with the divine. Such a relationship changes everything, including the way we react to the particulars of our day-to-day lives. It affects our ongoing feud with Aunt Martha and our feelings of betrayal in a collapsing marriage and our behavior toward that person who lords it over us at the office. This connection makes us gasp in wonder when there's a full moon on a cloudless night. We carry the spark of divinity within our own souls and know that it belongs there.

We end up abandoning our need to describe something that defies description and instead abandon ourselves to a love that defies abandonment.

Reflect: Look back over your faith journey and your expanding image of the living God. Accept that though you can never fully understand God, you can unite your spirit with the purity of divine love.

DECEMBER 8 • *From Worry to Wonder*

A wise adage claims that faith functions not to turn our anxiety into answers but to turn our anxiety into awe.

Fear, anxiety, and worry visit us daily—rapping on the door of our hearts and poisoning our peace. Many world religions remind us that faith and fear are antithetical to each other, that trusting God and existing in perpetual anxiety resemble oil and water that don't mix well.

Perhaps our angst arises from what we expect faith and trust to mean in our daily lives. Trust God to fix things for us? Have faith that we will always be protected from harm? Our expectations render the terms *faith* and *trust* powerless when we continue to encounter disruption and despair. So in what do we have faith? In what are we asked to trust?

These ongoing questions perplex all who seek deeper meaning in life and a deeper relationship with the divine Source of life. Perhaps part of the answer lies in our willingness to stand in wonder at the miracles that surround us daily—like the rhythmic beating of our own hearts or the astounding healing of a scratch on our arm. The power of healing, unexpected kindness, and irrational forgiveness should leave us awestruck. Then we live into faith and trust rather than try to measure it. No matter what happens to us, we choose love. No matter what someone does to us, we choose forgiveness. As we do that, we sense a presence that sustains us.

Worry takes a backseat. Are we concerned? Yes. Do we do everything we can to right the wrongs in this world? Yes. But we cling with childlike wonder to the beauty of an iris, to the sacrifice of one person for another, and to the loving Presence at the heart of reality. When worry leaves the premises, it leaves room for the entrance of wonder and for the turning of anxiety into awe.

Reflect: Notice today when worry overtakes you. Mentally take that worry and place it on a shelf amid objects of beauty. Allow it to fade in the face of wonder.

DECEMBER 9 • *Holding Life Lightly*

The clenched fist in our hearts slowly opens. Our grasping releases into gentleness. The need for control diminishes:

- We hold doctrines lightly, free to question their truth and relevance, remaining open to revelation, expansion, change.
- We hold nationalism lightly, no longer insisting "My country, right or wrong" but considering the perspectives of those in other nations, realizing they are equally loved by God.
- We hold our desires lightly, sensing the difference between wanting something and needing something.
- We hold outcomes lightly, acting from a wellspring of love and allowing results to unfold as they will. Expectations dissolve into hope.

- We hold goals lightly, proceeding from a place of integrity rather than a craving for success, all the while remaining alert for surprises and detours.

As if life were a tiny bird in the palm of our hand, we loosen our grip on our lives so that we can fly.

Reflect: Gently turn the palm of your hand upward; imagine a fledgling fluttering there. Imagine it is your life. Releasing the constraints allows it to fly.

DECEMBER 10 • *Savoring the Silence*

Silence is not empty. It resounds with the pulse of our own hearts and the pulse of the universe—all beating to the tempo of the Divine.

If we're never alone, we can't know ourselves or the God who created us. Silence gives us new ears and new eyes. When the thunder of our wandering minds begins to recede, we are free to hear the whisper of fresh thoughts and see the world with profound awareness. As we open ourselves to the voice of God in the vastness, we begin to hear the beckoning of our soul's true voice. We become aware of the immensity of the invisible world surrounding us and the aching beauty of the visible world in which we exist. And we sense that all of it is held in a loving embrace that sustains us and gives our lives meaning.

As the soul matures, silence and solitude combine to form a friendly refuge. Solitude allows us to retreat from the noisiness and introduces us to ourselves and to the God who longs to speak in the stillness. In that rich space, our fragmented selves become collected. We become present to the fullness of life in us and around us. We become deeply attentive, giving ourselves up to the mystery that permeates everything. We release control and simply let it be.

Reflect: Find a moment of solitude today. Take a walk in the park, steal a private moment at the office, or sit quietly in a chair. Make silence a priority. Today and every day. Exhale the static and inhale the calm.

DECEMBER 11 • *The One Thing Necessary*

Martha, Martha, you are worried and distracted by many things; there is need of only one thing. Mary has chosen the better part" (Luke 10:41-42).

The familiar story of Mary and Martha reminds us that we are essentially human beings, not human doings. Martha was taking care of business, providing food and housing for Jesus and the guests, being an efficient hostess. Mary sat at Jesus' feet, absorbing his presence and being attentive to his teachings. Jesus gives the nod to Mary's actions.

Our culture rewards productivity and efficiency—whatever it takes to get things done. However, for our actions to have lasting value, a rich state of being needs to fuel our doing. Loving motivation gives meaning to our worthy deeds.

So how do we go about being Marys in a Martha world? It's a matter of balancing these natural rhythms, of remembering that contemplation and action form a significant circle. This dynamic movement flows from inner to outer—both necessary for fullness of life. Contemplation and action go hand-in-hand, and one without the other is incomplete.

Here's a practical example. Suppose you're attending your child's soccer game. You can occupy a seat in the stands out of obligation (tinged with a hint of resentment at the interruption of your schedule), or you can be fully present to the child's experience with enthusiastic support. Either way, you are doing your duty by being there, but the motivations are decidedly different.

Paying attention to the practices that feed our Mary side—prayer, mindfulness, inspirational input—predisposes us to grace-filled action. Being present in the moment with a contemplative mind-set lends integrity to all our busy doing.

Reflect: Examine the events listed on the calendar today. Take a few moments to be with God in alertness and gratitude. Allow these moments to invigorate all that you do as you enter your activities.

DECEMBER 12 • *Good-bye to Guilt*

As we grow, the glaring light of truth begins to shine on our relationship with guilt. We begin to sense the difference between *meaningful* guilt (a failure to be true to our best selves) and *meaningless* guilt (a feeling of inadequacy based on the opinions and expectations of others). One invites us to grow and change; the other just nags and criticizes.

Meaningful guilt gently taps us on the shoulder and whispers, "You didn't speak up when you wanted to" or "You failed to say what you really meant" or "Your words and actions in that situation were contrary to your deepest values." Feelings like this prompt us forward, urging us to more authentic behavior.

Meaningless guilt runs the gamut from "They expected me to do that, and I disappointed them" to "They would like me better if I agreed with them on that issue." From "I really should host that dinner even though I don't have the money or energy" to "I must mow the lawn even though I'm too tired and want to put it off till Friday." And so it goes. Feelings like this propel us backward into patterns of dancing to someone else's tune or our own sense of oughtness.

Saying good-bye to guilt will be reflected in our everyday language—both our silent statements to ourselves and our verbal responses to others. Look for these words to disappear from your vocabulary: *I must, I should, I ought to, I'm supposed to, they want me to, they need me to, I've got to.* If these sentiments continue to fill your day, then meaningless guilt may still cling to your struggling soul with a nagging sense of disquiet.

Reflect: Monitor your internal and external chatter, keeping an eye out for those telltale phrases. Speak from your honest core, beginning statements with "I choose," "I want," and "I will."

DECEMBER 13 • *The Groove of Gratitude*

When our spirits are born anew, the groove of gratitude deepens. Moments of thanksgiving create a groove in our psyches and spirits—much like a wheelbarrow carves out a rut in a dirt road. The more thankful we are, the more thankful we become. Repetition reinforces the neural pathway and burrows it into our psyches, increasing the likelihood that our thoughts remain there. So even when circumstances take us out of the groove temporarily, we can slip back into it with ease and grace.

Of course, the same is true of our negative thoughts and litanies of complaint. They create a groove also, drawing us over and over again into worst-case scenarios and pessimistic reactions. As we grow in spirit, we establish new patterns of thought by repeatedly placing our attention on thankfulness, joy, and love.

Since our thoughts shape the way we see the world, our minds become more selective, choosing to look for the good in others and the hope in situations. As we go through each day, we pause to focus on graces that are both tiny and tremendous—finding the keys we lost, a fleeting look of affection on the face of our spouse, biting into a fresh tomato, as well as the giant swell of the tides and the warmth of the sun. Everywhere we look, we discover new delights that ignite our feelings of appreciation.

As the groove of gratitude shapes our hearts, we begin to see life through hopeful eyes. We greet even obstacles and challenges, once viewed as unwelcome visitors, with courage. We know down inside that it is all grist for the mill of growth. We expand from persons with a pool of blessings to those who swim in a sea of thankfulness. We go from saying "thank you" to radiating gratitude from the core of our being.

Reflect: Today, train your thoughts to slip into that deepening groove of gratitude. Feel the growing ease and seamlessness of the transition to thanksgiving.

DECEMBER 14 • *Response-Ability*

As our spirits continue to be reborn, we learn to be responsible for our response-ability. In other words, we engage our power of choice. We respond rather than react.

In life situations, whether trivial or tragic, a world of difference exists between responding and reacting. Reactions usually involve the blame-game. We all know how to play that one: "If he would just do this, then I could do that." "If she says that, then I'm going to fire back with this!" "Who made this happen to me—it isn't fair!" When we react, we bypass conscious choice. When we respond, we decide what action reflects who we really are, who we yearn to be, how God invites us to live—regardless of what the other person does or even what we perceive to be fair.

This maturing process usually involves a time delay—a pregnant pause—inhibiting many knee-jerk reactions that used to set us off. We are no longer at the mercy of volatile emotions, such as anger, revenge, and hurtful put-downs. We tend to refrain more and more often from impulsive advice-giving and rapid fix-it solutions. Reflexive judgments give way to attentive listening to another's point of view. A refreshing hiatus gives us time to consider a conscious reply rather than an impulsive comeback. When someone throws a hurtful comment our way, we don't automatically toss an equally mean-spirited rejoinder into the fray.

Response-ability implies that we reach for gracious resolutions to thorny situations in everyday life. For example, suppose your spouse wants you to go to a football game (or a shopping trip to the mall), and you don't want to go. You have a choice: Stay home and get some much-needed work done or accompany your spouse. Each choice has validity. It may be true that the lawn needs mowing or the laundry is piling up. On the other hand, perhaps you two haven't spent much time together lately, and you may choose to nurture the relationship through a joint venture. Done consciously, the interior dynamic moves away from projection and blame ("He'll be mad if I don't go" or "She knows I hate the mall") to the realm of thoughtful choice. Responding from integrity could mean either "My desire to be with my spouse trumps my desire to stay home" or "I feel more strongly about getting these home chores done." The point is to act from a position of choice rather than duty. Either way, it's a responsible decision made by an authentic person.

When we hold ourselves accountable for what we say and do, we disrupt the blame-game. We no longer shift responsibility to someone else. This frees us to make compassionate choices from a reservoir of love and kindness.

Reflect: Consider the state of your own response-ability. Notice the ways in which your spiritual journey has curbed your reactions and turned them into thoughtful responses.

DECEMBER 15 • *Simplicity and Subtraction*

During our journey to wholeness, our spirit will give birth to an acute desire for simplicity. We will begin to feel the crowding of too much stuff—cluttered closets, cluttered schedules, cluttered thoughts. Bustle and busyness may bother us; too many possessions may weigh us down. We increasingly sense the difference between permanent values and transitory values. Experience will reveal the truth that exterior clutter affects interior serenity, and we'll find ourselves making changes.

Chances are, we'll start giving things away with no strings attached. If we haven't worn a garment for a season, out it goes. If we're dusting stacks of books that we'll never want to read again, we send them off to libraries. If unused china and kitchenware cram our cabinets, we call the kids to pick and choose. We may even decide there's too much unoccupied space in our home and choose to downsize. A *For Sale* sign adorns the lawn.

Too much rushing around begins to bug us. With no contemplative time to reflect and no leisurely time to listen to friends, we feel compelled to trim a hustle-bustle schedule down to a manageable size. Meaningless activities that once brought delight may begin to bore us. Empty pursuits give way to projects that matter. Fostering relationships becomes more important than polishing our image. We dare to ask the questions, "Where is God leading me? What meshes with my time and talents? Is this activity in sync with the Spirit's messages in my soul?"

Even the workings of the mind shed their encumbrances. "If only it weren't like this. . . . " opens into "This is the way it is." "I wish I could make them do. . . . " becomes "I can't micromanage the thoughts and actions of others." We recognize that we can engage our influence in a responsible way but that control is an illusion.

As we move toward greater simplicity, we discover the truth proclaimed by sages through the centuries—the spiritual life is more about subtraction than addition.

Reflect: Notice the ways your life is becoming less chaotic and cluttered. Is that spaciousness making you more available to the Spirit's meaningful invitations?

DECEMBER 16 • *Treasures in Heaven*

Do not store up for yourselves treasures on earth, where moth and rust consume and where thieves break in and steal; but store up for ourselves treasures in heaven. . . . For where your treasure is, there your heart will be also" (Matt. 6:19-21).

Momentary pleasures are fleeting; profound fulfillment lasts forever. What is born in us is a clearer awareness of the difference.

Choosing to pursue spiritual goals goes against the grain of our culture and our conditioning. Investment in heavenly things comes through valuing what God values, longing to incarnate the qualities within ourselves that were present in Jesus. This requires giving ourselves to actions that foster justice, thoughts that inspire, words that encourage and build up others, relationships that reflect love, legacies that last. We develop the kind of ego transcendence that plants a tree under whose shade we will never sit or engages in works of compassion with no observable results or rewards. It means a capacity to feel delight in the delight of others, to be concerned about events not directly related to our self-interest. It means being willing to invest ourselves in tomorrow's world even though we may not be around to see it.

Our devotion to divine interests will cease to be motivated by what we can get out of it—even peace of mind or salvation. We will no longer seek stars in our crowns or glories in the sweet by and by or any kind of pay-off. The ego will let go of its voracious need to be satisfied and rewarded. Rather, we will begin to love God for God's self. We will feel the enormous draw of the ocean of love available to us simply by virtue of being a creation of a loving Creator.

Reflect: Look back over your spiritual journey to this point. How have your goals and yearnings changed? Think about the "treasures in heaven" to which the Spirit is inviting you.

DECEMBER 17 • *Loving the Unlovable*

The Sermon on the Mount presents some of Jesus' most difficult demands. Paraphrased in *The Message*, these words set forth a formidable challenge:

"I'm telling you to love your enemies. Let them bring out the best in you, not the worst. When someone gives you a hard time, respond with the energies of prayer, for then you are working out of your true selves, your God-created selves. . . . If all you do is love the lovable, do you expect a bonus? Anybody can do that" (Matt. 5:44-46).

Tough stuff. But as we grow closer to God, words like this will ring in our ears. They won't let us be our old mean-spirited selves. Rather than revert to retribution or revenge, we will seek ways to honor the challenge to love the unlovable without lying to ourselves and to God.

First of all, we realize that disagreeable people can be our teachers. They can provoke self-awareness as we ask ourselves, "Why am I reacting so negatively? Do their actions run counter to my cherished values of justice and mercy? Are they puncturing the bubble of my ego? Or did they just uncover a wound deep within me?" Encounters with disagreeable folks can teach us to set proper boundaries, to speak the truth in love, and to wrestle with creative conflict resolution—not always pleasant endeavors, but they build character and grow the soul.

Second, we come to understand the meaning of healthy detachment. Detachment doesn't mean we fail to care; it means we face the reality that we can't control others. Our acceptance of the fact that we can't fix a person or situation frees us to act with as much love as possible without enabling inappropriate behavior. Quite a balancing act. The slings and arrows of others tend to bounce off our tender egos when we realize they are living out of their own pain or dysfunction. Our motivation shifts from "How can I judge?" to "How can I help?"

We become less interested in interpreting persons' actions and behaviors. We're willing to tackle the tough task of sifting our own responses through a filter of loving-kindness.

Reflect: Think of a person in your life who is hard to love or to be around. Imagine viewing them with healthy detachment. Allow that spiritual posture to free you for loving responses.

DECEMBER 18 • *The Center of Consent*

A powerful voice inside each one of us carries commanding authority. That voice drives our decisions, telling us when to take action. It's our center of consent, controlled by our vital values.

If we want a life of financial success, our decisions will reflect that desire. If we want a life of luxury or safety or popularity, then we tend to live out of those basic longings. When our primary yearning is to love God and neighbor, it will shape our living.

The old hymn reminds us to "tune my heart to sing thy grace." As that tuning grows stronger it affects the inner voice, causing a dynamic shift in our willingness to change and grow. We stop protecting our old patterns; we stop making excuses; we stop blaming other people; we stop condemning the past. We're willing to face our fears and do what it takes to let them go or heal them. We grow up in grace and get on with our lives. In other words, we learn to say yes to life instead of no.

Our spirits become pliable, teachable, undefended. We stop our frantic efforts to deserve grace, to earn God's love. Though most of us were reared to believe God would love us if and when we changed, we begin to accept that God loves us *so that* we can change. Then we can let down our guard and consent to the flow of true transformation.

Life is change. Often we say we want to get better, to grow, but we hide behind barriers that keep us stuck in unhealthy attitudes and patterns. As we grow up in faith, we dismantle those defenses and take responsibility for our part of the growth process. We become willing to discover who we really are and live out of that identity. We thrill at the possibility of reflecting the love that blossoms within us.

Reflect: Imagine the core of your soul as a God-given voice that serves as your decision maker. Be honest about the things that are most important to you. Consider how they shape your decisions.

DECEMBER 19 • *Bouncing Back*

One of the graces of the growing human spirit is that of resilience, the capacity to regenerate and rebound from the stresses of life.

It's a divine pattern. Nature illustrates it for us every day—a daffodil peeks through a blanket of snow, green shoots spring from the ashes of a forest fire, a paper cut heals, a heart begins to beat after transplant surgery, tears of loss finally dry. Everything in creation leans toward life with primal force.

Amazingly, we too share this cosmic patterning. We learn that we are more than our mistakes, more than our sad story:

- When trauma steals our identity, we reestablish ourselves.
- When things fall apart, we slowly rebuild—whether it's our homes or our hearts.
- When our dreams are dashed, we discover new ones.
- When we think we are dying inside, we learn how to live.
- When life loses its luster, we open ourselves to the Great Light.

Our resilience nourishes what sprouts from the soil of our brokenness, transforming our darkest moments. Like the struggling sapling that emerges from a decayed tree stump, we choose life.

Reflect: As you ponder your times of suffering, think about the seeds of growth that lay buried in those experiences. Who have you become in spite of them? Who are you yet becoming?

DECEMBER 20 • *Unseating the Ego*

"Those who lose their life for my sake will find it" (Matt. 10:39). As our spirit matures, the ego loses its place on the throne. No longer the master, it is relegated to its proper place—that of a servant. It vows allegiance to the higher self, that soul center where God guides.

As this "unseating" progresses, self-consciousness diminishes. We will raise fewer internal questions such as: How should I behave? What image do I wish to present? How am I coming across? We will be more centered in our identity as a child of God, more comfortable in our own skin. In stressful situations, we will not always assume that we did something wrong or said something offensive. When something upsets us and we respond in an over-the-top fashion, a red light inside us will start blinking. We will succumb to this revealing litmus test: Every time our feelings get hurt, our needy ego has been punctured.

We cease to take things personally, realizing that it's not all about us. We become more independent of criticism as well as flattery. Others' opinions may disappoint or delight us, but they lose their power to tell us who we are. Deliverance from ego dominance frees us to be the authentic persons God created us to be.

When the ego recedes, we are finally free to disappear for God's sake; in losing the false self, we find the true self.

Reflect: Think about the times when your feelings have been hurt. How did your ego react? Consider how that is changing as you grow closer to your true self that is centered in God.

DECEMBER 21 • *Walking in Another's Shoes*

As we remove ourselves from the center of the universe, the door to genuine compassion swings open.

We dare to see the world through the eyes of others, becoming slow to judge and quick to understand. We imagine the life of the person who can't find a job or the exhaustion of the single mom after eight hours of waiting tables with dinner preparation and homework supervision yet to do. The scary looking guy asking for money may be a slave to addictions we can't fathom; the distracted person blocking the aisle in the grocery store may have been stunned by a recent biopsy report. As we step aside from our own prejudices and preconceptions, we slip into another's shoes and look at life through his or her eyes.

We will share their suffering in a visceral way. Our desire to be of service will stem not from guilt but from a need to share the love of God. We put legs on our compassion, acting from choice rather than duty.

A sense of kinship develops for all souls—without regard to race or culture or country. The yearning in our hearts is shared by all on a journey to the divine heart. We all participate in human life, all citizens of the same cosmos.

As compassion increases, we build bridges instead of borders. We move from arrogance to humility, from isolation to involvement.

Reflect: Look clearly at what happens inside when you see a person in distress. Feel the movement toward deeper compassion being born in your soul.

DECEMBER 22 • *Fostering Forgiveness*

Forgiveness becomes more than a lofty spiritual concept or a matter of saying the simple words, "I forgive." More than "I should, and so I will," forgiveness becomes a heartfelt, body-centered experience. We will feel increasingly imprisoned by unforgiveness and resentment, more sensitive to their toxic qualities. We come to understand that we can forgive people without condoning behavior.

I remember the moment that I "got it" about forgiveness. I had analyzed the word many times, acknowledging that forgiveness was not about condoning bad behavior; rather, it was about forgiving persons, not actions. I had studied the relevant scripture passages. I had prayed to experience God's healing forgiveness for myself. I had prayed to be able to forgive someone who had hurt me in a life-changing way. I knew that any Christian worth her salt should search for and strive toward forgiveness.

However, Frederick Buechner's words in *Wishful Thinking: A Seeker's ABC* helped me realize that I had not plumbed the depths of the process. I hadn't admitted to myself that, at its core, forgiveness is an act of radical self-interest. The wisdom of his words made my scalp prickle:

> Of the Seven Deadly Sins, anger is possibly the most fun. To lick your wounds, to smack your lips over grievances long past, to roll over your tongue the prospect of bitter confrontations still to come, to savor to the last toothsome morsel both the pain you are given and the pain you are giving back—in many ways it is a feast fit for a king. The chief drawback is that what you are wolfing down is yourself. The skeleton at the feast is you.[2]

My heart stood still at the power of the words. My truth bell rang in my head. I realized that the saving grace of God's forgiveness, while a free gift, required our center of consent, our voluntary participation, our vulnerable openness.

Something inside me raced ahead to anticipate the release—the reality of the biblical assertion that "the truth will make you free." I began to sense the value of accepting things as they were and as they had happened. I saw the bitter cost of unforgiveness: nothing short of the utter erosion of one's life. And, in my best self-interest, I wanted no part of it.

Which set me to thinking about something else. . . . Perhaps we could experience God's gift of self-preservation, of self-interest. as a benevolent guide instead of an ego trip (the negative tag of our self-judgment).Perhaps God had created us in such a way that to forgive another breaks the chains that bind *us*, to free ourselves from the prison that limits our freedom. Perhaps the sages asserted correctly that the gate to hell is locked from the inside.

The invitation to forgive reminds us that we hold the key.

Reflect: During a moment of quiet, see yourself stepping into the ongoing, eternal river of divine love. Take with you anyone toward whom you still hold a grudge. Swim in the freedom of forgiveness.

DECEMBER 23 • *Being Present with Presence*

Being wholly present to another person—with body, mind, and spirit—offers a holy gift beyond measure. An encounter of heartfelt listening is a meeting of souls wrapped in a container of utter and complete safety—no judgment, no fear of betrayal. That means the speaker pays no price for complete honesty, does not worry that the words will come back to haunt him or her. The speaker feels free to be outrageous, to rant, to weep, to laugh, to speak without editing, to disclose or not disclose. Even more important, the unspoken assurance of complete confidentiality ensures that the conversation will never be used for the listener's benefit. The secrets will not be whispered on the proverbial grapevine.

Being present means we get ourselves out of the way. Our whole self is present, yet absent. We don't divert the exchange by inserting, "This is how I handled that problem" or "Here's what I would do if I were you." We bracket our advice until requested; we suspend our fix-it solutions. Simply put, we serve as a sounding board to mirror the speaker's experience back to him or her. This encourages the speaker to tune in to the voice of his or her own soul.

As faithful listeners, we remain open to the divine presence, allowing that holy wisdom to sculpt our hearing and shape our words. It's as if we listen to the voice of God on another's behalf, allowing the greater Presence to be incarnated in the hallowed moment.

Reflect: Listen closely to someone today. Imagine that you hold their experience like a delicate bird egg in the palm of your hand, keeping it warm so that it can open into truth and meaning.

DECEMBER 24 • *Giving Your Gifts*

This season of gift-giving provides an appropriate time to imagine how you might offer your growing gifts of the Spirit during these often hectic days, when both people and packages fill our lives.

We can't give away what we don't possess. As spiritual gifts are born within us, we can bestow blessings on those around us out of the abundant overflow:

- Kindness—We can shower others with affirmation, encouraging the flickering candle of their best selves to burn more brightly.
- Patience—We can be tolerant when things go awry.
- Peace—We can fill the atmosphere with our own sense of peace, a calm amid the chaos, so that it summons the peace of others.
- Goodness—We can focus on the positives, rather than the faults, of those around us.
- Generosity—We can give our full attention to each person, one at a time, not omitting even the most troublesome.
- Self-control—We can commit ourselves to no outbursts, no irritating retorts.
- Faithfulness—We can be true to the blessed values of the Christmas season.
- Joy—We can be the source of smiles, laughter, and appreciation.
- Love—We can sift every thought, word, and action through the filter of "Is it loving?"

We participate in the gifts of God not only by what we say but by how we incarnate the life of the Spirit. From selfishness to sharing, fragmentation to wholeness, complaint to gratitude, hate to love, death to life. No matter how glittering the gifts under the tree may be, nothing shines brighter than the gifts of the Spirit.

Reflect: Today, in the midst of holiday hustle and bustle, breathe in the spiritual abundance that is yours and breathe out your gifts into the world.

DECEMBER 25 • *Embracing the Mystery*

In the beginning was the Word, and the Word was with God, and the Word was God. . . . And the Word became flesh and lived among us" (John 1:1, 14).

What a beautiful Mystery we celebrate on this Christmas Day, heralding the birth of Jesus. As we expand into the spaciousness of the world of Spirit, we feel less enthusiasm for trying to figure things out and more willingness to make friends with paradox, uncertainty, and ambivalence. Awe replaces our intellectual anxiety.

Divine mystery is not a problem to be solved but a reality to be experienced. Our growing souls become more interested in relationship *with* God than knowledge *about* God. This voyage of discovery is not as much about seeking other vistas as it is about seeing what's in front of us with fresh eyes—not so much learning something new as seeing the familiar in new ways.

This prayer captures our wonder:

> O God, sometimes the Mystery of the world of Spirit is too much for us to grasp. We stand in awe before it, knowing that your presence is both outside us and miraculously within us, that your Spirit reigns in the universe and wants to reign in our hearts as well.
>
> May it be so, loving God. May we nurture your image within us so lavishly that your heartbeat pulses through our veins and beats in our hearts, that our very lives become a prayer and our actions a mirror of your love and grace. Make us as the lilies of the field, open to your light, basking in your presence, willing to be who you created us to be—holding nothing back.
>
> Forgive us when we stumble, gracious God. Help us blossom in the freedom of your forgiveness, assured that when we make mistakes, you are waiting like a loving parent to restore us . . . to help us pick up the pieces and to welcome us home.

May we embrace the mystery that the Word that was incarnate in Jesus can be born in us as well. Amen.

Reflect: As you slowly meditate on the prayer above, allow your heart to swell with wonder. Give thanks that Jesus showed us how to live fully out of the spark of the divine placed within each of us.

DECEMBER 26 • *Radical Trust*

Trust in God is not about having a crystal ball that answers our questions or a detailed map of the future that erases anxiety. Trust is an elusive concept, difficult to nail down and even more difficult to live out. Spiritually speaking, it wiggles out of any straitjacket we put it in.

The meaning of trust is subject to astounding distortions. Many folks believe that trust in God assures that they can count on divine intervention to stop a tornado or shrink a tumor or protect them from financial collapse. Some believe that if they're good enough or pray hard enough, God will grant a solution to their current demands. Experience does not bear this out.

Still, we trust

- That God is—and will continue to reveal divine nature and truth.
- That God guides—prompting us toward avenues of deeper compassion and love.
- That God forgives—lavishly, abundantly, irrationally.
- That God abides— a Presence that never leaves or abandons us.
- That God creates—mysteriously infusing creation with dynamic life.
- That God loves—unconditionally, the author of a benevolent universe.
- That love triumphs—though we don't know how or when.

To live with this all-encompassing trust helps us rely on the grace available to us in each and every moment. Radical trust asserts, "There is no blueprint (because of free will), but I'll trust and pray anyway, casting my lot with a holy mystery that I can never completely understand, predict, or explain." For me, that's enough.

Reflect: As you affirm each aspect of radical trust, relax into the confidence of having faith in things unseen. Pray with this verse: "By faith we understand that the worlds were prepared by the word of God, so that what is seen was made from things that are not visible" (Heb. 11:3).

DECEMBER 27 • *Harvesting Wisdom*

So teach us to count our days that we may gain a wise heart" (Ps. 90:12). Most of us aspire to be wise. In fact, we prefer being wise over being smart or attractive or successful. The psalmist gives us a clue about how to move toward that lofty pinnacle.

We are to "count our days." Obviously, the psalmist points to something more than a number. One biblical translation uses the word *honor* rather than *count*. When we honor something, we look closely at it; we revere it, celebrating its value. So counting our days moves beyond quantity to quality—the pure gold of wisdom. We glean the nuggets of wisdom buried in our life experiences.

In a spiritual context, the following definition of wisdom from Webster's captures the heart of the process: "Wisdom is knowledge understood, experienced, and applied." In practical terms, we take the events of our lives, understand them by examining our experience, learn the lessons, and do something about it.

We know, however, that this is not an automatic process. It's possible to live a lifetime and never learn a thing in our "school of the soul." Even with our built-in yearning for meaning, we receive no guarantee that we'll pay attention to it. Given enough money, opportunity, and diversion, we do a bang-up job of avoiding questions that can produce wisdom. We can buy a bigger house, take a longer trip, get a new spouse, perfect our golf game—all worthy pursuits, so long as we don't use them as escape hatches from confronting issues of significance.

As we focus on what is being born within us this season, let's not forget to honor our days as the seedbeds of wisdom that they are.

Reflect: List some of the most memorable events of your life, both positive and negative. In what ways were they sources of wisdom? What lasting lessons have stayed with you?

DECEMBER 28 • *Freedom and Limits*

Freedom without limits invites selfishness. Limits without freedom stifle the flow of Spirit. It's a matter of balance. As our connection with the Holy One grows stronger, we learn to walk this tightrope with growing integrity. We become aware of the following challenges:

- Freedom from guilt—but not conscience
- Freedom from rules—but not responsibility
- Freedom from the expectations of others—but not the well-being of others
- Freedom to speak honestly—but not to demean people
- Freedom to take risks—but not to imperil others
- Freedom to be who we are—but not at someone else's expense
- Freedom to live out our deepest desires—but not to discard our moral compass

Our freedom comes through doing what we regard as loving, appropriate, and valid, then letting go of the outcome. Oddly enough, when we relinquish our attempts to control things, a strange serendipity often occurs. It sets free an inner dynamic, and the situation changes with no additional effort or input on our part.

When we embrace freedom with integrity, it's a good idea to incorporate an internal checklist to ward off self-centered behaviors: Is it honest? Is it true? Is it appropriate? Is it loving? By releasing the impediments to love, we are increasingly free to live out the principle of love.

Reflect: Think about the limits on your freedom as the Spirit flows through your days. Have you moved toward acting more spontaneously by taking more risks and loving more lavishly?

DECEMBER 29 • *The Authentic Self*

The birth of the authentic self is an occasion for fireworks and balloons. Shouts of celebration should ring from the rooftops. That pure child of God that has been hidden inside us all along finally emerges into fuller view. Then we can enfold it in our own loving arms, just as God does.

Sure, the birth is often messy. We can't think ourselves into becoming ourselves, and we can't rush the process. We experience rough patches: making mistakes and learning from them, discovering who we are not and regrouping, noticing what delights and debases that inner child and making appropriate changes, hanging in there when the birthing is painful.

As we get acquainted with our authentic self, we discover that we're not called to be a clone of anyone else—even Jesus. Following Jesus doesn't mean we become carpenters in Nazareth; rather, we become who we are called to be, just as Jesus was true to his God-given authentic self. And we also claim this sublime glory: that the God who created us loves us unconditionally, now and eternally.

Our acceptance of that wondrous reality creates a sublime ripple effect. We stop carping and complaining about ourselves, making fewer self-deprecating statements. By extension, our judgment toward others takes a nosedive. Even when we don't approve of others' actions or disagree with their views, our capacity to accept them as they are will expand. We will value diversity because it no longer threatens us.

It's not easy to be real. Authenticity involves being an informed citizen of our own inner landscape where God shows us who we are and loves us anyway. Secure in that knowledge, we can then summon the courage to move out of the shallowness of the false self and into the sacred space of the true self.

Reflect: Review the slow (and sometimes painful) process of coming to know your deepest, most real self. Celebrate your growing awareness of who that is.

DECEMBER 30 • *Living in Love*

Love is not something we trade . . . or bargain for. It's something we give away for free.

To love as God loves is a tough assignment, and it may not feel warm and fuzzy. It requires a bedrock resolve that seeks the highest good of others, even if we don't like them. Even if they are troublesome and unpleasant or evil.

We love because we're born to love, because we are loved by the One who created love. When we live in an atmosphere of love, we don't need to create it or generate it on our own. God is the Lover, the One who seduces us. We participate in a greater love and trust it as divine gift. In that mystical, yet practical, realm, pity is transformed into compassion, judgment becomes acceptance, hate is softened into goodwill. We know ourselves, lose ourselves, and find ourselves. We ask not what we can get but what we can give.

And our lives are swept into the divine flow of Love itself.

Reflect: Meditate on the words of this benediction attributed to Henri-Frédéric Amiel (1821–1881): "Life is short, and we don't have much time to gladden the hearts of those who walk the way with us. So be swift to love; make haste to be kind; and may the blessings of God the Creator, Christ the Son, and the indwelling Holy Spirit be with you." Realize that life is too precious for anything but love.

DECEMBER 31 • *Divine Unfolding*

As our individual lives unfold in the flow of the Spirit, we sense that the whole of creation is indeed "groaning in labor pains" (Rom. 8:22). This mysterious, divine unfolding is a process of spiritual evolution in which we participate with every loving impulse and action.

We take the first step on the spiritual journey with a sense of possibility, an intrepid (if flickering) hope that transformation can really happen. But then the landscape shifts, seasons come and go, and we often stumble on the potholed path. Along the bumpy road to meaning, we trip over barriers more than once, making us wonder if the journey is more fantasy than reality. Then along come those unexpected glimpses of the eternal that call us back to center and keep us going—a feeling of being in the right place at the right time, an impulse of pure love, a visitation from an invisible source, a sacred synchronicity that defies explanation. There are surprising moments when we feel aligned to the spiritual rhythms of the universe, so in tune with the divine music that life feels like one glorious song of grace.

When our hearts vibrate with the pulse of the Holy, we long to live in service to the highest calling there is—being part of the evolution of love. It means living in the present—yet more than that. It means loving and accepting others—yet more than that. It means honoring God as Creator and Sustainer—yet more than that. It's the unfolding of the Divine in and through all creation.

As we join in this unfolding, our earnest quest for self-fulfillment gives way to a passion for the greater good of people, the planet, the cosmos—the whole of life. When the rhythms of our own growth are tuned—even for one magic moment—to the rhythms of God, we yearn to be part of the creative force that animates all things, to be bearers of blessing and channels of unconditional love.

We sense God's signature on all of life, including the holy handwriting on our souls.

Reflect: May the incomparable love of the Spirit be born in us anew every single day so that we may be part of the divine unfolding of God's cosmos.

NOTES

A number of ideas, paraphrases, and adaptations were taken (with permission) from my previous books, listed below:

How Can I Let Go If I Don't Know I'm Holding On? Setting Our Souls Free (Harrisburg,PA: Morehouse Publishing, 2005).

How Can I See the Light When It's So Dark? Journey to a Thankful Heart (Harrisburg, PA: Morehouse Publishing, 2007).

How did I Get to Be 70 When I'm 35 Inside? Spiritual Surprises of Later Life (Woodstock, VT: SkyLight Paths Publishing, 2011).

Praying in the Messiness of Life: 7 Ways to Renew Your Relationship with God (Nashville, TN: Upper Room Books, 2011).

JANUARY

1. John Keats, Letter to George and Georgiana Keats (19 March 1819).

FEBRUARY

1. Andrew Newberg and Mark Robert Waldman, *How God Changes Your Brain: Breakthrough Findings from a Leading Neuroscientist* (New York: Ballantine Books, 2009), 154–63.

MAY

1. Wayne W. Dyer, *The Power of Intention: Learning to Co-Create Your World Your Way* (Carlsbad, CA: Hay House, 2004), 256.

JUNE

1. Basil Pennington, "Lectio Divina: Receiving the Revelation" in *Living with Apocalypse*, ed. Tilden Edwards (San Francisco: Harper & Row, 1984), 68
2. Marjorie J. Thompson, *Soul Feast: An Invitation to the Christian Spiritual Life* (Louisville, KY: Westminster John Knox Press, 2005), 25–26.

OCTOBER

1. Jerome Lawrence and Robert E. Lee, *Auntie Mame* (New York: Dramatists Play Service, 1999), 137.

2. Henri J. M. Nouwen, *The Return of the Prodigal Son: A Story of Homecoming* (New York: Image Books, 1994).

NOVEMBER

1. Henri J. M. Nouwen, "All Is Grace" in *Weavings: A Journal of the Christian Spiritual Life*, Nov/Dec 1992, 39–40.
2. Gregg Braden, *Secrets of the Lost Mode of Prayer* (Carlsbad, CA: Hay House, Inc., 2006), 83.
3. Lynne McTaggart, *The Field: The Quest for the Secret Force of the Universe* (New York: HarperCollins Publishers, 2002), 61–73.
4. John R. Claypool, *God Is An Amateur* (Cincinnati, OH: Forward Movement, 1994), 85–86.

DECEMBER

1. Frederick Buechner, *Wishful Thinking: A Seeker's ABC* (New York: Harper-Collins, 1993), 2.

for those who hunger for deep spiritual experience . . .

The Academy for Spiritual Formation® is an experience of disciplined Christian community emphasizing holistic spirituality—nurturing body, mind, and spirit. The program, a ministry of The Upper Room®, is ecumenical in nature and meant for all those who hunger for a deeper relationship with God, including both lay and clergy persons. Each Academy fosters spiritual rhythms—of study and prayer, silence and liturgy, solitude and relationship, rest and exercise. With offerings of both Two-Year and Five-Day models, Academy participants rediscover Christianity's rich spiritual heritage through worship, learning, and fellowship. The Academy's commitment to an authentic spirituality promotes balance, inner and outer peace, holy living and justice living—God's shalom.

Faculty trained in the wide breadth of Christian spirituality and practice provide content and guidance at each session of The Academy. Academy faculty presenters come from seminaries, monasteries, spiritual direction ministries, and pastoral ministries or other settings and are from a variety of traditions.

The Academy Recommends program seeks to highlight content that aligns with the Academy's mission to provide resources and settings where pilgrims encounter the teachings, sustaining practices, and rhythms that foster attentiveness to God's Spirit and therefore help spiritual leaders embody Christ's presence in the world.

Learn more here:

http://academy.upperroom.org/

CPSIA information can be obtained
at www.ICGtesting.com
Printed in the USA
FFOW05n1935120317

9 780835 813518